Stagecraft

Stanislavsky and External Acting Techniques

Stagecraft

Stanislavsky and External Acting Techniques

A COMPANION TO
Using the Stanislavsky System

Robert Blumenfeld

Limelight Editions
An Imprint of Hal Leonard Corporation

Published in 2011 by Limelight Editions
An Imprint of Hal Leonard Corporation
7777 West Bluemound Road
Milwaukee, WI 53213

Trade Book Division Editorial Offices
33 Plymouth St., Montclair, NJ 07042

Printed in the United States of America

Book design by F. L. Bergesen

Library of Congress Cataloging-in-Publication Data

Blumenfeld, Robert.
   Stagecraft : Stanislavsky and external acting techniques : a companion to using the Stanislavsky system / Robert Blumenfeld.
      p. cm.
   Includes bibliographical references and index.
   1. Method acting. 2. Stanislavsky, Konstantin, 1863-1938. 3. Acting. I. Title.
   PN2062.B65 2011
   792.02'8023—dc22

                                                      2010051074

ISBN 978-0-87910-384-2

www.limelighteditions.com

This book is dedicated with love to my wonderful, caring, brilliant friend, Christopher Buck, with profound gratitude for his constant love, support, helpfulness, and encouragement

Contents

PART THREE

SOME POST-STANISLAVSKIAN APPROACHES TO THEATER, CHARACTER CREATION, AND THE ART OF ACTING

Stagecraft: Internal and External Acting Technique

Backstage just before a performance, everything seems so mundane, so businesslike. The ambience is shabby, perhaps even a bit tawdry. It is dark. Work lights provide the only illumination. Ropes and cables are everywhere, and you have to be very careful not to trip over them. People are bustling about, and the dust gets up your nostrils. The excited hum of activity rises as curtain time nears. "Places!" is the call. Expectant, poised, alert, you wait for your entrance. In just a few minutes, the curtain will rise and the performance will begin. And the shabbiness, the dust, the rundown dressing rooms that the audience never sees, all will be forgotten for a brief space of time. You are suddenly in another world, in the wonderland of the play...

The theater is a magical world, a unique world with its own rules, inhabitants, customs, and lifestyle. It is a world in which magic and illusion are created by the use of practical, down-to-earth stagecraft—all those arts and crafts of the theater that make a performance possible. Lighting, costume and scene design, and the knowledge and skills required to run a show are all aspects of stagecraft that actors should become familiar with, because they are the necessary accompaniments and aids to their own art.

The techniques of moving around a performing area, finding the light, and making sure the audience can see you are a few aspects of the actor's own stagecraft, along with acting technique. The word "technique," like the Greek word *tekhnikos* (of art; with skill), from which it is derived, is polysemous: it has many meanings, both broad and narrow. *Tekhnikos* comes from the word for art, *tekhne*, which also means system, method, craft, and skill. And it means an artisanal trade. *Tekhne* includes the knowledge of an art, together with the skills needed to practice it. Actors in ancient Greece were called *tekhnitai*, artist-technicians. The description is still a good one.

Technique is a general system, method, or way of working in a particular field; we refer to acting technique, which can be used to create any character. And we talk of stage and camera technique, because each medium has its own demands. There are also specific techniques that form part of a more general category: acting technique includes vocal and movement techniques, for instance, and such specifics as holding for a laugh or timing an entrance. These are called "external" because they have to do with what the audience sees and hears. Internal techniques are the psychological methods and devices employed in sounding the depths of a character's mind and motivations. You cannot have one without the other: they work inseparably.

All the acting techniques taken together constitute the actor's craft. The actor's art lies in how the techniques are used in the personal interpretation and performance of a character: Every actor who plays Hamlet gives us *his* Hamlet.

I have discussed internal techniques in *Tools and Techniques for Character Interpretation: A Handbook of Psychology for Actors, Writers, and Directors* (Limelight Editions, 2006) and in the companion volume to this one, *Using the Stanislavsky System: A Practical Guide to Character Creation and Period Styles* (Limelight Editions, 2008). The system of acting elaborated by Constantin Stanislavsky (1863–1938) is laid out in detail and, I hope, with clarity.

The second part of the latter book is devoted to something Stanislavsky considered extremely important: period styles. The actor must personalize and internalize the social attitudes and manners of each era, and learn how to reproduce its deportment, as well as dealing with costumes and accessories.

The present volume provides more information on both internal acting technique and the vast subject of period styles, from ancient Greece to World War II. It also deals with basic aspects of the art for which there was no space in *Using the Stanislavsky System*: There is a thorough introduction to voice and movement techniques, and to such other externals of stagecraft as knowing how to speak verse, and how to utilize the built-in features of language (stress, intonation) to help create a character's manner of expressing him- or herself. Advice on the finishing touches that create the character's outward appearance is provided as well.

Every actor knows that without the external work, the internal work cannot be "read" or understood by the audience. So learning these aspects of the craft is of paramount importance. In fact, Stanislavsky thought that actors should take voice and movement classes all their professional lives, to keep their skills honed. These foundations of the actor's art are discussed in chapters 1, 2, and 3.

In order to interpret a character, you have to know what to look for in a script, and how to read its story. And you have to know how to rehearse, and what happens in performance. Much of this you can only learn from experience. This book includes information on how to proceed and what to expect, as well as on the specific techniques of performing in comedy and acting in musical theater, where the music makes unique demands on actor-singers.

Among Stanislavsky's important and influential successors are the Russians Michael Chekhov, Yevgenyi Vakhtangov, and Vsevolod Meyerhold, all of whom studied with him and then broke away from his ideas in different ways; and the Americans, Uta Hagen, Sanford Meisner, Stella Adler, and Lee Strasberg, all of whom expanded on his system. Their ideas are included in part 3 because they are of great use to contemporary actors.

The most important things in doing the work of an actor are the passion for the work, and the enjoyment of it. Love life! Fill yourself with compassion and empathy! You will infuse these qualities into your art. Always remember to be generous and giving to your audience, as well as to your fellow performers. And you will enjoy for a lifetime the work you are privileged to do!

Acknowledgments

I would like to give a special acknowledgement to Mel Zerman (1931–2010), founder and publisher of Limelight Editions. He was an erudite, courtly, and gracious gentleman, kind and compassionate, and he gave me my start as a writer by publishing my first two books. He is missed by everyone who had the privilege and pleasure of knowing him. Among those very dear friends who have contributed directly and indirectly to this book are Albert S. Bennett; Stephanie Cowell; Michael Mendiola and Scot Anderson; Peter Subers and Rob Bauer; Tom and Virginia Smith; Kieran Mulcare; Peter D. Kingsley, actor and writer, with whom I have had helpful discussions and debates on topics covered in this book; Suzanne Toren, a wonderful actor, award-winning book recording artist, and expert Feldenkrais teacher; Adam Cavagnaro, an excellent singer-actor who was very helpful on the Laban movement techniques; teacher and opera director Alan Hicks, with whom I had helpful discussions about acting in opera; and Robert Perillo, one of the great expert voice and speech teachers, who vetted my chapter on vocal technique and gave me excellent advice. My professional associations as a dialect coach on productions directed by the brilliant performer and opera director Dona D. Vaughn, artistic director of opera programs and director of undergraduate opera theater at the Manhattan School of Music; and by the wonderful Jay Lesenger, artistic/general director of the Chautauqua Opera and head of the opera department at Northwestern University, have provided invaluable and practical insight; as has the advice of my friend, playwright Ian Strasvogel. And I express my gratitude and thanks for their love and support to my wonderful family, and most especially to my father, Max David Blumenfeld (1911–1994), and to my mother, Ruth Blumenfeld. Both of them always encouraged my interest in language and theater, and I owe them everything. For their love and support, I thank my brother Richard Blumenfeld and his wife, my sister-in-law, Ming: my brother Donald Blumenfeld-Jones and his wife, my sister-in-law, Corbeau; my nephew, Benjamin; and my niece, Rebecca; as well as my mother's brother, my uncle, Seymour "Sy" Korn

(1920–2010), a brilliant and wonderful man and World War II veteran; and my cousin, Jonathan Blumenfeld. Many thanks are owed to my excellent project editor, Marybeth Keating; to my extremely helpful copy editor, Sarah Gallogly; and to the graphic designer of this book, F. L. Bergesen, who has done such a beautiful job. I want to thank my wonderful publisher, John Cerullo, who has now published six books of mine! And I want to thank editorial director Carol Flannery, who is always insightful and understanding. They are both a pleasure to work with, and they have both been terrifically supportive and helpful throughout. Lastly, I owe an incalculable debt to all the authors of the books in the bibliography, and to all the actors and directors I have worked with as an actor or dialect coach, as well as to the professors at Rutgers, who taught me elementary stage technique; and to the teachers I studied with when I decided to become a professional actor, notably Uta Hagen (1919–2004) and my very dear friend Alice Spivak. Most translations from French and German are mine. Any errors, mistakes, or misconceptions are my own.

PART ONE

Stagecraft and Stage Technique

On Acting
and Actor Training

Action: The Foundation of Acting

"The art of the dramatic actor is the art of internal and external action," said Stanislavsky.

By internal action, he meant purposeful thinking. By external action, he meant deeds done with the intention of accomplishing something.

The internal action of thinking may not result in an external action, but thinking itself can be very active, and filled with energy. Why is the character thinking? To solve a problem, or to resolve some issue, or to come to some decision. "To be or not to be..." To act or not to act...

You take action as the result of a stimulus that acts upon the mind, and provides motive, a sense of urgency, and impetus. And you take action because you have a need, a want, a desire. Your objective, your goal is to fulfill that need. The stimulus to action may be external: A fire breaks out, and you have to escape. The stimulus may be internal: You love someone, and you want that person to love you. Internal and external actions work in tandem: You have a psychologically motivated reason for everything you do. Why do you want what you want? Why do you do what you do?

Mental processes are internal actions that may be read in a character's eyes. "Ah," says the audience, "that's what is going on in his (or her) mind!" A wish to do something may or may not be carried out, as when one is in love or angry, but dare not express it. Yet these feelings cannot help but emerge at some point as a physical manifestation, perhaps in the look one character gives another, without saying anything. "Don't look at me like that!" exclaims Yelena to Uncle Vanya. "How else can I look at you, since I love you?" he replies. The audience will know that he loves her, because they, too, will have seen that look. And they will know how annoyed she is before she ever says a word, because her internal actions (observation; thought process) will have been as loud and clear as if she had verbalized them.

Actions are what a character does to get what he or she wants. Actions help accomplish an objective, reach a goal, carry out some task, fulfill some need, want, or desire, or find the solution to some problem. Internal action involves making decisions. External action involves carrying them out. Internal action is the mental life of the character. External action is the physical life of the character. Internal action is galvanic. External action is dynamic.

An external action may be verbal; for instance, in the form of a statement meant to elicit a response. A verbal action is filled with the character's intentions. "Speaking is action," said Stanislavsky. Or an external action may be physical: reaching out to touch someone, inspecting a crime scene, chasing someone down a street, or using a computer to find an answer.

When you interpret a role, you must select needs and actions that are logical and in consonance with the character and the circumstances. A series of actions—of steps taken—must follow a logical sequence. How and in what manner actions are carried out depends on both character and circumstance. For Stanislavsky, every action has to be "genuine": "internally justified, expedient, and productive."

How do you carry out the actions? The very word "action" implies dynamism, energy, activity rather than passivity. Acting is not the art of the inert, of the passionless, of the hollow. It is full of feeling, of desire, of commitment to behaving like the character, to doing what the character does!

Does the character carry out an action with passion, with high or low energy, weakly, strongly, reluctantly, or willingly? You can't try to be happy or sad! You are, or you are not. But playing the actions, really going after what you want, will awaken happiness or sadness. How much do you want what you want? What are the "stakes"—the character's emotional investment in attaining an objective? How much do you need what you need? How much is riding on the outcome? The higher the stakes, the greater is the energy put into pursuing an objective, and the more riveting is the pursuit for an audience.

In order to carry out the actions, you have to believe in the character. You have to believe in the given circumstances. Character determines how high the stakes are, and how deep your heart's desire. And circumstances determine whether you can fulfill it.

Work on the Self and Work on the Role

Acting may come naturally to you, but you still need proper training as an actor in order to have a clear understanding of what is involved, and to develop and cultivate your artistic skills. You must learn how to carry out actions, how to interact with others, and how to listen and respond. Elementary techniques, including those for rehearsing and performing, are covered in part 1, which is a guide to procedure, and to the actor's process and ways of working; but there is no teacher like the experience of actually doing something. As Constantin Stanislavsky knew, once you have the training, that is still the only way to discover what you really need to know, and how it really feels to act, and to create a character.

He believed that the actor had two basic kinds of work to do:

1. **Work on the self:** Training as an actor in internal and external technique; the development of the responsive instrument—mind, body, voice—through vocal and physical training, so as to develop flexible vocal and movement technique.
2. **Work on the role:** Interpreting and building a character; preparing for, rehearsing, and doing performances.

Moscow Rehearsals (Harcourt, Brace, 1936) by Norris Houghton is a seminal work on theater in Soviet Russia. Houghton visited the USSR and attended classes at the Moscow Art Theatre. And he summarized what he had learned were Stanislavsky's basic ideas on actor training. The elementary education and formation of an actor included work on the actor's personal psychology and self-control, as well as control of the nervous system, so that the actor could be in a muscularly relaxed and concentrated creative mood. The cultivation of the quality of "naïveté"; that is, "he [the actor] must believe in what he does and says," was paramount.

Learning the correct way to study the given circumstances in a script, so as to be able to make them specific, was also of supreme importance. Given circumstances are the factors that condition a character's life. They are supplied by the author. Emotional circumstances are internal, and include how the character feels in his or her relationships with the other characters, which involves the character's objectives. Physical, external circumstances include time, place, the weather, and the temperature. Stanislavsky included production elements (staging, scenery, lighting, costumes, etc.), as circumstances the actor had to deal with, quite aside from those in the script itself.

With regard to the circumstances in the script, Houghton uses the example of writing a love letter versus writing a business letter: the audience should clearly see which is which through the actor's physical behavior. The movement and gestures involved arise from the inner psychological state. The actor writing a business letter is organized, thinks clearly about what is being said, and goes about writing in a straightforward, foursquare manner. But when someone writes a love letter, there is a certain slowness to the movement, a certain dreaminess as the actor dwells on and visualizes the object of his or her love. There may even be a gracefulness to the movement, and a smile may play about the lips. What is written will be spontaneous, more or less unrehearsed, and will arise from the depths, whereas the business letter arises, usually, from immediate circumstances that must be dealt with in a concrete and forthright manner.

You must learn to listen, which means to hear what is really being said. Most importantly, you have to hear how it is being said: What does the other person mean to communicate beyond the actual words? And what is your character's reaction to the communication?

You must also observe and memorize emotions so as to be able to recall them when necessary.

And you must learn to have a sense of rhythm, pace and tempo that can be brought into the work on a scene, so that the pace will naturally happen satisfactorily as the scene is rehearsed.

In addition, you must study life in all its aspects, especially observing people from all walks and conditions of life, all professions and temperaments, so as to be in a position to understand people and, therefore, characters.

You must learn how to fuse, unite, and identify the self with the character—a fictional person you are to play in performances. Character is composed of the personality, moral fiber, distinctive attributes, and qualities of an individual, who lives in specific circumstances given in the script. You bring your own character into play when creating a character in fiction, and it is by means of your own character that you can understand the fiction. In his *Poetics*, Aristotle defines character as "that which reveals moral choice—that is, when otherwise unclear, what kinds of thing an agent chooses or rejects (which is why speeches [in a drama] in which there is nothing at all the speaker chooses or rejects contain no character)."

In short, to carry out an action as the character, you must use every actor's technique at your command. You must develop a "naïve" faith in the play's given circumstances of place, time and all the rest, using the technique of imagination to project yourself into them—as naïve as that of children at play. You must throw yourself wholeheartedly into the circumstances. You must build the character, discovery upon discovery, layer upon layer. And you must learn how to live through the actions and go through the journey the character takes. This is what you do in rehearsal. The process of creation is one of constant discovery. And that process is renewed for each new role.

Organic Behavior

Your goal as an actor is to create the conditions in which real, organic behavior can happen in performance; that is, behavior that appears to be spontaneous and unanticipated. And this is the paradox of the actor and of the art of acting! Because, of course, you will be aware of every moment in the character's journey. You will have assiduously rehearsed it!

Organic behavior in performing is the result achieved after the arduous process of the inorganic: making choices, rehearsing all the objectives and obstacles and actions, and deciding all the psychological constructs. Organic behavior is living in the moment. To be organic, you must let yourself alone, and allow actual behavior to take place. Everything—lines, movement, behavior, character, circumstances—will have been memorized. Acting is, after all, the result of memorizing everything about the play, not only the lines. Many actors have learned other people's lines as well as their own, sometimes without even realizing it. The creation lies dormant, and only awaits the moment when it is relived in performance.

The external, physical, plastic aspects of a role are inextricable from its inner, psychological side. You have to ask not only "What does the character do?"; "What does the character think, want, need, and desire?"; but also, eventually, "How does the character sound, move, and look?" The answer to the latter question should arise naturally as you rehearse; you should not have to predetermine any of those things.

In order to act, you have to know how to behave as the character in such a way that the audience can understand what is going on, and follow the story you are telling. Ultimately, that is why you are acting! And everything you do is for the purpose of communicating the character's inner life clearly to the audience. In fact, Stanislavsky referred to the audience as the "third artist" involved in a performance; the author and the actor are the first two artists of the theater. What the audience receives and then gives back acts in tandem with the actors' performances and creates the play. Without them and their active participation as spectators involved in the story, there is no realized work of art. Unless it has an audience, the script has not been, cannot be brought fully to life.

CHAPTER ONE

Voice and Speech; Acting with an Accent

The first thing you have to know about vocal technique is that when you get out on the stage, the audience has to hear you! If they don't, you have already lost them. They just look at each other and whisper, "What did he say?"

The second thing you have to know is that the audience has to understand you! You must speak clearly! Good diction is essential. Or else they murmur to each other, "What did she say?"

When asked what basic attributes anyone needs in order to be an actor, Tommaso Salvini (1829–1915), the brilliant Italian actor who inspired Stanislavsky, famously answered: "Voice, voice, and more voice." He was right. The first requirement, the first necessary attribute, for a career as an actor is a trained voice. Without that, how could you do eight performances a week of almost any role, let alone a demanding part like Stanley or Blanche in Tennessee Williams's *A Streetcar Named Desire*, or Hamlet or Juliet? And the way in which you use your voice is just as important as the organ itself: the best voice in the world, used poorly, will ensure failure.

Just as important: If people notice your splendid vocal technique, you are doing it wrong. Good vocal technique consists of concealing technique—in other words, of sounding as real and as natural as possible.

The actor's voice and body must be strong and supple, and the voice must have a good range of sound. Stanislavsky taught this as basic principle, as the elementary foundation of the actor's art, which must be studied even before the internal techniques of psychophysical action. He believed that only after you have learned to use your voice, and to pronounce the language well, with good diction, could you begin to create as an actor. Good vocal technique, including the ability to project the voice, must become a habit that you don't have to think about. And good technique will also help you to avoid strain and injury. Note also that the same techniques of breath control, placement of the voice in the mask, and modulation are just as necessary in the recording studio as on the stage; the only thing you don't have to do when recording is to project your voice.

In *The Art of the Theatre* (The Dial Press), published in English translation in 1925, the French actress and matinee idol Sarah Bernhardt (1844–1923) sets out her basic, very technical approach to acting. Perhaps surprisingly, it has much in common with Stanislavsky's ideas. Like him, Bernhardt emphasizes the necessity of understanding the character's actions, and decries empty declamation, while at the same time stressing the necessity for good vocal technique, which must become an unconscious habit for the actor. Her recordings are perhaps not the best guide to the fulfillment of those ideas, however, since they strike the contemporary listener as very declamatory. The speeches from classic tragedies are delivered with a heavy vibrato that makes them seem artificial, and even risible at times.

For the stage, Bernhardt advocates elegance and refinement of gesture. She tells us that a well modulated, powerful, well trained voice and superb diction are the most important tools of the actor in conveying the character's psychology to the audience. The following advice from the woman known as *la voix d'or* (the voice of gold) will be found in her appendix, "Hints on the Voice":

> It is necessary to have an excellent articulation...
>
> But what I must once more emphasize is this: when on the stage, the actor must forget that he knows how to articulate and how to breathe. He is no longer Mr. This who personates King Lear, nor is the actress Madame That who plays Esther. He *is* King Lear and she *is* Esther.

The only two vocal exercises Bernhardt recommends are the following:

1. Instead of worrying about placing the voice and about its best pitch, address an imaginary person who is at a great distance: "...everything, throat, mouth, jaw, and lips will instinctively fall into the position required."
2. "An exercise may be recommended which consists in pronouncing the vowel I [the French vowel, pronounced "ee," as in *meet*] in a long breath, keeping the sound steady and regular, and then, without taking fresh breath and preserving the same tone and sound through the teeth, gradually changing the I into E [the "e"

in *met*], then into U [the "oo," as in *boot*], then into O [the short "o" in *hot*, as it is sounded in British RP (see p. 29) or Canadian accents], and finally A [the back vowel "ah" as in *father*]." This should be repeated at least ten times.

For Robert Perillo, one of the most noted voice and speech teachers for actors in New York, the problem with Bernhardt's advice is that you already have to have had the training in voice placement and proper support before you do the first exercise. If you don't, you risk simply shouting. And you have to know how the vowels are produced before you do the second exercise. In addition, all the vowels, says Mr. Perillo, should be supported from below, by the belly muscle in conjunction with the diaphragm. In fact, as he says, the voice should always be so supported.

Vocal technique will help you develop your voice as an actor in general terms that are useful for all characters. But doesn't each character also have a specific, individual voice? Yes, of course, and that voice is determined in part by the rhythms of the character's speech. Does the character speak quickly, slowly, in even tones, loudly, softly? You will find all of that as you play the scenes in rehearsal, and as they develop a tempo-rhythm of their own. There are also certain individual ways of speaking written into the lines. So how do you find that voice, the timbre of which will not, cannot be so different from your own? Ideally, you should not have to calculate the voice. It should grow naturally out of the work on character.

The distinguished English actor Paul Scofield (1922–2008) describes in an interview in Helen and Lillian Ross's *The Player: A Profile of an Art* (Limelight, 1984) how he found the voice of Thomas More in Robert Bolt's (1924–1995) *A Man for All Seasons* (1960), the role he created on stage and in the 1966 film. He tells us that first he "had to find the way the man would feel; then I was able to find the way he would sound." As written, Scofield found the script somewhat dogmatic, and the lines for More made him sound like a "pompous and noisy man." Their rhythms and vocabulary, in other words, automatically gave the character an individual way of expressing himself. But Scofield thought the lines played against the overall character:

> If I said the lines with all the intensity they seemed to require, he would seem an aggressive man. And he was not an aggressive man. So I had to find a way of making the man sound not pompous and not aggressive. And yet he had to sound strong... Eventually, I

discovered that if I used a specific range of my voice, and characteristics of my voice that I had never used before, I might make him sound mild, even though what the lines themselves said was not mild... His dryness of mind, I thought, led him to use a sort of dryness of speech. It evolved as I evolved the character.

These technical vocal considerations, you will note, are quite apart from the exploration of objectives, obstacles, and actions. But, importantly, the voice "evolved as I evolved the character." Scofield's performance is unforgettable and powerful, and notable for his soft-spoken manner, even though he is in vehement opposition to King Henry VIII's usurpation of the religious power. Scofield also describes how finding More's spiritual side, human sensuality, and sense of humor further added to finding the character's voice: "the voice comes out in a certain way. It's a constant communication between thinking and feeling."

Technical Aspects of Voice Production

The voice is produced through the vocal cords, more correctly called *vocal folds*, because they are actual folds of muscle in the larynx. Air is sent from the lungs through the vocal folds in order to produce sound, either with the intention of uttering intelligible words, or simply to express in sound feelings of happiness or sorrow, anguish, pain, or the appreciation of humor with laughter. The colloquial term *voice box* means the entire larynx, including the vocal folds and epiglottis. Sounds are automatically, mechanically, and unconsciously controlled by the opening and closing of the epiglottis and by the sub-glottal pressure directing the stream of air coming up through them from the lungs. That stream of air is directed to a resonator, that is, to the bone surfaces against which the sound waves bounce, producing the vibrations that are then received as sounds by the ear.

Two paramount components of vocal technique in all methods are supporting the voice with the diaphragm (the muscular partition separating the chest and abdominal cavities)—in other words, consciously pushing up with the diaphragm as air is released from the lungs—in conjunction with the abdominal muscles around the belly button; and directing the airflow so that the voice is "placed" in the mask. This use of the diaphragm must become habit: automatic and mechanical, and not something you have to think about.

To achieve optimum vocal resonance, you need good placement. You must become aware of the use of the resonators in order to create your most resonant voice, full of the reverberation and enrichment of sound, amplified when the sound waves bounce off some solid object. The most important resonators for the voice are the bones in the front area of the face around the nose and cheeks, called the "mask." Like the use of the diaphragm, this awareness of placement must recede into the background of consciousness, and optimum placement should become a habit.

You must be able to control the voice's intensity automatically and without conscious effort; that is, to control the level of loudness or softness of sound, as well as the amount and quality of emotional feeling you infuse into a piece when singing or speaking. Everyone, audience and performer alike, shares the unconscious knowledge—absorbed in childhood when learning language—of the nature of the meaning of inflections and intonations in his or her own language. You thereby automatically communicate intentions, and what the character is going through without any extra effort being required.

Even though the actor knows how to project the voice, in the contemporary theater the actor must also learn to work with the microphone, which is a mechanical device that captures sound waves directed into it. The sound waves are instantaneously converted into electrical or electronic signals, and immediately reconverted to sound as they are sent through amplifying equipment and loudspeakers, whether the mike is used for broadcasting or recording, or to amplify the live voice. The mike is used in Broadway and other theaters for both general miking and for the amplification of the voices of individual actors, who wear a *head mike* or a *body mike*. The microphone is seldom used in opera houses, except occasionally for general area miking. One of the possible problems with the use of mikes is *feedback*, which is short for *acoustic feedback*: sound that, after emanating from an audio system, goes back into that system, causing an extra reverberation, heard instantaneously as a piercing whistle or squeak, emitted from a loudspeaker. This happens, for instance, when a person speaks too loudly into a mike, and the sound of the voice bounces from the loudspeaker back into the mike again. The habit of adjusting the level of sound when using a microphone must also be learned, so that it, too, is automatic. In other words, you must have the kind of flexible vocal technique that enables you either to project the unmiked voice or to use a mike, whichever is required.

Some of the principal methods used to teach correct, serviceable vocal technique, are:

1. **The Accent Method:** A way of teaching voice production developed by Danish speech pathologist Svend Smith (1907–1985), originally for the treatment of weak voices, but now used to train singers and actors as well in correct, easy breathing coordinated with the use of the vocal apparatus and bodily movement.

2. **The Fitzmaurice Method:** A contemporary approach to the use of the speaking and singing voice; founded by internationally eminent teacher, Catherine Fitzmaurice, who has taught at such prestigious schools as Yale, NYU, Juilliard, and London's Central School of Speech and Drama. The method includes work on and exercises for the development of physicality (awareness of the body); breathing and its central role in voice production; the vocal quality involved in interpreting texts and living in the moment; and, where necessary, vocal rehabilitation. It begins with destructuring: teaching physical awareness, breathing, and vocal expressivity; and the use of Tremorwork: a program of physical exercises and, sometimes, hands-on work by the instructor, which enables the student to feel what his or her body is doing); and continues with restructuring: promoting vocal production without physical strain and with maximum expressivity based in the text and in living in the moment.

3. **The Lessac Method:** Arthur Lessac's (b. 1909) vocal technique, clearly and succinctly outlined in his classic book, *The Use and Training of the Human Voice: A Practical Approach to Speech and Voice Dynamics* (DBS Publications, 1967). He created the Lessac Kinesensic Training for both body and voice. Beginning from the point of view that "*all* the vocal arts, *all* the speech skills should be considered a single discipline," he proceeds to develop the voice by way of establishing a good physical foundation, including the study of breathing and posture and the harnessing of energy, so that not just the voice but also "the whole person communicates." He deals with "tonal action," rejecting the traditional consonants M, N, and NG to bring about a sense of resonance, and instead using the semi-consonant Y to create that feeling of vibration in the mask, which he calls the "Ybuzz." This is useful for both speaking actors and singers. He compares the vocal instrument with those musicians play, and also explores all the sounds of the English language and their phonation (formation).

4. **The Linklater Method**: Developed by noted teacher Kristin Linklater (b. 1936), whose authoritative books, essential for actors, are *Freeing Shakespeare's Voice: The Actor's Guide to Talking the Text* (Theatre Communications Group, 1992), and *Freeing the Natural Voice: Imagery and Art in the Practice of Voice and Language*, first published in 1976, and revised in 2006 (Drama Publishers). She provides a step-by-step method of developing vocal technique, emphasizing the development of the actor's strength, flexibility and range.

Edith Skinner (?–1981), another brilliant teacher, detailed her ideas and methods in *Speak with Distinction* (Applause, 1990), a masterpiece that should be in every actor's library. Also wonderful is J. Clifford Turner's *Voice and Speech in the Theatre* (new edition; Methuen, 2009). Like Linklater's books, Skinner's and Turner's contain a wealth of exercises and foundational techniques, and inculcate excellent diction. Also extremely helpful for both actors and singers is Kathryn LaBouff's *Singing and Communicating in English: A Singer's Guide to English Diction* (Oxford University Press, 2008), an exceptionally clear, detailed text with many useful exercises.

One of the very best books on how to deal with verse drama, technically and organically, and particularly with Shakespeare, from whose works numerous examples are analyzed, is Cicely Berry's *The Actor and the Text*. Ms. Berry is a renowned expert and teacher, and the Voice Director of the Royal Shakespeare Company.

Elements of Vocal Technique

In addition to diaphragmatic support and the correct "placement" of the voice so as to bring out its greatest resonance, the elements of vocal technique include correct, sustained, and sustainable breathing technique; and the fluidity of a voice trained to be variable and flexible.

The trained voice moves around in the mask: in other words, its placement varies as the stream of air is directed to various areas, in order to express naturally, unconsciously, and without calculation what the character wishes. You won't have to calculate how to ask a question, or how to express anger: you do this automatically in real life, and you do the same things when you play a character; but you do them as the character would. The principal difference is that you have to project vocally; that is, to speak more loudly than you normally would.

An important caveat regarding the exercises in the following sections: You must take voice classes and study proper vocal technique with a teacher. Doing such exercises on your own is all very well, but as Robert Perillo points out, without a teacher, you will have no idea if you are doing them correctly or if you are achieving the desired results. He does think, however, that all the exercises suggested here are good ones.

Finding and Placing Your Voice

Here is a simple exercise for "finding" your best, that is, your most natural, pleasant-sounding voice:

> While standing, relax, breathe in deeply, and say "ah." Gently go up and down the scale, speaking on that vowel. Don't tense the muscles or tighten the vocal cords or hold the abdominal muscles. Just proceed with as little muscular effort as you can. Find out how high and how low you can go comfortably. Find the middle range where you are most comfortable. That is your best voice. You never want to go too low or too high, except for the purpose of creating a specific effect or doing a character voice. Also, it is the middle voice that projects best and is best heard in the theater.

You will begin to have a sense of the placement of your voice, all around the mask. The resulting sound is your voice at its most resonant; you should feel the bones of that part of the face vibrate. At the same time, the vocal cords will be relaxed, because you will be concentrating not on the physical sensation you experience there, but rather on the area where you feel the bones vibrate. You will be able to sustain the voice throughout a performance without fatigue to the vocal cords, and you will be able to vary the voice naturally. With correct breath support, you will also be able to project the voice with ease. As Robert Perillo says, "Every sound must be supported."

When you have correctly placed the voice, you should by no means experience the voice as nasal or as guttural, nor should it have an artificial sound, nor one that sounds too controlled.

Here is an exercise to help you place the voice correctly. Before you do it, you must know how the particular consonants in the exercise are articulated. They all fall into the category of continuants; that is, they can be continued as long as you have breath to do so. That and their natural placement explain their usefulness for placement exercises.

A consonant is nasal when you feel vibrations in the cavities around the nose, as with "m" and "n." The term "alveolar" refers to a place of articulation (where one part of the vocal apparatus, called an articulator, touches another) where the tongue touches the alveolar ridge, just behind the teeth. The term "velar" refers to a place of articulation where the tongue touches the velum, in the back of the mouth. An approximant is a consonant formed when the two parts of the vocal apparatus used to articulate it do not touch so closely as to cause audible friction, as with the consonant "l"; the word refers to the manner of articulation:

1. M: A bilabial [using both lips as articulators] nasal: a forward consonant formed by pressing the lips together, tongue relaxed, and extruding air between the closed lips.

2. N: An alveolar nasal: a forward consonant formed by pressing the tongue firmly against the alveolar ridge just behind the upper front teeth, lips parted, as air is extruded. The blade of the tongue is up and you should feel the palate vibrate.

3. NG: A velar nasal: a back consonant formed by raising the back of the tongue and touching it against the velum.

4. L: A lateral approximant: formed with the tongue raised and air extruded from its sides (laterally), while the tip of the tongue presses in a forward position against some part of the upper palate. There are different forms of this consonant in different accents and languages, formed and determined by where the different parts of the tongue press against the upper palate.

And now, here is the exercise. This will also be of use in helping you to maintain a steady, sustained voice as you control the airflow:

Remain standing, and begin humming the consonant "m." In the voice you have found, say, "am, I'm, ohm, ahm, ihm," dwelling on the "m" sound. You should feel the bones in the mask vibrate. Still dwelling on "m," begin reciting any text you have chosen. Do not worry for now about the meaning of the words or about how effective your reading might be. This exercise is purely for placement. Now repeat the exercise using the consonant "n," and again using the consonant "ng," and a fourth time, using the consonant "l."

Once you are sure of placing the voice correctly, make it a habit to do so when reading aloud or reciting lines. Then, most importantly, forget it. The habit you have formed should simply be there, and you should never have to think about it again. You can now concentrate on acting. The placement of the voice in the mask is not like the placement for singing, although it is akin to it. But in singing up and down the scale, the voice has to be in exactly the same basic place for all the notes. This is why some opera singers feel they have to speak by always placing the speaking voice in the same area of the mask, which makes them sound artificial and takes the audience out of its willing suspension of disbelief. Although the basic center of the speaking actor's voice placement is also in the mask, your speaking voice will go sometimes into the center, sometimes to the bottom of the mask, and sometimes to the top, without your being conscious of this, as you deliver the lines in the most natural manner possible, concentrating not on your voice, but on subtext, intentions, actions, and fulfilling your objective.

Supporting the Voice

As previously stated, you must learn to support the correctly placed voice from the diaphragm, in conjunction with the belly muscle, using its movement up and down to help you project the voice. Proper support for the voice involves a combination of the movement of the ribs in and out, as the diaphragm pushes upward; the lower muscles of the abdominal cavity are brought relatively less into play. Robert Perillo uses the term "belly muscle" in his classes, because the student can see it and feel it, whereas the diaphragm is inside the body and can only be felt. In other words, it is the belly muscle that the student can observe in action. To aid observation, he also recommends that people wear tights in class.

> To find correct support, stand comfortably, feet slightly apart, and breathe in and out while being very aware of the activity of all the muscles. As you expel the air from the lungs, more or less forcefully, the diaphragm will push upward. Try to concentrate on the action of the belly muscle. Repeat this exercise until you are conscious of the action of the diaphragm and feel you can control it. Use the portion of the abdomen where your belly button is, rather than the lower abdominal muscles, to help support and project the voice.
>
> Now sit down and repeat the previous exercise using the consonants "m," "n," and "ng," until you feel comfortable with the combination

of correct placement of the voice and the diaphragmatic support. This exercise will help teach you to place and support the voice correctly, without strain, in any physical position you may be in.

Breathing and Breath Control

Good breathing technique is essential for good voice production, and for sustaining the voice throughout a performance. The amount of breath you take for an utterance is very important: the more control you have, and the more air you can take in, the better. You will need it.

Breath control is also important for smooth phrasing and for sustaining vocal tone, as the following exercise will show you. By "phrasing," I mean how you speak a group of words that naturally belong together; a phrase can consist of any number of words, even one. Phrasing involves pacing, rhythm, and fluency of expression. When considering the phrasing of a text technically, you will ask yourself, "Am I going to sustain a long phrase on one breath? Or will its meaning be clearer if I break it up into its separate clauses?" This can be particularly important when performing Shakespeare or other verse dramas. Ideally, phrasing is an unconscious natural phenomenon arising organically from the nature of the text. With good breath control, phrasing that is natural will be easy, and you should not have to calculate it except in particularly difficult cases.

Here is an exercise to help you develop breath control:

> Choose a sonnet by Shakespeare. Say the first line on one breath, then stop, even if you feel you can go on. Take another deep breath, and say the first two lines on one breath without stopping. Now stop, and take another deep breath, then say three lines on one breath without stopping. Continue in this way, adding lines, until you find the natural limit of how many you can say on one breath. Repeat this exercise periodically, and after some time you will have developed more control than you might have imagined possible.

Developing Variety and Flexibility

Variety results from varying pitch and tempo. Flexibility means being able to switch back and forth at will between pitches, without having to think about it.

Here are two exercises to help develop both:

1. Take any text you choose, and purely for vocal effect, read it aloud with a staccato rhythm, then with legato phrasing. Do it with different rhythms and in different tempi. Read on alternately high and low pitches, varying the pitches from low to high, then from high to low.

2. Now read the text aloud again, giving it the meaning it should have. Read with varying intentions and subtext that you invent. You should find that you have automatically added variety to your reading.

Paralinguistics: How to Do Different Voices

Paralinguistics deals with aspects of sound production that are related to language, but are not directly part of speech. These phenomena include the general rhythm or tempo of an individual's speech as well as the quality of his or her voice, including its high and low timbres, its shrillness or soothing effect, and whether an utterance is whispered, croaked, etc. The way in which emotions are expressed through intonation patterns is also a paralinguistic phenomenon, one connected to the communication of subtext, as are expressive vocal sounds such as cries, sobs, and shouts. These *voice qualifiers*, which make a delivery hoarse, drunken, sick, whining, raspy, loud, soft-spoken, high-pitched, obsequious, or drawling, all communicate a condition or relationship. For example, a hoarse voice may indicate that a person is sick. Actors can use these phenomena to great advantage in recreating behavior. They may be decided technically, but they must be incorporated in an organic way during the rehearsal process.

In order to change your voice so that you can do a character voice, you must consider several things, all of which involve manipulating the muscles inside the mouth and directing the flow of air:

1. **Placement: nasal, throaty, etc.** Imagine that the voice is placed where you wish it to be, and feel the placement simply by concentrating on the physical sensation your imagination has produced.

2. **Direction of the air:** You must direct the air coming up through the vocal cords to a particular area: down into the chest; up into the area behind the eyes (for a nasal voice), etc.

3. **Tightening or loosening of the vocal cord muscles:** Tighten them at the top for higher voices, and lower down at the bottom for

lower voices. This requires some practice. It helps to close your eyes as you concentrate on feeling where the muscle area is.

Changing the voice involves changing its natural pitch and its natural placement. This demands some concentration on the muscles of the vocal cords, which is exactly what you want to avoid in your general placement of the voice.

Of course, many actors simply do different voices naturally and unconsciously, just as some people are naturally good at doing impressions or imitations. You want to avoid undue strain on the vocal cords, although there will be some strain in any case. Therefore, while doing the following exercises keep a glass of water handy to help you keep the vocal cords thoroughly moist.

1. **The stage whisper:** Say "hah" as loudly as you can, voicing the vowel. Now repeat the exercise without voicing the vowel, which will give you a loud, but whispered sound. Repeat this as often as you like while directing the flow of air to the upper part of the mask. Now add some voice to the whispered "hah," and you will have what is called a "stage whisper."

2. **The creaky voice:** On the sound "hah," direct the stream of air so that you feel it going through the top of the vibrating vocal cords. This will begin to give you the high notes of your range. Tighten the vocal cord muscles at the top, so that you have the feeling of holding them. Now direct the stream of air through the tightened vocal cords so that you really feel the cords vibrating. You can now begin to play around or experiment with the resulting rough, raspy, creaky voice. Use a line of text for practice.

3. **The gruff, gravelly, or hoarse voice:** On the sound "hah," direct the stream of air so that you feel it going through the bottom of the vibrating vocal cords. This will begin to give you the low notes of your range, and the beginning of a gruff, rumbly voice. Tighten the vocal cord muscles at the bottom, so that you have the feeling of holding them. Now direct the stream of air through the tightened vocal cords so that you really feel it through the bottom of the cords vibrating. You can now begin to play around or experiment with the resulting voice. Use a line of text for practice.

4. **The high old person's or sick voices:** On a high pitch, start whining on the syllables "ah" and "ooh." Go up and down the scale,

almost as if you were imitating the cliché of a ghost. At a comfortable pitch stop and repeat any phrase of text. You should find your voice beginning to quaver or tremble slightly, because of the tightness of the vocal cords. A caveat: You will want to avoid the usual sorts of clichés indulged in for the portrayal of feeble or ill people.

Diction

No matter what the accent you or the character speaks with, good diction and pronunciation, consisting of clear vowels and well-articulated consonants, makes everything you say easy to understand. Clear pronunciation is a requirement of paramount importance, even in heavy regional accents, which must usually be altered somewhat for the stage or screen, for the sake of intelligibility. The mumbling, slurring, and generally poor diction one hears nowadays from some young film actors is appalling and distracting. Spectators should not have to strain to hear and understand you: they should be able to concentrate on the story as it unfolds. If they don't understand you, they spend time thinking about what you might have said, and lose what is happening while they are thinking.

In Shakespeare, and indeed in all Elizabethan verse plays, clarity of articulation is essential. The language is hard enough to grasp, and scarcely needs the added difficulty of faulty diction. If you are an American actor, you don't need to do Shakespeare with an English accent—dropping post-vocalic "r" and pronouncing such words as "can't" and "ask" with a broad, open-throated "a"—anymore than you would need to do his plays with an American accent if you happen to be English. Contemporary English accents are not the same as they were in Elizabethan days in any case.

Sometimes whether you will use the clearest diction or not depends on the character you are playing, although, once again, the audience still has to understand you. But if you are playing a drunk scene, or doing a character from a lower social class, like the gravedigger in *Hamlet*, or someone with an accent, native or foreign to the language, your diction will be adjusted accordingly, as with the French, Irish, Welsh, and Scottish accents required in *Henry V*. But in general, I repeat, good diction and vocal energy are essential, particularly since the language is archaic. Vocal energy requires diaphragmatic support and the energetic use of the tongue and lips, as in a Gilbert and Sullivan patter song, without overdoing it by moving them too much out of their natural positions. The articulation of the consonants (when one part of the vocal apparatus touches another) has to be clean, crisp, and clear, as in the sounds of d, t, b, and p, for instance. The same principles apply to recording, with the caveat that the recording artist must not over-articulate. This is as bad and as distracting a fault as not articulating enough.

W. S. Gilbert may not be Shakespeare (of whom, by the way, he was not overly fond) but for practice in crisp, clear diction, with strongly articulated consonants, take any patter song from a Gilbert and Sullivan operetta. "My name is John Wellington Wells" from *The Sorcerer* is a good one.

> Oh! my name is John Wellington Wells,
> I'm a dealer in magic and spells,
> > In blessings and curses
> > And ever-filled purses,
> In prophecies, witches, and knells.

In a phrase like "blessings and curses," we want to hear all the consonants! Indeed, we want to hear them clearly articulated throughout. And link the "r" in the word "dealer" to the word "in": "deale rin."

In *Trial by Jury*, the Learned Judge, having explained how he became a judge, sings:

> It is patent to the mob
> That my being made a nob
> Was effected by a job,
> And a good job too!

The words nowadays are a bit obscure, and an audience might have difficulty understanding them even with the best diction, but they have no chance at all without it. (You almost need a translation: It is obvious to the mob that my being made a wealthy man was brought about by a confidence trick, and a good trick, too.)

Remember that in this context the first syllable of the word "patent" is pronounced with a long diphthong, like the word "pay." For clear diction, dwell on the "n" in the word "nob"; and pronounce the final "b" very clearly, with strong articulation. Do the same with the consonants in the word "mob": dwell on the "m" and the "b." The final "d" in "made" should also be very strong. This technical advice does not preclude delivering the material organically, especially if this diction is absorbed during rehearsal, and becomes simply a habit.

Here are some of the hallmarks of good classical stage speech and diction:

1. Pronounce final consonants strongly and distinctly. We tend to drop them or use a naturally soft version of them in everyday discourse. Make them stronger than usual, without overdoing it.

2. Pronounce all consonants in consonant clusters more strongly than you usually would; we want to hear the "st" in "lost" and the "pt" in "swept," as well as the "pts" in "accepts," the two "st" sounds in "vast stretches," the "t" and the "m" in "trust me," and—one of the most difficult combinations—the "pths" in "depths."

3. Pronounce both syllables in such two-syllable words as poem, ruin, believe, police, jewel, cruel, and duel, and all the syllables in such multi-syllable words as library, museum, February, believability, jewelry, cruelty, vegetable, and natural, but don't overdo it; in other words, don't overemphasize consonants. (Incidentally, if you were doing the Major General's song from *The Pirates of Penzance*, you would be obliged to pronounce the word "vegetable" with all four syllables.)

4. Use the diphthong commonly known as the "liquid u" in such words as "new" and "duke": nyoo, not noo; dyook, not dook.

Make sure we hear the consonants that we usually drop or elide slightly in the middles of such words as "recognize" and "completely" in everyday speech, unless the character would not pronounce them. But they still have to be clearly spoken! Be very careful to avoid consonant assimilation, coalescence, and consonant dropping. Assimilation and coalescence take several forms:

1. One consonant can disappear into another in such phrases as "quite determined," where the "t" in "quite" would simply be dropped and elided into the "d" of determined;

2. Similarly, "s" or "z" coalesces with "sh" in such phrases as "this shoe" or "these should go here";

3. Assimilation also takes place when "t" or "d" is followed by "y" and changed into "tsh" or "dzh" in such phrases as "can't you

tell" (kæn choo); or "get your book" (ge chər) or "did you see that?" (di dgoo);

4. Consonants in consonant clusters are frequently dropped in such phrases as "hold fast," where we should hear the "d" and "t," or "the first thing I want to tell you," where we should hear all the final "t" sounds, even though in normal speech we would not hear the final "t" in "want" before "to."

In normal speech, of course, some consonant assimilation is natural, and you would certainly use normal speech in speaking dialogue so coalescene will occur, but be careful to keep diction clear. Some of the most salient examples of consonant dropping, assimilation, and coalescence are heard in certain regional accents: In New York City, "Did you eat yet?" becomes "dgee che?" with the "t" in "yet" glottal stopped. A glottal stop replaces a "t"; it is formed by the quick closing and opening of the glottis, the "t" not being articulated. In a heavy London Cockney, "That's all right, isn't it?" becomes "ass aw roy ni?" with both the "t" in "right" and "it" glottal stopped. In Australia, "Made your bed yet?" becomes "my dguh bi dgi?" with the "t" in "yet" glottal stopped.

Prosody and Phonation

You must study and understand the *prosody* of the language, which is particularly important when doing verse plays. Prosody includes the language's system of versification, which depends on various linguistic features, especially stress patterns; see chapter 2 for a discussion of meter. More generally, prosody includes the linguistic features, aside from phonetics (e.g., vowel and consonant sounds), that determine how versification and prose work. These factors include *stress*—a result of the amount of force or loudness placed on a syllable when forcing air up from the lungs and through the vocal folds during speech. And stress depends in part upon the length (literally, the temporal duration) of syllables, and creates the rhythmic pattern of a language. Prosody may also include *pitch patterns*, also called *intonation* patterns. Which words are stressed and what intonation is used depend on the speaker's intentions. For more on this subject, see the next chapter.

The study of phonation is also very important: it details the way in which a speech sound is formed, produced, and uttered, i.e., by the vibration, and the oscillatory opening and closing of the vocal folds. They open and close as air is sent from the lungs upward through them, and directed to a particular part of the vocal apparatus: *vowel phonation*; *consonant phonation*. You will find examples of phonation in the discussion of the consonants m, n, ng, and l on page 17.

The study of phonation patterns (an aspect of phonetics) is essential when working on an accent: vowels and consonants are similarly but differently phonated in different languages, and the differences may be carried over into the new language, creating the accent.

In fact, as you develop vocal technique, you should simultaneously learn general phonetics, which is the scientific study of human vocal sounds, especially speech sounds. Phonetics includes the analysis of their source, production, and manner of utterance. It also includes the classification of sounds into various categories, as well as the transcription of the classified sounds into the symbols called letters. The symbols have been refined in the *International Phonetic Alphabet (IPA)* to reflect sound as accurately as possible.

Singers must know at least the phonetic systems of the languages they sing. It is also a good idea to learn the prosodic features of the languages, and, best of all, to learn the languages fully. The quality of sounds in other languages differs from English sounds because of the way in which the vocal musculature is used in phonation; e.g., French generally "feels" more forward in the mouth than American English does. The nature of vowels is conditioned by the extent and shape of the mouth opening, which, again, differs somewhat in each language. The nature of the consonants (although similar in each language) is conditioned by the hardness or softness of articulation, and therefore also differs somewhat from language to language. Also, the application of sound values to letters (orthography, i.e., spelling) differs in every language, although such applications often coincide. But in German, for instance, the letter "d" at the end of a word represents its voiceless equivalent "t," whereas it represents the voiced sound in English.

For a general introduction to the science of phonetics, and for further information on all the sounds of English, consult Beverly Collins and Inger M. Mees's *Practical Phonetics and Phonology: A Resource Book for Students* (Routledge, 2003).

Vocal and Diction Exercises

Remember Hamlet's advice to the actors: "Speak the speech, I pray you, as I pronounced it to you, trippingly on the tongue; but if you mouth it,

as many of your players do, I had as lief the town-crier spoke my lines."
That is still good advice—and you can use that speech as a vocal exercise.

First, exercise the muscles of the mouth by moving the lips from side
to side with the mouth slightly open; then repeat with the mouth open
wider. Open and close the jaw, and stick the tongue out and back in.
Make chewing motions with your mouth closed.

For simple diction practice, repeat each exercise at least five times,
varying the pitch and stress patterns, and using different subtexts and
intentions of your own devising:

1. He thought he saw a Banker's Clerk
     Descending from a bus:
   He looked again, and found it was
     A Hippopotamus:
   "If this should stay to dine," he said,
     "There won't be much for us!"
          (from *Sylvie and Bruno* by Lewis Carroll)

2. There was a Pig that sat alone
     Beside a ruined Pump:
   By day and night he made his moan—
   It would have stirred a heart of stone
   To see him wring his hoofs and moan
     Because he could not jump.
          (from *Sylvie and Bruno Concluded* by Lewis Carroll)

3. Having been a wicked baronet a week,
   Once again a modest livelihood I seek,
     Agricultural employment
     Is to me a keen enjoyment,
   For I'm naturally diffident and meek!
          (Robin Oakapple, from act 2, *Ruddigore* by Gilbert and
          Sullivan)

4. Poor children, how they loathe me—me whose hands are certainly
   steeped in infamy, but whose heart is as the heart of a little child.
          (Sir Despard, from act 1, *Ruddigore* by Gilbert and Sullivan)

5. I don't like compliments, and I don't see why a man should think
   he is pleasing a woman enormously when he says to her a whole
   heap of things that he doesn't mean.
          (Lady Windermere to Lord Darlington, from act 1, *Lady
          Windermere's Fan* by Oscar Wilde)

6. So, my good window of lattice, fare thee well: thy casement I need not open, for I look through thee.
   (Lord Lafeu to Parolles, from act 2, scene 3, *All's Well That Ends Well* by William Shakespeare)

7. Jeremiah, Obadiah, puff, puff, puff,
   When she goes her messages she snuffs, snuffs, snuffs,
   When she goes to school by day she roars, roars, roars,
   When she goes to bed at night she snores, snores, snores,
   When she goes to Christmas treat she eats plum-duff,
   Jeremiah, Obadiah, puff, puff, puff.
   (old English nursery rhyme)

8. A guardian there was, and a crab was he,
      Fal de ral, de ral, lal, la;
   He kept his ward under lock and key,
      Fal de ral, de ral, lal, la.
   He tried to plague her all the day,
   But she danced and sang the hours away.
         Fal de ral, de ral, lal, la.
      (from the poem "The Guardian" by George Colman the Younger)

9. To be avoided, unless specifically required for a character, is the *monotone*, which is flat, unvaried speech, spoken on one pitch. But for the purposes of this exercise, take any of the above texts, and recite it all on one note. Then recite it again a half tone up, then a tone higher, and so forth. Then recite it on successively lower tones. Lastly, recite the text as you would ordinarily wish to do.

Acting with an Accent

Everyone has an accent, because nobody could possibly speak without one. An accent is simply a pattern of pronunciation. It is a person's habitual way of speaking. We recognize accents as being of a particular place, as belonging to a specific social class, and as having particular linguistic characteristics. So accents are also models of pronunciation patterns.

There are two kinds of accents: those native to a language, and those used by someone who has learned the language, called foreign accents. Although native accents are usually associated with geographic place and social class, many people learn to speak with a neutral accent. This pronunciation model is often thought to be a standard "best" accent, and to be suitable for newscasting, documentary narration, broadcast journalism, announcing, or book recording. The idea of the "best pronunciation" is a sociological one; that is, the accent usually so named is used by the upper economic classes, who constitute a dominant minority. But characters who speak with other than the so-called standard accents are ubiquitous in performance projects of all kinds.

It is difficult to lay down hard and fast rules when it comes to accents of English, and English has many words with more than one pronunciation. Nevertheless, you must be aware of what the standard sounds of the language are. By standard sounds we mean those perceived or observed as being used by the majority of speakers. There are a number of so-called standard accents (which always vary somewhat from speaker to speaker). Among them are General American or Canadian, if you are North American, used by the majority of speakers; or British Received Pronunciation (RP; also called BBC English), if you are British, actually natively used by a small minority. It is gradually disappearing and being replaced by Thames Estuary, an upper-class accent much influenced by London middle-class accents. You can learn one of those accents, if it is not your own, and it is a good idea to be able to do more than one. To help train yourself, listen to recordings or films made by the many British, Canadian, and American actors and authors with superb diction: Martyn Green, in Gilbert and Sullivan recordings from the late 1940s and early 1950s; the entire Redgrave family; Ronald Colman; Robert Donat; Maggie Smith; Edith Evans; Edna St. Vincent Millay, in recordings of her poetry; Langston Hughes reading his poetry; Walter Pidgeon; William Powell; and Ruth Draper in her monodramas. Listen as well to the rich voice and marvelous diction of Welsh poet Dylan Thomas in his many recordings.

A character's accent is a given circumstance, and is simply the way a character speaks, whether the accent is native or foreign. It should be selected to be as specific as possible to the individual. And it should be worked on as early as possible so that it can become a habit. In fact, it should become so ingrained that the actor can pick up any piece of material and read it with the accent, or conduct a conversation using the accent.

An important point, usually left out of the equation: People who are speaking a language not their own listen differently from people who are speaking their native language. They listen more carefully, even after years of speaking the learned language, because they have to be absolutely sure they understand. The listener is usually unconscious of doing this, but it does condition responses, however slightly. People who really have the accent with which they are acting do this automatically. But Anglophones who learn a foreign accent have to factor it into the equation to add a sense of reality. If you listen in too relaxed a manner, the way you usually do, you give the lie to the idea that you are a foreigner who has learned English, and this unreality communicates itself to the audience without anyone's being consciously aware that this is so.

Learning an accent is a technical exercise, but the accent itself should become organic. As a dialect coach, I usually teach the particular placement of the accent first; that is, I tell the actor specifically what sounds resonate where, and what the muscles of the vocal apparatus are doing. I may then have the actor do brief exercises in order to get the correct feeling of the accent in the mouth.

After that, I concentrate on the salient characteristics of the accent, for instance, important rhythmic patterns. In Hungarian, words are stressed at the beginning, with the following syllables being evenly stressed, and this trait is often carried over into an accent in English, as with Zsa-Zsa Gabor or Bela Lugosi. A French accent works differently: In French, the language communicates by means of rhythmic phrases that are stressed on their last syllables (the phrases may be long or short), except when that syllable contains the sound of the schwa (the sound of "e" in the word "the" before a consonant: the story; IPA symbol: ə), in which case the preceding syllable is stressed. Example: In the rhythmic phrase *la table* (lah TAH blə) the syllable "tah" is stressed. In the rhythmic phrase Alexandre Dumas (a lehk sahn drə dü MAH), only the last syllable is spoken with a primary stress. There is also secondary stressing in French, as there is in other languages. These traits often, but not always, carry over into a French accent in English.

Inseparable from these rhythmic considerations are the intonations, or pitch patterns, that are specific to an accent. A rising pattern at the end of a question and a falling pattern at the end of a statement are traits common in English, but not always in other languages. And if your words are to be heard, you cannot drop your voice at the end of an utterance, no matter how authentic the intonation!

At the same time as I deal with rhythmic and intonational patterns, I teach the necessary sounds (the phonetics) of the accent. For instance, some consonant and vowel sounds are important features of an accent because they do not occur in the learner's native language: the "th" sounds of English, for example, do not exist in many languages. What does the speaker substitute for the "th" sounds? Also important are the differences in vowel sounds, for instance in the northern and southern accents of the United States.

You can work on an accent technically in the way I have described, using, as one always should, actual models. Listen to recordings, or to people who have the required accent. And you can use such books as my own, *Accents: A Manual for Actors* (Limelight, 2002), with its two CDs of exercises bound to the inside back cover.

Uta Hagen's principle regarding foreign accents, as expressed in *Respect for Acting* (Macmillan, 1973), is important: Everyone learning a language tries to speak without an identifiable foreign accent. Everybody tries to speak as well as possible. Ingrained, unconscious native linguistic habits interfere with developing a perfectly native-sounding accent in the new language (although this can be done). To put it another way, people do not always hear accurately, and even if they do, they are not always able to use the muscles automatically to produce a new pattern of sounds that would be perceived as native by a native speaker. A linguistic habit is a muscular habit: the way the vowels are automatically shaped by the mouth, and the manner in which consonants are articulated, are the result of the earliest learning, as children begin to speak at the age of about two. Such habits are very hard to break.

People who speak with an accent, by which a foreign, class, or specific regional accent is usually meant, often do not know they have such an accent. This is the case, for instance, with Eliza Doolittle in George Bernard Shaw's (1856–1950) *Pygmalion* (1913), and in the Lerner and Loewe musical made from it, *My Fair Lady* (1956). She is a London Cockney who is taught upper-class speech by a phoneticist, Professor Henry Higgins, and passed off as a high-society lady. The play was written in an era when the entrenched class system in Great Britain was very difficult to overcome, and when accent indicated social class and all that it implied about educational background, manners, and vulgarity. Anyone doing the play or the musical must immerse him- or herself in the social and political mentality of the era, in its accents, and the manners, etiquette, and ways of behaving.

Really good accent work does not draw attention to itself. In the BBC dramatization of George Eliot's *Adam Bede*, for instance, the accents, which are mostly those of rural England in the late eighteenth century, are superbly done. They may not actually be period accents (we don't know exactly what the accents were back then), but they are rustic, and entirely convincing, especially when one knows that the country accent is not the real accent of such brilliant actors as Jean Marsh. There are dialectical features that have been completely assimilated, such as the use of the word "summat" to mean "something." Altogether, this is very satisfying work.

There is little that is more distracting to an audience than bad accents. They take the audience out of their suspension of disbelief and into a consciousness of the artificiality of the whole proceeding. In the magnificently done 1999–2001 British television miniseries adaptation of C. S. Forester's *Captain Horatio Hornblower*, you will hear superb accent work. This is not at all the case with the 1951 Hollywood film, which is done with the worst accents imaginable. Not the least of its egregious faults is that not one of the Spanish characters is played by a Hispanic actor. The swarthy makeup is caricatural, the characterizations are stereotypes, the accents in both English and Spanish are abysmal, and it is obvious, since these characters speak Spanish a lot, that not one of them really speaks Spanish! Only some of the French characters are played by French actors, who really do speak the language, of course; the others are caricatures. Most of the English characters don't even try to do the accents (this is probably just as well), and those who do are bad. Since one or two of the actors actually are English, their authenticity shows up the falseness of the others immediately. On the whole, this is what the Russian actor Mikhail Shchepkin (1788–1863), known for his realistic acting, called "actoring" at its worst—hack work.

There is no excuse for such poor work. It is incumbent on you to study and reproduce the required accent as accurately and, above all, as convincingly as possible. Often, a light accent is all that is necessary, involving a few sound shifts. But the important thing is always a consistent placement of the sounds. Where the sounds resonate makes the accent what it is: In some accents the flow of air is directed forward, in some it is farther back, or in the middle of the mouth. Equally important and an inseparable part of the accent is how the muscles of the tongue and lips are held—more or less tautly, with more or less tension during speech.

If the placement is consistent the accent will be convincing. If it is not, the accent will fail, no matter how accurately it may be done in other respects, for instance, using certain sound shifts. It is inconsistent placement, involving inconsistent use of the muscles, that gives the lie to the accent and distracts the audience: this is what is meant by being "in and out of the accent." Accent work is sometimes neglected, but it is actually essential, because in almost every project, various native or foreign accents are required.

CHAPTER TWO

Reading the Script and Finding the Subtext; Technical Aspects of Language; Speaking Shakespearean Prose and Verse

How Stanislavsky Learned to Read Chekhov

"I will describe life to you truthfully, that is, artistically, and you will see in it what you have not seen before, what you never noticed before: its divergence from the norm, its contradictions," Anton Chekhov (1860–1904) told his friend Lydia Avilova (1864–1942), author of the posthumously published memoir *Chekhov in My Life: A Love Story* (Harcourt, Brace; 1950).

Chekhov achieved his artistic goal with astounding truthfulness and beauty, and his stories and plays still resonate today, in another time, and in many cultures. In the last letter he wrote to Lydia, he said, "Above all, keep cheerful and don't take life too seriously; very likely, it is much more simple. And, anyway, does the life we do not know deserve all the tormenting thoughts which corrode our Russian brains? I doubt it." We may dream as much as we wish, but who could guarantee that if our dreams came true they would really give us what we long for? And just what is it we long for? Do we actually know?

Those are some of the major Chekhovian themes, and at first, few theatergoers or theater professionals seemed to understand them. *The Seagull* failed abysmally at its premiere in St. Petersburg in 1896, so different did it appear from any play written up to that point, and so difficult to comprehend. Chekhov fled the theater in shame, not daring to take the customary opening night bow. It was not until Stanislavsky and Vladimir Nemirovich-Danchenko (1858–1943) produced the play at their newly founded Moscow Art Theatre two years later that its success was assured.

But Nemirovich-Danchenko, who loved the play, had had to persuade Stanislavsky that it was worth producing at all. Stanislavsky had not seen the play's merits, and thought it monotonous, boring, and unplayable. So Nemirovich-Danchenko spent many evenings explaining the inner life of the characters to his unenthusiastic colleague. Chekhov's psychologically profound style, alternately terse and poetic, meant nothing to Stanislavsky at first. When the light finally dawned, Chekhov had no more enthusiastic supporter, and nobody could have appreciated or admired Chekhov's genius more. On the other hand, the author often thought that the director/actor had continued to misunderstand what he was reading when presented with the writer's later works.

The way in which Chekhov wrote characters was innovative. He depended much more on subtextual implications than had previous playwrights. His full-length pieces are full of "indirect action"—events that happen offstage, like the sale of the cherry orchard or Vanya's stealing the drug from Astrov's medical kit. Indirect action is a common playwriting device, used since ancient times. In Greek tragedies, murders took place offstage. But Chekhov uses it in a startling way sometimes: In *Three Sisters*, the unfaithful Natasha has an entire love relationship offstage with Protopopov, who never appears. Yet we can flesh out the whole affair in our imaginations.

His plays are also full of symbolism: the clocks, one of which gets broken, in *Three Sisters*, for whom time is running out; the cherry orchard, which stands for the established sociopolitical order; the samovar in act 1 of *Uncle Vanya*, which represents domestic tranquility and harmony, and which grows cold waiting for people to come and gather around it for tea, warmth, and love at the family table. And the plays are full of dramatic and psychological irony: it is ironic, for instance, that Constantine in *The Seagull* is in love with Nina, the would-be actress who in some ways resembles Constantine's mother, the famous actress, Madame Arkadina; both behave in a very rejecting way with him. But this relationship is also a psychologically astute creation on Chekhov's part, although it has become a contemporary cliché to say that men unconsciously marry their mothers, as they pick women who resemble them.

It was sometimes more difficult to discern immediately the given circumstances in Chekhov than it was in the plays of Shakespeare or Molière, where things were more clearly laid out. Stanislavsky readily admits in *My Life in Art* (Little, Brown, and Co., 1924) that it took him time to understand "the depth and richness of Chekhov's laconic remarks." In *The Seagull*, he played Trigorin, a ladies' man and the successful writer of romantic and probably rather pedestrian fiction, in an impeccably clean, elegant, white costume; and he had made himself up to look as handsome and dashing as possible. But Chekhov, who told him he was wonderful, added that he should play the part in "torn shoes and checked trousers." This was a major clue to the character's mentality, and therefore to the given circumstances of the milieus in which he circulated. Puzzled at first, Stanislavsky later realized that the torn shoes and checked trousers are the real and symbolic outward sign of Trigorin's disordered inner mental activity; of his romantic dreams, which lead him to write his stories; and of the insecurity that leads him to be a Don Juan where women are concerned, in order to overcome a sense of inferiority that remains with him despite the commercial success he has enjoyed as an author.

This was not the last time the playwright would feel misunderstood. In 1899, when Stanislavsky, who was directing and playing Astrov, had told Chekhov before rehearsals for *Uncle Vanya* that he had decided the actor playing Vanya should wear an old coat and heavy riding boots, and carry a whip, because that is what the loutish boors of the landowning class were like, the writer said in astonishment, "Didn't you read my play? It's all in there. Vanya wears a natty silk tie. That should tell you all you need to know!" And, indeed, as with his remark about Trigorin, it does. This is a case where the actor has to use his imagination, but once you know what to look for when you read, it suddenly becomes obvious what Chekhov meant when he supplied this telling external technical detail; and aspects of the character begin to fall into place.

The silk tie indicates that Vanya takes some trouble over his appearance, and that he wants to appear elegant in order to impress Yelena, with whom he is in love, and to show her that not all landowners fit the picture of a boor—the very portrait Stanislavsky had just painted for Chekhov. Vanya is, in fact, the exact opposite of that picture: he is sensitive and intellectual and refined in his tastes. And he happens to be masochistically in love with another man's wife, that man being the widower of Vanya's dead sister, whom Vanya had adored. Living in the provinces far away from the sophisticated city doesn't mean that one is naïve or ignorant or loutish. And Chekhov explained further that the landowners he knew were not boors, but were very much the way he had depicted Vanya as being.

One lesson to be learned here is "Avoid clichés!" Look at the individual character as specifically as possible. The brilliantly conceived 2003 Russian television miniseries adaptation of Feodor Dostoevsky's *The Idiot*, available on DVD, is an object lesson: every character is uncannily real, individual and specific, and consequently quite devoid of any clichés associated, for instance, with army officers or aristocratic ladies.

Even Chekhov's wife, the actress Olga Knipper (1868–1959), was not always sure how to interpret her husband's works. During the preparations for *Uncle Vanya*, Chekhov, a perpetual invalid who suffered from tuberculosis and who dared not attend the rehearsals in Moscow, wrote to her from Yalta on September 30, 1899:

> ...you ask me about Astrov's last scene with Elena. You write that Astrov addresses Elena in that scene like the most ardent lover, "clutches at his feeling like a drowning man at a straw." But that's not right, not right at all! Astrov likes Elena, she attracts him by her beauty; but in the last act he knows already that nothing will come of it, and he talks to her in that scene in the same tone as of the heat in Africa, and kisses her quite casually, to pass the time.

It is at that point that Vanya walks in and, surprising them in the act, thinks there is far more going on between them than there actually is. He is so bitterly disappointed and upset, because he is so in love with Elena, whom he had considered a paragon of virtue, that he displaces his anger onto her husband, the Professor, and that is one of several reasons why he tries to shoot him at the end of the act.

With any author, including Shakespeare, you must learn to read between the lines. You have to find the subtext, the intentions, and to see what the indications in stage directions tell you about the character and the moment. You can ignore them until you know what they really mean, and whether they are relevant to what you are doing. Actors using Strasberg's Method customarily draw a line through stage directions. But they can be useful, depending on who is writing them. Shaw's stage directions are novelistic, and can be read for what they tell us about given circumstances. With Chekhov, they are particularly useful for character interpretation: his directions can be as subtle as that for Vanya's cravat.

You must be a combination of psychologist and detective. You must learn to be a great observer not only of what an author writes, but of the life that it reflects. This is also what Stanislavsky thought. He wanted actors to look deeply into the life around them, and to draw models for characters not only from within themselves, but also from the people they knew and observed every day; in short, from all available sources. It is a good idea to keep a notebook of observations, since you never know what will prove to be grist for the actor's mill.

Chekhov thought of his plays as comedies, but many others read them as dramas with comedic elements and tragic overtones. His comedy tends to be subtly ironic and depends partly on the limited vision of the characters, who cannot see beyond the limitations of their circumstances, while the audience clearly perceives that their problems could be solved if only they understood and could rise above the contradictions in themselves as well as in their situations. If only Madame Ranevskaya could rise above her inertia and do something, perhaps she could save the cherry orchard from destruction! But, of course, she can't; she is unconsciously self-destructive, for one thing. Psychological insight and understanding, clearly shown and embodied in true to life characters, and in the subtext beneath the text, are Chekhov's great gifts to actors and audience alike.

Script Analysis

As Constantin Stanislavsky wrote, from the moment you read the first page of a play that you will be bringing to life—and even before, when you learn that you are going to work on it—your mind will be stimulated. You will feel inspired intellectually and even physically. And you can hardly help beginning to daydream about the play and about your character. All kinds of thoughts about them will revolve over and over in your mind. In the course of organizing and ordering these chaotic and disordered impressions, you will find that some ideas prove useful, while you will discard others. But it is helpful to write them all down. Every one of them. Be assured that you will forget many of them otherwise.

In *The Illusion of the First Time in Acting* (Putnam, 1915), William Gillette (1853–1937), the writer and actor remembered for his stage portrayal of Sherlock Holmes, says:

> No one on earth can read a Play... The Play—if it is a Drama—does not even *exist* until it appeals in the form of Simulated Life. Reading a list of things to be said and done in order to make this appeal is not reading the appeal itself.

A script is no more a play than an architect's blueprint is a house, or a printed score a symphony. The script is a set of directions for putting together a play. They tell you what characters say. They tell you something about the circumstances of their lives. They tell you if the characters are in a Victorian drawing room or wandering through the forest glades of Arden. But that's all they tell you. They don't tell you how to do anything. Or how to be a character. Or how to play a moment. Yes, there are sometimes directions such as "sadly" or "joyfully," but they mean nothing until the actor finds out why the character is sad or joyful, and can infuse the moment with life.

As with reading a map before setting out on a journey, you have to know how to proceed in order to get where you want to go. In *Using the Stanislavsky System*, I outlined Stanislavsky's basic method of deconstructing a script: going from the large to the small picture, in order to put each moment together so that the larger picture is then reconstructed. This is actually an external technical exercise, since the actor does not yet inhabit the character, which must be fleshed out as the play is brought to life in the course of rehearsals. The internal, imaginative techniques discussed later in that same book will then be employed to give reality to the character's inner life. To recapitulate: First, read the play for its story as a whole; then read it again for your character's place in it. Next, divide it into large sections (episodes); then divide those into small sections (events), then into smaller, more manageable sections (scenes; units within scenes). Within each event something happens, and the character wants something (the character's objective). Something stands in the character's way (an obstacle), and the character does something to get what he or she wants (the physical and verbal actions).

Defining the Given Circumstances

When you read a script for its story, you know even before you start that the plot is a given circumstance: you cannot change its outcome. At the same time, you begin to think about the other given circumstances that are specific to your character's life. These facts are usually immediately accessible or easily deduced from the script. Such circumstances as place, time, weather, historical epoch, and all the circumstances that go with them are indicated from the outset. (A list of necessary questions regarding historical period will be found at the end of the introduction to part 2 of *Using the Stanislavsky System*.)

You must begin to answer the question "Who am I, the character?" Certain answers are obvious: name, profession, marital status, etc. But "Who am I?" in the psychological sense and in relationship to the other characters remains to be discovered, and will not be answered until you are well along in rehearsal.

Use the following list to help you. Obviously, some questions will be irrelevant. For instance, it is evident that Romeo and Juliet do not have children: they are children. But the questions about their parents and their childhoods are extremely relevant.

A point of external technique that leads directly to internal technique: Think in terms not of he or she, as many actors do, but of yourself. In order to create an immediate sense of identification, refer to the character as "I":

1. What is your age?

2. Who were your parents? What were they like? What is your relationship with them?

3. Who are your family members? What are they like and what is your relationship with each of them?

4. What was your childhood like? Where did you live? Where did you go to school, and what was that like for you?

5. What is your state of health? Are there any disabilities?

6. Profession or job? What work do you do? How do you view your work? Do you like it or hate it?

7. Economic circumstances?

8. To what social class do you belong?

9. How do you spend your time?

10. Marital status?

11. Do you have children and, if so, how many? What are their names, ages, and so forth?

12. Living arrangements? Where do you live? What are the living quarters like (how furnished, etc.)?

13. Educational background?

14. Religious beliefs? How strongly do you feel about them?

15. Political ideas and beliefs? How strongly are you committed to them?

16. Opinions about people and life.

17. What sort of personal habits of cleanliness do you have? (There are characters in Feydeau farces who never wash, for instance, and this is the subject of jokes.)

18. How do you dress, and what is your taste in clothing? Are you neat or sloppy?

19. What do you like to eat and drink? Do you like to eat and drink?

20. Do you have vices, such as smoking?

21. What, if any, are your artistic and musical interests?

22. Are you pessimistic or optimistic?

23. Are you an honest, forthright person? Or devious and as hidden as possible?

24. Do you relate well to others?

25. Are you warm, loving, caring, compassionate; or cold, filled with hatred, uncaring, and indifferent? Much of this may be decided in rehearsal, and certainly need not be decided in advance. Nor need you be negatively judgmental about the character: people who are indifferent to the suffering of others justify their indifference, often on an unconscious level.

26. What is your sense of humor like?

27. How do you feel about sex and sexuality, your own and other people's? How does your character feel he or she is looked on as a sexual being?

28. What is going on with you emotionally? Analyze each event or happening provisionally in terms of your character's general inner life and state of mind during the event. This is intimately connected with the objectives the character wishes to attain; the obstacles in the way of attaining them and how the character feels about those obstacles; and the actions taken in pursuit of them. Be open to the answers changing: They will evolve as you explore these aspects of the character in rehearsal, and receive direction regarding moves and positioning on stage.

Words, Subtext, and Intentions

"What do you read, my lord?" asks Polonius. "Words, words, words," replies the ironic, knowing Prince of Denmark. Words can be exhilarating, exciting, life-giving. Words can make you feel loved and cherished. And words can wound. And words can kill—they can drive a wedge of anguish, misery and despair into your heart that time itself will never heal.

"Words can stimulate our five senses," said Stanislavsky. Sight, sound, taste, touch, and smell are all aroused by words. Think of adjectives—dazzling, cacophonous, scrumptious, slimy, reeking! Such words set your imagination on fire! But so do all the more ordinary adjectives: hot, cold, sleepy, happy, sad. How do you feel when you think of these words? And there are the verbs, common ones like sleep, make love, drink, eat. When you eat, do you devour, chew slowly, or relish and savor your food? Words are like tastes: their deliciousness should linger on the tongue. What sensations do those verbs evoke when you think of them? What visions do they bring, what tender, haunting memories, or tormenting remorse do they arouse?

By the end of the rehearsal period, you will know the playwright's words backwards, forwards, inside and out. You will say them in your dreams! But, as Lee Strasberg said, "To give words meaning, you must first know the reality, the thoughts, sensations, and experiences that the words stand for."

In *The Illusion of the First Time in Acting*, William Gillette says:

> [The actor] is fully aware—especially after several performances—of what he is going to say. The Character he is representing, how-ever, does not know what he is going to say, but, if he is a human being, various thoughts occur to him one by one, and he puts such of those thoughts as he decides to, into such speech as he happens to be able to command at the time. Now it is a very difficult thing... for an actor who knows exactly what he is going to say to behave exactly as though he didn't...

How can you achieve this behavior? By saying lines with the intentions that inform your verbal actions, in pursuit of objectives: If you are involved in the actions, you will feel as if you are saying the lines for the first time. Remember what Claudius says in act 3, scene 3 of *Hamlet*, as he is trying to pray: "My words fly up, my thoughts remain below; / Words without thoughts never to heaven go." It is the intention that counts! Thoughts and words must be of a piece. You cannot think of your grocery list while you are playing a riveting love scene. Well, you can. But the scene will probably not be quite so riveting. It is true that some nineteenth-century star actor-managers said they were counting the house while delivering their impassioned soliloquies. In fact, they were notorious for it. But if your thoughts as the character/actor do not inform the words you speak, your performance will be as hollow, leaden, earthbound, and unconvincing as Claudius feels his prayers are.

The subtext—the thoughts and feelings buried just beneath the words—determines how the text is uttered. The subtext is what gives the text its meaning. In what manner and with the intention of obtaining or doing what do you speak? Are you making a point, pleading for something, expressing love, making a joke, being sarcastic, praising, insulting, cajoling? The words of a play are never uttered in a general way, but rather in the specific way the character would say them. "The subtext is what makes us say the words," says Stanislavsky. And it makes us say them in a particular way, with specific intentions. "How are you?" can have any subtextual intention you like, depending on circumstance and relationship. Why do you say what you say, in the way that you say it?

Let us be clear: subtext is not, as some people think, merely the concealment of a feeling or intention, the opposite of which is expressed in the lines. What is going on with the character may indeed include such concealment: the character may be lying, for instance, as Iago is. But Iago, like every liar, wants to be convincing! Subtext gives us the reason for the intention: It gives the words we say their color, their energy, and their actual emotional meaning, which goes well beyond simple dictionary definitions. "Speaking is action," Stanislavsky tells us. Intention is purposeful. It is verbal action in pursuit of an objective, dynamic and forceful.

The wonderful British actor George Rose (1920–1988) said in a 1974 interview with James Day on PBS that he always explored what the character *doesn't* say, what the character *doesn't* do, what is concealed, and, importantly, what the character avoids saying and doing. That is, he explored what is *not* in the immediate subtext or intentions, but is in the hidden depths of the character's unconscious.

But Rose always started by analyzing the text. He pointed out that he began with the actual words that are said, rather than beginning with psychology or with actions and objectives. The text leads to everything, including what the character doesn't say, as well as the manner of playing the actions. This process gives great depth to the interpretation of character and is a great aid to concentration as well. There is so much to think about that you simply can't help concentrating, so that the ability to concentrate becomes thereby a part of your very nature as an actor.

Subtext can include layers of psychological complexity and complication. To take a simple example, just because Kulygin (a part I had the pleasure of playing) in Chekhov's *Three Sisters*, says "I am contented," doesn't mean that the character is actually happy. Nor does it mean that you, the actor, will feel happy when you say the line. How contented can Kulygin be, when his wife Masha, whom he loves—or thinks he loves, but that is another question—is betraying him, and when he is deeply upset by the betrayal? You will feel whatever you feel; that is all you can do. And you will say what he says. Kulygin's subtext, his intention, is "I want you to believe what I am telling you, namely that I am happy. I want to believe that myself!" But what is Kulygin not telling us? What does he not say, perhaps even to himself, on a conscious level? "She doesn't love me after all, and I am so unhappy. In losing her, I am losing everything." He also says aloud, "Masha loves me. My wife loves me." Again, the subtext is "Believe what I say!" But is Kulygin trying to convince others or himself? Perhaps both.

You must never forget—never!—that the words are conditioned by what goes on inside, internally, in the actor/character's heart and brain, emotionally and cognitively. What goes on in the mind is the cause of what the character says. The words don't come from nowhere! And the external technique of analyzing and dealing with language is inseparable from the internal technique of psychophysical motivation.

How Language Communicates: Grammar

As Stanislavsky wrote in volume 3 of his *Collected Works*, "The actor works with words on stage with the help of intonations (rises and falls), accents (force) and pauses (stops)." Along with vocal technique, a knowledge of the technical aspects of language is the foundation on which you can build your analysis of how to say the lines. This technical knowledge works in tandem with your vocal technique. It should be part of you. And then you can forget it: you can allow the information to recede to the level of the preconscious, to be recalled when you need it.

An actor should know his or her own language, and how it works. This means that you must be familiar with grammar, which is the essential means by which the language communicates. You must know the parts of speech and how a sentence is put together to create meaning. The following necessarily incomplete summary, which deals with the most elementary aspects of English grammar, should prove useful as a refresher in the nature of grammatical functions.

In English, the parts of speech are as follows:

1. **Adjective**: A word that modifies a noun—that is, changes the meaning of the noun in some way; also called a *modifier*, which is a more general term, used also for adverbs. When more than one adjective modifies a noun, the adjectives are called "compound adjectives": *a happy, satisfied person*. An *article* or *determiner* (a, an, the), which indicates definiteness or number, is a kind of adjective.

2. **Adverb**: A word that modifies or qualifies a verb, telling us, for instance, how an action is performed; a kind of modifier. Many adverbs end in "-ly": *fortunately, happily*. An adverb may also modify or qualify an adjective: *The duly processed papers were on file*.

3. **Conjunction**: A word that serves to connect or link one thing to another in some way, such as "and," "but," or "that."

4. **Interjection**: An exclamation or outburst of some kind, usually indicating surprise: "Oh!" "Ah!" "My goodness!" Also called an *ejaculation*.

5. **Noun**: A substantive, that is, a word that denotes something having solidity and substance, such as a person, place, or thing; or that indicates a state of being, e.g., happiness, sadness; or a proper name, such as that of a person or place; hence the term *proper noun*.

6. **Preposition**: A word that denotes position or direction, such as "on" or "to." Prepositions are followed by their objects: An *object* is a word that tells us why the preposition is used; that is, what or where something is, or the direction in which it is going: *on the table*; *to the door*.

7. **Pronoun**: A word that takes the place of a noun that it represents or stands for, such as "her," "him," or "it": rewritten with pronouns, *Romeo met Juliet in the garden* would read, "He met her in the garden."

8. **Verb**: A word that indicates an action, or a state of being. Verbs of action are called *dynamic*. Verbs denoting states of being are called *stative*.

A. Some verbs that denote actions may take an object, and are called *transitive* verbs: *He hit the ball.* Some verbs that denote an action do not take an object, and are called *intransitive* verbs: *He went to the store.* Verbs that denote a state of being do not take an object, and are therefore intransitive: *I am happy.*

B. Verbs have tenses; that is, they tell us about time: past, present, future; e.g., a simple past tense: *I went.*

C. Verbs in the present tense in English have three *states*:
   a. The *simple* (merely stating a fact in the simplest way): *I go.*
   b. The *emphatic*, as shown by the use of the verb "do," is an *auxiliary* or *helping verb* in this context; that is, it helps the main verb by emphasizing what is happening: *I do go.* The emphatic state may also occur in the past: *I did go.*
   c. The *progressive*, indicating continuity, and informing us through the use of the conjugated verb "to be" of an action that is ongoing, or that someone is in the act of performing; it may also have an emphatic effect, particularly when the verb form of "to be" is stressed by the speaker: *I am going. I AM going.* The progressive state may also occur in the past or the future: *I was going. I will be going.*

D. In English, the past tense is often indicated by auxiliary or helping verbs, such as "have," which, when used as an auxiliary before the *past participle* of the verb, informs us that the action of the sentence took place in the past: *I have often gone there.* The helping verb "will" tells us that the verb is in the future tense: *I will go there.*

E. Verbs also have *moods* that tell us something about possibility or actuality: the *indicative*, that is, denoting something that definitely is, was, or will be; the *conditional*, telling us something that could or might exist under certain conditions, often denoted by the simple past of the verbs *can* or *will*, "could" and "would": *I could do that, if I wished. I would do that, if she wanted me to.* The *subjunctive* mood tells us that something depends upon something else; in other words, it is a kind of conditional that informs us of hypothetical or contingent action. Also indicating subjectivity, the subjunctive in English is far less used now than it used to be: The phrase "If I were" (subjunctive) is often heard as "If I was" (indicative), now considered quite correct usage: *If I were to go to that store, I might find what I wanted. If I was to go to that store, I might find what I wanted.*

The word "object" refers to something acted upon in some way. Objects are *direct* or *indirect*: In the sentence "He hit the ball," the word "ball" is a direct object, because it has been directly acted upon. In the sentence "He gave him the ball," the word "ball" is still the direct object, and the word "him"—with the preposition "to" implied—is the indirect object. The indirect object serves to identify the reason for the direct object, that is, for or to whom or for what motive the object is acted upon.

The parts of speech listed above are used in the different parts of a sentence, the major large unit for communicating ideas, which is divided into its *subject* (what the sentence is about: who or what performs an action); its *verb* (what the subject is doing); and its *predicate* (completes the sentence and, often, tells us how the subject acts upon something). *I* (subject) *went* (verb) *into the house* (predicate). The foregoing is the simplest kind of *declarative* sentence; that is, one that makes a direct statement about something that happens, has happened, or is expected to happen. But most sentences (like this one) contain *clauses*, which are sections that add to, clarify, or in some other way modify its meaning; clauses are separated by conjunctions or by punctuation marks, such as the semicolon in this sentence, that link them to the other clauses. Sentences may be *passive* (the subject is acted upon), or *active* (the subject acts, or performs an action): *The ball was hit by the batter.* (passive) *The batter hit the ball.* (active)

Punctuation, Intonation, and Stress

Stanislavsky knew the importance of observing punctuation. In *An Actor's Work* (translated by Jean Benedetti; Routledge, 2008), he says, "Words and speech have their own nature which requires a corresponding inflection for each punctuation mark." By inflection, he meant a particular intonation, or pitch pattern. The study of intonation patterns is quite an important one. When doing accents, for instance, the intonations patterns are salient features, whether the accent is one native to the English language, or from a language other than English. Someone from Liverpool naturally has a different intonation pattern from a New Yorker; a Parisian has a different intonation pattern from someone who hails from Marseilles—even when speaking English. Someone from

Vienna sounds different from a person from Berlin, whether in his or her native German, or when speaking English with an accent.

Says Stanislavsky, "There is great expressive power in all these inflections [intonation patterns]." Inflection always arises naturally, as an expression infused into intention. Some actors' analysis of a character's intentions remains on the surface, as an external divorced from motivation. "Do I shout now?" "Do I speak softly here?" are technical, superficial questions such actors ask. They are not asking about the purpose that informs the intention, but only about how to read the line technically. In performing Shakespeare, for instance, this kind of actor prefers to dwell on the mechanics of speaking verse dynamically, rather than on the character's psychology. But this approach is something you should avoid. Concentrate instead on what gives rise to the intentions, all the while knowing the technical aspects as well.

Intimately linked to intonation patterns are the rhythmic patterns of an utterance. The rhythmic pattern is created by the stress patterns: which word or words are emphasized. The stressed words convey the intention, as Stanislavsky pointed out. The stressed syllable of the most important word—the one that makes the point—from the speaker's point of view is called the "nuclear tone." The nuclear tone also has a lengthened vowel. It is towards this word, and this nuclear tone, that the speaker goes, de-emphasizing the words around it. They are spoken on a more even pitch pattern, while the stressed word is spoken on a differentiated higher or lower pitch than the others. I must emphasize that stress or rhythmic patterns ought ideally to arise from the organic process of exploration in rehearsal, and not to be calculated or contrived beforehand. There may be cases, however, where one must calculate such patterns, particularly if the actor is stuck and cannot seem to find the moment. Sometimes, limited rehearsal time dictates that the director intervene, as Stanislavsky sometimes did. But in general, allow such things to happen naturally and spontaneously.

Stanislavsky noted several rules for stress, which were not original to him, but which he had observed:

1. An adjective qualifying a noun should not be stressed more than the noun it describes, usually. In Hamlet's speech (see p. 65), for instance, do not stress the adjectives "windy" or "forced," although there is room to color them with visual meaning, for instance by drawing out the "I" sound in the first syllable of "windy," but see rule 3: avoid overstressing.

2. If, however, it is meant to bring out an antithesis, the adjective might be stressed: She is a *good* person, but he is a *bad* one.

3. Do not overstress words: let the stress happen naturally, organically.

4. Do not understress words: again, let the stress happen organically.

To work on finding stress technically, he recommended that the actor not stress anything in particular at first, but give everything an even stress, until the underlying intention is clear. In other words, don't pretend to know something and don't act as if you know until you really do. This is similar to the neutral attitude of actors beginning Sanford Meisner's famous "repetition exercise": wait to see what happens and go with it, accordingly.

Punctuation and stress are interdependent, and punctuation marks also provide some indication of pitch/intonation patterns:

Punctuation Marks and Their Uses

1. A **period** demands a full stop, however brief. But usually you must not drop your voice even for a full stop, but keep the volume up so that the audience hears you, and also knows that more is coming, either from the speaker or from the person spoken to.

2. A **semicolon** also demands a full stop, or may demand a shorter pause, as after a comma.

3. The placement of a **comma** or of the three dots called **ellipses** or points of suspension is of paramount importance: these punctuation marks show something that is going on in the character's unconscious mind, and that results in a pause of some kind, with some meaning in that pause.

4. A **question mark** shows that an answer of some kind is required and even demanded by the speaker. In the case of a rhetorical question, the speaker may simply want the other character to be thinking the obvious answer. There is usually a rising pitch at the end of any question, but there may sometimes be a drop in pitch, depending on intention. The question "How are you?" may have any kind of intention underneath it, depending on circumstances. It may be abrupt, warm, or cold; a simple inquiry or a command; a concerned question, or an indifferent, thrown-away remark, delivered offhand, and as if the person to whom it is addressed is interrupting whatever is going on.

5. A **colon** requires that the speaker pay attention to what follows it, and modifies the statement before it in some way. The final word before the colon is therefore usually spoken on an upper pitch representing inconclusiveness.

6. An **exclamation mark** demands a response, sometimes one of agreement with the speaker; or the following of some order given in the form of an imperative verb. The pitch and stress patterns are usually very strong.

7. **Parentheses** require you to drop your voice to a lower tone, which communicates a thought as incidental to the main thought.

8. **Quotation marks** around a word or phrase may show sarcasm or irony, and the intonation pattern will reflect those attitudes. Or they may simply show that the speaker means the words to stand out, so the pitch will be higher or lower on those words.

Although it is unusual to stress a conjunction, you can do so to create a specific effect, get attention, or make a point. In the television film of *Macbeth* (2010), Sir Patrick Stewart stresses the word "and" twice at the beginning of the soliloquy from act 5, scene 5 (on the advice of Sir Ian McKellen): "Tomorrow and tomorrow and tomorrow..." As Stewart says, 'the relentless weight of time," and the sadness, weariness, and disillusionment of the character, thus emerge with great clarity.

Punctuation and the Pause

A pause, often indicated in the writing by a comma or by ellipses, is a brief, motivated stop in the speaking, filled with some suspense and/or with some action done silently; that is, without vocal utterance. It is never unmotivated, never empty. It is always filled with something: anticipation, desire, thinking, a physical action or activity. And it is very important to know how to deal with pauses. There are strategic, telling pauses throughout Chekhov's plays, and the British dramatist Harold Pinter (1930–2008) employs many long, intriguing pauses, of which he is the great master. They must all be vibrant with thought, intention, and meaning.

Although, as Stanislavsky points out, ordinary grammatical patterns do not usually require or even allow pauses in such sentences as "I'm a man," a "psychological pause" would indeed allow a stop after "I'm."

In a longer sentence, such as "I'm a man who knows what he wants," a pause after the word "man" will immediately attract the audience's attention, and make them listen harder. And the length of a psychological pause is indeterminate: it can be as long as the character/actor feels it is necessary, although a director may intervene and insist that the actor tighten it up, that is, shorten the pause.

Also, as Stanislavsky says, a pause must aid the audience's comprehension and not be a distraction from it. The use of pauses must not create confusion, or be mere self-indulgence, "messy and overextended," because the actor wishes to create an effect or draw the audience's attention.

The pause is inseparable from intention: it is part of the surface under which the subtext lies in wait. In comedy, for example, the technical setup of punch lines in jokes is partly dependent on taking a pause in the right place: when and how the setup line is delivered determine the timing of the punch line. How long a pause does the person with the comic line take before delivering it? Rehearsal and, even more, performance, will determine this, but even when looking at the script, certain determinations may be made based on punctuation, as in the following example of a simple joke from Oscar Wilde's *The Importance of Being Earnest*, in which Algernon and his friend Jack are awaiting the arrival of Algernon's aunt and cousin for tea. Backward slashes indicate possible (brief) pauses after periods. In the last line, the pause helps Algernon set up his own punch line:

> ALGERNON: ... Please don't touch the cucumber sandwiches. \ They are ordered especially for Aunt Augusta. (*Takes one and eats it.*)
>
> JACK: Well, you have been eating them all the time.
>
> ALGERNON: That is quite a different matter. \ She is my aunt.

Choices, choices! There are many choices, always to be arrived at organically, if possible. But here are some technical considerations: What words should be stressed in the first line? Stress also means differentiating the pitch. The word "Please," if emphasized, immediately stops Jack from taking a sandwich. Jack is bound to pay attention: he is stopped by Algernon's word, by the verbal action, by the differentiated pitch. Algernon might even take the briefest of pauses after "Please," before continuing. And the words "touch" and "cucumber sandwiches" could also be stressed, continuing the verbal action, but uttered slightly less emphatically than "Please." In the second sentence, the word "especially" almost cries out for emphasis, as do the words "Aunt Augusta." Jack might stress the word "you" in the line "You have been eating them all the time," helping to set up the necessary stress on "my" in Algernon's last line, without which the joke would be lost. In his surprise, Jack could be outraged, or sulky and annoyed. Another choice: Perhaps this entire exchange would be more effective with no pauses, and with the words just tumbling out.

Sometimes, particularly when an actor is in difficulty, line analysis is required. Vasili Toporkov, in his book *Stanislavsky in Rehearsal* (Routledge, 2004), describes Stanislavsky's working with him in an analytical way, to help the actor find variety and nuance. Because Toporkov was overemphasizing every word, Stanislavsky went so far as to have the actor "anatomize" some of the lines, discovering the most important words, which would then be stressed—not overly stressed, warned Stanislavsky—to make the character's point. In ordinary circumstances, the line should come out naturally without such a predetermined idea behind it. You want to remain free to act! However, Stanislavsky demonstrated not merely the value but the absolute necessity of specificity.

Figurative Language

In all plays, from those of ancient Greece through the classic plays of the Elizabethans and on up to contemporary plays—in the long sentences of Eugene O'Neill or George Bernard Shaw, or the terser prose of Tennessee Williams, Arthur Miller, and David Mamet—you must observe the punctuation, and the stress and intonation patterns the punctuation indicates. And you must deal with heightened language that is more colorful and unusual than the everyday variety. The rhythms of modern and contemporary prose are no less a part of its structure than are those of Shakespearean writing; they are simply different. You will notice in contemporary plays carefully crafted antitheses and juxtapositions, artful language and metaphors, similes, and other figures of speech no less complicated than those of the Elizabethans or Jacobeans. And you must learn to understand figurative language, which is the use of words in other than an everyday, standard, communicative way in order to amplify and create meaning in both literature and ordinary discourse. All actors should be familiar with the following elementary terms, as well as with the nature of meter, discussed in the section on Shakespearean verse tragedy:

1. **Allusion**: A passing, unidentified reference to a work of art, person, event, object, or place. An allusion, which is meant to be germane to the work of art, play, or film in which it is mentioned, refers to something outside the world of that work of art, and is meant to be a reminder of something expected to be well known to the audience.

2. **Anticlimax**: The intentional deflationary rhetorical device of proceeding from high to low, when the audience expects the reverse; also called *bathos*. As M. H. Abrams defines its use in his magisterial *A Glossary of Literary Terms*, an anticlimax "denotes a writer's deliberate drop from the serious and elevated to the trivial and lowly, in order to achieve a comic or satiric effect." And he cites George Gordon, Lord Byron (1788–1824) deflating "the would-be gallantry of Juan's father" in canto 1, verse 9 of *Don Juan*:

   > A better cavalier ne'er mounted horse,
   > Or, being mounted, e'er got down again.

3. **Aphorism**: (A-for-izm) A laconic, pithy, memorable statement, maxim, or adage, often reducing a situation to a comment on it, or stating a principle or opinion, usually with a moral aspect to it, e.g., Oscar Wilde's dictum, "What is a cynic? A man who knows the price of everything and the value of nothing." (*Lady Windermere's Fan*, act 3)

4. **Apostrophe**: An address to something or someone who is absent, or believed to be so, e.g., Juliet's speech in act 2, scene 2: "O, Romeo, Romeo, wherefore art thou Romeo?"

5. **Epanorthosis**: (ehp-uh-nor-THOH-sis) Immediate rephrasing, for emphasis and reinforcement, as in the famous toast by the English poet, wit, and inventor of a system of shorthand, John Byrom (1692–1763):

   > God bless the King! (I mean our Faith's Defender!)
   > God bless! (No harm in blessing) the Pretender.
   > But who Pretender is, and who is King,
   > God bless us all! That's quite another thing!

6. **Epigram**: Originally, a short witty or amusing poem or couplet, like Benjamin Franklin's well-known rhyme from *Poor Richard's Almanac*: "Early to bed, early to rise, makes a man healthy, wealthy, and wise." But in contemporary terms, an epigram is a

concise witty phrase that has a twist to it: an unexpected but satisfying ending, as in Oscar Wilde's famous one-liner, "I can resist anything except temptation."

7. **Euphemism:** The substitution of an unobjectionable or sensitive term for an objectionable, blunt, or potentially unpleasant one. In Edward Albee's *Who's Afraid of Virginia Woolf?*, the idea of euphemism as a form of squeamish censorial puritanism is made fun of when the toilet is referred to as "the euphemism."

8. **Malapropism:** The unconscious, unintentional use of a wrong word in place of the right one that was intended. The term comes from the name of the character Mrs. Malaprop in Richard Brinsley Sheridan's *The Rivals*: she is always using a word that is close in sound to the one she really means to use, as in what is probably the best known of her malapropisms, "She's as headstrong as an allegory on the banks of the Nile." Her name comes from the French phrase *mal à propos*, one meaning of which is "inappropriate."

9. **Metaphor:** An implied or implicit comparison of one thing to another in a non-literal, suggestive way: the winter of our discontent (Shakespeare, *Richard III*, act 1, scene 1); the whirligig of time (Shakespeare, *Twelfth Night*, act 5, scene 1); in my flower of youth (John Milton, *Samson Agonistes*).

10. **Metonymy:** (meh-TAH-nih-mee) The replacement of one word with another that is suggested by it, and "with which," as M. H. Abrams tells us, "it has become closely associated because of a recurrent relationship in common experience": *He sets a good table*, i.e., he serves good food; Abrams's example from Shakespeare's *As You Like It* (act 1, scene 4): "Doublet and hose ought to show itself courageous to petticoat." The term **synecdoche** is similar in meaning to and often confused with metonymy.

11. **Onomatopoeia:** (ah-noh-mah-tah-PEE-ah) The use of words suggestive of sounds heard in nature, as in "the buzzing of bees"; "bow-wow" or "meow" for the sounds dogs and cats make; and in such phrases as "the murmuring stream" and "the rustling leaves."

12. **Pathetic fallacy:** The attribution of human emotions, qualities, or intentionality to inanimate nature, natural phenomena, or animals; sometimes as if nature were sympathetic to human fate;

constantly used in metaphor in verse drama: "Good things of day begin to droop and drowse" (Shakespeare, *Macbeth*, act 3, scene 2). "Blow, winds, and crack your cheeks!" (Shakespeare, *King Lear*, act 3, scene 2).

13. **Ploce**: (PLOH-see) The repetition of a word, for rhetorical effect, as in "Make war upon themselves; brother to brother / Blood to blood, self against self," from Shakespeare's *Richard III* (act 2, scene 4).

14. **Pun**: A joking play on words that deliberately exploits their similarity. Shakespeare's *Richard III* begins with a pun: "Now is the winter of our discontent made glorious summer by this sun [son] of York."

15. **Simile**: A direct comparison using the words *like* or *as*: "My love is like a red, red rose"—Robert Burns.

16. **Stichomythia**: (STICK-oh-MIH-thee-ah) Rapid-fire exchanges of sharp, pointed dialogue, as in some sections of ancient Greek tragedies, where it was used in antagonistic exchanges; e.g., Aeschylus's *Agamemnon*. It also occurs in Noël Coward's plays, e.g., *Private Lives*; Tom Stoppard's *Rosencrantz and Guildenstern Are Dead*; and Shakespeare's *Richard III*, act 4, scene 4, in the confrontation between Richard and Queen Elizabeth; each line of dialogue here is a *hemistich*, which is half a line that ends in a *caesura* (a rhythmic break for sense in the middle of a verse), and continues metrically into the next line of dialogue:

    K. RICH.: Now, by the world—
    Q. ELIZ.:   'Tis full of thy foul wrongs.
    K. RICH.: My father's death—
    Q. ELIZ.:   Thy life hath that dishonor'd.

    Stichomythia is much the same as the *botta e risposta* (smart rejoinder, delivered like a shot from a gun, and the quick-witted response/reply/riposte to it) of commedia dell'arte.

17. **Synecdoche**: (sin-ECK-duh-key) The use of one word substituting a whole for a part, or a part for a whole, e.g., Hollywood, for the film industry; the theater, for the entire industry and everything connected with it. Or to substitute the specific to mean the general, and vice versa, e.g., tragedian, for actor; theater, for auditorium. Synecdoche is often confused with **metonymy**.

Speaking Shakespearean Prose and Verse

Before you can begin to deal with the technical aspects of textual analysis, stress patterns, and intentions in classic plays, you have to know something about their grammar and vocabulary. You have to absorb the old-fashioned, archaic language, to make it yours, to feel it in your bones. The grammar of Shakespeare's Early Modern English is very close to our own, and easily comprehensible. But where there are differences, the actor sometimes needs to work technically to make meaning clear to the audience. Actors performing Shakespeare should have David and Ben Crystal's exhaustive *Shakespeare's Words: A Glossary and Language Companion* (Penguin, 2002) on their library shelves. Aside from being a complete dictionary, it has concise discussions of Elizabethan grammar, and provides fascinating information on obscurities of the language.

Elizabethan Stage Directions

Elizabethan stage directions need to be understood by directors and actors. They may or may not be useful in productions, but at any rate, they are a help in visualizing scenes. And of course you have to know what they mean when you see them in a play script. Sometimes they refer to what we presume was the way in which theaters were constructed. At other times they clearly indicate what actions were performed. There is a useful, if brief, sidebar on the subject in *Shakespeare's Words*, but a more exhaustive study is Alan C. Dressen and Leslie Thomson's *A Dictionary of Stage Directions in English Drama, 1580–1642* (Cambridge University Press, 1999). The following brief list should prove helpful:

1. **above** The upstage balcony, presumably an acting area in an Elizabethan theater, although the sketch of the Swan Theatre—the only authentic one we have from the period—shows spectators sitting in that area. The above could be concealed by curtains that would be opened to "discover" a scene. This area is also called the *inner above*. The direction "above" indicates that a scene takes place there, or that some actors in a scene are blocked to be there. Actors may be directed to "enter above" or "aloft." Another direction indicating that a scene took place above is "on the top."

2. **alarums and excursions** Military action. Alarums were the off-stage sounds of trumpet fanfares, drums, and shouts calling to

arms. Excursions were the onstage, choreographed movements of soldiers.

3. **alone** By oneself (on the stage), as in the direction "Enter alone." In act 3, scene 2 of *Romeo and Juliet*, we see Friar Laurence *alone with a basket*. And in act 1, scene 5 of *Macbeth*, we read the direction for Lady Macbeth to be *alone with a letter*.

4. **aloof; apart; aside** To one side; a short way away from the other actor(s).

5. **below** The acting area beneath the upstage balcony, but on the main stage platform, in an Elizabethan theater. It could be concealed by a curtain, opened to reveal actors and perhaps pieces of scenery. (In the Swan Theatre drawing, there are two doors in the wall below the above, indicating that they may have been used for entrances, but that no scene could have been played there.) This area is also called *inner below*. The direction "below" indicates that an entire scene takes place there, or that actors in a scene that uses the main stage are blocked to be there. Actors may be directed to "enter below." The term also refers to the area beneath the stage platform, the "cellarage," the area where the Ghost in act 1, scene 5 of *Hamlet* is heard: GHOST. (*Beneath*) Swear.

6. **discover** To reveal; used of someone removing a disguise to reveal his or her true identity; or of a scene that was hidden behind a curtain (perhaps in the inner below), or otherwise concealed, and is now shown to the audience: *Here* [now; at this point in time] *Prospero discovers Ferdinand and Miranda, playing at Chess*. (*The Tempest*, act 5, scene 1)

7. **exit** (Latin) He or she leaves (the stage).

8. **exeunt** (Latin) They leave (the stage). Also, *exeunt omnes*: They all leave.

9. **flourish** A horn or trumpet fanfare, usually indicating the presence or entrance of royalty or some other important personage(s).

10. **forth** Onto the stage, or off the stage; used with verbs, as in the direction in act 1, scene 2 of *Romeo and Juliet*: "They all but the Nurse go forth." That is, everyone but she leaves the stage.

11. **like** Disguised as: *Ariel like a water-Nymph* (*The Tempest*, act 1, scene 2).

12. **manet** He or she remains (on stage, after others leave).

13. **manent** They remain (on stage, after others leave).

14. **off** Offstage; used when someone or something is to be heard from offstage; e.g., a sennet. The "flourish and shout" acclaiming Caesar in act 1, scene 1 of *Julius Caesar* is meant to be heard off.

15. **sennet** Trumpet fanfare preceding a procession.

16. **severally; several ways** Separately, i.e., in different directions. To enter or exit severally is for two or more actors to come onstage or to leave in different directions, or to leave in the same direction by different exits.

17. **tucket** A trumpet call.

18. **within** Either offstage, or, more usually in Elizabethan staging, in the area directly below the balcony, the inner below, with its (presumed) curtain closed. Sounds may be heard "within" indicating that someone is about to enter, or the area may have been used for actors who concealed themselves as part of the action, as in act 1, scene 5 of *Hamlet*, where Horatio and Marcellus are "within" while Hamlet is onstage with the Ghost; or in act 4, scene 2, where Rosencrantz and Guildenstern are looking for Hamlet, and we hear them calling his name "within."

Shakespearean Prose

In Shakespearean prose, the punctuation was often inserted by the editors of the original editions. In many cases, the lack of punctuation can make interpretation difficult. But observing what there is, rather than ignoring it, can be very helpful for clarity and comprehension. When the punctuation is not there, and because the language is in some ways so far removed from our own, the actor must sometimes calculate where to put in punctuation. You must figure out technically how to divide sentences so as to make their meaning clear to a contemporary audience. In addition, you have to elucidate Shakespeare's metaphorical style and his use of other poetic linguistic devices.

In act 1, scene 1 of *The Tempest*, Gonzalo, "an honest old counselor" (a part which I had the pleasure of playing), tries to instill confidence in his fellow shipboard passengers by talking ironically about the blunt, outspoken Boatswain, who has told them to prepare to die in the great storm that is buffeting the ship. But perhaps Gonzalo is simply trying to reassure himself; or maybe he is just talking out of fear, and is trembling in terror; perhaps all three. Or perhaps he is actually talking to himself—a weaker choice, also from the technical point of view of having to be heard over the noise of the storm. The word "hath" is still easy for us to understand, even though we say "has" nowadays:

> I have great comfort from this fellow: methinks he hath no drowning mark upon him; his complexion is perfect gallows. Stand fast, good Fate, to his hanging! make the rope of his destiny our cable, for our own doth little advantage! If he be not born to be hanged, our case is miserable!

Technically, this speech must undoubtedly be shouted, so that Gonzalo can be heard over the howling wind and the noise of raging waves, especially in modern productions with sound effects.

Before we interpret or translate some of the more obscure meaning of this prose speech, let us notice the punctuation. The colon after "fellow" indicates a slight pause, and a rising inflection, telling us the thought is not done and will continue. His hearers will thus want to know what he has to say next: why does he find this surly, unmannerly boatswain, who is nevertheless intent on doing his job, someone who provides comfort? There follows a joke: because the Boatswain is destined to be hanged, not drowned! This means they will all survive! Notice the semicolon, and take the slight pause indicated by it.

The Shakespearean metaphor of the cable of Fate—particularly the rope (hanging is again implied) of the Boatswain's destiny—being the cable for all of them, is another ironic indication that needs explaining: why should his cable also be theirs? Because the physical cable to which they cling so as not to be thrown overboard grants them only a precarious hold on life that could break or snap at any moment.

The actor preparing the part may immediately understand all this, but it will only be clear to the audience if he actually observes the exclamation points and makes those sentences excited, loud outbursts, partly with the objective of overcoming the noise of the tempest. Perhaps pauses between the sentences, indicated by the extra spaces between them (after the words "gallows" and "advantage"), are warranted, if the tempo of the scene as rehearsed and directed allows for them. Also, this is an example of verbal action, and the correct stressing of the words will make all of this clear—quickly spoken, no doubt, in the urgent tempo required by the scene. All of this technical analysis is based entirely on the inner motivation and given circumstances, as the punctuation helps us to understand them. Notice that after "hanging!" the word "make" is not capitalized: it was a convention of punctuation both in this period and for several centuries to regard some exclamation marks as being internal to a sentence. Therefore, the following word did not need to be capitalized, particularly when—as here—the thought is continued.

Shakespearean Verse Tragedy

A tragedy is a drama about life lived intensely and passionately, on the edge of a precipice, with disaster looming, often just outside the purview of those on whom it will descend with a mortal impact. An unhappy, indeed catastrophic, but unforeseeable ending is in store for the protagonists. As Aristotle tells us in his *Poetics*, this ending results from error on the part of the protagonists, and from guilt—the guilt of immoral actions taken by them, that is, actions taken without regard to ethics and consequences, actions meant to ensure immediate gain, while ignoring long-term implications. In classic terms, the tragic hero or heroine—as the protagonists of a tragedy are called—always has a tragic flaw, that is, a blind spot in a character's self-perception that leads him or her to disaster. Aristotle's word for this is *hamartia*. The fault or flaw is often that of hubris: god-defying pride and overly high evaluation of the self, that goeth before the flawed hero's fall. Hubris is a combination of the sense of complete entitlement to whatever the tragic hero desires and a blindness to the consequences of his actions. The needs of others are ignored, and the tragic hero goes self-confidently forward to his own destruction, deflecting warnings from the gods or from other people. And the stakes for everyone are the highest possible—as they are in farce!

This is the moralistic basis on which tragedy, from the ancient Greek to Shakespeare to contemporary stories, is to be understood. Tragedy is a warning to the beholder not to overstep the bounds of ethics and propriety, to think before one acts, and to consider the long-term consequences of action. But when playing tragedy, the actor must be aware of the usually unconscious nature of the hero's tragic flaw. The tragic hero is unaware of his hubris, and instead simply feels that psychological sense of entitlement, and the urgent need to forge ahead.

Hamlet's tragic flaw has been seen as his indecisiveness, but this is only one interpretation among so many. Actually, he decides to do a lot of things, but he acts to avenge his father's murder only when he is enraged and can do only that, since his own death, instigated by his father's murderer, is already imminent, after he is stabbed with the envenomed sword. Othello's tragic flaw has been seen as his trusting nature, combined with a tendency to mordant jealousy. He murders his wife in order to relieve his feelings of rage and hurt, but this results not in any kind of relief—how could it?—but in despair and in his own self-murder. Such analyses are important for understanding and following the character's throughline (see glossary), and the arc of the part.

Elizabethan verse tragedy presents unique problems for the performer. The verse must be spoken with a sense that it is heightened and beautiful language, but without the exaggeration that would falsify it immediately in the audience's mind; in other words, without declamatory phoniness. The words must be heartfelt. And they must be spoken with love: that is the true secret to speaking verse, loving it and loving the words.

In his fascinating book *Shakespeare's Advice to the Players* (Theatre Communications Group, 2003), the great English director Sir Peter Hall deals extensively with the technical aspects of analyzing and scanning verse, with which words to stress according to the meter of the verse, and with the nature of figurative language. Hall emphasizes that these are historic techniques for interpreting and delivering verse that should not be lost in the mists of time—rather than prescriptions that preclude those internal aspects of character psychology that provide real interest to both actor and audience. On the contrary, he talks about how breaks in the lines are there for sense and meaning, and emphasizes that there are emotional changes that the actor must learn to understand when a caesura separates a line.

Performing verse drama requires you to deal with specific rhythms, namely the classical meters in which verse plays were written. Meters are rhythms that alternate strong and weak stresses in a predetermined, recurring pattern, called a "foot." A metric line of verse is named after the number of feet it contains: a tetrameter contains four feet; a pentameter, five; a hexameter, six; a heptameter, seven; and so on. (The second syllables of the words ending in -meter are stressed when the words are pronounced.)

One of the most commonly used meters is "iambic pentameter." An *iamb* (pronounced "I-am"; but "iambic" is pronounced "eye-AM-bik") is a foot containing one weakly stressed syllable followed by one more strongly stressed syllable; there are five iambs (or iambic feet) in a line of iambic pentameter, in the following rhythm: te TUM / te TUM / te

TUM / te TUM / te TUM. Shakespeare's verse in his plays is usually iambic pentameter.

There are three other standard feet that you should be familiar with, because you will find them all at one point or another in verse plays, along with free, unrhymed verse, which uses no uniform metric pattern at all:

1. The **anapest,** consisting of two weak syllables followed by one strong syllable: ta ta TUM.

2. The **trochee,** consisting of one strong syllable, followed by one weak syllable: TUM ta.

3. The **dactyl,** consisting of one strong syllable followed by two weak syllables: TUM ta ta.

Iambs and anapests are said to be written on a rising rhythm, because the strong syllables are at the end; and trochees and dactyls are referred to as being written on a falling rhythm, because the weak syllables are at the end. Although the pitch on which those syllables are spoken may also be higher or lower, you should not drop your voice on the ends of lines, unless it is absolutely necessary to do so. In most cases it is best not to reinforce the meter, but to leave it alone; it will be heard anyway. For more information, see the cogent entry "Meter" in M. H. Abrams' *A Glossary of Literary Terms* (Heinle & Heinle, 1999), one of the most useful, thorough reference books I know.

Two other important poetic devices are the *run-on line,* meaning that a thought is continued into the next line, as you will see in some of the examples below, and the *caesura,* which is the end of one thought and the beginning of another somewhere in a line, such that a pause is necessitated in the reading of it, as you will also see below. The use of run-on lines and caesuras facilitates enormously the task, and the pleasure, of performing verse drama, and of providing subtextual reality.

The iambic pentameter in which the free (unrhymed) Shakespearean verse is usually composed cannot be ignored, but it should not generally be dwelt upon, or it will sound labored and artificial. Instead, divide the sentences so that the meaning is as clear as possible. The run-on lines and caesuras in many of the verses will help you to sound real and natural. As Stanislavsky points out, the rhythm must live inside you, and you must exist within it: it must be part of you, whether you are speaking or are silent: "The whole performance must be charged with rhythm." This means that you don't actually have to dwell on the rhythm of the verse, so much will it have become part of you in rehearsal, and so much will you be full of the rhythmic feeling, without having to make a point of it. Take, for example, this selection from Lady Macbeth's monologue in act 1, scene 5, in which she plans to murder King Duncan when he arrives as a guest, so that her husband and she can become king and queen of Scotland:

> Stop up the access and passage to remorse,
> That no compunctious visitings of nature
> Shake my fell purpose, nor keep peace between
> The effect and it! Come to my woman's breasts,

The richness of the language and its rhythms even in this brief excerpt show the exciting material the actor has to make come alive. Lady Macbeth speaks of evil, and steels herself to murder, but in such an exhilarating way that whoever plays the part must be filled with fire and enthusiasm. Everything works together: rhythm, tempo, pace, and emotion, fury, and concentration on the objective.

The second and third lines are run-on lines, and they alter the rhythm of the verse as spoken, because the thought and the sentence are continued from one line to the next. In the last line, where the thought is broken and a new sentence with a new thought begins in the same line, we have an example of the caesura, the pause between the thoughts.

In contemporary terms, Lady Macbeth is a psychopath, which is what the English literary critic and essayist William Hazlitt (1778–1830) implies when he says that she is "not amenable to the common feelings of compassion and justice." One of the other attitudes and feelings that epitomize psychopathy is that psychopaths do not see people as terribly real, with their own fears and desires. To Lady Macbeth, people are only pawns in the vast game of chess she plays. Everything must be sacrificed to her ambition. Everyone in her life is there to be manipulated to her ends, including her weak-willed, miserable, puny, small-hearted husband— another psychopath. The one thing that might redeem her is that some-where deep down is a lurking ability to feel guilt and remorse for her evil deeds; it is this that will drive her mad. The fact that Lady Macbeth can ultimately feel guilt is implied—and will be borne out later in the play—by the lines:

> ... Come, thick night,
> And pall thee in the dunnest smoke of hell,

That my keen knife see not the wound it makes,
Nor heaven peep through the blanket of the dark,
To cry, "Hold, hold!"

As I have said, when punctuation is supplied, it not only helps clarity, but also should absolutely be observed. Notice, for instance, the comma in "Hold, hold!": it calls for the briefest of pauses. A louder, slightly longer stress is required on the second "hold," since it is followed by the exclamation point.

In the following example from Othello, act 3, scene 3, used by Stanislavsky himself in *An Actor's Work*, there are quite a few commas. (He played the role, as well as directing a production of it.) It is therefore up to the actor to follow what is there and to put in any necessary breath pauses; that is, to take the slight pauses and use the inflections that will give the speech its sense and make it completely comprehensible to the audience. Othello has succumbed to Iago's manipulations and swears that he will never change his mind, but will pursue vengeance to the bitter end. You will notice that Othello's reply to Iago's statement "your mind, perhaps, may change" is not followed by an exclamation point, but simply by a period. This indicates that he does not shout, and is steeled to calmness. Single and double backward slashes indicate possible longer and shorter breath pauses for clarity and sense. The actor's breathing also gives the audience time to absorb the meaning.

Never, Iago. \\ Like to the Pontick sea, \
Whose icy current and compulsive course
Ne'er feels retiring ebb, \ but keeps due on
To the Propontic and the Hellespont, \\
Even so, \ my bloody thoughts, \ with violent pace, \
Shall ne'er look back, \ ne'er ebb to humble love \
Till that a capable and wide revenge
Swallow them up.

The phrase, "ne'er ebb to humble love," can be very emotional, as Othello recalls the circumstances of his love for Desdemona instantaneously, and portrays himself as humble in his love. Such emotion justifies the pause at the end of the line, which also aids comprehension, because it gives the audience a chance to absorb the archaic language. You will notice the archaism "till that" in the penultimate line, where we would leave out the word "that": this means that you should never stress "that," but gloss over it quickly, so that the stress on the first syllable of "capable" is very strong.

Cicely Berry has a wonderful discussion of this speech in *The Actor and the Text* (Applause, 1992), and she thinks that "it would be possible to speak them [the lines] naturalistically making sense of each phrase." Alternatively, the actor could "honor each of these small phrases, yet ride the whole sentence on one breath . . . That is the skill we need, yet without ever losing the spoken impulse, for it should not sound rhetorical." This latter way would bring out the metaphor of the surging current of thought, like the raging sea, in which Othello is caught up; thus "we will come close to the elemental nature of that thought."

In Shakespeare's *Advice to the Players*, Sir Peter Hall gives such technical advice on speaking verse as how the actor must "make every line scan" and "work out a breathing pattern so that you always have breath in reserve": "Breaths whether small or substantial should only be taken at the end of the line." And he advises actors to "Keep the line whole and play lines rather than words." This does not preclude finding the stress patterns that would allow the actor to emphasize and play with certain words. Rhyming couplets not only end scenes, they can emphasize a point being made, or create doubt and therefore suspense in the audience's mind. Rhymes must be "used and enjoyed," he tells us. I remind you, however, that dwelling on rhymes should be as lightly done as possible, or they will simply seem heavy-handed: the audience will hear them anyway, without your having to make an extra effort to stress them.

Having learned and absorbed the technical aspects of speaking verse, you have to make them so habitual that you no longer think about them, are no longer conscious of them. This can only come from experience.

Shakespeare and Subtext

It is a common notion nowadays that there is no subtext in Shakespeare, that everything is directly stated on the surface. But as long as lines have intentions—which they always do—this cannot possibly be true. In any case, there are not only motivated immediate intentions, but psychological situations that give rise to the motivation. And there is always room for different interpretations. No two actors will approach a role or a moment in exactly the same way. In fact, it is a fascinating exercise to compare the interpretations that have come down to us either in the form of written accounts, or, since the early twentieth century, have been preserved on sound recordings, film or in versions made for television.

In act 1, scene 2 of *Hamlet*, the prince, in mourning for his father, the late king, has accepted the truth of his mother's statement that "all that lives must die, / Passing through nature to eternity." Gertrude then asks, "If it be, / Why seems it so particular with thee?" And Hamlet replies:

> Seems madam? nay it is, I know not seems.
> 'Tis not alone my inky cloak, good mother,
> Nor customary suits of solemn black,
> Nor windy suspiration of forced breath,
> No, nor the fruitful river in the eye,
> Nor the dejected behavior of the visage,
> Together with all forms, moods, shapes of grief,
> That can denote me truly. These indeed seem,
> For they are actions that a man might play,
> But I have that within that passes show—
> These but the trappings and the suits of woe.

The speech has been seen as a reproach to Hamlet's uncle, Claudius, King of Denmark, even before Hamlet suspects that his uncle has murdered Hamlet's father. Hamlet just doesn't like his uncle, and of course hates the fact that Claudius has married Hamlet's mother. That is clear, and should be in the playing, but the best and wisest course would be to veil the loathing from Claudius and the others. Remember, people try to hide their feelings, most particularly in a public situation such as the one in this scene, where prestige and respect for the royal house are involved. Hamlet dare not be too openly sarcastic. The line about "windy suspiration" was interpreted by the American Shakespearean actor-manager E. H. Sothern (1859–1933) as referring to the king as an empty blowhard, and the promptbook for his 1906 production indicates that Claudius "glowers at Hamlet," who has glowered at him, to the surprise of the court. They understand Hamlet's implication that the king is insincere. The line about "actions that a man might play" also refers obliquely to Claudius, but must be delivered in such a way that Hamlet could, if questioned, ask, "Why, what do you mean? I had no intention of insulting the king!" Claudius, however, well understands at whom Hamlet is aiming his barbs. Nevertheless, veiling his discomfiture and anger, he tells Hamlet that it is "sweet and commendable" that the prince pays such dutiful homage to his late father. The anger is subtextual, and the intention in the lines is to play the action of being conciliatory. This is also an example of playing opposites, discussed on p. 130.

A more subtle playing of these moments would certainly work even better than Sothern's promptbook indicates was the case in his production. The point is that what we have in Hamlet's speech is all in the intentions, which one actor may interpret as simply to describe false and hypocritical mourning, as opposed to Hamlet's true mourning—perhaps he thinks Claudius is also sincerely sorrowing. Another actor will deliver the speech as barbs directed at Claudius for his callous insincerity covered over by a false show, and those barbs will be subtle, spoken as veiled allusions and innuendo. The second interpretation is no doubt stronger and more active. But, whatever interpretation is used, the lines are hardly devoid of subtextual psychological meaning and intention. And the intentions will be communicated in part by the stress patterns.

To reiterate, how a speech is delivered, and why it is delivered in a particular way, constitute its subtext: in other words, there is a reason why the speech is delivered in one way and not another, as chosen by the actor, and that reason is the subtext. As Iago manipulates Othello, his lines have the subtext of his true intentions: to convince Othello that the lies he tells are the incontrovertible truth. When he talks to the audience, he is more direct, but there is still the question of his unconscious psychological motivation. Why is he behaving like this to Othello? Why does he hate him so? These are enigmas not necessarily to be solved in the reasons he gives us, but rather to be discovered by the actor playing the part.

Actors must "by indirections find directions out," as Polonius in act 2, scene 1 of *Hamlet* instructs his servant Reynaldo to do when he sends him to Paris to spy on his son, Laertes. Polonius means that Reynaldo should ask questions of people who know Laertes, and that he will by such an indirect method get direct answers that Laertes himself might be reluctant to give. In terms of acting, you must use your powers of logic and deductive reasoning to question the text about the subtext.

We don't know how Shylock was originally played by Richard Burbage (1598–1619), the role's presumed creator, known as the first actor to play Hamlet and Othello. At any rate, in the century or so following its premiere, it was played as a comic, caricatural part, a trickster or a clown, sometimes by well-known comic actors, often made up with a red wig and beard, and in altered versions of the play. Indeed, the full title of this play, with its loaded, uncomfortable history, is *The Comical History of the Merchant of Venice, or Otherwise Called the Jew of Venice*. For a discussion of anti-Semitism and *The Merchant of Venice*, see chapter 9 of my book *Tools and Techniques for Character Interpretation: A Handbook of Psychology for Actors, Writers, and Directors.*

The Anglo-Irish playwright and actor Charles Macklin (1699/1700?–1797) changed the traditional comic portrayal, with some trepidation as to how his performance would be received. In 1741, he chose to give the audience Shakespeare's original text, and to play Shylock as a human being, flawed and implacable, a person of "unfathomable cunning," as the astute German traveler and observer of the English theater scene, Georg Lichtenberg (1742–1799), tells us. Macklin was known for the realism and power of his acting, and the following technical details concerning vocal and linguistic technique and stress patterns are of interest. Such line readings may be imposed technically or they may arise organically in rehearsal. Probably, the former was the case with Macklin:

> He wears a long black gown, long wide trousers, and a red tricorne, after the fashion of Italian Jews, I suppose. The first words he utters, when he comes on to the stage, are slowly and impressively spoken: "Three thousand ducats." The double "th" and the two sibilants, especially the second after the "t," which Macklin lisps as lickerishly [greedily] as if he were savoring the ducats and all that they would buy, make so deep an impression in the man's favor that nothing can destroy it. Three such words uttered thus at the outset give the keynote of his whole character.

No doubt, Macklin took the full stop indicated by the period at the end of "Three thousand ducats." And note that he stressed all three words. The subtext in the line "Three thousand ducats" is in Lichtenberg's description of Macklin, "as if he were savoring the ducats," and reveals what Macklin wants us to know about the character from the very first.

The Venetian ducat of the era was a gold coin, although the first ducats were minted in silver in the twelfth century. When the play was written (1596 or 1597), three thousand ducats was a yearly income for the wealthy (a Cardinal's annual salary was four thousand ducats, for instance). An aristocrat's yearly income varied between one and four thousand ducats. And later in the play, Shylock refers to a diamond as being worth two thousand ducats. If we go by comparative Elizabethan values representing the yearly income of the wealthy (see p. 221), three thousand ducats could amount to more than a million dollars in today's currency.

We have accounts of many other great Shylocks, including that of Sir Henry Irving (1838–1905), whose 1879 London production ran for a record 250 performances. Over the next twenty-four years, he would play Shylock "over a thousand times," as his personal assistant and business manager, Bram Stoker (1847–1912), the author of *Dracula*, tells us in *Personal Reminiscences of Henry Irving* (William Heinemann, 1906).

The acerbic, bigoted American theater critic William Winter (1836–1917), friend and biographer of Edwin Booth, wrote a couple of books on Shakespearean performances, *Shakespeare on the Stage* (Moffatt, Yard, and Company, 1911, 1915). He goes into great detail as he describes Irving's readings of certain lines. In accordance with the acting practice of the era, the readings appear quite calculated, but they must have been internalized in order to create the illusion of reality that was important to him. The subtext and intentions in act 1, scene 3, are indicated by Winter, who tells us that

> ...the mention by *Shylock* of the ducats desired by *Antonio* was made in a lingering caressing tone, involuntarily expressive of his love of money...The first speech, "Three thousand ducats:—Well?" only noted the sum, with an accent of inquiry; the second speech, "For three months:—Well?" indicated watchful expectation of something to follow; but the third speech, "*Antonio* shall become *bound*," was uttered with a strong emphasis on the merchant's name and on the word "bound," accompanied by a momentary flash of lurid fire in the dark, piercing, baleful eyes...

Winter indicates as well how Irving stressed words in other lines:

> "How like a *fawning publican* he looks" was spoken with a loathing sneer, a peculiar long, soft emphasis of contempt and scorn being laid on the word "fawning" but that sneer instantly gave place to a stare of reptile hate as the avowal of bitterest animosity was harshly snarled forth, with significant and appropriate stress on the second word of the second line:
> I *hate* him for he is a Christian,
> But MORE, for that, in low simplicity,
> He lends out money *gratis*

In act 3, scene 1, where he learns of his daughter's elopement and Antonio's disaster:

...there was no yelling, and there was no rushing to and fro. The utterance of "There I have another—*bad match*" expressed the infinite of loathing. The ominous words "Let him look to his bond" were spoken in a lower tone than was used in speaking the associated sentences, and in the final iteration every word was uttered separately. "Let—him—look—to—his—*bond*!"

Despite what seems from Winter's description to be the melodramatic nature of his performance, it is clear that the stress patterns used by Irving are meant to reveal what is going on internally and subtextually—an example of Stanislavsky's dictum, "Speaking is action." The line readings seem very theatrical, but as Robert Perillo points out, when it comes to Shakespeare, "There's nothing wrong with a theatrical line reading. If you don't have some, it's pretty dull, but you should always speak from the heart." And, of course, you can't have too many theatrical line readings, or the play becomes all bombast, and unlistenable.

Movement and Gesture; Posture; Positioning

"On entering the court *Shylock* advanced a little way, paused, and slowly gazed around until his eyes found *Antonio*, upon whom his look then settled, with evident gloating satisfaction,—a cruel, deadly look of sanguinary hatred,—and then he stepped a little forward and gravely bowed toward the *Duke's* throne." It is thus that in *Shakespeare on the Stage* William Winter describes Henry Irving's entrance in act 4, scene 1, the trial scene in *The Merchant of Venice.*

The 1879 opening night review in *The Spectator* tells us that throughout the first part of the scene, Irving was:

> standing almost motionless, his hands hanging by his sides ... his gray, worn face, mostly averted from the speakers who move him not; except when a gleam of murderous hate, suddenly and deadly, like the flash of a pistol, goes over it, and burns for a moment in the tired melancholy eyes.

At the end of the scene, Irving "moved slowly and with difficulty" (Winter) and nearly fell, tottering, offstage into the wings. Just before he did so, he lifted his head and glanced for an instant with "ineffable, unfathomable contempt at the exulting booby, Gratiano" (*The Spectator*), the anti-Semite who vulgarly insulted him. Bewildered, shocked by what had happened to him, having lost everything, with "the expression of defeat in every limb and feature," he dragged himself along, head bowed, and left the stage with a last "deep, gasping sigh." Shakespeare gave him no words to say during that exit. No words were necessary.

The physical life of a character is of equal importance with the mental life, which it reflects: Just as the internal state determines external behavior, so the physical life communicates the internal psychological state. In performance, the language of movement and gesture must be so clear as to be read even in the back of the auditorium. Movement communicates prior to spoken words, and body language can tell us what is going on as effectively as the lines. The raising of a finger may be a telling moment. And the slightest movement of the head is expressive and significant. On the screen, the flicker of an eyelash is full of meaning. "The language of the body is the key that can unlock the soul," said Stanislavsky.

Movement, gesture, and posture all work together to communicate character. And a particular movement or gesture can indeed "unlock the soul." Emotion and feeling can be awakened from their dormant state. Look down. Do you feel neutral? Do you suddenly feel sad? Do you feel apprehensive? How do you feel? Look up and to your right. What feelings are aroused? Run down the street! Jump into the air! Fold your arms across your chest! How do you feel? When you do a play, the feelings and emotions will depend, of course, on both character and the circumstances in which the movement is carried out.

Law enforcement personnel trained in the forensic science of psychological or behavior profiling can presumably spot a liar by observing that a suspect looks down, or to the right or left when speaking, that the person looks away, that he or she does not blink, or blinks too much. When a suspect remembers truthfully, the person may look up and to the right. These are real, unconscious reactions that people often cannot control and are not aware of. They can be of use to actors, who might even play against them: Is the character a good or a bad liar, for instance, and therefore in control of such movements or not? In the hit television series *NCIS*, there are many interrogation scenes. Watching the suspect in the interrogation room from the other side of the glass are observers who often note the suspect's body language and comment on it. It is worth your while to watch these scenes and to pay close attention to what the observers see, and to why they have the impressions they have.

The body language of posture and gesture plays a great role in allowing us to understand circumstances, but you will want to discard the many clichés from your movement vocabulary. People supposedly tap their fingers to indicate impatience, or stroke their chin when trying to make a decision. But how many people have you ever seen actually doing those things, except perhaps on stage? We perceive a person with arms crossed as unhappy, uncomfortable, feeling defensive, or creating a barrier against someone else. People who are bored often tilt their head to one side. Further clichés have it that a person walking briskly is self-confident, a greedy villain rubs his hands together in anticipation, and someone standing with her hands on her hips is impatient. These clichés may even sometimes be manifestations of actual behavior. But unless such clichéd movement is real and organic, it should be avoided. It is nonspecific and therefore meaningless. You have to find the movement and gestures that are specific to the character.

In *An Actor's Work*, Stanislavsky talked of "working on the bodily apparatus we use for physical embodiment and its outward technique." As an actor, you have to learn to move all over again. On a stage, most people become self-conscious. Their movements are stiff, awkward, and unreal. In life, people are not usually aware of their movements, unless a specific physical condition makes awareness necessary, if you have sprained an ankle, for instance, and have to be careful when walking. When you create a character, you have to be as unself-conscious as possible in your movements, just as we are in everyday life. Even in such extreme characters as Shakespeare's Richard III, you have to know that the way Richard limps slightly and the posture he adopts because of the bent bones of his hunched back are habitual. Richard is self-conscious about his appearance, but he moves in the way that is natural and specific to him.

The brilliant designer and theoretician of the theater Gordon Craig (1872–1966), the son of Henry Irving's leading lady Ellen Terry, saw Irving perform often and worked with him as an actor. Craig tells us in *Henry Irving* (Longmans, Green, and Company, 1930), that he was a great original, who pronounced the language in his own, somewhat eccentric way. As Shylock, for instance, Irving said "Cut thrut dug" for "Cut throat dog."

Craig describes Irving's way of moving on stage. It was specific to him, and dance-like: he even counted every step he took, as dancers do. And his movement, constantly remarked upon by theater critics, constituted "a whole language":

> His movements were all measured. He was forever counting—one, two, three—pause—one, two—a step, another, a halt, a faintest turn, another step, a word. (Call it a beat, a step, a word, all is one—I like to use the word step.) That constituted one of his dances. Or seated on a chair, at a table—raising a glass, drinking—and then lowering his hand and glass—one, two, three, four—suspense—a slight step with his eyes—five—then a patter of steps—two slow syllables—another step—two more syllables—and a second passage in his dance was done.

Technical and self-conscious as this kind of thing is, it was Irving's personalized way of working, his own system. In order to create the illusion of reality, which he believed was the essence of what acting is all about, the sort of movement pattern Craig describes has to have been internalized, and to have become fluid and unself-conscious. Irving's minutely detailed, individualistic physical behavior was meant to reflect the character's inner life. And the study of movement is meant to help all actors do exactly what Irving defines as the actor's job, in his essay "The Art of Acting" (1885):

> The actor's business is primarily to reproduce the ideas of the author's brain, to give them form, and substance, and color and life, so that those who behold the action of a play may, so far as can be effected, be lured into the fleeting belief that they behold reality.

Movement

You must take movement classes and study the way the body moves. And you must use all available physical, external means and techniques in order to be able to communicate "the life of a human spirit." For Stanislavsky, these external techniques were of paramount importance, because it is the external, physical behavior that the audience sees. Once again, what Stanislavsky called "the life of a human body in a role" communicates what the character is all about, in conjunction with the spoken words.

An essential place to begin the study of movement is with the body's anatomy. You must understand the connections between the body's moving parts, how the joints work, and how the muscles function. Among other things, this will help you avoid strain and possible injury. A good, concise analysis of human anatomy, accompanied by drawings, is provided in the opening section of a book that should be in every actor's library, *Movement from Person to Actor to Character* (The Scarecrow Press, 2009) by Theresa Mitchell. Mitchell emphasizes correct spinal alignment and breathing, and discusses how to center yourself in the character so that the movement flows naturally. She draws the concept of a character's center from Michael Chekhov: it is one of his main techniques of character creation. Mitchell also gives excellent advice on warm-ups, and the many exercises she provides are essential for the mastery of movement technique.

In its simplest aspect, human bodily movement is the motion of muscles: they contract and expand as the result of the energy used when the central nervous system consciously or unconsciously directs them to move. In the classic Stanislavskian sense, movement is action: a series of muscular motions made with the purpose of accomplishing something, whether it be a bit of stage business, or the fulfillment of a large or small objective.

It is also important to note that the muscles remember; more precisely, the neurological system remembers the muscle movements the body makes to accomplish something, particularly such simple tasks as walking. This is called "procedural memory," a long-term memory usable over a lifetime (walking, riding a bike, typing); or for as long as it is needed, as in the case of the movements required of an actor in a particular stage production (blocking, stage combat), a dancer in a ballet, or a musician in playing a piece.

Sense memory includes muscle memory: the memory of what happens when one is drunk, for instance, involves the muscle movements that have been part of the experience. Movements in accordance with it will thus be made when, for example, a class exercise is done miming the experience. The muscle memory will then come into play. It will also be aroused when you mime the sipping of a boiling hot drink or simulate being doused with freezing water. Even though you are not using actual props, the muscle memory is reactivated. Emotional memory also involves muscle memory. Such simple reactions as crying or laughing, for instance, immediately activate the muscle groups that the body learned long ago are used in these expressions of feeling.

Of all the different kinds of movement an actor makes, the most important from Stanislavsky's point of view is walking. It is the movement used most often on stage, yet most people get up on a stage and forget how to walk in a natural, real manner. They suddenly become self-conscious and walk stiffly, in a way they never do when they are hurrying through the streets on the way to the theater, or going down a supermarket aisle in search of cereal. On a stage, they have to learn how to walk all over again. If you have a purpose when you walk, a goal, your walking will immediately become more natural.

A character's particular walk can be a very telling, revealing part of his or her nature, and a natural, specific walk for a character can develop organically in the course of rehearsals. Does the character glide along, prance; walk stiffly, jerkily, smoothly, slowly, or quickly? Does the character waddle? Is the character bowlegged, which conditions the walk? Circumstances condition tempo: walking quickly or slowly is in part determined by the situation.

Never waste movement! Movement in terms of acting should always mean something. It should always be relevant and specific, not general, and certainly not a cliché or unconscious mannerism or what the actor does when he or she is nervous and doesn't know what is going on in the scene. If you have a mannerism, become aware of it and get rid of it by concentrating on the circumstances, actions, and objectives. Don't fidget or move one leg back and forth unless there is a reason and a purpose for doing so. Stillness is fine, and can even be very significant and telling. As Lee Strasberg said—and his remark applies to more than just movement—". . . don't fiddle around on stage, which is involuntary nervous expression." You immediately take the audience out of its suspension of disbelief as they notice that awkward face-scratching or that mechanical stance, or the extra "Uh" or "I mean" added to the beginning of a line.

Very important: Every movement you make must be filled with intention. This is true of the ordinary movement of a contemporary character as it is of a character in a period piece doffing a plumed hat, using a snuffbox, hiding the face with a fan, or gesturing elegantly with a glove. These movements should mean something!

Remember, too, that if you go away from something, you are going toward something else. If you move to get away from someone, what are you moving toward?

The basic elements of the actor's physical and movement abilities include mobility, poise, flexibility, agility, speed of reactions, coordination, physical balance, and above all, control of the body, which involves all of the foregoing elements. A sense of rhythm is also essential.

Movement takes place in space and time—that is elementary. The place is always of prime consideration, both the performance space, and the fictitious place in which the piece is set. Place helps the actor determine both the size and amplitude of the movements. How long does it take to get from one area to another in the space? Movements must be timed technically, and then incorporated into the actor's score (see p. 123), so that they become automatic and instinctual, and can be carried out in every performance as rehearsed.

There are two general categories of movement: involuntary, which is uncontrolled and automatic, such as the reflex activated when flinching before a blow; and arbitrary, which is subject to the will of the mover, as when pouring a drink or striding across a room or turning the pages of a book.

Every movement has its own direction, speed, and tempo, which depend on circumstances; and is done with a particular energy, or power. Each movement involves several groups of muscles, and also has a particular amplitude and character. Every actor should be familiar with the following classification, which expands on the idea of involuntary and arbitrary movement:

1. **Emotional (mime) movements:** These are most often involuntary, as in automatic facial expressions assumed when laughing or crying; but they may also be arbitrary, as when reaching out toward a loved one in order to embrace that person. Facial expressions can communicate to the audience without any other movement being necessary.

2. **Illustrative movements:** Gestures usually accompany verbal actions and are meant to make something clearer, as when pointing to an object or in a particular direction, or shaking the head to indicate "no," or nodding it to indicate "yes." While some illustrative movements are involuntary, most are arbitrary.

3. **Locomotive movements:** These are movements meant to take a person from one place to another, as when walking or running, jumping, or climbing.

4. **Semantic movements:** These are movements that have particular meaning, as in the gestures used by a team in the *NCIS* television series to tell which members where or in what direction to go in a dangerous situation where silence is required; or as in winking significantly, smiling with love, or frowning in puzzlement or anger.

5. **Working movements:** These are the most conscious of all the arbitrary movements; involuntary movement is involved in their execution. Working movements are those used in pursuance of a particular action or actions, as in boxing or fencing. But they are also the locomotive movements used in Romeo's scaling the wall into the Capulet's garden, and in climbing onto Juliet's balcony.

Movement may be further classified as being either *concentric*: movement directed towards a center; or *eccentric*: movement directed outward and away from a central point. While this is very much part of

Delsarte's virtually useless system (see below), the concept was also used by Laban and by Meyerhold, and it may be of use to actors in search of a general Michael Chekhov psychological gesture (see p. 316). A sense of concentric, inner-directed movement may be useful for a character who is introverted; a sense of eccentric movement may serve for a more outgoing, extroverted character.

Like speech and gesture, a character's movement comes from the interior life of the person. This is true of both the general unconscious way the character moves, and of any specifically necessitated movement, such as those attributable to a particular condition like injury, disease, a war wound, or old age.

The French inventor, early cinematographer, cardiologist, and scientific theorist Etienne-Jules Marey (1830–1904) published his groundbreaking ideas on the nature of movement in *La machine animale* (The Animal Machine: A Treatise on Terrestrial and Aerial Locomotion) in 1873. Among other things, he talks of the way in which the muscular system works, and discusses at length the contraction and expansion of the muscles activated by the central nervous system.

If you sift through Marey's book, you will find all kinds of useful information. For instance, in connection with what happens to the muscular system as the body ages, and how this affects movement, the following passage is revelatory:

> What then, is the change which takes place in the muscular function during the different periods of life? Everyone knows that, except in the very rare cases in which the man keeps up the habit of gymnastic exercises, the muscular functions become more and more restricted— at least, as far as the extent of movement is concerned. The articulation of the limbs, and those of the vertebral column, undergo normally a sort of incomplete anchylosis [immobility or stiffening of a joint, perhaps as a result of abnormal bone fusion], which continues to lessen more and more the flexibility of the trunk.

If the objective is to move, and to move well, this condition constitutes a physical obstacle, and the action of moving becomes more difficult as the muscular tensions and stiffness in the joints have to be overcome. This is very often what happens as one ages, and movement is also impeded with the development of such conditions as osteoporosis, as well as the weakness inherent in broken bones that have knit, or as the result of surgery, trauma, accidents, or mishaps. These gives specific possible causes for the kind of halting movement one sees in certain people in old age, one that the actor who wants to be specific and not general will want to study. There are many older parts played by young actors, although often people who are around the right age are cast. But a character like the eighty-year-old Firs, the servant in Chekhov's *Cherry Orchard*, is usually played by someone much younger, although Morris Carnovsky played the role when he was eighty-seven! Also, being eighty at the end of the nineteenth century was often quite different from what it is today, with advances in medicine and healthier lifestyles, so that eighty is the new sixty. In *Uncle Vanya*, the title character, who is forty-seven, says, "Why am I so old?" In the days when life expectancy was not what it is today, he meant it. He also tells us that he expects to live perhaps another thirteen years, and wonders what he will do with that vast amount of time. And, unlike Chekhov himself, who died at the age of forty-four of tuberculosis, Vanya is in good health and leads an active lifestyle as an estate manager who constantly goes out walking and riding to inspect the fields and orchards.

The specific moves or blocking given to the character by the director or improvised in the course of rehearsals must be incorporated into the actor's score and internalized: as I said above, going somewhere involves going away from something, and going away from a place involves going to another place, for a reason connected with character motivation. This is elementary and axiomatic, but it is a principle too often forgotten. Actors frequently do not motivate moves, but move simply because the director has told them to do so. Every time you move, there must be a reason for doing so: the character's inner life does not stop. The actor may disagree with the director: "I don't think my character would do that." But in the last analysis, it is part of the actor's job to justify the direction.

Acting and behavior are first perceived as movement. As Stanislavsky said, "You cannot see feeling." You can see movement. On stage or on screen, movement is more powerful than sound. Our eye goes first to what moves. In theatrical terms, movement is the action of going from one place to another; or of using a body part to gesture; or of assuming a particular physical posture; or of performing some physical action. Something as simple as pouring a cup of tea attracts the eye even before the words that may accompany the action attract the ear. If two people are sitting and conversing in a drawing room, and a servant enters with a tray, our eye goes immediately to the servant, and we stop listening to the dialogue for a second. This means that the servant's entrance must be perfectly timed with the dialogue, so that we lose nothing essential. It helps if the two seated characters stop talking when the servant enters, for the motivated reason that they do not want the servant to hear what they are saying. But if they continue talking, we will lose some of the words.

There is an anecdote about a young actress who had a wonderful role, and would enter and go downstage to deliver her opening lines. But they had no effect on the audience. She wondered why, until a friend informed her that the star of the show was in back of her fiddling with the window curtains, moving a vase to a different place on a table, tossing her hair, and so forth. The next time the young leading lady entered, instead of going downstage, she stood near the star, and, as if inadvertently, put her foot on the hem of the star's long gown, so that she could not move without tearing the dress. This time the young actress's lines were greeted with prolonged applause. Afterwards, she was summoned to the star's dressing room. She went in with some trepidation, and the star fixed her with a glare, then smiled. "You're learning!" she said.

Staging for large theaters is essentially done with the balcony in mind. Those spectators sitting above the stage tend to look first at the back of the stage, so the movements of the actors or singers at the back have to be planned with that in mind. This would seem to be a note for the director, but it is important for the actors at the back to realize that what they do will be observed, and they have no right or reason to slack off or to think that what they are doing is not as important as what the principals may be doing at the front of the stage. Everyone has to work together.

Movement Exercises

Aside from the absolutely necessary movement classes specifically designed for actors, classes in various forms of dance, including ballet, modern dance techniques, jazz, and tap dancing, are extremely helpful. In fact, there is no better training for inculcating flexibility and variety of movement. And, needless to say, if any actor wants to do musical plays, especially Broadway musicals, knowing how to dance is necessary, even for the nondancers, who may be called upon to participate in dance numbers. Dancing is also a necessary skill in operetta, for instance in the works of Gilbert and Sullivan or Offenbach, where there are frequent dances included both by themselves and as codas to musical numbers. Opera requires less dancing of its singers, but even there, for the title role in Bizet's *Carmen* or for some characters in Offenbach's *Les contes d'Hoffmann* (The Tales of Hoffmann), dancing may be required, in a rather limited way. And in the latter opera, the soprano playing the mechanical doll, Olympia, must learn the movements of the automaton, and coordinate them with the singing of her difficult coloratura aria. Every soprano in the many productions I have seen has actually done this perfectly!

If you have specialized training in acrobatics and can do stunts, like Burt Lancaster, who did many of his own stunts in the movies, then you have all the movement training you need as an actor. You will move with grace and agility and be able to carry out almost any physical action. But among actors such training is relatively rare. Gymnastics is far more common; it, too, is an excellent basis for athletic movement and flexibility. But even if you are not an athlete, exercise and movement classes are a necessary help in inculcating body awareness and variety.

General calisthenic and aerobic movement exercises are used not only in actor training but also as limbering-up exercises before rehearsal and before performance. The spine should be well aligned, and the actor should be physically relaxed, so as to eliminate the possibility of injury. Not every actor does such exercises, but for many it is a useful way of making sure that the body is responsive and flexible. Aerobics is meant to help develop the actor's endurance and stamina, and to ensure the good functioning and health of the cardiovascular and respiratory systems. Aerobic exercises ensure that the body remains in good shape generally: walking and swimming are two of the best such activities. Do not strain when doing any of the following well-known exercises! Exercises 2 through 7 should be done with at least ten repetitions each, increasing to twenty or thirty as the actor wishes:

1. **The Isolation Exercise:** Lying flat on your back, eyes closed, begin at the feet and work upwards, becoming aware of each body part and how it feels. This is not strictly a movement exercise, although it can be accompanied by some movement of the legs, arms, and stomach, so as to release further awareness.

2. **Stretches:** These are done standing up. Begin by lifting the arms, one after the other, and stretching with them as high as you can, lowering each arm and alternating the stretch with the other. Then do the same thing by moving up and down on both firmly planted legs, bending the knees in time to each arm movement. Next, stretch the arms to the side from the shoulders, both arms at the same time. Now do a transverse movement, stretching the

arms first to the right, then to the left, turning the chest and shoulders in whichever direction you move.

3. **Neck and Shoulder Rolls:** Roll the neck around to the right, then to the left. Roll both shoulders forward, then backward. Roll each shoulder separately, forward then backward. These exercises ensure that the joints are flexible. Be careful not to strain or tense up when doing the exercises. They should help to eliminate tension.

4. **Side Swings:** Standing with the arms crooked in front of you, fingers clasped, swing around, first to the right side then back to the front, then to the left and back to the front, moving quickly and going as far as you can without straining.

5. **The Back Curl:** Stand straight up, without tension. Bend slowly forward from the waist, stretching the arms toward the floor, and curl slowly and carefully back upward until you reach the position from which you started.

6. **Back and Front Stretch:** Standing with your hands clasped behind your back, stretch slowly backward, then slowly forward, as far as you can go without straining.

7. **Leg Lifts:** Lying with your back on the floor, lift the right leg straight up and lower it; then do the same with the left leg. Then do the same with both legs. Turning onto your side, rest your head on your hand, and lift, then lower, the leg. Turn onto the other side, and do the same thing.

All of these exercises should be done with the utmost care and awareness so as to avoid aches or pains, injury or strain. The last thing you want to do is pull a muscle or a tendon. Undue tension should be eschewed, and you should remain concentrated and constantly aware of what the muscles are doing. Anyone with back problems or other muscular problems should be particularly careful. A doctor should be consulted before embarking on a course of exercises. Using the services of a knowledgeable, empathetic physical trainer is an excellent idea. Therapeutic massage can be particularly useful in easing aches and pains and in eliminating tension.

Rudolf Laban and His System of Movement

As the Hungarian theorist and choreographer Rudolf Laban (1879–1958) points out, echoing Stanislavsky, every movement reveals some aspect of the actor/character's inner life. Influenced perhaps by Vsevelod Meyerhold's "biomechanical" approach to movement (see chapter 15), Laban was among the great movement teachers, and his methods and principles are still taught. He was also a difficult, irksome egomaniac, and not the brightest penny in the stack: Laban supported the Nazis, until his own iconoclasm and emphasis on individualism led to his falling out of favor with them. Still, he had a great deal to teach that was valuable.

Laban analyzed the elements of movement, which he divided basically into effort and action, and he taught flexibility as a necessary habit. The actor must be able to adjust his or her weight and shift the center of the body's gravity not only in general, but also specifically, when creating the physicality of a character. He developed a complicated system of movement analysis and exercises, but one must be wary of taking what he had to say as gospel, and recognize the limited usefulness of all such analysis: the way a character moves should arise naturally, and not according to some predetermined plan.

Despite that caveat, his division of "body movements" into "steps, arm and hand gestures, and facial expressions" is useful, if obvious. All such movements work together and can only be separated for purposes of analysis. The important questions for Laban were:

1. Which body part is moving?
2. In what direction is it moving?
3. How fast is it moving?
4. How much energy, particularly muscular energy, is needed?
5. How much energy is actually being used to make the movement? (Perhaps less is required, and the actor could conserve energy by using less of it.)

Among Laban's exercises are those which cover movements in various planes and dimensions; e.g., pulling up and down in a one-dimensional plane, or pulling transversely, in more than one dimension, out and over. He also analyzed what movements are used in performing various actions. And he divided movements into two basic types with regard to the weight or weightiness of the movement:

1. Firm and strongly resistant
2. Gentle and weakly resistant

In between are various amounts of resistance and hardness. A further element of movement is the amount of time it takes:

1. Sudden
2. Quick
3. Sustained in time
4. Slow
5. Protracted and indulgent

For Laban, movements may be either direct; i.e., in more or less a straight line, and characterized by inflexibility and rigidity; or indirect, that is, characterized by flexibility, turns, and curves.

Laban further categorizes movements by how these (ultimately insep-arable) elements are combined in various ways that exist in planes and dimensions:

1. Firm, direct, sustained
2. Gentle, direct, sustained
3. Firm, indirect, sustained
4. Gentle, indirect, sustained
5. Firm, direct, sudden
6. Gentle, indirect, sudden

To understand viscerally and physically how simple Laban's seemingly complicated system of classification actually is, you must take classes and experience working with the Laban system. He devised a series of exercises that he felt the actor would find most useful for training in flexibility and suppleness, as well as for extending the actor's repertoire of movements. Having absorbed the system, the actor would then be able to move freely with the motion required at any time by the character's psychological desire or need, and by his or her physical condition.

Jacques Lecoq and His Ideas on Movement

Jacques Lecoq (1921–1999) came to theater from sports, his passion as a youth, as he tells us. More far-reaching than Laban, because he was less parochial, Lecoq was one of the most influential theorists and movement teachers in the latter half of the twentieth century. He began his pedagogic career in 1947 by teaching classes in physical expression.

One of his main interests was how to translate movement into character. He was fascinated by all forms of theater. In 1948, he was invited to teach in Italy, where he studied commedia dell'arte and its techniques of movement and mask work, and discovered Greek tragedy. In his ideas and approach, he belonged already to the French modernist tradition of training and technique taught at the Théâtre du Vieux-Colombier under Jacques Copeau (1879–1949) and Louis Jouvet (1887–1951). Continuing the tradition, he had taught in Grenoble with Copeau's nephew, Jean Dasté (1904–1994), who wanted to bring innovative theater to the provinces. In Italy, Lecoq worked with several important playwrights and directors, and studied the commedia with the Piccolo Teatro di Milano, where he worked with the influential director Giorgio Strehler (1921–1997), also noted for his opera productions. Lecoq helped establish its theater school. In 1956, he went back to Paris and founded his peripatetic School of Mime and Theater, which at last found a home on the Rue du Faubourg St.-Denis. Lecoq used the school not only for teaching, but also as an experimental laboratory for the study of movement. Eventually, he also founded a Laboratory for the Study of Movement, known as the LEM, from its French initials.

His important book, *Le corps poétique* (The Poetic Body), published in 1997, was translated into English under the title *The Moving Body: Teaching Creative Theater* (Routledge, 2000). Simply reading it is a broadening experience, and it should be on every actor's bookshelf alongside the works of Stanislavsky and Michael Chekhov. In it, he outlines extensively his ideas on movement and movement technique, along with his theories of the drama and different kinds of performance, from mime to tragedy. The book also contains many useful exercises, and schematic drawings of movements and positions.

Aside from discussing what he calls "dramatic acrobatics" and other specialized forms of movement, he also talks at length about the foundations of "natural everyday movements," which he conceives of as occurring "in everyday life: *undulation, inverse undulation,* and *eclosion.*"

Undulation is the foundational "first movement" of the body, utilized also by fish and snakes. "Humans in an upright condition continue to undulate," Lecoq says. As people climb stairs, for instance, the up and down movement involves undulation, which takes the leverage from the ground and applies it to the accomplishment of the task of getting up the stairs. But undulation applies to all movement that starts from the ground up. When a person walks, for instance, undulation is apparent in the pelvis. Says Lecoq, "Undulation is the driving force behind all physical effort manifest in the human body, which comes down to pushing/ pulling." Pushing and pulling are important complementary movements that every actor needs to be aware of. They are universal oppositions that we all use to accomplish tasks.

Whereas undulation starts from the ground and moves upward, inverse undulation starts from the opposite place, the head, "which initiates the movement by taking its lead from something outside me that sets me in motion." He uses the example of someone watching a bird in flight. As one watches, "the whole body is mobilized" and concentrated. Undulation is voluntary action, as in climbing stairs, even though it uses the involuntary neurological system that activates the muscles, but inverse undulation is the result of reaction, and it thus "expresses dramatic reaction." Most importantly, for the actor's study of movement, Lecoq tells us: "Undulation and inverse undulation share four main body-positions as the movement unfolds: inclined forwards, drawn up to its full height, inclined backwards and hunched."

Lecoq had his students assume each of those positions consciously when executing both kinds of movement. They suggest the different ages of humankind, as in Jaques' famous speech in act 2, scene 7 of Shakespeare's *As You Like It*, "All the world's a stage." For Lecoq they are "infancy, adulthood, maturity, old age." Furthermore, "The body in forward position, back arched, head thrust forward, suggests an image of childhood or the figure of Harlequin." An upright position suggests neutrality and adulthood. The last two positions—inclined backwards; hunched—suggest the decline into old age.

The third movement category mentioned above, eclosion, also suggests neutrality, although it "opens up from the center." It involves "moving from one position to the other without a break and with each segment of the body following the same rhythm." The entire body feels this movement, which is thus a "global" one.

Lecoq devised exercises for all these categories, which are useful in carrying out the actions a character needs to perform. The exercises make the actor aware of the body and its movement possibilities, and inculcate flexibility and creativity. Finally, for Lecoq all movement involves *"expansion and reduction, equilibrium and respiration, disequilibrium and progression."* Correct breathing (*respiration*) creates balance in the body (*equilibrium*). All movement *progresses* towards something, and as equilibrium ends, disequilibrium leading to the next movement is created. And by *reduction*, Lecoq means contraction. The student doing a movement exercise will begin from a neutral position to *expand* the movement to its maximum, and will then proceed to reduce it back down. All the qualities of movement will be in play, and the actor's awareness of what he or she is doing will be greatly increased, allowing for easier bodily control. This also seems a good way of eliminating unwanted mannerisms or personal tics that interfere with concentrating on the character.

How does Lecoq's theory and practice of movement apply to character creation? For one thing, the movements are meant to bring out and communicate character in terms of movements and the positions that result from them, and not in an inorganic or technical way. This approach is the opposite of the Delsarte technique, described below. By attitude, Lecoq means "a powerful moment of stasis, isolated within a movement." He uses the word to mean particular physical positions, and says that each attitude must have a dramatic justification; that is, it must ultimately be justified as part of a character's psychology. This is the connection to character creation that all actors' movement is meant to inculcate.

In classes at the school, masks might be used to help the actor learn about movement and how it communicates. The mask is an artificial, removable facial covering made of any number of materials, from paper to plastic. In the ancient Greek and Roman theater, masks were used to indicate who the character was supposed to be, and eventually an elaborate system of masks was worked out. Masks are also used in some forms of Asian theater, such as Japanese kabuki, as well as in Italian commedia dell'arte, where half masks were also used to show which character an actor was portraying. And they are used in improvisational classes where acting students are taught how to work with masks. Masks set up a particular personality, and give the actor a feeling for character, as well as a sense of freedom, since the face is not seen. They oblige the actor to use his or her full body to express the range of the character's emotions, hence their use in teaching movement.

There are specific cases of movement that has been worked out for a particular genre, such as the *lazzi* in the commedia dell'arte that was such a revelation to Lecoq when he encountered it. *Lazzi* (the singular is *lazzo*) is the Italian term for tricks, standard bit of comic business, droll facial expressions and grimaces, mugging, and comedic embellishment of all kinds. They were originally improvised; the most successful were standardized.

Commedia dell'arte, which is Italian for "comedy of art," is a form of improvisational comedy and a genre of scripted comic play based on standard, formulaic scenarios using stock characters, such as Harlequin,

Columbine, Pantaloon or Pantalone, Punchinello, and Scaramouche; it began in the late sixteenth century. Many of the characters wore masks or half-masks. The term *commedia dell'arte* was not actually heard until the eighteenth century, when the Venetian playwright Carlo Goldoni (1707–1793) used it to refer to scripted plays that he had written—many of which were based on well-known commedia stories—as opposed to the *commedia dell'improviso*, or comedy of improvisation. For full information, consult John Rudlin's admirable *Commedia dell'Arte: An Actor's Handbook* (Routledge, 1994).

The Piccolo Teatro di Milano with which Lecoq was associated during his sojourn in Italy keeps the tradition alive, and often performs the plays of Goldoni. Their commedia playing is delightful, with stylized movement and gestures, as I saw when they came to the McCarter Theatre in Princeton, New Jersey. You hardly needed to understand a word of Italian to appreciate and enjoy the comedy, lazzi, and the slapstick humor. In one scene of Goldoni's *Il servitore di due padroni* (The Servant of Two Masters), a character wishing to hide threw himself down on all fours with his back to the audience and covered himself with a cloak. Harlequin, mistaking him for a chair, sat on him, to reflect and debate with himself over some issue. In pain, the man on all fours hit the stage floor with his hand several times. Harlequin, distracted from his thoughts, immediately said "Avanti!"—Come in!—and we howled. He looked around, shrugged his shoulders, and resumed his contemplation. Again, the hand banged the stage. Again, Harlequin looked up and said "Avanti!" The simple, corny, technical trick, this lazzo, was done with grace and elegance and style, and with perfect timing. Even when it was repeated several times, we burst out laughing each time. One of the reasons for our laughter was that the trick was done with such fulfillment of the characters' inner lives, and with such completeness and reality that we could not help but be drawn in.

Similar comic bits and tricks were used all the time in vaudeville and farce. Doing bits is always a technical exercise: they can never be entirely organic, because of the fact that they have to be done by the numbers, like a stage fight.

Some Elementary Stagecraft: Specific Stage Movement Techniques

It is of paramount importance to know how to prepare for a move on stage, without showing the audience you are doing so. You must anticipate a cross and prepare for it. Just a short time before the cross, put a slight amount of weight on the leg that will remain stationary when the other leg moves to begin the walk: on the left leg if you cross right; on the right leg if you cross left. When turning to cross, always turn downstage, not upstage, unless you are otherwise directed.

When a character crosses past you, do a slight counter-cross—a move in the opposite direction from the person who has just crossed—to adjust the stage picture automatically and unobtrusively. And move on the upstage foot first, whether you are going further to the center or away from it. Also, as Meyerhold points out, you should anticipate your exit: "Get closer to the door before you exit! Even closer! That's axiomatic. The closer you are to the door, the more effective your exit. In moments of climax, the seconds of stage time and centimeters of stage floor decide everything."

As he knew, the actor must always adjust to the particular space, whether on a proscenium stage or in the round. Any actor who has ever been on a bus and truck tour playing one-night stands can tell you that it is imperative as soon as you arrive to explore what the playing space is like physically, and to time moves and entrances.

As Meyerhold also importantly noted, the actor should take pleasure in executing the movements, and should enjoy them. This pleasure is communicated unconsciously to the audience, who will also then be able to enjoy the spectacle being presented. "If the spectator is bored," he said, "it means the actors have lost the substance of the scene and are playing out the dead form of it." Meyerhold classified his biomechanical movements into various types that actors working with him, or using his system, had to learn. In chapter 15, his concept of biomechanics is discussed further.

When you have to sit down, feel the seat with the back of the thigh and, in most cases, sit down smoothly without looking around. If you cross to a chair, prepare the cross as described above, then continue the move smoothly, making the cross and the sit one continuous move, unless you are required to pause or to stop the move for some reason. When you are seated, generally speaking, cultivate the habit of sitting up straight, and place yourself in a forward position toward the front edge of the chair, unless for some reason of character a different kind of position is called for. For instance, the Dauphin in Jean Anouilh's (1910–1987) *The Lark* (1952), a play about Joan of Arc, slouches and lolls about on his throne like a child. But good posture is always called for in comedies of manners, such as those of Oscar Wilde, and it is a definite help to character, especially to those high-society characters who are more conservative, like Lady Bracknell in *The Importance of Being Earnest*. If you are seated in a forward position, it will be easier for you to gesture, and to rise. In period pieces, rising is generally accomplished in a graceful manner, and depends in part on the costume. Also, while you are sitting, one leg should be slightly in front of the other, and your feet should not be too far apart. The foot of the leg that is farther back should be bent slightly and placed under the edge of the seat, while the front calf is vertical, with the foot firmly planted on the floor. This way of sitting on stage, depending once again on character, should be a habit, so that you don't even have to think about it. You must also ask yourself how your particular character would sit and stand.

Stage Combat; the Stage Fall

Stage fighting involves specialized movement that requires training, which many actors do not have. But specific fight moves are taught in rehearsal by the fight director or fencing director of a production, and general movement training and flexibility will be serviceable. Classes in such skills as fencing are necessary for any actor who wants to play in period pieces or in the classics, where duels and other forms of fighting are often required as part of the action. Duels and sword-fighting are common in Shakespeare's plays, as are various forms of fisticuffs. He even has a wrestling match in act 1 of *As You Like It*. Duels are also frequent in operetta, such as those in Offenbach's *Barbe-bleue* (Bluebeard) or Charles Lecoq's *Le petit duc* (The Little Duke); and in opera, as in the pistol duel that results in Lensky's death in Pyotr Ilyich Tchaikovsky's *Yevgenyi Onegin*.

The first rule is always safety. This is why stage fights and combats, whether with weapons or with bare hands, must be choreographed by a fight director, who understands the timing, rhythm, and style of the particular form of combat. A fight scene between two individuals, or in groups, must be rehearsed to the nth degree, and its choreography always adhered to. No improvisation! Stage combat is a very technical exercise. Particularly in the case of individual swordfights or fisticuffs, it is often rehearsed just before every performance, to keep it absolutely fresh in the actors' minds, even though they have done it dozens of times. The most skilled, trained actor in the company is usually designated as the fight captain, and is in charge of such rehearsals. Bear in mind that one false move can lead to injury or worse. Concentration is therefore also absolutely essential.

Also of paramount importance is the knowledge, training in, and practice of the delivery and receiving of stage slaps, punches, and blows. These depend more for their effect upon the reactions of the actor being struck than on the actions of the actor doing the striking, and they must be correctly carried out as rehearsed. But if the actor being struck anticipates the blow, or does not react in a physically correct manner, the audience will not be convinced. Sometimes it is the actor being slapped who actually makes the sound of the slap by striking his leg with his hand and simultaneously throwing back his head, more or less forcefully depending on the strength of the blow. The result is a resounding hit that looks real. Another way is to have the actor being struck clap one hand against another, sometimes with his or her back to the audience. In either case, the hitting arm completes its motion but does not actually strike the other actor with any great force, despite appearances. A light slap might, however, be done for real, as would a light stage punch.

The stage fall is also a necessary tool for the actor. It must be done technically, in such a way as to avoid injury: When taking a tumble, the actor must land first on one leg and one arm, allowing the relaxed body to crumple to the floor, all in one smooth move. George E. Shea gives the following advice on how to fall on stage in *Acting in Opera* (G. Schirmer, 1915)—a book that is actually so anti-acting, and so old-fashioned, that it is not to be recommended except for some of this sort of technical advice:

> Suppose you fall on the right side; the right foot is somewhat advanced, the knees bent out to the right; the body topples over, and the order of contact with the floor is—
>
> Right knee (exterior face), right hip;
>
> Left hand (cupped, palm down) strikes floor in front of right shoulder;
>
> Right hand (cupped, palm down), the right arm having been extended straight out to right or at a 5/8 elevation; the triceps muscles, the bunch of muscles at back wall of armpit, and those covering ribs below it, cushion the body's impact; and you are prone with a crash (and amid dust, alas!).

This is exactly the kind of fall that is useful in scenes where your character is shot, as in the duel in Tchaikovsky's opera *Yevgenyi Onegin*; or in sword-fighting or hand-to-hand combat scenes.

Methods and Techniques of Achieving Awareness and Relaxation and Expanding the Actor's Ability to Move

Aside from taking actors' movement classes, you can help yourself relax in other ways. There are various schools of massage that will help relieve muscular tension; and you can also practice exercises learned in the different schools of yoga, which inculcate bodily awareness, flexibility, and the relief of stress. All these methods include body management techniques and an awareness of breathing and its physical effects. For an excellent discussion of the many kinds of massage and other systems of bodywork now available, consult *BodyWork: What Type of Massage to Get—and How to Make the Most of It* by Thomas Claire (William Morrow, 1995). At some length, he discusses the Alexander, Feldenkrais, and Rosen Methods, as well as many others. Among the bodywork techniques currently in use, and very popular with actors, are the following:

1. **The Alexander Technique:** Perhaps the most widespread technique studied by actors, this is a kinesthetic method of relaxation and of freeing, aligning, and balancing the body, allowing for efficiency and economy of movement. It was devised and developed by F. Matthias Alexander (1869–1955), an actor who left his native Tasmania and moved to London in 1904, where he was a noted Shakespearean. Medical doctors were unable to help him overcome his tensions. In an attempt to deal with his own vocal problems and muscular tenseness, he expanded on the idea that the actor could control his movements and achieve proper, unforced balance and posture through complete awareness of what was going on physically. His first step was to become aware of exactly what was causing the problem, and then to relax with regard to it: it could be solved, and he would solve it. To that end, he devised a way of working with the muscles and with correctly aligned spinal posture. The Alexander technique is currently used as part of actor, singer, and dancer training in Great Britain and the United States. Every actor should take at least one course in the Alexander technique under the guidance of an experienced teacher. During each forty-five minute session, the student, dressed comfortably, lies on a padded table, while the teacher, sometimes with gentle touching, and always by verbal instruction, teaches the student to be aware of bodily tension, and to develop

new, more relaxed ways of moving. The student stands, and is taught to be aware of the spine and its alignment, and to develop good, relaxed posture.

2. **The Feldenkrais Method**: Named for its originator, Moshe Feldenkrais, D.Sc. (1904–1984), the method is a physical approach to awareness of one's whole self through the body. The Feldenkrais method is practiced by people of all professions, either one on one with a teacher, where the work is called "Functional Integration," or in classes, which go under the heading of "Awareness Through Movement." It has been studied with great benefit by actors and other performing artists. The object of the teaching is to create "somatic awareness" and to teach the actor how to move with less effort, and at the same time to be aware of what the entire body is doing to help or hinder the movement. As Thomas Claire says, "it aims to help you learn how to learn." The Feldenkrais practitioner works with movement through focusing attention on the client's skeleton. "The emphasis is on skeletal alignment, rather than muscular strength," says Suzanne Toren, a Feldenkrais practitioner since 1991; she has also been teaching the Feldenkrais method at Mike Nichols's New Actors Workshop. As Ms. Toren says, the philosophy of the method is that "when the skeleton is organized, movement necessarily becomes not only easy, but also graceful and elegant. Think for example of a cheetah, which goes from rest to sixty miles an hour in a twinkling, and uses all of itself—whatever is appropriate to achieve its goal." The aim is to extend the available repertoire of the actor's movement, and also to lessen the pain that can result from a lack of awareness of what the body is doing, so this way of working is very gentle: no forcing, no undue pressure. Feldenkrais believed that our characteristic, inflexible movement patterns are set unconsciously in early childhood, based in part on what we see our parents doing, and that we can learn to be more flexible, and to experience the repertoire of available movements. It is interesting to note that Feldenkrais himself worked with Peter Brook's company for a time, on freeing the jaw and breathing.

3. **The Rosen Method**: This was devised by Marion Rosen (b. 1914), based on her fifty years of experience as a physical therapist and health educator. Her method uses music to induce a state of relaxation and to inculcate relaxed breathing, good alignment of

the musculature, and flexibility. It is meant also to increase the body's vitality and to provide a sense of "physical and emotional awareness."

Among other methods currently used to teach movement is *eurythmics*, consisting of rhythmic games, dances, exercises, and gymnastics intended to inculcate a sense of movement and rhythm. It was first designed by the Swiss musician Émile-Jacques Dalcroze (1865–1950) as a method of experiencing music viscerally through movement exercise. Eurythmics had an influence on public education and on education for the theater. The exercises are useful for actor training, especially for developing the actor's sense of tempo and rhythm.

Gesture

Gestures should be natural and organic, not calculated, except when certain gestures are specifically called for, as in a comic bit or stage combat, where timing is of the essence. Certain technical habits of stage-craft, on the other hand, should be learned early: for instance, the actor should develop the automatic habit of gesturing with the upstage hand, so as not to conceal the face or body.

Stanislavsky's principle of the correct psychophysical action arousing the desired emotion also applies to the action we call gesture; and the correct gesture, even if done technically, can be a very useful tool. The superb, versatile British actor Gary Oldman (b. 1958), interviewed by Conan O'Brien (b. 1963) on the *Tonight Show* on January 11, 2010, demonstrated how he fended off the unwanted attentions of paparazzi by pretending to be menacing: He looked down, looked up, raising his head slightly, then, making his eyes assume a threatening expression, he fixed them menacingly on the eyes of the offending photojournalist. In low tones, he said something like, "Please don't take a picture of me." It worked every time, said he. And no doubt following the steps in order led to his feeling certain emotions as well.

In the seventeenth century, the famous English actor Thomas Betterton (1635–1703), in his putative autobiography *The History of the English Stage* (published in 1741 as a work written by Betterton, but probably actually penned by its publisher, the bookseller and writer Edmund Curll [1675-1747]), tells of a learned Jesuit who had made quite a study of gesture and expression, and passed his knowledge on to Betterton.

Based on this, Betterton practiced exact positions of the arms and hands and facial expressions in a mirror. Nowadays this is anathema.

In the nineteenth century, there were a number of theoreticians who tried to define and set out in detail their ideas on body language, movement, and gesture, among them the Irish clergyman, scientist, and educator Gilbert Austin (1753–1837), whose book *Chronomia; or, A Treatise on Rhetorical Delivery: Comprehending Many Precepts, Both Ancient and Modern, for the Proper Regulation of the Voice, the Countenance, and Gesture* (1806), based on classical models such as Quintilian and Cicero, was highly influential. Also very well regarded was *Theoretische lessen over de gestikulatie en mimiek* (Theoretical Lessons Concerning Gesture and Mimicry), a tome published in 1827 by the Dutch actor and painter Johannes Jelgerhuis (1770–1836).

But it was the method devised by François Alexandre Nicolas Chéri Delsarte (1811–1871) in the mid-nineteenth century that caught the imagination of the theatrical community, and had taken over actor training by the end of the century. Like the other methods, it was extremely technical, and called for posture, stance, gestures, and movements to be calculated in advance so as to create a particular effect for the audience: in other words, posing, instead of being or behaving.

If Stanislavsky was perceived as an incredible innovator and iconoclast, it was partly because the Delsarte system had been so influential. One of the reasons actors and others found the Delsarte system so alluring was its supposedly scientific nature, in the age of burgeoning scientific theorizing and categorizing, even more so because he combined his supposed science with his religious faith.

Here is how Delsarte himself analyzed one of his discoveries, supposedly made through minute observation of people's behavior:

> Now, how does surprise cause us to lift our arms? The shoulder, in every man who is agitated or moved, rises in exact proportion to the intensity of his emotion. It thus becomes the thermometer of the emotions. Now, the commotion that imprints a strong impression, communicates to the arms an ascending motion which may lift them high above the head.

Even if it were true that surprise caused us to lift our arms, and there is reason to doubt that this is always so, why should an actor calculate such a gesture? Playing the moment as if he or she were actually surprised will certainly communicate that fact to an audience. For Stanislavsky, surprise can be expressed organically in any number of ways, none of them calculated in advance. But for Delsarte, all that is necessary is a standard way of indicating a particular feeling. The actor can reproduce the same predetermined pose, invented by Delsarte, every time, like a dancer repeating choreography. He or she would feel something when performing the movement, but Stanislavsky's ideas of emotional recall, and psychologically motivated actions that would naturally arouse the desired feelings, as the actor pursued an objective, are foreign to Delsarte's thinking.

At one point in his researches, Delsarte made a startling observation:

> I noticed nurses who were distracted and indifferent to the children under their charge; in these the thumb was invariably drawn toward the fingers, thus offering some resemblance to the adduction which it manifests in death. With other nurses, more affectionate, the fingers of the hand that held the child were visibly parted, displaying a thumb bent outward; but this eccentration rose to still more startling proportion in those mothers whom I saw each carrying her own child; there the thumb was bent violently outward, as if to embrace and clasp a beloved being. Thus I was not slow to recognize that the contraction of the thumb is inversely proportionate, its extension directly proportionate to the affectional exaltation of the life. "No doubt," I said to myself, "the thumb is the *thermometer of life* in its extending progression as it is of *death* in its contracting progression."

This is, of course, the most preposterous pseudoscientific claptrap. A moment's observation of mothers carrying their children will suffice to demonstrate that these "observations" must be entirely invented. Nevertheless, Delsarte's influence in practical terms was enormous, and the theatrical practice of the day no doubt benefited, at least in the hands of the great practitioners of the art of acting.

The *Delsarte System of Oratory* (Edgar S. Werner, 1882) was edited by his disciple, the Abbé Delaumosne, who sets forth Delsarte's method in his own way. Here is what he has to say about the movement of the head, which, he informs us (unscientifically) "has nine primary attitudes, from which many others proceed... These nine attitudes characterize states, that is, sentiments, but sentiments which are fugitive":

1. If a forward movement, it ends in an upright one, with elevated chin, and indicates interrogation, hope, appellation, desire.

2. The same movement with the chin lowered, indicates doubt, resignation.
3. A nod of the head, a forward movement, means confirmation, *yes*, or *well*.
4. If the movement is brusque forward, it is the menace of a resolute man.
5. The head thrown back means exaltation.
6. If the movement is brusque backward, it is the menace of a weak man.
7. There are rotative inflections from one shoulder to the other; this is impatience, regret.
8. The rotary movement of the head alone signifies negation, that is *no*.
9. If the movement ends toward the interlocutor, it is simple negation.

Genevieve Stebbins (1857–1914?), a student of Steele MacKaye (1842–1894), the man who brought Delsarte's system to America, was an innovative modern dancer and a precursor of Isadora Duncan (1877–1927), herself influenced by Delsarte. Stebbins wrote the influential *Delsarte System of Expression* (Edgar S. Werner, 1887), which went through several editions. There were drawings illustrating such necessary areas of knowledge as "the attitude of the head" and even "the attitude of the eyeball"; the attitudes and gestures were hardly subtle. To express "supplication" one knelt on one knee, with the arms held forward and apart and the head tilted slightly back and up. The actor stood to express "discovery," with one arm thrown up and forward, while the other arm was held down and back, and the head was thrust forward and slightly down. And "horror" was portrayed by standing with one foot slightly in front of the other, the head forward, one arm bent with the hand, palm spread, near the top of the head, while the other arm is stretched out and up to the side, with the hand raised, palm outward.

A brief quotation from the *Delsarte System of Oratory*, in which we can read the only five chapters he finished writing before his death, will suffice to show you how very different Delsarte's approach was from Stanislavsky's:

> The artist should have three objects: To *move*, to *interest*, to *persuade*. He interests by *language*; he moves by *thought*; he moves, interests and persuades by *gesture*.

You will notice that creating a character truthfully, with an inner life and psychology, is not among Delsarte's "objects."

A word about touching, which is a special form of gesture, often expressing affection: The rules, usually unspoken, about who could touch whom, when, and in what circumstances, vary with different historical periods. Until the modern era, touching between the sexes was generally confined to private situations. Any such intimate gesture as a touch expressing affection was usually strictly prohibited, particularly in the Anglophone world, until the modern era, when physical expressions and gestures of affection are ubiquitous. In certain other cultures, such as those of France and some places in South America, touching was permitted, particularly in the form of hand-kissing in situations involving royal receptions or greetings to visitors. The kiss often did not involve actually touching the lips to the hand, but rather miming the gesture of doing so. And the buss on the cheek as a form of greeting between males was also not uncommon, between people of the same rank. But in the mid-Victorian era, for instance, when young couples were accompanied regularly by chaperones, touching of any kind was virtually out of the question, particularly in England and North America; hence the idea of a stolen kiss. By the end of the nineteenth century, the rules had relaxed, but only a little. In modern times, men often hug when they greet each other, and in France, a kiss on one or both cheeks is de rigueur between good friends and family members, but that is not the case in many other cultures. Shaking hands is common also, between men. But any more affectionate form of intimate touching is generally avoided, nor is any of the touching to be prolonged. With regard to these matters, and depending on the period, behave on stage as you would in real life, unless the director tells you otherwise.

In a production of an Oscar Wilde play for which I was dialect coach, the leading actor actually touched the leading lady on the breast during a performance, although this had not been rehearsed. She was outraged, and slapped him. Afterwards, he apologized profusely, and explained that, as the character, he had felt like doing this. But had be been truly in touch with the mores of the late Victorian era in which the rather dated play was written, and in which it was set, he would never have touched her in that way, even though the two characters were in private. If the scene had been in a brothel, that would have been a different matter. The moral of the anecdote: Know the customs of the period, and stick to them!

Charles Darwin's *The Expression of the Emotions in Man and Animals*

Charles Darwin (1809–1882), the great theorist of evolution, published his far-reaching, analytic masterpiece, *The Expression of the Emotions in Man and Animals*, in 1872, the year after Delsarte died. It still makes fascinating reading, and the actor might learn much from perusing it.

Among other things, the book would be useful for the famous animal exercises, which involve the improvisational reproduction of a non-human animal's physical characteristics as a way of exploring a character. Devised originally at the Moscow Art Theatre school and developed also by Michael Chekhov, they are used both in the classroom and as a tool in rehearsing a play. The following questions are asked: First, "If my character were an animal, what animal would he or she be?" The selected animal is then observed, either in its natural habitat or in a zoo. Next, the actor asks, "What are the characteristics of that animal that I associate with my character?" and "How might I incorporate them into my character's physicality?" As classroom exercises, animal improvisations are useful for developing powers of observation and imagination. In rehearsal, they may help the actor get into the character, but of course they should never be apparent in the final performance.

Among Darwin's findings is the fact that certain human emotions are expressed cross-culturally in the same way: laughter; smiling to express pleasure; frowning as a frequent sign of thoughtfulness, puzzlement, or anger; and so forth. But other manifestations of human actions and emotions that we take for granted in most Western cultures are less widespread: kissing, for instance, was unknown among the natives of various South Pacific countries before the arrival of westerners.

Darwin analyzes the physical expression of each emotion and explains how the body's nervous system automatically reacts to produce it. When you have understood this, you will realize that emotions can be aroused or evoked technically by performing the correct physical actions, in accordance with the Stanislavskian idea that action arouses the emotion. If you know a character is worried and you frown, worry will assert itself: it is the body's habitual response, and it has become automatic. It may be a physical cliché to do so, but it is at the same time a truthful one. Sometimes one needs to use such technical means as a way of launching oneself into the situation in the scene.

As Uta Hagen points out in *Respect for Acting*, when people are very upset and want to cry, they also restrain themselves, and it is the attempt not to cry, and then the weeping that bursts forth because it cannot be contained, that are effective in portraying such suffering. In chapter 6, "Special Expressions of Man: Suffering and Weeping," Darwin has this to say on the subject of weeping:

> The corrugators of the brow... seem to be the first muscles to contract; and these draw the eyebrows downwards and inwards towards the base of the nose, causing vertical furrows, that is a frown, to appear between the eyebrows; at the same time they cause the disappearance of the transverse wrinkles across the forehead. The orbicular muscles contract almost simultaneously with the corrugators, and produce wrinkles all around the eyes... Lastly, the pyramidal muscles of the nose contract...
>
> The [almost simultaneous] raising of the upper lip draws upwards the flesh of the upper part of the cheeks, and produces a strongly marked fold on each cheek...

For actors who have difficulty weeping, beginning with the eyebrow muscles and working down, as Darwin describes, while simultaneously attempting to restrain tears, may be a useful technical way of getting into a crying scene, where such crying and weeping do not first arise naturally from the given circumstances. This may be especially useful, for instance, during a long run.

Darwin also describes what happens physically when we laugh:

> During laughter the mouth is open more or less widely, with the corners drawn much backwards, as well as a little upwards; and the upper lip is somewhat raised. The drawing back is best seen in moderate laughter and especially in a broad smile.

While this may seem obvious, its use technically for an actor is that by opening the mouth and raising the upper lip, the impulse to laugh may be aroused, and the actor may then proceed to utter "ha ha ha" sounds in a more less staccato manner, which, with practice, will begin to sound real. As with crying, this technique can be useful if laughter does not come easily, as long as the result sounds real, spontaneous, and natural.

On the other hand, during long runs, the habits of weeping and laughing will have been pretty much set after a period of time, no doubt a different one for each actor. All the actor will have to do is to arrive at the moment requiring laughter or tears, and the correct behavior will almost automatically be aroused. This is not to say that such weeping or laughter should be automatic: it must still arise organically from the situation.

At any rate, Darwin's scientifically based descriptions, coming from his observations, are not confined to the purely physical manifestations of emotion, but also deal with the mental reasons for them. There are other books on the subject of the physical manifestations of emotions in humans, but Darwin's has not been surpassed. One more example:

> The partial closure of the eyelids ... or the turning away of the eyes or of the whole body, are likewise highly expressive of disdain. These actions seem to declare that the despised person is not worth looking at, or is disagreeable to behold ...
>
> The most common method of expressing contempt is by movements about the nose, or round the mouth; but the latter movements, when strongly pronounced, indicate disgust. The nose may be slightly turned up, which apparently follows from the turning up of the upper lip; or the movement may be abbreviated into the mere wrinkling of the nose.

This description, while obviously accurate, may smack of at least potential clichés. And you want to avoid clichés, which are mechanical and inorganic. But it is absolutely true that if the actor partially closes the eyes and turns them slightly downward and away from the object of scorn, anger, derision or contempt, the relevant emotions will indeed be aroused. The actor may then proceed with the playing of the scene, without worrying about feeling, and further emotion will be aroused in the course of playing the actions. The difference between this and Delsarte's approach is the difference between real science and pseudo-science, between using the technique suggested here to arouse emotion and putting on or indicating feeling.

The Character's Posture and Movement

Posture, which the actor studies in movement classes in connection with balancing and centering the body, is the habitual way in which the musculature of the body is held when sitting, standing, or walking. It is automatic and develops over a lifetime. Some people have posture inculcated into them from an early age: "Sit up straight!" and "Don't droop your shoulders!" are commonly heard instructions to children. Some people develop an optimum posture that enables them to breathe and move freely, neither too stiff nor too relaxed. The actor must become aware of his or her habitual posture, so that it can be adjusted as necessary, particularly when assuming the posture of a character. Period costume plays a part as well in how the actor can stand and move. The strictures imposed by particular garments determine posture.

Health also plays a great role in posture: A person who is unwell or suffering from a specific disease will have a specific posture. Age also makes a difference, as it does with movement, and all of this must be explored in rehearsal, not decided ahead of time. The result of advance decisions on such matters is usually a cliché and a mechanical reproduction of physical behavior, inaccurate as often as not.

The distribution of weight creates posture, in conjunction with the sense of balance, which results in the body having a center of gravity. All of this will vary on an individual basis. Like all the technical aspects of performance discussed in this book, posture must be "forgotten," enabling the actor to concentrate on the essentials of the given circumstances and of the actions and intentions to be played. Particularly useful for general relaxation, awareness of posture, and the development of good posture for optimal vocal production is the Alexander technique, discussed above.

Some Elementary Stagecraft: Positioning Yourself on Stage

Part of believing in the character and the circumstances is behaving as if you are in the place or places where the story unfolds. You must endow the performance space with the necessary attributes. The stage is not the Athenian wood in *A Midsummer Night's Dream*. It is not Hamlet's castle, nor a Venetian courtroom, nor a dreary apartment in a rundown section of New Orleans. But you can learn to behave as if it were any of those places.

Remember, too, that the windows, doors, and openings in a set, whether real or abstract, represent "the borders to different worlds," as playwright and first president of the Czech Republic Václav Havel (b. 1936) said. There is a world within the play that is outside the world of the set, and it, too, is part of the play's given circumstances. You must imagine the offstage places where part of your character's life happens.

The theatrical experience for both performer and audience depends on the architecture of the theatrical space, and most especially on how the space is set up for the project. The space may be a proscenium stage, or a theater in the round, or three-quarters round; the theater may be indoors or outdoors. The performance must be adjusted technically to the space and its acoustics. These physical adjustments, which are external to interpreting the character, precede making the adjustments an organic, automatic part of the performance. How loud will you speak? How will you be able to move in the space? How can you time the entrances to make sure you are there at the exact right moment? What is the pattern (blocking) of your movements? Where do you go, and when? When you "walk the space" to find out how the blocking works, you will be imaginatively projecting yourself into that place, making it personal and particular to yourself. You will believe in it as the space it is supposed to be.

On a proscenium stage, positioning will be different at the back of the stage, where it is harder for the audience to see the actors, than at the front, where facial expressions can be read immediately. At the back of the stage, the movements, gestures, and stance must therefore be slightly larger than at the front, so as to ensure communication. All of these adjustments should become automatic and habitual.

In a theater in the round, turn slightly as you speak to include automatically all areas of the audience, without making an obvious point of doing so. This may involve an actual slight stepping movement.

In other words, you have to be aware of the parameters and limitations of the performing space. In your imagination, the stage is the place where the play is happening. But in your actor's reality, it is a particular space that you have to navigate, and you must be as aware of its topography as you are of the rooms you live in. Even if you have to be uncomfortable as a character, you have to be comfortable as an actor on the particular stage that you will come to know intimately as the run proceeds. This is a technical matter, and the technical side of negotiating the particular space will have to be absorbed into your score and become unconscious: You must be aware without being aware, so to speak, once you have learned and memorized the space. Where is that creaking board that you have to avoid? If the stage is raked, where and how do you stand so that you don't begin to slide?

For purposes of blocking and positioning actors, the proscenium stage floor is divided into the following nine areas:

1. **Upstage:** the area farthest from the audience, at the back of the stage; divided into upstage center (UC), also called *up center*; upstage right (UR), also called *up right*; and upstage left (UL), also called *up left*.

2. **Center stage:** the area just below backstage, going towards the front; divided into center (C); right center (RC); and left center (LC).

3. **Downstage:** the area at the very front of the stage, nearest the audience; divided into downstage center (DC), also called *down center*; downstage right (DR), also called *down right*; and downstage left (DL), also called *down left*.

The stage is also divided into numbered planes that correspond to the wings (1, 2, 3, 4, or more on large stages), beginning at the front of the stage: "down in one" means that an actor is in plane 1 downstage—that is, in the acting area in front of the curtain. "In two" means that a scene is played just below the wing in plane two, and so forth.

To be seen by the audience, who will then "read" the actor's expression, and so understand what is happening for the character emotionally, you must often "cheat," or turn out towards the spectators, even though this does not feel natural to you at the moment. To the audience, on the other hand, it will seem perfectly natural, provided you make it seem so, having absorbed it into the score of the part. Always cheat out as much as possible, so as to be facing downstage; do not upstage yourself.

Always find the light. This can be done without the audience's perceiving that you are doing it. Notice where the hottest, i.e., brightest, spot nearest to your position on the stage is, by looking down slightly, then step into it. During technical rehearsals, you may also look up and actually see the light that is trained on that particular spot. If you have not found the light, and are standing in semi-darkness, the director may tell you to move into the light, or completely out of it, if you are required to be in shadow.

You must always be aware of your positioning on stage with regard to that of the other actors, and must adjust the stage picture so as to preserve a proper distance between the actors. Such awareness is an essential component of stagecraft.

All of the foregoing would be useless, no matter how adept you are at moving, gesturing, and positioning, if it did not serve you to infuse physical life into a character, a physical life that may differ from your own. And the physical life must be a reflection of the character's psychological life, so that the audience can understand your characterization. As Stanislavsky wrote, his entire system depended on the "close unity between the internal and external, where the feeling for a role is also summoned by creating a life for the human body."

CHAPTER FOUR

Rehearsal and Performance Techniques

Rehearsal in History: Some Highlights

In 1708, John Downes (?–1712?) published his *Roscius Anglicanus or an Historical Review of the Stage* (usually known as *The English Roscius*); the original Roscius—Quintus Roscius Gallus (126–62 BCE)—was the most famous actor of ancient Rome. The book is a listing of the plays performed during the Restoration and early Augustan eras, and of the actors in them, by someone intimately involved with the theater of his day. A loyal friend and supporter of Thomas Betterton, Downes was bookkeeper and prompter from 1662 to 1706 in Sir William Davenant's (1606–1668) company, the Duke's Men, "at his Theatre in Lincolns-Inn-Fields." Among other jobs, Downes copied out the parts—we would call them sides—for the actors; this was one of the prompter's jobs. In fact, the prompter was really the equivalent of a modern assistant producer, stage manager, and prompter combined: in addition to being on book and prompting lines during performances, he organized rehearsals and made sure the scene painters and carpenters did their jobs. As the introduction by John Loftis to the Augustan Society's 1969 reprint informs us, Downes "wrote accurately about subjects that no one else bothered to say anything about." This is true despite the value of a number of other period sources, including the hilarious memoirs of Colley Cibber and accounts of performances by Samuel Pepys.

We learn from Downes in his introduction that actors rehearsed in the mornings and performed the plays in the afternoons. But we don't know what the rehearsal process was, beyond what we can deduce it must have been, since the actors were expected to have memorized their lines before rehearsals began. The old plays were revived and run sporadically, and a new hit play could have a record run of twelve performances. One of the entertainments presented at Lincoln's Inn Fields was "The Rivals, a Play, Wrote by *Sir William Davenant*; having a very Fine Interlude in it, of Vocal and Instrumental Musick, mixt with very Diverting Dances." And we find this interesting account of a Shakespeare revival, which Samuel Pepys saw in 1664; he thought the play was "made up of a great many patches":

> *King Henry* the *8th*, This Play, by Order of *Sir William Davenant*, was all new Cloath'd in proper Habits: The King's was new, all the Lords, the Cardinals, the Bishops, the Doctors, Proctors, Lawyers, Tip-staves, new Scenes [scenery]: The part of the King was so right and justly done by Mr. *Betterton*, he being Instructed in it by Sir *William*, who had it from Old Mr. *Lowen*, that had his Instructions from Mr. *Shakespear* himself, that I dare and will aver, none can, or will come near him in this Age, in the performance of that Part.

"Old Mr. Lowen"—also spelled Lowine, Lewen, Lowyne, or Lowing—was listed in the Shakespeare First Folio: he was John Lowin (1576–1659?), a highly respected actor in the Lord Chamberlain's Men, in which he had two shares. There were twenty shares altogether, distributed among six to eight "sharers," who divided the profits and paid the company's bills and debts. The acting company also included journeymen, hired for the job, and apprentices. Burbage and Shakespeare each had four shares.

A rather portly man, to judge by his portraits, Lowin was known for his playing of comic soldiers and villains, and most probably created the part of Iago opposite Burbage in the original production of *Othello*, and of Falstaff in both parts of *Henry IV* and in *The Merry Wives of Windsor*. He presumably created the role of Henry VIII, under Shakespeare's instruction.

Note that before the modern era, the word "instructions" was used for what we now call "directions": actors were instructed in their roles—often equivalent to coaching—rather than directed. And actors frequently worked without even that much help. William Charles Macready (1793–1873), a celebrated star actor-manager, describes in his *Reminiscences* how he attended the reading of a new play by its author, in 1817. The author's reading of his play was usual practice, and took place sometimes days before the first rehearsal. Immediately afterwards, "the written parts were distributed to their several representatives... and to work I went upon it with my usual determination."

On January 2, 1833, we find this rather surprising diary entry:

My performance this evening of Macbeth, afforded me a striking evidence of the necessity there is for thinking over my characters previous to playing, and establishing by practice, if necessary, the particular modes of each scene and important passage.

One would have thought that the obvious way to proceed! This tells us how much actors were expected to be able to direct themselves, and how little rehearsal there usually was with the other cast members. But Macready was so dedicated to his art that even on walks from his country house up to London, he passed the time in going over scenes from *Othello*. On March 13, 1834, he played Hamlet: "When I have a part like Hamlet to play my whole day is absorbed by it. I cannot give my thoughts to any other subject..."

Before the Victorian era, when systematic, regular, organized daily rehearsals under the supervision of a director were instituted, actors in Europe and America worked on their roles largely on their own. They memorized the lines in advance of the elementary rehearsals, which consisted mostly of arranging and running through entrances and exits, and rehearsing special scenes involving stage combat or complicated farcical tricks. This meant going through the choreographed moves that they had worked out among themselves, often under the supervision of the playwright, master actor, manager or patron of a company, or theater owner, who "instructed" them.

Actors knew how to project their voices, how to move on a stage, and how to adjust their positions as necessary. From the Elizabethan era and into the eighteenth century, they often followed conventions for stock characterizations that they had learned as apprentices from their masters. David Garrick's biographer Thomas Davies (1712–1785), for instance, tells us in *Memoirs of the Life of David Garrick, Esq.: Interspersed with Characters and Anecdotes of His Theatrical Contemporaries: The Whole Forming a History of the Stage: Which Includes a Period of Thirty-Six Years* of the various character types that Garrick had rehearsed on his own when he was just starting his career: "The Clown, the Fop, the Fine Gentleman, the Man of Humor, the Sot, the Valet, the Lover, the Hero, nay, the Harlequin, had all been critically examined, and often rehearsed and practiced by him in private."

Starting in the middle of the nineteenth century, and in the days of the great actor-managers, such as Sir Henry Irving, we know something of what went on during rehearsal sessions. Memoirs by actors and other professional figures in the theater, as well as texts about acting, began to proliferate. There are many eyewitness descriptions of performances. And, as with the Restoration period, we have many promptbooks of productions that tell us what the blocking or staging was like. It would have been arranged by the actor-manager or the company manager, such as Sir William Davenant, the equivalent of a modern artistic director. We know what sound cues were used—bells and whistles, for instance, to signal the orchestra to play or the crew to move scenery—and in which grooves the flats were to be placed. There are costume and set designs, and period engravings of production scenes. However, with the exception of some information about Garrick's rehearsal methods (see chapter 12), only in the twentieth century do we really get sources that tell us fully about rehearsal procedures and techniques.

In 1931, Mrs. Katherine Goodale, whose stage name was Kitty Molony, published *Behind the Scenes with Edwin Booth* (Houghton Mifflin), her recollections of the days when she acted with the "Eminent Tragedian." Her book tells us a great deal about the general conditions of working in the theater, touring with a repertoire of productions, and a little something about how rehearsals were conducted. She and two other young ladies of the company shared Booth's private train car in the 1886–1887 forty-week tour of the US. The tour was arduous and exhausting, but at the same time exhilarating and inspiring, as she got to know Booth as a person and as a consummate professional.

The handsome, debonair actor Lawrence Barrett (1838–1891), who often alternated Iago and Othello with Booth, and played Cassius when Booth performed Brutus in *Julius Caesar*, was the managing director of the company, and Booth's business partner for the tour. He usually ran the rehearsals, but sometimes Booth would want to "take" the rehearsal himself. Barrett had had his own company, in which he played Hamlet and Shylock, and "was itching to 'take' these rehearsals. He ached to put some of the big scenes through, to whip up the actors as he did in his own company; but his restraint was perfect," says Mrs. Goodale, who had been a member of his company as well. Occasionally, newer company members would have to be "instructed." But Booth's experienced actors knew their lines and blocking. They would run through several plays before they broke for the day: "Three tragedies in a four-hour rehearsal was nothing to them."

Blocking was determined by where the star chose to position himself in a scene, and he controlled the staging. At one point, for instance, Booth asks Kitty to stand with her back to the audience in a scene from *The Merchant of Venice*, in which she played Jessica to his Shylock.

When he is not on stage, he says, she may do as she likes. Supporting roles were just that: lesser characters who surrounded the protagonist and made sure the main part or parts stood out. Iago and Othello were of equal importance, and two stars often alternated in the roles, as Booth did with Barrett. But the rest of the actors were clearly subordinate to them, however important their roles.

Mrs. Goodale informs us that "Ten days proved enough to get the company letter perfect in *Richelieu, Macbeth, Hamlet,* and *Othello.*" *Richelieu* (1839) is a verse play, much admired in its day, by Sir Edward Bulwer-Lytton, 1st Baron Lytton (1803–1873); it contains the famous line "The pen is mightier than the sword." Eight other plays were also part of the repertoire. Rehearsing in such a short period of time and in this way is a far cry from the methods developed by Stanislavsky and others, and was no doubt partly responsible for the sort of facile, declamatory delivery of the verse, as well as for the indicating and "mechanical" acting, that he decried. In fact, this method is close to the way operas are still rehearsed when productions are revived, after the initial presentation, which has been rehearsed by the director. The stage manager runs the singers through their blocking, and there are music rehearsals. Often, a star who has been brought in to sing a role will simply do it his or her own way. Despite all this, the operas are often well received, and well reviewed, as Booth's company was wherever it played.

The Meiningen Company's Innovative Productions and the Autocratic Director

The Meininger Hoftheatertruppe (Meiningen Court Theater Troupe), known as the Meiningen Company, was founded in 1866 by its artistic director, Georg II, Duke of Saxe-Meiningen (1826–1914). The company's work had a great influence on Stanislavsky's thinking. Former actor Ludwig Chronegk (1837–1891) was the autocratic director who ran the company with an iron hand, with the help of the Duke's third (morganatic) wife, the musician, actress, and coach Ellen Franz (1839–1923). They insisted upon realistic characterizations from every actor. But it was the scenery, accurate historical costumes, and especially the fluid handling of elaborate, carefully orchestrated crowd scenes that made the company world-famous.

In 1874, the Meiningen Company, which had previously confined its activities to the court theater, began what turned out to be sixteen years of international tours, starting in Berlin. Stanislavsky attended performances in 1890 in St. Petersburg, during the company's second tour of Russia. He made notes about the productions, and sketches as well, in notebooks that he took with him to the theater. Some visitors were allowed at rehearsals, and he attended a number of them.

Among their many famous productions were Shakespeare's *Othello*, *The Merchant of Venice*, *The Winter's Tale*, *Twelfth Night*, and *Julius Caesar*; Schiller's *Wallensteins Tod* (Wallenstein's Death), *Die Jungfrau von Orleans* (The Maid of Orleans), and *Wilhelm Tell*; and Goethe's *Faust*. On June 1, 1881, an anonymous *New York Times* journalist wrote a laudatory article about the company, quoting from the London newspaper *The Standard*, which had reviewed the opening of *Julius Caesar* at the Drury Lane Theatre:

> It will be very near truth to say that last night "Julius Caesar" was played in England for the first time as Shakespeare had conceived it. Instead of being unmanageable, the multitude representing the Roman people, as trained by Herr Chronegk, raises and subdues its voice, sways to and fro, has significance in its looks, and eloquent meaning in its gestures... and the *crescendo* and *diminuendo* in the explanations with which it responded to the two speeches of Mark Antony were wonderfully effective.

The company got mixed reviews. Other London critics quoted in the article thought the principals were excellent, but not astonishing, and that some were actually weak. But the *New York Times* journalist thought the actors playing Caesar, Brutus, Cassius, and Mark Antony "far superior to any English Shakespearean actor now living." And that included Booth and Irving, whose work with stage crowds was influenced by Chronegk thereafter.

Chronegk was a martinet to the actors he directed. He expected absolute discipline and demanded long hours. Rehearsals started and ended at the scheduled times. No actor dared be late, on pain of losing the role he or she had been assigned, which would be reassigned to another actor while the latecomer was relegated to a lesser role. The crowd scenes, perfectly drilled and meticulously choreographed, required that the actors pay attention to every minute detail. Small groups of extras were rehearsed separately, then assembled into larger crowds. Actors rehearsed in costume, as soon as costumes were available. Chronegk was not afraid to stage actors with their backs to the audience, and critics remarked on his innovative realistic touches.

It took many weeks to rehearse, which was most unusual for the period. If Booth's company rehearsed three plays in a four-hour rehearsal session, as we have seen, Chronegk could rehearse one scene for eight hours when he thought it necessary. He also refused to allow actors whom he coached to indicate emotion, no matter what role they were playing. And he insisted on long and demanding rehearsal sessions where actors would do the kind of work ordinarily done at home in those days: that of interpreting their characters. The company even enforced fines when the actors had not performed exactly as he had directed them to do. The actors had no freedom, as we do today, but had to follow rigidly and inflexibly every movement, every gesture, and every intonation and line reading demonstrated to them by the director, all of which the actors had to justify, no matter how they felt and how much they might disagree with what the director had asked them to do.

Stanislavsky and His Changing Rehearsal Methods

Stanislavsky himself began his directorial life as a tyrant, influenced by what he had seen of the Meiningen Company. But he came to realize that the actor, as a member of a collaborative team, should have the freedom to create with the guidance of a director, as opposed to being under the thumb of a dictator, and he learned how to get what he wanted by suggesting and counseling, leading and guiding, rather than by imposing his will with line readings and insisting that the actors behave in certain ways.

As the system evolved, Stanislavsky suggested an exhaustive, all-inclusive method for rehearsal, which he later modified considerably, since it proved unwieldy and, most of all, impractical in terms of actual working conditions in the commercial theater. He felt that a year was the ideal amount of time to rehearse a play! You can find his twenty-five-step system for directors to use when working with actors outlined in an appendix to *Building a Character* (Theatre Arts Books, 1949). Not until step fourteen did he allow the actors to read the play for themselves, and not until step eighteen did he allow them to read the actual text to each other. Step twenty-two was the first one in which the actors were actually able to begin finding the character's activities, which constitute the character's physical life. Most of the rehearsal time was devoted to discussions and improvisations revolving around the play.

Stanislavsky called his last, unfinished rehearsal method "active analysis," because it involved getting actors on their feet much sooner than he had done earlier. He had finally realized that his previous ways of working, although thorough, could be counterproductive. After ages sitting around a table talking, the actors would get up and freeze. They were inhibited; they couldn't act. Everything they had discussed at such length suddenly went out the window. Why? Because they had *done* nothing; they had not put into action what they had discussed, and were therefore unable to perform truthful psychophysical actions. What actors needed to do was to act: to discover through doing. So Stanislavsky, ever open to change, revised his rehearsal methods. There was minimal discussion, and the actors would get on their feet almost immediately, by the second or third rehearsal, and begin exploring the objectives and psychophysical actions of their parts through the use of improvisations based around the text, and then, much sooner than before, they would start rehearsing with the text itself. The rehearsal process was therefore shorter, and led to results that were just as truthful as the longer process. But improvisation remained a very important rehearsal tool for Stanislavsky, whatever rehearsal procedure he used.

While based firmly in the text, which Stanislavsky thought was paramount, his method of improvisation called for études (exercises) constructed around it. He came to the conclusion, which would be emphasized by Stella Adler in her teaching, that script analysis and interpretation were the actor's primary tasks before he or she could begin to decide what exactly to do physically when dealing with the actual creation of a character. Analyzing a script imaginatively is indeed at the heart of the Stanislavsky system, and from it all else proceeds.

The use of emotional and sensory recall, and of substitutions, which he had developed already as part of his system, he deemed necessary, particularly in the early steps of working on a role. But in playing the actions found through improvisation, the substitution would gradually disappear, to be replaced by being alive in the present moment, and really relating to the acting partner. Still, to remember how it felt to be standing in a beautiful garden on a moonlit night would help the actors playing Romeo and Juliet to find the actions indicated in the given circumstances of the text in the balcony scene. The logical, consistent physical life of the character would awaken Romeo's ardor, his passionate love and desire for Juliet, and hers for him. What Iago and Rodrigo do to arouse Brabantio's household in the opening scene of *Othello* required not only the physical actions, which would awaken the emotions of trepidation and the feeling of being in a dangerous situation that might have dire consequences, but would also require the memory of place and time that would have to be substituted in the actor's imagination for a dark Venetian night—helped by the stage set and the lighting even in a production that is more abstract than realistic in design.

Stanislavsky was continually evolving and growing, never satisfied that he had found the ideal way of rehearsing. In a very interesting letter written in 1936, translated by Rose Whyman in her book *The Stanislavsky System of Acting: Legacy and Influence in Modern Performance* (Cambridge University Press, 2008), he sets forth yet another idea for rehearsal:

> It involves reading the play today and tomorrow rehearsing it on stage ... A character comes in, greets everybody, sits down, tells of events that have just taken place, expresses a series of thoughts. Everyone can act this guided by their own life experience ... and so we break the whole play, episode by episode, into individual actions ... So the internal life of experiencing is outlined.

Stanislavsky finally came to feel that carrying out actions aroused the desired emotion for the situation and that, when there were eight performances a week to be gotten through, the correct psychophysical action, correctly carried out, would serve the actor best.

The Director in the Contemporary Theater

In Nicolai M. Gorchakov's *Stanislavsky Directs* (Limelight Editions, 1991), he tells us that Stanislavsky said, "The most important function of the director, as I understand the definition, is to open all the potentialities of the actor and to arouse his individual initiative ... The director must constantly excite and kindle his actors' imagination." He wanted the director to be knowledgeable in all fields, to have a broad cultural background, and to be a great observer of life, so that he or she could bring all of this to an analysis of the script. Only then would the director be in a position "to advise the actors on playing," and to help them bring the play to life.

The director in the theater has several functions and jobs to fulfill, including the political one of managing all parties to the creative process, and bringing harmony to the proceedings, encouraging everyone to work as a team under his or her leadership. First and foremost, the director is an interpreter of the material, and knows how each role fits into the story he or she wants to tell. The director is in charge of telling the story, and guiding the actors in their interpretations, according to his or her view of the playwright's script. Finally, the director is the general overseer of all aspects of the production, from staging to all the design elements. Nothing in the theater—not a costume, or a light level, or a piece of scenery or a prop—is as it is without the director's approval.

If it is your job as an actor to know the character in specific, minute detail, it is the director's job to help you reveal the character through the staging. And, because it is the director who is telling the playwright's whole story, it is also your job to justify directions you are given, even if you disagree with them.

For Stanislavsky, part of the actor's and director's ethics is to serve the playwright's text faithfully. Still, even he rewrote lines when he felt he had to, as he did in the opening scene of a production of Ibsen's *Ghosts*, much to the outrage of Nemirovich-Danchenko, who thought the writer should be supreme and the text sacrosanct, and argued with Stanislavsky on the subject more than once. The often-heard remark in the contemporary theater made by actors to playwrights, "I don't think my character would say (or do) that," amounts nowadays to a risible cliché. But in the past, actors rewrote lines and indeed whole scripts on occasion. With so little systematic rehearsal in such a short time, it was only natural that actors who had not even had time to memorize their lines thoroughly would improvise, out of necessity.

The director will help build the scenes and the play as a whole so that climaxes can be reached and have their effect. In that regard, the only thing you have to worry about as an actor is not entering on such a high note of vocal and/or physical energy that you have no place to go in building the scene. In other words, when you work on your own on actions, intentions, and objectives you must also be aware of how they develop technically. And they usually start on a low and build to a high.

The last thing you want to do as an actor is to use words and feelings in a calculated, set way, or to calculate line readings and delivery: they should arise naturally and organically in the course of rehearsals. However, it is usual for a director to say "Keep that!" when the actor has found a particularly felicitous way of expressing a line or performing a moment. The ability to repeat—in other words, to remember and reproduce something as exactly as possible—is an important aspect of the actor's art and craft, in both rehearsal and performance. But no repetition is ever exact, since each must be done as if it were new, and the actor must "live" in the moment, without being mechanical. Still, the basic shape and idea of a moment must remain the same.

Rehearsal is not run as a democracy: nobody votes, and the director is he or she who must be obeyed. The director may simply be faithful to the writer's ideas, or may place his or her heavy stamp on the production, coming to the foreground, instead of remaining in the background as the loyal servant of the play. But most directors are aware that it is their job to serve the audience and illuminate the material, rather than simply to display themselves and their own vision. When Alan Schneider directed the original production of Edward Albee's *Who's Afraid of Virginia Woolf*, for example, back in 1964, the writer's play and the acting were first and foremost for the audience, and afterwards, when the play was done, one could say that he had directed it brilliantly, so engrossed were we by the story itself, and so riveted by the actors' performances.

Albee's own revival production of the play, which he directed in 1976, was also memorable and revealing. Ben Gazzara played George, while Colleen Dewhurst played Martha, and Albee directed them with great attention to their particular personalities and needs as actors, according to Gazzara. He describes the production and the rehearsal process in his generally instructive and fascinating autobiography, *In the Moment: My Life as an Actor* (Carroll & Graf, 2004). Albee made the cast feel at home, comfortable, and confident that "Our staging would be tailored specifically to our cast. I simply cleaned up my diction and let the witty and acerbic dialogue carry me along." Of course, he did a great deal more than that—and received a Tony nomination for his gripping performance. Yet his point is well taken: Albee never pushed for results, and allowed the actors to find their way through the labyrinth of his play.

Contemporary Rehearsal Procedure in the Theater

The exciting day has arrived. The show has been cast, the team is assembled. For the next few weeks you will follow a schedule, laid out for you by the stage manager. You will no longer be "resting," as the British say, but in rehearsal. Oh, sweet relief—to have a job in the theater after all that time spent auditioning!

For many of us, rehearsal is the most exciting part of putting on a show. We take delight in the pleasantly organized, though arduous, process of exploration, discovery, practice, and repetition, and in the interaction with our fellow actors. And then, the intramural exercise is over. We have arrived at the first public performance. Performance has its own, different delights: the spectators will now be our collaborators, taking what we offer and giving back to us. And the audience will of course be different every night. Yet we must appear not to know they are there most of the time, allowing them to peer at us through the famous fourth wall.

Lee Strasberg outlined a four-week method of rehearsing a play in stages that is useful for the contemporary, commercial theater when four full weeks are allowed. In week one, the actors would do readings and table work. The second week would be devoted to blocking and memorizing lines. In week three, there would be line-throughs and run-throughs. And in the final week, there would be dress and technical rehearsals. Since in today's theater there are often only three weeks of rehearsal, weeks one and two are condensed into two weeks, with only one or two read-throughs at the beginning, and the rest of the time devoted to blocking and perhaps early run-throughs. If the play is a musical one, time is of course allowed for learning and rehearsing the music prior to numbers being staged.

As Jason Robards, Jr. (1922–2000), a superb Tony and Academy Award-winning actor known for his performances in Eugene O'Neill's (1888–1953) *The Iceman Cometh, Long Day's Journey Into Night*, and *Moon for the Misbegotten*, said in an interview in *The Actor Speaks* (Greenwood Press, 1994), "I know a lot of actors, they shouldn't even be acting with other people! Acting is a cooperative business. It's not competition; it's cooperative, and it's the giving and the taking." Nowhere is this more evident to begin with than in the rehearsal period of a play. Often, people are meeting each other for the first time. And everyone must now work together to get the play mounted, just as everyone must work as a team during performances. A closeness, a professional camaraderie will develop that is part of the process. We must behave like a functional family, or the show will never happen. Theater is a collaborative art, and we forget that at our peril.

The first rehearsal often begins with a *meet and greet*, at which the actors and various personnel make each other's acquaintance. Then there is usually a read-through, during which the stage managerial staff, director, actors, and perhaps designers sit around a table or in a circle of chairs.

The actors read the play aloud, and make the abstraction of words on pages begin to seethe and shine with reality. They begin to enter the world of the play, its universe peopled with unfamiliar characters and unfamiliar places that will grow familiar. They will begin to see the world through the play's vision of it. The stage manager often will read any relevant stage directions. The director will sometimes interrupt to make a point, but, generally speaking, the actors are allowed to proceed without much interruption.

The reading may continue after lunch, or there may be *table work*: discussion between the director and the cast about the play, its themes, the characters, and other germane material. If the play is a period piece, there will be a discussion of the era. Perhaps there will be more reading of scenes as well. The process of breaking the play down into manageable units has begun.

At an early rehearsal (hopefully), the designers show costume and set plans, often in the form of a working model, to the actors. The table work will continue for as long as the director deems necessary. Stanislavsky would have the actors do various scenes as improvisations using their own words instead of the text. But nowadays, rehearsals often continue with general preliminary blocking, and the director gives the actors their moves and tells them when to sit or stand. The actors will then begin to experience the play, as they must. As a result, sometimes an actor will say, "I don't feel as if I [or "my character"] would stand here." The director may or may not insist. Sometimes, the director may ask the actor when he thinks he should stand, and will allow the actor the freedom to do so. During the blocking rehearsals, also called staging rehearsals, moves are sometimes improvised by the actors, depending on the director's methods of work. But often, the director will have worked out the schema of physical moves and actions in detail.

After the entire play has been gone through and blocked, rehearsals continue with individual scene rehearsals, until an entire act is ready. It is usually run through at that point. Then the next act is worked through and run. Sometimes so much time is spent on the first act that the second is given short shrift, and rushed through rather than worked and then run through.

Once all the scenes are blocked for each act, they may be worked out of order, and only the people in them may be called for rehearsal. The act will then be run as an act.

When all the acts are done, if there is time, they are worked through again. The acts are then run through again as acts, with as little stopping and starting as possible. Then the play as a whole is rehearsed. There may be more work-throughs of individual parts that are not yet satis-factory, if time permits, during which there are continual stops and starts. These later rehearsals are often walk-throughs, which are fairly slow run-throughs. Finally, there are run-throughs at full pace. Costumes will be added for final run-throughs, but hopefully you will have had them well before that.

Early rehearsals usually take place in a studio, with the floor spiked by the stage managerial staff to represent the set. That is, playing areas of the set have been delineated with tape so that, for instance, doorways, other entrances, and stairways are clearly visible. Once the show moves into the actual performance space, the experience will be quite different. Entrances have to be retimed and vocal adjustments made for projection. Blocking may have to be altered to accommodate sightlines. There will ideally be several run-throughs on the set before the actors have to make further adjustments for lighting and other technical matters.

Finally, there are technical rehearsals using lights, scenery, and costumes, which are sometimes only partially ready. Adjustments are made as the "techs" proceed. Then come the tech-dress rehearsals in full costume, and ten-out-of-twelve days; and the dress rehearsals when the show is run fully without stopping, short of a disaster, such as a light or a piece of scenery falling. In opera especially, there is a "designer run": a run-through especially for the benefit of the set, costume, wig, makeup, and lighting designers. There is usually a final dress rehearsal, perhaps two or three, the last often being an invited dress, to which the actors and other personnel are allowed to invite guests.

During the tech rehearsals, even if you are going "cue to cue"—that is, from lighting cue to lighting cue—with very little time in between, do not let down your guard or your concentration. Use these rehearsals as your opportunity to act, to refine moments, to continue exploring, in whatever time is given to you.

At last, there are preview performances for commercial productions before the play opens officially for the critics. Daytime rehearsals to iron out difficulties or to resolve problems may be called during the preview period, since the play has not yet opened. During the run of a play, understudy and replacement rehearsals are regularly called. There may be rehearsals for the regular company at the discretion of the management, if they feel the play is not going well or is not being run as rehearsed. And there will usually be a company rehearsal to put in replacements. The actors may be called for periodic brush-up rehearsals, or for a line-through or speed-through rehearsal, especially after a day off, where this is not prohibited by Equity rules.

Some Elementary Stagecraft: How to Rehearse

Stanislavsky set ethical standards for rehearsal and performance that we still observe today: The actor must serve the theater, the writer, the play, and the audience. In accordance with these ethical standards, there are certain elementary, self-evident principles and rules that an actor must heed because they are a necessary part of the work. They are logical rules that consider everyone's well-being.

The first rule of rehearsal is: Be on time. And always sign in when you arrive, so that the stage manager knows you are there. When rehearsals begin on stage, do not leave the set or backstage area until you are told you may do so, when it is certain that the scene you are in will not be repeated. In fact, always ask the stage manager's permission to leave rehearsal, if you have to do so at any time for any reason. Being on time actually means being early, arriving before rehearsal is due to begin, so that you can be ready to start on time. Don't run in at the last minute, out of breath and slightly disoriented; this is simply a disservice to yourself. Also, although it should be unnecessary to point this out, being late is highly discourteous to everyone else.

The second rule is: Always go to rehearsal prepared. No excuses! Do your homework, the nature of which will have emerged from the day's work. You will have discovered what you have to develop, and what depths you have to plumb, and where you have work to do. And you will do that work as a preparation for the next day's rehearsal.

Although at first you may not know what to expect in rehearsal, unless you have worked with the same actors or director before, you will no doubt quickly orient yourself to the methods of both the director and your fellow actors. Whether the atmosphere is tense or relaxed, creative or strained depends on various factors, including the attitude of the director and how accessible he or she is, and on the amount of time allowed for a project before it is presented before the public. But whether tense or relaxed, rehearsal is always a joy, and I have found it the most interesting and enjoyable part of the experience, sometimes even more so than performing. There is the exciting aspect of finding a moment that has eluded you, of discovering a new psychological or emotional aspect of a character, and of plumbing one's own depths in order to find substitutions. And there is all the interaction with one's fellow performers, and the great pleasure of getting to know them as people, as well as artists and colleagues.

A cardinal rule in rehearsal is to respect your colleagues' process, and not to give another actor directions. Leave that to the director, or to the stage manager, as the case may be. If you have a problem, it is possible of course to discuss it with your partner in a scene, but a better policy is to bring it up with the director, either privately or during the rehearsal, whichever is appropriate. But an actor who says, "I need you to do this at this moment" is on the wrong road for several reasons: First, that actor is not the director, and it can only be the director who determines what should be happening at any given moment in the story being told. Second, the actor who can say this has set his or her performance, or moments, or line readings, and is not living in the moment or allowing for spontaneous interactions and reactions when listening and responding. On the contrary, that actor is being selfish, egotistical, and not part of the team that is trying to create the play so that everyone is in the same world. That being said, it may well be that the script indicates in some way that the actor does indeed need his or her performing partner to be doing something in particular. But if the other actor has not felt this way, or has not yet been able to find the moment, then that actor must be allowed to pursue the process. Perhaps the actor must indeed be instructed by the director to fulfill a moment in a particular way, and must then take the direction and find it in as specific a manner as possible. In other words, always take what you are given and use it: listen and respond. The director will make the necessary adjustments.

Always prepare for the very first rehearsal by analyzing the text and making provisional decisions, so that you are ready to take direction and make the instant adjustments required by the director. Such early decisions on your part will always be subject to change, as the play and your part develop themselves in the course of rehearsals. But you need to have a good, logical place to start from by the time you sit down at the table to do that first read-through. And then you need to listen to the director and understand his or her vision of the play and the story.

What Stanislavsky said with regard to rehearsal and to actors preparing for a role cannot be repeated too much: "Never begin with results!" Never! You have to find the results! And you have to find them not only by analyzing the text, but by rehearsing: discovering by doing. It is only by working that inspiration will present itself. When you find something that causes you a sensation of delighted surprise and excitement, self-consciousness disappears: that is exactly what you want.

What you find may not always work. This is one reason why inspiration is not a reliable guide: you can count neither on its being awakened nor on its accuracy. Your initial results may have to be discarded. You will find others. And, to repeat what Lee Strasberg said, "Never force or push for a result."

Results are, after all, the end of the work. No matter how little time you have to prepare a role, always begin at the beginning, go on until you come to the end, then stop—as the King of Hearts sagely advises in Lewis Carroll's *Alice's Adventures in Wonderland*. Indeed, when you act, when you prepare a script, you enter wonderland, a fantasy world, a dream that you have created using the text and yourself.

For that first read-through, especially, do not set anything! Keep an open mind! To set even one line reading is to stifle your creativity and to limit the process of discovery in rehearsal. You don't yet know how a scene or your entire role will be shaped, which means you don't yet know how to play them. You may be tempted to set moments or line readings out of insecurity and/or the desire for approval, especially from the authority figure who is the director, but setting anything at this point will only backfire and will interfere with the process of exploration and finding the character. So don't pretend you understand something when you don't: In other words, don't read lines with authority, anger, joy, or other emotions, the specifics of which can only be found in the course of rehearsals. You will only be indicating, and putting those emotions on— in other words, acting from the outside in—as opposed to finding them, or allowing them to happen as a result of having played an action a particular way. And your acting will be general and clichéd instead of specific! At the first read-through, concentrate on paying attention to the other actors. Let their intonation patterns—which show their intentions—"land" on you, and absorb them before replying instantly, in a spontaneous way. This is similar to Sanford Meisner's famous repetition exercise. The last thing you want to do is to come in with everything set, even if you have been asked to memorize the lines in advance because of a short rehearsal period. You can memorize them by doing preliminary analysis of objectives and actions, including verbal actions, which will help you to remember them, but you still are not obliged to set readings: you must be open to reacting to what the other actors bring to the table.

Try not to allow memorizing lines too early, even if you are required to memorize them, to restrict or ruin your imaginative approach to playing: stay as open as possible, and, again, don't set things rigidly. I was once in a production of *Hamlet*, and the actor playing the Prince of Denmark came into the first reading with his lines memorized and, as it turned out, his line readings all set in stone; they did not vary from performance to performance during the three-month run. It seemed that he never lived in the part at all, but rigidly and mechanically recited it, with a facile display of put-on emotion. He must have been terrified at tackling this daunting test role, but his solution prevented him from ever experiencing the role or enjoying the performances, and deprived him of any individuality: his playing was generalized, not specific. He did not seem to realize that actors who have been successful in the role have each taken a very individual approach, and all their approaches have been valid interpretations. In fact, it is the greatness of this play and the genius of Shakespeare that the role lends itself to so many different interpretations. This actor was doing his job only in the sense of walking onto the stage, saying the lines, and going through the motions. The audience may even have found him very effective, but I thought his performance an abysmal failure, because it was much too declamatory, and lacked that essential element: life.

Another elementary technique: Always write down everything that directly affects your character's movements, and your position on stage at any given moment. Use pencil, since everything is subject to change until it is set. The symbol "X" is commonly used for "cross," the actor's move in any direction: R (right); C (center); L (left); D (downstage, or down); U (upstage, or up); DL (downstage left); UL (upstage left); UC (upstage center); LC (left center); and RC (right center). Hence XDL (cross downstage left). The letters stand also for the actual position the actor occupies on stage: "Stand DL" or "XDL, stand." If you are already in a position at D and crossing to downstage left, "XL" will do nicely. In the rehearsal studio, you will be working on a floor that has been spiked by the stage manager. And furniture is placed as it will be on the actual set.

Once you start to get the play on its feet, you need to follow certain ways of working with the director. Among other elementary rehearsal techniques, you should always stand downstage of the director when she or he is demonstrating an action or movement, so that you see it from the spectator's point of view. That way, you will be aware of how it looks from out front, and you will able to adjust your position with that in mind; you do have to know what the audience will be seeing. This technical principle is in accord with Stanislavsky's idea of including the actual playing space, the theater, and the audience in the given circumstances. I stress again that you must take account of them, even though you are concentrating on being in the world of the play itself.

In the course of rehearsals, you will find everything: all the moments, the ways of playing actions, the emotions aroused. And you will find all the given circumstances, and the offstage circumstances that lead to your entrance. These you neglect at your peril. Why does the character come into the scene? Where are you coming from? What are you doing there? Once you get there, once you are in the scene, you can try anything you want that comes into your mind. You should feel free to do this even in a short rehearsal period. Rehearsal thus becomes in part a process of elimination, as you and the director decide what works and what doesn't, and discard the ineffective results of an experiment.

As rehearsal proceeds, you will also be creating and compiling the score of your part. And you will revise the score as a result of what you discover when rehearsing the scenes.

The score is the order of the beats in a script. A beat, also called a unit, is a piece or bit of a scene: it is the amount of time during which a conflict in a scene is played out. The term also means the beginning of a specific moment when an action is begun. If and when a small objective has been attained, or if and when it has not, there is a change of beat. When one beat comes to an end, another begins immediately. Characters can have individual beats (moments when an action starts), that differ from the longer beats in a scene. You will often hear directors say, "Let's take that beat again," meaning "Let's do that part of the scene again," giving the specific reasons why, and explaining what you should be looking for.

You can use the margins or the blank pages of the script to score your part. Begin by writing a list of the events and episodes of the story, and of the scenes in which you appear. You then "score the beats" (i.e., write them down in order), and their accompanying actions, in each scene. Be sure to include what happens to the character between the scenes.

In justifying the directions you are given, there may be times where the director talks in terms that are general: "Do that faster, please." You have to translate (Alice Spivak's term) what the director wants into your own acting terms. If you are told to do something more quickly, you can simply add a sense of urgency to the situation, and increase your need for speed.

Tempo-Rhythm: Finding the Pace of a Scene

As Stanislavsky said, every character, every person has his or her own inner and outer rhythm and tempo, and those two rhythms may not be the same: someone may think fast while walking slowly, or walk fast while thinking slowly. Finding these rhythms in a scene is an organic part of the rehearsal process. How much time is allowed for any action or speech is a function in part of the dynamics of a character's needs and desires, as well as of the necessity of accomplishing the action in a particular time frame. Also, a play cannot be allowed to drag, or it will lose the audience.

The individual actor/character rhythms condition the general tempo and pace of the scene. The rhythms can be worked on consciously, but it is better if they arise from the given circumstances, naturally. If the scene as a whole does not have the dynamic tempo it should have, then the actions are not dynamic enough. One solution is to play the scene with more energy.

A scene naturally develops its own tempo and pace in the course of rehearsals. If the correct tempo, from the director's point of view, is not happening, the director may resort to any number of devices to help it along. I once worked with a director who sat there with a bass drum and beat time on it with a drumstick, until the actors were performing at the pace he wanted, whether or not we had really found all the moments. "The bloody play is under the stage cloth! Pick it up!" he would yell. We were rehearsing a fast-paced British farce, *See How They Run* by Philip King, and he wanted us to do it at breakneck speed and peak physical and vocal energy, in performance as well as in rehearsal. We had to develop a sense of the manic nature of the proceedings, and after a while, not even to think. We also had to have our lines memorized very early in the process, so as to facilitate carrying out the action up to speed, without hesitation. His directorial technique was actually reminiscent of the classes on tempo-rhythm described in Stanislavsky's *An Actor's Work*.

Stanislavsky used the term "tempo-rhythm" because indeed the two are inseparable. In music, the rhythm of a piece is determined by its time signature, but the tempo, which is the rate of speed at which the music is performed, varies with the conductor or soloist. Everyone interprets the music with the tempo deemed appropriate, which will help to give the piece its feeling and emotional content for the listener. With regard to tempo, playing scenes is analogous, because the pace/tempo at which a scene is played automatically arouses feelings in the spectator: a fast car chase in a movie keeps the spectators on the edge of their seats, and a slow, languorous love scene can be relaxing and lulling.

Like emotion and feeling, tempo-rhythm cannot be forced. It must be discovered, usually by playing a scene and letting it happen. Questions to ask yourself include, How urgently do I want this? With how much energy do I pursue this objective? How quickly do I need this to happen? The character's physical condition will also condition the tempo-rhythm. Age, illness, a particular physical infirmity, or a state of drunkenness will all help to determine the tempo-rhythm, as will circumstances of light and darkness. The tempo-rhythm of a burglar moving through a darkened room at night, with perhaps only moonlight shining through the window as a guide, will be different from that of a welcomed visitor walking into the room in bright daylight. And the visitor's tempo-rhythm will be different from that of a police detective investigating the burglary and politely questioning the victim, whose tempo-rhythm when looking around the room in chagrin will be different from that of the police detective.

The slow and stately entrance of the court in a Shakespearean play will contrast in tempo-rhythm with the scene that follows it. In *Hamlet*, for instance, the court enters to one tempo-rhythm, and each actor to his or her own tempo-rhythm. The court then settles down. The tempo changes when Claudius speaks, is different again when Polonius speaks, and so on. And Claudius's tempo-rhythm, as the person who leads the scene and is in charge of the proceedings, is quite different from and more dynamic than those of the bystanders, including Gertrude, who remains alert and perhaps wary, observing her son. Hamlet's tempo-rhythm, as he bides his time in melancholy and distress, is much slower outwardly than those of Claudius and Gertrude, but his mind is racing, so that his inner tempo-rhythm is very fast. That of Polonius may be slow both outwardly and inwardly, depending on the actor's interpretation.

Given circumstances are determining factors in tempo-rhythm. Place and temperature are among the conditions that help determine it: people move differently on a hot day in the tropics than on a cold winter day in northern climes. A funeral scene, a love scene, a meal at a restaurant, or a stroll in the park will each have a different tempo-rhythm as a scene, regardless of the inner tempo-rhythm of the characters. It is usually up to the director to decide what the tempo-rhythm should be, and to adjust it when the pace is not helping to carry the play along. But often, the tempo-rhythm and pace will happen automatically, without having to work specially for them.

In the chapter on tempo-rhythm in *An Actor's Work*, the teacher Tortsov (Stanislavsky) has a student do an exercise in which he is "a traveler hearing the first bell to announce the departure of a long-distance train." This immediately arouses an energy in the traveler, who had been sitting and waiting for it in the station. The character's tempo-rhythm changes from one of outer slowness to a more dynamic one as he heads towards the train. But the bell also arouses certain visions and emotions regarding the trip and his destination. And the tempo-rhythm changes again if the traveler is rushing into the station, afraid to be late for the train. If he only arrives on the second or third warning bells, for instance, his tempo-rhythm will be different each time, as in the Uta Hagen demonstration in which she realized she would be late for a class across town from her house. First she has ten minutes to get there, then five, then, in the third demonstration, it is already time for the class to begin. Her tempo-rhythm is different each time, and so are the emotions aroused in her by the playing of the actions (packing her purse, rushing out the door). It was a very revealing and instructive demonstration, and taught us everything we needed to know about the necessity of being specific. Even a few minutes makes a difference, and conditions behavior.

Props and Objects and Their Uses: Details and Specificity

In *Respect for Acting* (MacMillan, 1973), Uta Hagen applies Stanislavsky's idea of specificity to physical objects and props; this is an important cornerstone of her interpretation of Stanislavsky. Every single thing you handle, from a pen and paper to a glass of water to a dagger or sword or fan, must have a personal meaning to you as the character, and therefore to you as the actor. If you are at home, drinking tea from a cup, you know where and when you acquired the cup, and what it means to you. It should be the same when you are handling a prop teacup as an actor/character. Technically, you must learn to integrate its use with whatever action you are playing and to time its use with the dialogue, without thinking too much about it, unless that is called for specifically. In other words, you must use props in a natural way, particularly in a realistic or naturalistic play. The "cup and saucer dramas" of Tom Robertson (1829–1871) provide salient examples. This was a particular genre of nineteenth-century Victorian realistic play, theatrically revolutionary in its day, in which tea was served, and the characters sat around discussing social issues. One of his most successful problem plays was *Caste*. In act 3, POLLY *meantime has poured out tea in two cups, and one saucer for* SAM, *sugars them, and then hands cup and saucer to* HAWTREE.

Props and objects, and especially how they are used, should ideally reveal the character's inner life. In other words, they have a heightened symbolic value for the audience. In rehearsal, you should, if possible, use an equivalent to the actual prop you will be handling: if you are supposed to walk with a cane, ask the producer to supply one, or bring your own.

In the French film *Plus tard tu comprendras* (One Day You'll Understand, 2007), Jeanne Moreau handles props in a very telling way. She (the character) has collected objets d'art and decorated her apartment with them. When she prepares a meal, she pays less attention than she ought to a hot casserole, and burns her fingers slightly as a result. Nearly every object she handles, from her son's briefcase to a shawl she takes off, is more or less thrown where she wants it, with some show of carelessness, and she displays complete indifference to almost every material object she deals with. Actually, there is an element of anger in what she does, and it appears to be unconscious on her part—a brilliant touch. The way she handles the props is very real, very natural, and also very telling: the character's indifference to the outer, material aspects of life, even to art objects she finds beautiful, and her deep anger are portrayed vividly through this use of objects. She dwells in her mind on the past in Nazi-occupied France, on what happened to her Jewish parents while she survived as the wife of a Christian—none of which she ever talks about. Her son searches for and unearths the past, and when she knows she is about to die, she reveals some things to her grandchildren, even showing them the yellow Star of David she was obliged to wear, which she confides for safekeeping to her grandson. This object she handles with great care. At the same time, everything she does with props is so natural that the viewer absorbs her personality unconsciously. Only when observing her performance closely, for purposes of writing about it, did I notice her brilliant use of objects in portraying the character's internal life, and then only when I decided to concentrate on what she was doing with them, because everything she did was so perfectly organic and unself-conscious.

Hyppolite Girardot, playing her son Victor, also used props and objects superbly: He handles his mother's papers, as he searches for the history of what happened to his Jewish grandparents, very carefully, in exactly the reverse of the way his mother deals with such objects. And his touching of the wallpaper in the room in the provincial hotel where his grandparents were arrested by the Nazi German soldiers and the collaborationist French police is also very psychologically telling—not in an obvious way, but rather in a communicative way that the spectator immediately absorbs. Touching the wallpaper seems perhaps to be an unnatural, even artificial gesture that nobody in real life would do, but it becomes somehow real and acceptable in the circumstances as they are presented to us.

In other words, both Moreau and Girardot endow the props with personal meaning. They particularize and personalize every object, and this is one of the things that gives such life, such reality, and such psychological depth to their portrayals. And this has to do once again with a combination of external and internal techniques, based on analysis of the text and of the given circumstances. And it comes from total immersion in those given circumstances. This is both harder and easier on film than on the stage. It is easier because the camera picks up the minutest of movements, which might not even be seen beyond the front row in a live performance. It is harder for the same reason: any bit of unreality is picked up by the camera and glaringly breaks the illusion of reality. And, secondly, whether a film is shot in or out of sequence, it is always shot in bits and pieces, and the actor must have the best memory in the world to be able to pick up exactly where he or she left off. This is helped by whoever is in charge of continuity, who will have noted everything down in the minutest detail, one hopes. Both these conditions must have obtained in the shooting of *Plus tard tu comprendras*.

When it came to props and even to the specifics of every moment and every object, Stanislavsky warned that the actor should not be overly meticulous about absolutely everything: such overindulgence in every trivial detail, concentrating on each thing, is as bad for the reality of living in and through the given circumstances as not concentrating on anything. This is not generally the way people are in real life, and much of their knowledge of objects remains on the preconscious level: they don't think all the time about where that coffee cup came from or how long they have had it, but they know this unconsciously, and that knowledge conditions how they handle it.

Finding the Character: Some Further Suggestions

As Lee Strasberg said, "When a character is fully created, the audience can walk away and speak about that fascinating person that lives on separately from the actor." One thinks of Hamlet, Othello, Romeo, Ophelia, Desdemona or Juliet, Amanda Wingfield, Blanche DuBois, Stanley Kowalski, George and Martha, and so many others in classic and contemporary theater and cinema.

In the media, there is often very little time in which to find the character. You have to rehearse on your own, when there is little or no rehearsal time allowed in a hectic schedule. Modern technology thus harks back to the old-fashioned system in place in the centuries before systematic rehearsal in the theater! Hence the usefulness of noted acting teacher, coach, and actor Alice Spivak's *How to Rehearse When There Is No Rehearsal: Acting and the Media* (Limelight, 2007), on which I collaborated with her. Firmly based in the Stanislavskian system discussed here, it details an essential way of working that you can use in a short period of time, and that is also useful for long rehearsal periods. Understanding the character's background and biography, which are given circumstances, you also work on the character's objectives, obstacles, and actions, both overall and in each scene. In film work, as Ms. Spivak points out, you "accumulate" the character, playing scenes that are often filmed out of script sequence, and your experience of the character is therefore quite different than when you do a play and sustain a character from the beginning to the end of his or her story in one continuous performance. Nonetheless, the same methods of analysis and work in character creation apply in both the theater and the media. The book is also full of specific tips and techniques.

Actors Studio member, actress, producer, and noted acting coach and teacher Susan Batson (b. 1944) founded the theater school Black Nexxus, with branches in New York and Los Angeles. And she has written a brilliant book that should be in every actor's library, *Truth: Personas, Needs, and Flaws in the Art of Building and Creating Characters* (Rugged Land, 2006). Using original exercises, as well as some drawn from Strasberg, and firmly grounded in Stanislavskian principles of sense memory, public solitude (the fourth wall), personalization, and script analysis, her approach is nevertheless a distinctive system of character creation. Among other things, the actor works on the character's "face," which is the public persona he or she presents to the world; the character's underlying hidden "need(s)," masked from the world much of the time; and the character's "tragic flaw," which is usually unknown to the character and constitutes an obstacle to the character's achieving what he or she needs and wants. This is to simplify an approach that you can read about more fully in the book, but it is a good place to start, after you have dealt with given circumstances, because it deals directly with the character's psychophysical motivations, and helps determine the character's actions, in the classic Stanislavskian sense.

I would suggest that you can do a great deal of work at home on the character's psychology, as well as on making the given circumstances real and truthful. What is going on with the character unconsciously? In other words, what are the character's unconscious motivations? Remember that we need the unconscious: To be conscious and aware of everything would drive anyone crazy. We need to be able to block out certain memories, just as we need to block out extraneous sound and light, or we would be bombarded by sensory impressions. What is the character blocking out? Even the fictitious mind of a fictional person has an unconscious that includes the character's ambiguity and ambivalence, discussed below in connection with playing opposites.

The study of psychology and of the character's sexuality are of supreme importance to the actor, yet most people neglect these aspects of character, and know little about psychology or psychoanalysis. But, as I suggest in *Tools and Techniques for Character Interpretation: A Handbook of Psychology for Actors, Writers, and Directors*, the findings of psychological theorists and practitioners, from Freud's psychoanalysis through such contemporary schools as cognitive and existential psychology, are not only helpful in interpreting character, but essential. Just as the psychology of psychopathy underlies the characters of Iago and Richard III in Shakespeare, and the psychology of prejudice informs *The Merchant of Venice*, so what Freud called "the psychopathology of everyday life" informs every play written, not to mention films and television sitcoms, daytime and nighttime dramas.

A Rehearsal and Performance Technique: Playing Opposites

As Robert De Niro said in an interview in *Actors Talk About Acting*, "Never indicate. People don't try to show their feelings. They try to hide them." In other words, people often behave in a way that directly hides their emotions and reactions, sometimes even appearing to feel the opposite of what they really feel. To play a scene this way as a character is to give it depth and reality. This technique is an aspect of what is called "playing opposites," also discussed in *Using the Stanislavsky System*. This form of playing opposites is also called the technique of "playing against" a particular condition or situation. Uta Hagen points this out in *Respect for Acting*. People don't try to cry; they try not to cry, and their resistance, which may lead to outright sobbing, is very real and convincing. People who are drunk are extra careful, so they won't fall down or break a glass, though their efforts are not always successful.

Playing opposites or playing against begins perhaps as external technique—in other words, a choice that is calculated—which is then transformed into an organic way of playing a scene or a moment. Or it may simply occur naturally in the course of rehearsing a scene, and not be calculated at all.

Playing opposites has to do also with our natural, characterological ambivalence, about which the German pioneer psychologist and friend of Sigmund Freud Georg Groddeck (1866–1934) wrote a great deal in *The Book of the It* (Vintage Books, 1961), which I recommend to all actors. The word "ambivalence" means the simultaneous existence of seemingly contradictory or mutually exclusive feelings, such as love and hate. The terms "ambivalence" and "ambiguity" mean very similar things, but ambivalence is unconscious, and ambiguity is ambivalence made conscious.

For Groddeck, love and hate exist together, and are found side by side. Ambiguous feelings may exist with regard to particular circumstances. And one can be ambivalent about another person, or sometimes about oneself, when narcissistic self-love and self-loathing exist together in the unconscious.

There are ambivalent feelings in every relationship. The noble, high-minded Brutus in *Julius Caesar* is the only conspirator to have acted out of principle and not, like the others, out of envy. And he is filled with ambivalent feelings about Caesar, some of which intrude into his consciousness in the form we call ambiguity: Brutus is at "war with himself" over the moral dilemma of assassinating his revered friend, and this fills him with pain, but he accedes to what he conceives to be the higher good. Still, he is filled with ambivalence even after the deed is done.

In Chekhov's plays, Vanya's relationship with his mother is full of ambivalence, as is Constantine's relationship with his mother, Madame Arkadina, in *The Seagull*. How does Masha in *Three Sisters* really feel about her husband, Kulygin? She resents his continued existence, since she loves the army officer Vershinin, but she knows that Kulygin, for all his faults, is basically a good-hearted person. Part of her still loves Kulygin, but in the end she remains with him because she feels she has no choice, and cannot leave with Vershinin when the army departs: this is ambiguity. But in her unconscious there is also ambivalence: She regrets having married Kulygin at all. But she knows that he loves her. All of this, in acting terms, is subtextual meat for the intentions of the lines and for the way the actions are played. As for Kulygin, he smiles when he wants to cry.

As an actor's technique, playing opposites is also usually defined as behaving in a way contrary to what would be expected when expressing a character's feelings, thus adding reality and depth to the portrayal in the playing of specific moments. Playing opposites is one of the most useful tools in acting. For instance, a person who is full of rage may speak softly, but the menace underneath, having been felt and experienced by the actor, will be readily apparent to the audience. A person may be happy and convivial in one scene, and depressed and irritable in another. Happiness might be expressed with a frown, as when a character is joking or teasing; and irritability with a smile, showing that the character is perhaps afraid to express annoyance directly to another character.

Playing opposites also includes playing characters as a whole in a way that recognizes a character's ambivalences, and acting them when appropriate; for example, appearing to be the opposite of what the character is, so that a villain, for instance, may be a charming, urbane, well-mannered psychopath, not easily detected by the other characters. A hero, a person of great courage, may appear unassuming and modest, and even distracted or slovenly, but will act in a heroic manner when called upon to do so. For example, in Oscar Wilde's *An Ideal Husband*, Lord Goring, who poses as a superficial if witty man about town, proves in reality to be a deeply moral person capable of great acts of kindness and friendship, which, out of modesty, he would prefer other people not to know about.

Another example: In 1983, I performed in George Steiner's *The Portage to San Cristóbal of A. H.* at the Hartford Stage Company. In the play, Israeli commandos are bringing Hitler, who has been discovered alive in a jungle in South America, back to Israel to stand trial. The commandos are pursued by the forces of other countries, who also wish to capture Hitler, and, as time is running out, the Israelis hold a trial right there in a clearing. Sitting still at the side of the stage at a reading desk with a single lit lamp, I played the part of Lieber, an Israeli official broadcasting to the commandos in the jungle, in order to embolden them and to remind them why they are doing their task.

When I began rehearsing the play, I was very emotional, and I had all I could do not to weep during my long speeches about the Holocaust: "In Maidanek 10,000 a day..." My obstacle, I told myself, was that I needed to control myself and found it difficult because of the horror of the events. But Mark Lamos quickly put me on the right path. "If you cry, or even show us that you are trying not to cry," he said, "the audience won't." And he directed me to deliver the material dispassionately, almost coldly, simply building the speeches to their climaxes, but without any affect or emotional involvement. My objective and the action I played were to remind them, to remind them, and to remind them again, not by pounding away, but by simply telling them the story, by simply making points: This is why you have gone after the maniac! This is the way it was—"At Maidanek 10,000 a day..." This also allowed the audience to absorb the images and to imagine events for themselves, which is what you as an actor and they as spectators want. And it is another good example of playing opposites: I felt deeply upset by what I was relating, but I related it as if I were not upset, but simply narrating facts. And it took rehearsal and direction to help me find this way of playing the part.

Relaxation and Concentration

In order to be able to act at all, you must be able to relax; that is, to have an inner sense of being at rest, so that you can turn your attention to concentrating on the role. This sense of being at rest must be accompanied by the feeling that you are ready and eager to work. These feelings of relaxation and commitment to the job are further accompanied by a sense of excitement and even of exhilaration as the time for the performance nears. Importantly, you must overcome fear, manifested as stage fright or "butterflies" in the stomach, and other personal issues to arrive at this creative state. We all fear adverse judgment, and we all want applause. We want to be told how wonderful we are. But in order to get that applause, you have to concentrate on doing the job you are there to do. And performance is exhilarating! It is such great fun, even in a tragedy!

There is so much to think about when you create a character. But when you perform, you have to "forget" everything you thought about, and just do it. As Meryl Streep said in a *New York Times* interview program broadcast on the CUNY channel on February 19, 2010, about the film *Julie and Julia* (2009), she was so concentrated on carrying out such actions as chopping onions or making love that she didn't even think: she just acted.

And here, I think, we must distinguish actions from activities, which are stage business. True, activities are actions in the sense that they are physical deeds, such as pouring a drink or knitting a scarf, and they fulfill immediate, minor objectives. But they are not the kind of actions that are done in pursuit of a major objective. These underlie the entire scene, perhaps without even being directly expressed externally. Chopping onions was more than an activity. It was an action because it was part of Julia Child's process of learning to be an expert cook. It was one of the things she did to help her get where she wanted to go. And she chopped those onions with a concentration and a vigor, and in the specific way she had been taught at cooking school. What she did and how she did it was a lesson: every action must be carried out with full commitment, and with specificity and an attention to detail.

In order to "forget," you need to be in a state of concentration on the play, while remaining aware of being on a stage, in front of all those people. They are looking at your every move. Oh, my... There is always an underlying muscular tension, of which the actor is often unconscious. Although it is impossible to get rid of it entirely, Stanislavsky maintained that we could fight it, principally with the weapon of concentration.

He talked about different but interconnected "circles of concentration." Concentration is focused attention, and he thought that there were broadening circles of attention that the actor dealt with:

1. **Small circle:** Concentration on the self, on the character's immediate inner needs and desires; and/or on the actions being carried out, and how or in what manner they are being enacted; as well as on the acting partner and the immediate needs of the relationship, and on what the other person is doing.

2. **Medium circle:** This involves "switching attention" from one object to another, as each demands attention. The attention is directed outward and away from the self; for example, in a swordfight, when the fighter must battle several opponents at a time. There is active connection or contact with the object, usually within a limited area.

3. **Large circle:** Attention and concentration that is inclusive of more than one object—in other words, on generalities; for instance in a party or ball scene, where the concentration may be on the actor's immediate partner, and at the same time be diffused, so that attention is also paid to the refreshment buffet, the dancers, and the other people who are there.

4. **Subliminal concentration on the reality of the surroundings:** On a more subliminal level, there is attention paid to the audience for

whom the actor performs without acknowledging their existence, except in cases of direct address to them, as in some Shakespearean soliloquies. The actor is always aware on some level of the presence and responses of the audience. This can interfere with the performance, and it is a danger that must be dealt with by even deeper concentration on the circumstances.

The actor also must be aware of changes that take place spontaneously during a performance, so as to be able to adjust to them: when such things happen, the actor who adjusts his or her performance is really acting in the moment.

To begin with, you must choose to concentrate in order to be centered within the role. But you may choose and yet not be able to achieve the state of feeling concentrated. However, there are techniques that will enable you to concentrate even though surrounded by distractions. The first technique is to accept mentally and emotionally that these distractions are there, and to include them in your attention span, which you will gradually narrow as you enter the world of the play.

In order to concentrate, you have to relax. In order to relax, you have to concentrate on the given circumstances, which include the actual environment: the state of the dressing room and what it is like to be in the wings or the backstage area waiting to go on.

What Happens in Performance During the Run of a Show

If you are committed to doing the show, to carrying out the correct psychophysical actions, the audience will be riveted. You have to remember that they are there, and you have to forget that fact at the same time. This is one of the prime techniques of performing. But how do you get there? You perform with precision, with dynamism, with truth, and with commitment, as Stanislavsky said. During rehearsals of Molière's *Tartuffe* at the Moscow Art Theatre, as Toporkov tells us in *Stanislavski in Rehearsal*, Stanislavsky particularly praised the actors, who had been improvising, for doing just that: "This is no longer theatre. This is genuine real-life action, full of concentration and commitment."

When Stanislavsky talks of a "circle of concentration," he means a kind of protective shell that the actor builds around him- or herself during performance, in order to avoid anything that might distract from playing the part, and in order to be able to concentrate on living through the given circumstances as they unfold from moment to moment. On stage you are helped by lighting, and by the fact that, usually, the audience is in darkness, so that the world of the play is delimited by light. You simply look at certain things, and shut everything else out of your purview, while remaining aware, as one must, that those things are there—collapsing scenery or a fire backstage cannot, after all, be ignored. The show must go on, unless the theater is burning down.

In order to help concentration, you will find the technique of the fourth wall serviceable, and at times even absolutely necessary, first during rehearsal, and second, sometimes, during performance. The fourth wall refers to the missing wall of a proscenium set, but it is also useful in the round or in three-quarters round. The technique consists of imaginatively placing imaginary objects directly in front of you. If there is supposed to be a window or a particular painting on the wall, this becomes obvious, but where nothing in particular is indicated in the script, you are free to place anything at all on the fourth wall—hopefully something connected to the play, something that makes sense in the context.

The audience will change the nature and impact of the performance, depending on their reactions, which may even have a determining effect on its rhythm and tempo. An important principle is never to look at them directly, even though you are constantly aware of their presence and reactions: Instead, if you must face front, select a spot over their heads and all the way in back. That way they feel included, but are still able to look on as spectators. Of course, if you have a soliloquy, this may include a direct address to the audience. Nevertheless, the same idea of selecting a spot above and behind them applies: Try not to look anyone directly in the eyes, as this interferes both with your concentration in playing, and theirs in watching, since it removes both you and them from the situation and into the more potent reality of life itself.

During the run of a show, and at rehearsals, you should behave professionally at all times. Professional behavior consists of a commonsense code of conduct that actors are duty-bound to abide by, and that the discipline of show business requires. The first rule is to be courteous, considerate, and respectful to everyone, backstage, on stage, or in the studio; in rehearsal, and in performance: From that, all else follows. Know, understand, and abide by the terms of your contract. Remember that you are there to serve the play. To begin with, when you arrive, always sign in for both rehearsals and performances, so the stage manager knows you are in the house; and for auditions, when required. Nobody may sign in for another actor: the actor must sign in personally.

You are expected to be at the theater at half hour, at the latest, which means half an hour before the official curtain time. But the curtain usually goes up ten to fifteen minutes after the announced time. And the stage manager or an assistant will announce fifteen- and five-minute calls to curtain, and then "Places," in the US, or "Beginners" in the UK, which means that you have to be on deck, ready to enter when the curtain rises, or whenever your entrance is. Always say "thank you" to whoever gives the calls before a theater performance (unless, of course, they are only given over the PA system), to acknowledge that you have heard and understood them. But you should always make an effort to be ready well before all of the calls. Arrive at the theater at least an hour before curtain time, if not two, especially if you have to apply makeup. You will find this a help to relaxation, and for getting into and soaking up the backstage atmosphere that you include in your preparation for the performance. And never miss an entrance: there is no excuse for such unprofessional conduct.

During the show, do not upstage your fellow performers (or yourself) or steal scenes. Do your job: play your role as you rehearsed it, bearing in mind that your organic performance will cause you to experience the role slightly differently every time you perform. Staying alive within the world of the play will help you avoid the cardinal sin of anticipation—expecting the next event before the character is in a position to do so, instead of allowing it to happen. A common form of anticipation is cringing at an unexpected blow that the other character has not even started to deliver. Anticipation reveals to the audience the artificiality of what is going on, of acting itself, and immediately breaks their concentration and cracks wide open the illusion of reality, the stage convention that has lulled them into attention on the proceedings and inattention on the reality of their own lives and even their surroundings. Still, your obligation to stay "in the moment" does not give you the right to throw your fellow actors off by doing something startling, new, and completely unrehearsed, because you supposedly "felt it." A severe reprimand from stage management usually follows such uncouth behavior. And you should always say all your lines exactly as they were written, or rewritten, by the author. While there is sometimes room for an ad lib, that is, for a spontaneous improvised, off-the-cuff line or bit of stage business, this is usually inappropriate, especially in a tragedy, and certainly in a verse play, or with music. And remember, acting is acting: at no time do you have the right to hurt your fellow performer or put him or her in any danger.

In the wings, concentration is essential. The creative mindset is conducive to concentration as soon as you arrive there to wait for your entrance. Some people get there early—but unless the theater is a large one and there is plenty of backstage space, you may create traffic problems. Therefore, you will have to time entrances so as to be there later than you might perhaps find ideal, but you will easily adjust to the situation as the run proceeds.

Another way to relax before a performance is to use music: sing something softly to yourself that suggests the emotional state of the character, or listen to music that does that. When you warm up vocally, do it with music that helps bring you into the character, arousing the emotions you want, so as to be in the state of mind the character is in. As you listen and concentrate, use headphones and you won't disturb your colleagues.

When you arrive at the theater for a performance, concentration begins in earnest. It may even have started before, when you are on your way there. In fact, the day is spent gearing up for the performance, whether you are conscious of this or not. You will find that you pace yourself and conserve your energy throughout the day. When you arrive at the theater, include all of the circumstances: What is the backstage area like? Who is there when you arrive? What state is the dressing room in? If you share a dressing room, include all the other occupants in your circle of concentration. Excluding anybody or anything, at the beginning of the process of preparing for a performance, is unhelpful, because it puts those things and people in the position of being intrusive, and, when they inevitably do intrude, that destroys concentration.

You must respect anyone who obviously wishes to be left alone to concentrate. If you are the kind of actor who wishes to be left alone, you can still include everyone in your peripheral vision, so that you will not experience them as disruptive or intrusive. You have every right to keep yourself to yourself, especially as you go on deck to prepare for your entrance. At that point, everything but the entrance should only be a peripheral part of your environment, pushed into the background. You will have entered the given circumstances as much as you possibly can before actually being in them, out there on the stage.

Always keep your dressing table as neat as possible, so you can find whatever makeup you might be using quickly and efficiently. Always store your costumes neatly, and make sure everything is in its proper place before you leave the theater after the show. Don't make extra work for the already overworked wardrobe department. Keep your personal props in order, and if you pick up a prop from the prop table, always put it back in its proper, marked place when you exit, unless of course you have left it on stage. Or hand it to a props department person or assistant stage manager under whatever arrangement has been made.

During the performance, even when you are offstage, stay in character. If you don't, it will be that much harder to get back into character when you have to make an entrance. During a long run, after a few months, you will probably have no difficulty in getting right into character immediately, no matter what you have been doing just before an entrance. But it will still be more helpful to you to concentrate on the performance the whole time. In any number of shows, and especially in musicals, there are quick changes of costume and sometimes of makeup to be effected in a matter of minutes. Until you get so used to these, you may not be able to remain in character while the technical demands of the changes are being met. But eventually, there will be no problem in dividing your attention between the character and the backstage demands of a quick change. Rapidly putting on makeup or another costume during a performance, either over the one already being worn or replacing it, so as to be able to enter immediately, will become second nature. Quick changes are also called lightning changes, or wing changes, because they are most often done directly offstage. They are usually done in a small enclosed space or booth, curtained off from the rest of the backstage area, where the actor, sometimes with the help of a dresser, can effect the required transformation. This little space is also called a quick-change booth or an onstage dressing room, and it requires getting used to. But once this is done, all you have to do is concentrate and everything should run smoothly and effectively. Never appear in costume or makeup outside the theater: to do so shows a lack of respect for the profession and the project. And it is part of your job to be there for the curtain call, even if your part had only one scene at the beginning of the performance, unless you are specifically excused.

Once the production opens, the director usually leaves the actors on their own to do the shows. The director may return to check on the show from time to time. Most actors are quite happy not to have to deal with the director after the production is up and running, even if the director is a personal friend. But dealing with the person who functions as the director's deputy, the stage manager, can be quite difficult. It is one of the stage manager's jobs to maintain the play as directed, and consequently to give the actors notes as necessary, after the performances. If you don't get along well with the stage manager, or don't respect him or her, or if you disagree, you may find yourself in a rather unpleasant situation, but you are duty-bound as a professional to obey in any case.

A caveat, especially for inexperienced actors, but also for some of my more experienced colleagues: After a performance, when we all want applause and praise from others, we tend to be our own harshest critics. We all have our insecurities. But try not to be too critical of yourself. For one thing, you really don't know how you did. You only know how you feel, and that is not always a reliable guide. People who saw you are in a better position to be objective about your performance. That does not include those on stage with you, who are also involved in the performance and therefore not in a position to be objective. If you don't get the praise you want, you may feel miserable and begin to doubt yourself. Or you may feel you were great and unappreciated, but you may have been off. "What happened to you out there tonight?" is a question sometimes asked of an actor who thought he or she had delivered a terrific performance. Conversely, you may feel off, but someone may say, "Wow! You were really cooking tonight!" On the other hand, do be analytical, as objectively as possible. You will undoubtedly know how you feel specific moments worked. You will always want to continue working on, refining, and improving your performance. No matter how much praise you receive, you don't ever want to rest on your laurels. And you will want to try new things that are within the framework of what has been set up. There is always the next performance!

How to Make a Long Run Interesting

In books of interviews, several actors have given the following advice: approach the part each evening as if you were really doing it afresh. Look for something new. This keeps you constantly alert. Remember, too, that no moment can be repeated exactly. So in reality, everything *must* be done afresh: there is no choice. We never come to the theater in quite the same state of mind we were in the day before. And we are never the same twice in a performance, even though the architectonics of the role have been worked out in rehearsal, and the basic shape, arc, and journey of the character remain the same.

Famed actor Alfred Lunt (1892–1977), who always acted with his wife, British-born Lynn Fontanne (1887–1983), interviewed in *Actors Talk About Acting*, answers the question as to what keeps his interest going during a long run: "Oh, it's because you never feel you make it

anyway, from the beginning. I mean you never give a satisfactory performance from the time you start. Something always goes wrong."
Therefore, the actor strives every time to give the perfect performance,
and this is one way of keeping up the desire to perform each time. Also,
Lunt points out that there is a different audience each night. Their
expectations also help the actor want to perform as well as possible.

Ms. Fontanne says in the same book, when asked to define acting
technique, "You just read your part with as much reality as you can—
truthfulness—a little louder than in an ordinary room and don't bump
into each other, that's all." If you adhere to this, you will require of
yourself the effort to infuse reality and truth into your playing. And in
every performance you will live from moment to moment in the given
circumstances of the play and the production. And be very careful not
to bump into the scenery or furniture, unless you are playing Yepikhidov
in Chekhov's *Cherry Orchard*!

CHAPTER FIVE

Performing Comedy

As some theater wit said long ago, and many have repeated since, "Dying is easy. Comedy is hard!" And finding out who said that is impossible! There is a legion of candidates, of whom the most plausible is...But I digress. Hard as it may be, comedy is also a most enjoyable thing to play. It's fun! You get to laugh inside yourself all evening, and to enjoy the audience's laughter. And that is the key and the secret to playing comedy: Enjoy yourself! If you don't, oh melancholy swain, you can be sure that the audience won't. And they will go home cursing and spluttering, "I thought this was supposed to be funny!"

It may be difficult to play a comedy for the five-hundredth or even the fiftieth time. But you have to do it! It's your job! So get out there and enjoy yourself, damn it! And if you should be playing a comedy for the five-hundredth time, remember how lucky you are to be doing so!

In an article entitled "Random Rules for Comedy" in the magazine *The Dramatist* for November/December 2005, playwright Paul Rudnick begins with this advice to playwrights and directors, "Use funny actors. It is absolutely impossible to urge or trick someone into being funny when it's just not part of their particular arsenal." He is right, of course. But what is funny? Who is funny? And why? Who knows? And how do you know you're funny? That one is easy to answer: If people laugh when you tell a joke or play a comic scene, you know you're funny.

Humor may be droll, dry, sly, clever, witty, pointed, acerbic, comic, amusing, wry, rueful or outrageous, salacious, riotous, obscene, or hilarious. But for all the words used to characterize it, the nature of humor remains elusive. What people find funny and what makes them laugh depends on their individual temperaments—see Freud's *Der Witz und seine Beziehung zum Unbewussten*, translated as *Wit and Its Relations to the Unconscious*, or *Jokes and Their Relation to the Unconscious*.

In Gilbert and Sullivan's *The Yeomen of the Guard*, the strolling jester Jack Point—rather a sad sack, because he is unhappy in love, and desperate to find a permanent job as somebody's personal jester—sings of his profession in the patter song, "Oh, A Private Buffoon Is a Light-Hearted Loon":

If you wish to succeed as a jester,
You'll need to consider each person's auricular.
What is all right for B would quite scandalize C,
for C is so very particular.

Rigoletto would no doubt have disagreed. Just tell any horrid, sarcastic joke you want about anybody, to anybody, for anybody, he would have maintained. He did. And look where it got him! Jack Point really says it all: You have to know your audience. And in performing comedy, you have to know how to play a real character, however heightened the situation, however unreal and absurd. You must also know the specific external techniques of playing comedy, such as holding for a laugh, that are quite apart from the psychophysical actions, but must be incorporated into the acting score. And you have to know where the laughs come, but you cannot anticipate them. If you do, they will most probably not be there.

A Funny Thing Happened

Comedy is the art of the incongruous. The juxtaposition of one inappropriate thing with another can be hilarious. A funeral is not funny, but if a character behaves outrageously and inappropriately at one, while pretending to be involved in the ritual of mourning, the situation provokes laughter, perhaps somewhat shocked, nervous laughter born of the audience's discomfort. Grace behaves completely inappropriately at funerals in episodes of the television series *Will and Grace*. So do the King and the Duke in the many adaptations of Mark Twain's *Huckleberry Finn*. And we laugh.

Another example of the incongruous and the inappropriate: Two divorced spouses, who have each remarried, find themselves sharing adjoining balconies at the resort hotel they have gone to for their honeymoons with their new consorts. The situation is incongruous, but not impossible. It could happen! The very facts provoke the anticipation of laughter even before we hear all the brilliantly witty, pointed, acerbic, inappropriate exchanges in Noël Coward's *Private Lives*.

The erroneous assumptions of a character can be funny. Mistaken identity is one of the prime occasions for erroneousness. Such a useful device for playwrights, and such fun to act! When characters act on false information or presuppositions, and the audience knows the truth, the scrapes the characters get into are funny—to the audience. Not to the characters involved!

Farce and drawing-room comedy are both full of surprises, of incongruous situations, and of erroneous impressions on the part of the characters. But there are techniques required for playing farce that are different from those required for drawing-room comedy, even though they have some techniques in common, such as timing a laugh and doing a double take. Farce is a manic genre, and drawing-room comedy is a milder, more leisurely, more decorous form. Its humor depends on wordplay and repartee, on rapier sarcasm, and on the ability to handle words wittily and to deliver a punch line in a casual, offhand, perhaps even snobbish and arrogant manner, betokening an attitude of superiority. The words in a drawing-room comedy must come "thick and fast," like the oysters tumbling onto the beach in Lewis Carroll's "The Walrus and the Carpenter." But the humor in farce depends more on physical excess than on verbal prowess; patently absurd situations; physical actions; and the fast-paced movement of the play in a furious tempo-rhythm, with everybody scrambling to achieve certain results that have either been put off too long or are necessary because of emergencies, as in Feydeau's farces, where all the characters run to get behind the right door so as to avoid discovery. This is outrageous, silly, and absurd, but it could happen! It is possible!

Both drawing-room comedy and farce also depend on a sense of humor shared by all the actors, who can therefore play together with the consciousness of what is funny and why. And, just as importantly, comedy and farce depend on character, and character must be played truthfully and for real. Or else it's not funny! This brings us to the major point about playing comedy: you must have seriousness of purpose.

Comedy Depends on the Reality of Character and on Serious Commitment to the Reality of the Situation

Christopher Guest (b. 1948) has made a number of mockumentaries, which are satirical films that purport to be documentaries and parody the genre as well as burlesquing the subjects they treat. Cowritten with comedian Eugene Levy, who also appears in the films, Guest's hilarious movies are brilliant and supremely funny. Guest and Levy write the stories, Guest directs, and apparently much of the dialogue is improvised by the superb comedy ensemble cast that plays in all the films. They include the 1984 mockumentary *This is Spinal Tap* (made before the partnership with Levy), in which Guest plays Nigel Tufnel, the lead guitarist of Spinal Tap, the rock group of the title. In *Waiting for Guffman* (1996), Guest plays Corky St. Clair, the extremely fey director of a small-town musical in a community theater setting. He is always taking about his wife (!), who is never around. This is certainly incongruous: the fact that he claims to have a wife at all is incongruous.

In *Best in Show* (2000), Guest plays Harlan Pepper, the owner of a hound whom he exhibits at a dog show. My brother and sister-in-law, Donald and Corbeau Blumenfeld-Jones, raise and show prize-winning Rhodesian Ridgebacks, and they assure me that the people in the film are really like the ones at the dog shows they go to, and that Guest is exactly like the owners of hounds they have met. For this role, Guest looks rather like a hound, with a very long face. "It's not a mockumentary; it's a documentary!" Donald jokingly says, and he adds, "It's scarily accurate."

A Mighty Wind (2003) is about a reunion of old-time folk musicians from a number of groups, forty years after the height of the folk music movement's popularity in the 1960s. They have been asked to participate in a film honoring the recently deceased iconic manager Steinbloom. Guest plays folksinger Alan Barrows, and he had little preparation to do, since he used to play that kind of music in Greenwich Village's famed Bitter End nightclub.

In *For Your Consideration* (2006), Guest plays Jay Berman, a Jewish movie director who is making a film about a Southern Jewish family, *Home for Purim*. And this man, munching on a ragged corned beef sandwich, gives directions in a real New York accent. Guest never overdoes the character, whose pedestrian creative juices are always flowing as he obsesses about his project.

There is a common thread that runs through all Guest's characters: they are so completely caught up in their world, whether it be that of community theater, heavy-metal rock, or dog shows, that they see little beyond it. Guest said in a 2002 interview with Gary Dretzka of MCN, "I am interested in the notion that people can become so obsessed with their world that they lose sense and awareness of how they appear to other people. They're so earnest about it." Obsession and single-mindedness can be funny! But not to the person who is obsessed and single-minded.

How does Christopher Guest do it? Obviously, he observes people with a fine eye for the details of their behavior. He sees how they move, how they walk, and he can imitate them perfectly. But, just as obviously, he understands the psychology that gives rise to the movement and appearance. He understands his characters' inner lives, their defense mechanisms and obsessive-compulsive neurosis. He knows what people either unconsciously repress or consciously try to conceal about themselves, such as Corky's blatant homosexuality, which the character may not even understand is there: we are never sure if he is being hypocritical, or is actually unconscious of who he is and how people perceive him, or if he just doesn't think it matters. This ambiguity is very real, and very funny as a result.

As the brilliant and dryly hilarious W. C. Fields (1880–1946) said, in a rare sober and serious moment, "Comedy is other people's tragedy." I might say that tragedy is sometimes other people's comedy—this may be the case with farce, and a clue as to how to play farce. There are outrageous, overdone characters in farce whose lives must be tragic, so outlandish are their quirks and compulsions, and so unhappy must they be in their feelings of isolation, born of their inability to establish communication with other people. Our laughter at such creatures may arise from the discomforting, largely unconscious knowledge that we could have been like them, had our circumstances been like theirs. As Sir Despard and Mad Margaret sing in Gilbert and Sullivan's *Ruddigore*, "We were the victims of circumstances!" At any rate, Fields's quip is a great clue as to how to approach comic parts: with seriousness, if not solemnity. More solemnity than a situation calls for is funny. Less is also funny.

When you play comedy, you must be invested in the situation, however absurd, silly, or outlandish it may be. And you must have high stakes for the objectives. Also, funny characters often have a disapproving attitude, which they are not afraid to express in a sarcastic or ironic way, and their disapproval is very serious—to them. Their inner stakes can be very high: perhaps they want to feel superior, because somewhere deep down, they feel inferior. At any rate, insults and put-downs, if they are not truly cruel and unbearably malicious, can be very funny to audiences.

Comedy depends on the commitment to situations. You have to believe in the situations, in the given circumstances. But just as importantly, as I have said, comedy depends on the reality of character. Christopher Guest is the perfect example.

One more example of other people's tragedy: People often feel as if they are losing control both of themselves and of what is going on in their lives. In comedy, this can be very funny, particularly as such things proliferate and multiply. In farce, everyone can be out of control at once, as pandemonium and chaos ensue. The audience laughs. We've all been there!

Lucille Ball, playing the character of Lucy whom we have come to know and love so well, takes a job at the conveyer belt of a candy factory.

The incongruity of her always wanting to get into show business and to be a star, then taking that job, is funny in itself. In addition, there is the incongruity in the tempo of the conveyer belt, which speeds up so that she can barely do her job. She is out of control! Way out of control! She is panicky and desperate! Now that's funny!

All of these comic elements—incongruity, inappropriateness, erroneousness, misconceptions, lack of control—depend for their humor on another aspect of comedy and jokes: the element of surprise. The audience is set up to believe one thing about a character or situation and is surprised when something occurs that is outside or opposite to its expectations. They are taken unawares, so they laugh. The conveyer belt in the Lucy episode begins at normal speed. She does her assembly line job. Everything is fine. Gradually, the belt speeds up. Suddenly, it seems to be going at breakneck speed. We didn't expect this development any more than Lucy did. We immediately empathize because we know we would have reacted as she did, and we laugh because we are surprised. She fulfills every part of the situation perfectly and with complete reality. She believes in the circumstances. So their patent absurdity becomes absolutely hilarious, as we also accept their reality. The axiom applies: If you believe in something, so will the audience. If you don't, they won't.

The audience may also expect a reaction, and when it happens, they laugh. This is the case, for instance, with the unfortunate Fontanet in Feydeau's *Un fil à la patte* (Caught by the Heel, 1894), who smells because he doesn't bathe. We anticipate that every character who approaches him will react to his odor, and each does in his or her own specific fashion. And the oblivious Fontanet has no idea why people react to him as they do. But we have been informed by another character, who warns some of the others about Fontanet, and we laugh! Then there are the unwary, uninformed characters who go up to him. Some of them don't quite know where the stench is coming from. But we do! And we laugh as they approach Fontanet, because we know what they are about to go through.

Comedy Depends on Tempo-Rhythm: Timing the Laugh

Tempo-rhythm and the timing of laughs play the most important part in comedy in performance. Everything depends on timing, and the whole play is shaped by its tempo-rhythm in a way that tragedy is not. In tragedy, you can take your time. In comedy, you have to allow time and timing to govern you. Speeding up or slowing down tempo and pace unduly are funny phenomena. Such variations in tempo usually have to be worked out carefully in rehearsal, although tempo will change in reaction to audience responses. If you don't get a laugh where you expect it, for instance, building to the next laugh may be harder, and the tempo will have to be serendipitously changed because of the change in circumstances; that is, the change occasioned by the audience response must be dealt with on the spot.

Rudnick also says, "There are certain actors who are shameless, indefensible, amoral laugh whores. Worship them." I can guarantee you that those actors know how to make the audience laugh by not telegraphing that a laugh is on its way. The laughs are incidental from the characters' point of view: the situation and what is happening in the moment are important. In "So That's The Way You Like It," the great parody of Shakespearean tragedy done in the British revue *Beyond the Fringe*, which played on Broadway from 1962 to 1964, if the actors had not done the absurdly silly lines and played the situations for real, we would not have laughed. Groaned, perhaps, but not laughed, at silly, punning lines like, "Oh saucy Worcester, dost thou lie so still?" Worcester, saucy or not, has just been killed, and the delivery was as tragic as could be: the death of a young hero, slain before his time.

The most important external comedic technique is timing a laugh, and holding for it to subside. To begin with, when you deliver the laugh line, stand still! Remember, the audience notices movement before it hears words, and movement is distracting. It takes a second or more for people to go back to listening to what is being said after they have seen movement. Fidgeting, gesturing, taking a step—all are distracting. You must simply be standing there and talking with your acting partner. But if you do move, stop deliberately: This stop draws the audience's attention to you. Deliver the line while you are still. No other movement on stage should distract the audience, either. And all of that advice applies no matter what the pace or tempo-rhythm of the scene. It is a simple, technical procedure, and pure stagecraft. The stop and the way of delivering the line must be incorporated into the acting score.

Once the audience has been put in the mood to laugh by the first joke, they will continue in that mood and be inclined to laugh again. It helps as well if the audience is large. People are more comfortable laughing when they are surrounded than if there are only a few people in the house.

When the audience laughs, you have to stop the action—you should already be still in any case—and go into freeze-frame mode as you hold while they roll in the aisles. You have to time the laughter out, and this timing will be different at every performance: It depends entirely on the audience reaction. Holding for a laugh requires a deliberate, timed cessation of the play's action while the laughter rises to a peak, and until it dies down sufficiently for the comedy to proceed. When it is perhaps halfway down towards its ending, you will begin speaking. But for all that time, which may seem like an eternity, you must remain frozen in place and stay in character. Stand still! A gesture or a movement will cause the audience's laughter to start dying down. You might move when you want this to happen. The pause while you hold must be filled, and, I repeat, it is most important that you stay in character. You must not lose momentum or energy, and you must be poised for action, like a panther about to spring upon its prey. The skill required can only be acquired through experience: good, hard, practical work. No amount of teaching or reading can substitute for doing.

That supremely funny comedian, filled with a true sense of the ridiculous, Bert Lahr (1895–1967), best known for his performance as the Cowardly Lion in the film *The Wizard of Oz* (1939), said in his interview in *Actors Talk about Acting* that timing is rhythm. Timing is indeed a function of pace and tempo. It is the ability to do or say something at the exact right moment. And that is not as simple as it sounds. Again, even when you have the instinct for good timing and the necessary sense of rhythm, experience is the great teacher.

More Essential Comedic Techniques

The art of comedy also depends on setting up the jokes, which arise from the situation. Setups are done technically, in a tempo-rhythm established in rehearsal, which leads to the climax of the punch line as surely as a piece of music leads to its coda. The setup is not supposed to be funny, usually. But it can be, and the joke will then be even funnier. Both of you doing the joke—the person setting it up and the person delivering the joke's punch line—have to know it is funny, but you can't let the audience know you know. Of course, you think about getting laughs, and you know where you think they should be. Now let the audience discover what's funny, which they will never do if you "comment" on the material by a knowing wink, an intonation that says "Laugh here!" or "This is funny—wait for it!" or other similar antics and devices.

There are always exceptions to every rule. Even when doing a stage play, the British music hall comedian Frankie Howerd (whose performance in Gilbert and Sullivan's *Trial by Jury* is discussed in chapter 6), would connive with the audience, whom he would momentarily include in his purview, by looking at them and uttering his trademark "Ooh!" as if to say, "Would you believe it?" In fact, he often added those very words. He got away with it because he was just so hilarious! But this is a rare kind of thing, and should generally be avoided. Then there are those witty characters in Oscar Wilde plays who know they are funny, and they let the stage audience—the other characters in the play—know they know. But they are not professional comedians, simply characters who want others to perceive them as funny.

There are techniques used in comedy of consciously asking for a laugh: "putting a button" on a line or moment, which is emphasizing or stressing the line, and perhaps making a finalizing physical gesture. Another technique is to say the line and then briefly look front, perhaps with raised eyebrows, as if you were reacting to yourself, but at the same time you are making the audience complicit and having them share your point of view. If you are a comic actor, or a would-be comedian, study and analyze how the great comedians did it. Why do you laugh at their jokes or antics?

Another point of comic style, and a technique: If you have two possible laughs in a line, get the first laugh as if it were the only one, by using a finalizing intonation pattern that says, in essence, "This is it. That's all I have to say." Then, when you have timed the audience's laugh, proceed with the second half of the line, almost as if it is an afterthought, or a completely new idea—whatever is appropriate to the situation. Another technique for getting two laughs is to react to something someone says: that brings on the first laugh, which, as always, must be timed. When it is the right moment, say your line, which will get the second laugh. This was a technique perfected by Bea Arthur (1922–2009) in her television series *Maude* (1972–1978) and *The Golden Girls* (1985–1992), both available on DVD. It worked every time, because she was absolutely real in her reactions. As the lesson of Bea Arthur shows graphically, the comedic style arises from the behavior; indeed, it is the behavior. In order to get the laughs, you have to play real scenes for real, as in Neil Simon's best plays, some of which can have an endless series of side-splitting guffaws.

Among the most important comedic techniques is the "take," which is a sudden, surprised, serious or comedic reaction resulting in a fixed stare, involving recognition of someone, some thing, or some circumstance. The take depends for its effect on the exact rhythm and tempo of the moves:

1. The *double take* is a comic bit in which a look of blank incomprehension is instantly followed by a second look of immediate surprised comprehension. This take, done in three units or beats, involves looking at someone or something, looking away, and instantly looking back at the object of attention.

2. The rarer *triple take* involves turning away from the object of attention, turning back, turning away again, and finally turning back and fixing the attention on the object—all done in a twinkling.

3. The *spit-take*, used especially in farce, involves a person drinking a liquid, and, being shocked or surprised while the liquid is still in the mouth, forcibly expelling it and spraying it all over the place, usually with a loud spluttering sound, e.g., when being clapped on the back by someone entering a room.

4. The *swallow-take* consists of audibly gulping while swallowing saliva, often accompanied by bulging eyes and a gesture of loosening a shirt collar, followed by dropped jaws, as a reaction of fright or surprise. It is very effective in film, e.g., when the camera can focus on the victim's prominent Adam's apple going up and down.

But beware, beware, beware! These takes should be real, and should not be a comment on the material. Remember this commandment: Thou shallt not telegraph or comment, lest thou lose the laugh!

To comment is to let the audience know in some way during a performance what the performer thinks of the character, the play, the other actors, or the direction. Commenting usually destroys, rather than creating the desired effect. In comedy especially, it destroys what is funny. To put it another way, play comedy like a high-security secret: on a need-to-know basis. The audience doesn't need to know the joke, or even that there is a joke, until the right time.

Knowing how to punch a joke, that is, how to deliver a line in order to elicit laughter, is a basic part of any comedian's technical toolkit; a habit and way of working that do not have to be thought about. To "punch" means simply to emphasize or stress certain key words that constitute the joke. The intonation pattern is also a help as you rise in pitch slightly at the end of the line (not always; don't overuse this technique). And I cannot stress enough that the essence, the very basis of performing comedy, and the only thing that will make it funny to the audience, is to play it seriously, as you would a drama, even though you know it is funny. And you must take delight in its being funny. You want to communicate this delight to the audience indirectly, by holding your own pleasure in the back of your mind, out of the direct view of the audience, but as a twinkle in the eye.

Deadpan, the kind of comedy, and of comic playing or performing, in which a comedian uses a neutral expression, is perhaps the ultimate in the serious performing of comedy. The twinkle in the eye that communicates the comedian's pleasure and delight in being funny is almost hidden from the audience when uttering a joke or doing funny bits of business. But it is there. You just have to look extra hard to find it. Such underplayed comedy depends on an expressionless face and flat but pointed delivery of lines, never telegraphing a joke. Buster Keaton is the prime example of a deadpan comedian, with his hangdog look and poker face; you can see him in many films, and in excerpts on YouTube. His timing was impeccable, and somehow, you knew he thought he was funny, but he never communicated that fact by the slightest sign. Yet he had to know, because he always got huge laughs.

The question of a character's sense of humor is often ignored, unless the part is written specifically with wit and jokes in mind. What does a character find funny, and why? What does the character's sense of humor tell us about his or her unconscious? Does the character use humor to get approval or disapproval, or to be the center of attention? These are all questions for the actor to ask when exploring a character, particularly one who is supposed to be funny.

The Different Genres of Comedy

In each of the comedy genres, despite the use of elementary comedy techniques in all of them, a different style of playing is required. Uta Hagen wrote in *Respect for Acting* that "style is the dirtiest word in the actor's vocabulary," and should be banished from it forever; but it is not the province of only "critics, essayists and historians," as she thinks. True, in one way she is absolutely correct: if actors think in purely technical, external terms about doing a period or acting or comedy style, their thinking is wrongheaded, because style has to evolve organically from the rest of the work on character, and to be personalized and internalized. In other words, style has to be integrated into the performances, and to be inherent in the world of the play. In actors' terms, period style is behavior characteristic of a particular era. What Uta Hagen meant to warn against is superficial, imposed, contrived, artificial, indicated stylization that is meaningless, mechanical, and imitative, whether a particular acting style or a period style.

Each comic playwright has his or her own style: the terse subtlety of Noël Coward is different from the aphoristic subtlety of Oscar Wilde, different yet again from the one-liners of Neil Simon. Yet each follows the technique of setting up the jokes and punching them. And each has his share of put-down, insult humor. Some of the differences also lie in their distinct linguistic and sociocultural eras.

As I said, each theatrical period and genre of comedy demands a different approach, but with the same underlying seriousness. The ways of behaving, of showing deference, social and class attitudes may be different, and these condition the mindset of the character, the knowledge that forms the background of the play. Oscar Wilde's drawing-room comedies, set against the background of Victorian imperialism and sexual repression, and the rigidities of the class system, demand a different way of playing than a seventeenth-century Molière farce, grounded in the even more inflexible social mores and class distinctions of the France of Louis XIV. Although the audience sees behavior that differs for each period, the universality of the human condition and amorous desires makes these plays relevant in today's world.

Kinds and Genres of Comedy

1. **Absurdist; theater of the absurd:** An artistic movement in playwriting lasting from the late 1940s through the 1960s, which took as its starting point the nihilistic and existentialist ideas that life is basically meaningless and impossible to understand: life has only the meaning we choose to give it; in other words, taken by itself, life is an absurdity. Its seminal authors were Samuel Beckett and Eugène Ionesco, and its present practitioners include Edward Albee and Tom Stoppard.

2. **Bedroom farce:** A sex comedy involving outrageous but plausible situations, fast-paced action, and lubricious characters. Georges Feydeau's (1862–1921) farces provide many examples.

3. **Black comedy:** A play full of grim, mordant, sarcastic humor about the human condition, but without a tragic hero or a tragic ending. Subjects that are usually the occasion of sadness, tragedy, or misery, such as death, disease, drug abuse, war, domestic and other forms of violence, terrorism, insanity, murder, and the like, are treated satirically, ironically, or humorously. They are often

done in a deadpan style, so that the audience is sometimes not sure if what they are seeing is even supposed to be funny. See, for example, the film *American Psycho* (2000), with Christian Bale as a bitterly sarcastic and narcissistic serial killer with an evil sense of humor, who appears normal, especially to the unobservant. The Coen brothers' horror film *Fargo* (1996) is another example of black comedy. Indeed, some of the old-time Hollywood horror films sometimes seem like black comedies nowadays, even though they were undoubtedly not made with comic intentions. But they do take themselves very seriously indeed, perhaps too seriously, and this lends them comic overtones.

4. **Burlesque:** 1. A satirical piece or play that parodies or mocks an existing play or persons. On television, Rowan Atkinson's hilarious *Blackadder* series is, along with its social satire, a burlesque of historical dramas and films. 2. A form of theater that combines vaudeville comedy sketches, musical numbers, and ladies who strip for the audience, especially in a *burlesque house*. 3. To parody or lampoon an existing play or persons.

5. **Comedy of character:** A play, film, or television show that depends for its humor on the specific persons involved in the situations, as opposed to one that relies more on plot, e.g., such television sitcoms as *The Honeymooners, I Love Lucy, The George Burns and Gracie Allen Show*, and *The Golden Girls*. The situations are still important, of course, but we watch these shows more for the characters and how they go through the sometimes outlandish scrapes they get themselves into.

6. **Comedy of humors:** A Jacobean subgenre, popularized by Ben Jonson (1573?–1637), dealing with what we would now call psychological humor, i.e., the humor that arises from people's personalities, foibles, etc. It was based on the concept of the four humors in medieval medicine and physiology: a humor is a biophysical element that made the body function as it does: blood, phlegm, black bile, yellow bile. These humors were thought to determine a person's temperament, which could be sanguine, phlegmatic, choleric, or melancholic, depending on which element was dominant.

7. **Comedy of ideas:** A play that revolves around a debate concerning ideas of politics, philosophy, religion, and the like, but in a humorous way. Characters often represent different points of view in the debate, as they do in the plays of George Bernard Shaw.

8. **Comedy of intrigue:** A play in which the plot is all-important, and the characters—memorable though they may be—less so than the situations in which they are involved, as in some of the nineteenth-century farces of Georges Feydeau.

9. **Comedy of manners:** A play that deals with upper-middle-class or upper-class mores, usually in a sophisticated, witty, sometimes even arch style. The setting is always in a society stratified by class, and class differences and behavior are readily apparent. Many Restoration plays are examples, as are some plays by Molière, the late-nineteenth-century comedies of Oscar Wilde, and some of the twentieth-century plays of Noël Coward, such as *Private Lives*.

10. **Comedy of morals:** Comic plays that deal with ethical issues in an amusing way, e.g., Molière's *Tartuffe* or Oscar Wilde's *An Ideal Husband*.

11. **Commedia dell'arte:** [Italian: comedy of art] An Italian form of improvisational comedy and comic plays based on standard, formulaic scenarios and using stock characters, such as Harlequin, Columbine, Pantaloon or Pantalone, Punchinello, and Scaramouche; it began in the late sixteenth century. Many of the characters wore masks or half-masks. The term *commedia dell'arte* was not actually heard until the eighteenth century, when the Venetian playwright Carlo Goldoni (1707–1793) used it to refer to scripted plays that he had written—many of which were based on well-known commedia stories—as opposed to the *commedia dell'improviso*, or comedy of improvisation. For full information, consult John Rudlin's admirable *Commedia dell'Arte: An Actor's Handbook* (Routledge, 1994). An important aspect of commedia plays is the *lazzo* [Italian: trick; plural: *lazzi*], the clown's trick, standard bit of comic business, ad lib, and comedic embellishment of various moments in commedia dell'arte plays. Lazzi were originally improvised; the most successful were standardized.

12. **Drawing-room comedy:** A play featuring witty banter and airy persiflage, as well as a complicated plot, that takes place in a middle- or upper-class milieu; sometimes referred to as high comedy; often seen as synonymous with comedy of manners. There are always formal scenes in a drawing room or salon, at a reception or other high society event, as in Oscar Wilde's *An Ideal Husband* and *The Importance of Being Earnest*.

13. **Farce:** A fast-paced comedy that involves unlikely, far-fetched, and extreme situations, which are nevertheless plausible. The actors in a farce must behave with complete conviction and reality in extravagant circumstances. Supporting characters are often eccentric, with quirky character traits. Sexual innuendo, broad physical humor, wordplay, chase scenes, slapstick bits, mistaken identity, frustration, and misinterpretations of people and events by characters are some of the elements associated with farce. Absurd and silly as it is, the farce can nevertheless be realistic, as with Molière's pieces or Chekhov's *Marriage Proposal*; or outlandish, like some of Ionesco's plays. Dating back to fifteenth-century secular comedies, a *French farce* is a bedroom farce or sex comedy, e.g., those by Georges Feydeau. *Knockabout farce* contains rough-and-tumble physical action, slapstick, and physical gags.

14. **High comedy:** Witty, jocular plays dealing with the upper strata of society and their romantic problems, e.g., comedy of manners; drawing-room comedy.

15. **Light comedy:** An amusing, delightful play or film that depends on witty dialogue rather than physical business, and does not have much depth or point, but abounds in laughs, e.g., Neil Simon's *Barefoot in the Park*; Noël *Coward's Hay Fever*.

16. **Low comedy:** 1. Crude, coarse, tasteless humor. 2. A vulgar farcical play that includes elements of slapstick, bad jokes, garish costumes and makeup, and a lack of subtlety or sophistication. 3. An actor's unsubtle performance: *a low comedy performance.*

17. **Parody:** A piece that satirizes, mocks, spoofs, and/or imitates another piece, as in mock opera or ballet performances.

18. **Restoration comedy:** English plays written after the restoration in 1660 of King Charles II to the throne; the era ends around 1700. The period is known especially for the comedies written by such authors as Colley Cibber, William Wycherly, William Congreve, and Sir George Etherege, among others.

19. **Romantic comedy:** A play or film dealing in a lighthearted, humorous, amusing way with love and its complications.

20. **Satire:** A piece that mocks or makes fun of social customs, mores, habits, and ways of behaving.

21. **Satyr plays:** Lewd ancient Greek comedies and farces that were part of the religious rites involved in the worship of the lubricious

god Dionysus. According to Aristotle, these rites were the origin of comedy. Later, such plays were preformed after the tragedies at the Dionysia.

22. **Screwball comedy:** An outrageously farcical piece with eccentric characters and situations; e.g., the film *My Man Godfrey* (1936). The 1930s was the heyday of the genre in Hollywood.

23. **Sex comedy:** A comic play that revolves around sexual encounters and complicated love affairs, graphic in its physical and verbal humor; a bedroom farce.

24. **Situation comedy:** A comedy that depends for its humor on the circumstances that unfold and that the characters find themselves involved in, willy-nilly. The term is applied especially to half-hour episodic television series that are meant to be funny, done for a season or more using the same regular cast of characters and various guest stars; broadcast weekly during primetime evening hours, or rerun on late-night television; called a *sitcom*, for short. The regular viewing audience knows the characters well, so the humor in these episodes depends on both character and situation.

25. **Sketch:** A short act of spoken dialogue in a television comedy show, such as *Saturday Night Live*; or in a vaudeville evening or revue; also called a skit.

26. **Stand-up comedy:** Humorous routines and solo acts performed by an individual comic who tells a series of jokes or does an act or a routine in various venues, such as nightclubs, cabarets, comedy clubs, old-time vaudeville theaters and music halls, television, or a Broadway theater, e.g., Jackie Mason's or Dame Edna's Broadway shows; called *stand-up*, for short. In clubs where they perform, the comics stand and deliver their jokes, often using microphones in the larger venues.

27. **Tragicomedy:** A hybrid genre of drama that began in the Elizabethan theater, crossing comedy and tragedy and emphasizing the ironic and the humorous in human destiny; sometimes called a *heroic comedy*. Such plays often have a rueful ending: not tragic, but not happy either. Scenes of low comedy are interspersed with serious dramatic scenes, e.g., in Shakespeare's *The Merchant of Venice*, in which characters of different social classes mingle and interact; or Chekhov's bittersweet play *The Cherry Orchard*: the

Ranevskys lose everything they have held dear, but their lives are not threatened, and Lopahin, the former serf, has triumphed over his former adversity.

The Bottom Line

Enjoy yourself! That's the bottom line. To repeat—and this is the second bottom line—the comedian must know that what he or she is doing is funny, even hilarious, but that knowledge must remain somewhere in the back of the mind, and must never be telegraphed to the audience. The third bottom line is that you must be thoroughly conversant with the comedy techniques discussed above. And the fourth is that you must believe in the circumstances, however absurd they are.

I remember seeing a supremely silly, uproarious comedy, Miriam Hoffman's *The Maiden of Ludmir*, at the Folksbiene (People's Theater), the Yiddish theater, in 1997. It was so funny that I remember details of the production all these years later. The cast enjoyed itself hugely. Their antics and the jokes made us positively howl with laughter (I understood about eighty percent of the dialogue). And no joke was ever telegraphed! You couldn't see it coming, despite the ridiculousness of the situations!

One of the principal characters was a wonder-working rabbi, always poring over his books. And when I say poring, I mean he pored. Nobody ever pored more, or with more seriousness. What he had to pore over, we never learned. He never told us. He had a servant with a stooped posture, a halting gait, a cringing servile attitude, and a high-pitched, whiny voice—all funny in themselves—and the actor was absolutely as convincing as he was ridiculous: this was a real person who had been battered into submission by life, and you sensed the tragedy of everything that had brought him to this point. His life never varied. Day after day, moment after moment were the same—monotonous, oppressive, and boring. But that voice! As soon as he spoke he was funny!

The rabbi had an endless stream of clients, and every time someone wanted to gain entrance to the inner sanctum, the servant would enter sideways, like a crab, and say tremulously, "Rebbe, es shtayt aroys a mensch..." [Rabbi, there's somebody outside...] As if to say, "Don't hit me. It's not my fault." To which the rabbi always replied in an incredulous tone, implying that his browbeaten servant was an incompetent idiot, "Nu? Vos shtayt ihr? Fuhr ihn arein!" [Well? or So? (The word "nu" can be translated any number of ways.) What are you standing there for? Or, What are you waiting for? Bring him in!] It was droll the first time, but by the third it was irresistibly funny, and we were in stitches. Each time, the servant and the rabbi did the lines and played the moment in exactly the same way, as if such an incredible thing as someone arriving to consult the rabbi had never happened before. This was perfect comedy, or rather farce style, and pure Stanislavsky technique. The actors believed absolutely in the truth of what they were doing, and so did we.

Another really dumb joke that had us in stitches had to do with a woman client, played by that superb actress Mina Bern (1920–2010), who came in carrying a fake prop chicken in a basket. The chicken had a string attached to its head, and when it was pulled, the chicken nodded up and down. The chicken was supposed to be a real chicken. She claimed the chicken was her husband. The rabbi looked at her as if she were nuts, but he patiently asked her to explain. She told him that one day her husband had left the house and not returned, and when she went out on the road to look for him, she saw a chicken waddling along. The chicken had the same walk as her husband, and nodded its head in just the same way, so she knew her husband had been bewitched and turned into a chicken. She wanted the rabbi to turn the chicken back into her husband. The rabbi, still naturally incredulous, asked her if she were absolutely sure the chicken was her husband, to which she replied indignantly, "You think I wouldn't know my own husband?" After all the dialogue that had gone before as a perfect setup, that line brought the house down. Of such trivialities is the broadest farcical comedy made.

CHAPTER SIX

Acting in Musical Theater and Opera

A talented young opera student during a coaching session for an operetta said to me, "I don't really have to act. I'm a singer!" I was slightly taken aback, as you may imagine. My immediate response was, "No, no, no, no, no! You are playing a part on stage! What do you think you do when you sing a song or an aria? You are singing about something! You are singing for a reason! And that involves acting! And in this piece, you have to speak! You have to play scenes from beginning to end, as well as sing."

Acting in a musical theater piece presents unique technical problems and demands. During musical portions of the piece, which may even be through-composed, the rhythm of the acting is determined by the rhythm and the tempo of the music. The actor-singer must follow the tempo—the speed—set by the conductor. The way actions are carried out depends not only on the tempo-rhythm of the music, but also on its melody. The expressive pitch pattern of the melody reflects what the character is living through emotionally. Although these limitations are imposed from without, the rhythm, tempo, and melody must be internalized so that the acting is smooth. The music and words must become one, just as the spoken word and its intention are one. The intention is in the music, as well as in the words! If there is spoken dialogue, the transition into and out of the music must be incorporated into the acting score. Those transitions must be seamless, and (within the accepted artificiality of theatrical convention) appear real and natural.

Sometimes singers are called upon to dance, at least minimally, as in Bizet's *Carmen*, or operettas by Johann Strauss, Offenbach, or Gilbert and Sullivan. This is often very difficult for actor-singers who have little if any dance training, even if they have studied movement technique. Also, to be an opera singer, you must have the ability to project passion and emotion that seem larger than life, but that everyone in the audience will be moved by. And singing itself has its difficult and demanding technical side. It is no wonder that some opera singers neglect acting because they are worried about and concentrate on their voices.

Each number or song in a musical theater piece tells its story, just as each scene in a drama has its own small story to tell that is part of the whole story. So the actor-singer must have determined the objectives, obstacles, actions, and intentions exactly as if there were no music, and must then confine him- or herself to carrying them out within the constricted time and space allowed by the score. The singer cannot, as speaking actors do, take any amount of time that feels right and comfortable and organic. On the contrary, time takes the singer. But within the delimited time, moments should be as real as they are for the speaking actor.

The stress pattern provided by music, which determines what individual words are emphasized, is invariable. There may be some variation when the singer uses rubato (from the Italian, meaning "robbed"), which varies from the strict tempo in which the music is performed, so that when a note is slowed down or prolonged, it "robs" the time from another note. But there is always a return to the tempo as it has been set up by the conductor, so that nothing is lost as the music surges inexorably and pitilessly forward, carrying all with it.

The brilliant opera singer Lotte Lehmann (1888–1976) says in her book on lieder, *More Than Singing: The Interpretation of Songs* (Boosey and Hawkes, 1945), that "a phrase must always have a main word, and with it a musical highlight." Furthermore, "every phrase must be sung as a sweeping line, not just as a series of words that have equal weight and no grace." This way of singing is also a way of acting the sung line, and takes account of how the language would be spoken.

In acting terms, sung words can be treated like spoken words: they have intentions and subtextual meanings. In such music dramas as Richard Strauss's *Der Rosenkavalier*, Italian verismo, Wagner's operas, and many contemporary operas, the musical setting facilitates acting. But even the singers in early- to mid-nineteenth-century bel canto and romantic pieces must act, using the florid coloratura passages to portray changes in emotion.

The idea that the meaning of the text should be clear, and that the acting should be full of passion, is by no means new. Eighteenth-century Italian singing teachers had a motto, "Chi pronuncia bene, canta bene": Who pronounces well, sings well. They meant that if a singer has good, clear diction and excellent articulation, he or she can sing well. Without excellent pronunciation and enunciation (in any language), there is no chance. As with speaking on stage, excellent diction is of paramount importance: the words must be understood.

The famous opera baritone Manuel García (1805–1906), son of the renowned Spanish tenor of the same name, was a teacher of bel canto technique, which he had originally learned from his father. In 1840, he wrote an important manual, *Traité Complet de l'Art du Chant* (Complete Treatise on the Art of Singing), published in English as *Hints on Singing* (Ascherberg, Hopwood, and Crew, Limited) and released in a new and revised edition in 1894. It is in the form of questions and answers, illustrated with numerous musical examples. *Bel canto* is the general Italian term for "beautiful singing," the style of singing especially associated with mid-seventeenth-century baroque music through nineteenth-century romantic opera. It is characterized by beautiful, even tones throughout the singer's range, as well by the technical skill and breath control required for negotiating the ubiquitous, florid coloratura passages; the smooth and seemingly effortless singing of high notes; and ornamentation that is integral to dramatic expression. By extension, it means the style of composition that demanded such singing: *bel canto opera*.

Part 2 of the *Hints* is entitled "Singing Coupled with Words." García answers the question "Of what importance are words to melody?" in the following way:

> To express any particular feeling or idea, we must make use of words. Hence the importance for the singer of delivering these with the utmost distinctness, correctness, and meaning, under the penalty of losing the attention of the audience [if this advice is not followed].

He then goes on to analyze vowels and consonants in a very technical way. But you will notice that he attaches importance to the "meaning" of the text, and this involves subtext and interpretation; in other words, acting.

García distinguishes three different styles of singing, any of which might be suitable for either chamber recitals, church, or theatrical singing (the three venues he mentions):

1. The florid [Italian: *fiorito*], which "abounds in ornaments."

2. The declamatory [Italian: *declamato*], "dramatic singing" that can be either serious or comic.

3. The *canto spianato* [Italian: smooth, plain singing]; this is the "noblest of all styles," a plain, legato style of singing, devoid of ornamentation, which he calls the most demanding because it "is

based entirely on the degrees of passion and the variety of musical light and shade."

Aside from detailing the strenuous and demanding vocal technique required for bel canto singing, he also talks about the interpretation of the text, and communicating with the audience. To the question "How can a singer transmit his emotions to the audience?" he answers: "By feeling strongly himself." When it comes to the repetitions that are found frequently in all kinds of vocal music, where the same words and music are heard in succession more than once, he has this to say: "To avoid monotony, they should be submitted to various interpretations such as the subject of the piece might suggest, thus giving rise to a variety of coloring."

His advice, although obviously calling for an external, technical way of creating variety, also can bring about variety from the inside, in an organic way, as the various changes are internalized and new feelings constantly awakened during performance. This is pertinent to the interpretation of every kind of aria, and there are many types, including such standard kinds as the *aria di vendetta* (vengeance aria), in which the changes of emotion must be observed and built towards the aria's climax, or the aria loses its impact. Think for instance of such varied set pieces as the Queen of the Night's "Der Hölle Rache kocht in meinem Herzen" (Hellish Vengeance Boils in My Heart) from Mozart's *Die Zauberflöte* (The Magic Flute) or Don Pizzaro's "Ha! Welch' ein Augenblick" (Hah! What a Moment!) from Beethoven's *Fidelio*. These vengeance arias are very different in style, the Mozart piece being a florid coloratura soprano aria, and the Beethoven a dark, impassioned example of the romantic school. Yet they have something in common besides the theme of vengeance: they show a series of changing emotions. As the characters grow ever more vengeful, each section into which the aria is divided must be different, and in repeat sections those emotions must be further varied by being deepened, even though expressed in the same words and melodies.

The same principle holds true for the singing of bel canto ornamentation: no repetition should be exactly the same, but each comes from a different emotional place, if the singer is truly acting at the same time as singing. In the case of bel canto coloratura passages, the despair or happiness of the character may increase markedly, leading to its emotional expression in the ornamentation provided by the composer to show the nature, intensity, and depth of the character's feeling.

Lotte Lehmann says in *More Than Singing* that the words you sing are of the utmost importance. They are the reason you sing. They are what you sing about. They are what inspired the composer to write the music. Lehmann was a thrilling soprano and superb actor, known for her performances in Wagner and Richard Strauss, and for such heroic roles as Leonora in *Fidelio*. Incidentally, it was she who discovered and encouraged the Trapp Family Singers to perform in public; they were later immortalized in Rodgers and Hammerstein's *The Sound of Music*. She has this to say about technique and art, which applies just as well to acting as to singing:

> Certainly no one can question that technique is the all important foundation,—the a b c of singing . . . But realize that technique must be mastered to the point of being *unconscious*, before you can really become an interpreter.

Notice that last, most important word: interpreter. You must work constantly to perfect your vocal technique, and you must also work constantly on interpreting the material. Furthermore, her advice on how to approach a song can also apply to the art of interpreting the musical portions of any lyric theater piece, whether it be an opera, operetta, or a Broadway musical:

> The fundamental basis of my conception is this: never approach a Lied just as a melody. Search for the ideas and feeling which underlie it and which will follow it. Out of what mood or situation was the poem born? What drama, what dream, what experience was the inspiration for its conception?

You must use your imagination to project yourself into the circumstances of the song, as you do of a role. Also, you must not forget your partner, the accompanist with whom you work closely. No more can you forget the other singers or the orchestra when you perform in an opera or other music theater piece.

Even if you are in a concert, singing songs, you are telling stories. The song *is* a story, with a beginning, middle, and end, just like a play in miniature. And if you sing one of the great song cycles by Franz Schubert (1797–1828), for instance—*Die schöne Müllerin* (The Beautiful Maid of the Mill) or *Die Winterreise* (The Winter Journey)—you are telling a story more extended than that confined to a single song. You are acting. You are playing the character whose story you are telling in a direct address to the audience. How much more so, then, are you acting when you play a character in a staged musical theater piece, whether it be a

Broadway musical or an opera, in which you have to play a complete character, with costume and makeup!

What is an opera, after all, but a play set to music, and meant to be sung and acted on stage with instrumental, usually orchestral accompaniment? Most operas are through-composed; that is, almost every word is set to music, as in the operas of Giuseppe Verdi and Giacomo Puccini. There is solo and, in most cases, ensemble singing, with the dialogue being sung in recitative, which consists of sung lines of conversation or soliloquy: the musical setting is supposed to mirror a conversational tone, and some recitatives are underscored with dramatic music. But in many operas, the dialogue is spoken, as it is in the Viennese *Singspiel*, such as Mozart's *The Magic Flute*, or in the French genre of *opéra comique*, which simply means opera with spoken words in between the numbers, and is not to be thought of as comic opera, which is *opéra bouffe* in French. Opéra comique includes some very serious pieces, such as Bizet's *Carmen*.

There are also subgenres of opera, principally serious and comic opera. And there are through-composed music dramas, such as those by Richard Wagner, that eliminate the separation between aria, ensemble, and recitative, as opposed to the "number operas" that alternate the two, like those of Verdi and the great bel canto composers, Rossini, Donizetti, and Bellini. The "grand opera"—nineteenth-century pieces that included vast sets, elaborate staging, huge ensembles, and the obligatory ballet sequence—is what many people think of when they think of opera, but that is only one type of number opera, and it is particularly associated with the Paris Opéra. Among the most famous grand operas are those by Giacomo Meyerbeer, such as *Les Huguenots*.

Opera singers/actors must be trained in classical vocal technique, requiring great control, agility, and beauty of tone, as well as the flexibility necessary to express vocally the range of emotions demanded by the musical settings. The technique and aesthetic style involve learning how to place the voice in the mask, and to control the changing muscular tensions involved in the shifts between the chest voice and the head voice. This kind of singing is called legitimate singing, or legit, to distinguish it from the more popular vocal styles, such as crooning or belting, often heard in Broadway musicals, where legit may also be required. Belting involves singing out loudly and powerfully, using a lot of chest voice, as opposed to controlling the different registers. To croon is to sing in a low, soft, evenly modulated, soothing voice, drawing out the sounds almost seductively, using more of the head voice than the chest voice. It is the opposite of belting.

Opera's variant, operetta, which is really a light opera, usually includes spoken dialogue. The stories are comic or seriocomic, and often romantic in nature; with lush ballads and vivacious dance tunes. The music can be very operatic, or rather schmaltzy and popular in tone and feeling.

Operettas include those of the early and late Viennese schools by such noted composers as Johann Strauss, Franz Lehár, and Emerich Kálmán; the French operettas of Hervé, Edmond Audran, Charles Lecocq, Jacques Offenbach, and so many others; and, in Victorian England, the delightful and decorous pieces of Gilbert and Sullivan. And the genre includes American pieces by such composers as Victor Herbert, John Philip Sousa, Jerome Kern, and Sigmund Romberg.

Like opera, operetta requires legitimate singing, as opposed to the techniques demanded in many Broadway shows, which often need singers who have the versatility to sing in various popular music styles, such as ragtime, jazz, folk music, gospel, rock, and blues. A musical, like an opera or operetta, is a play in which vocal and instrumental music and dances are an essential part of the show, usually with spoken dialogue in between the numbers. Although there are many English and European examples of musical comedy, the term is often used to refer to the American, and especially the Broadway variant of the operetta, like the pieces by Rodgers and Hammerstein, Lerner and Loewe, or Sondheim. It is a cliché, but true, that when a character in a musical feels such great emotion that he or she can no longer speak, the character bursts into song!

Many Broadway shows have been adapted for the screen; and many musical comedies were written directly for the movies, especially in the 1930s and '40s, the "golden age" of the Hollywood movie musical. These make very instructive viewing.

In the different areas of musical theater, different working conditions and rehearsal procedures prevail. An opera is not rehearsed in quite the same way as a musical comedy on Broadway, for instance. And different unions cover different venues. But the point is that, no matter what the genre of musical theater, the pieces are all plays set to music, and meant to be acted, as well as sung.

Playing Comic Opera and Operetta: Gilbert and Sullivan; Offenbach

The nineteenth-century comic operas of Jacques Offenbach or Gilbert and Sullivan are quite different from each other in style, tone, and content, just as they are different in their musical idioms from the mid-twentieth-century American musical comedies of Rodgers and Hammerstein or Lerner and Loewe. These are different from the early-twentieth-century Viennese operettas of Oscar Straus, Franz Lehár, and Emmerich Kálmán. And all of them are different from today's musical theater pieces, with their rock rhythms and occasional forays into a lush, pseudo-operatic pop style. But Gilbert and Sullivan and Offenbach have something in common not only with each other, but also with the satirical operettas of turn-of-the-twentieth-century Berlin and Vienna: They are all very funny. And they share as well the necessity to perform them ultra-seriously, with specificity, with an attention to detail, and with a knowledge of the period in which they were written, which provides the objects and raison d'être of the satire.

There is an interesting CD, *La Grande Époque: Rare Recordings of Delmas, Héglon, Lafitte. Simon-Girard*, which includes 1903 recordings by Juliette Simon-Girard (1859–1954), who created the title roles in *La fille du tambour-major* (1879) and *Madame Favart* (1878), from which she recorded one of the great numbers, the "Ronde des vignes" (Grapevine Rondo); the CD is available from Pearl (GEMM 9113; 1994). The recordings show what Offenbach, who directed most of his own productions, wanted from his singers: superb singing, and a true sense of droll, tongue-in-cheek comedy. One can actually hear in Madame Simon-Girard's recordings that she knows she is funny, but she sings everything very seriously, with an underlying sense of humor and comedy. This is the essence of comic opera style.

Offenbach's mythological satires, *Orphée aux enfers* (Orpheus in the Underworld, 1858; revised 1874) and *La belle Hélène* (Beautiful Helen, 1864), not only send up Greek mythology, sacrosanct to the intellectuals of the time, and taught in school to everybody in that era, but also parody the government of Emperor Napoleon III, and his personal peccadilloes and philandering ways. The indignant, not to say vitriolic denunciations with which critics lambasted Offenbach (critiques not unmixed with anti-Semitism), for daring to stoop so low as to mock the sacrosanct classics, brought the public flocking to the theaters to see what all the fuss was about. And the universal themes of love and betrayal, as well as the gorgeous music, ensure that these pieces have attained a kind of immortality, and are often revived, with great success.

The satirical and fantasy scenes in these works have to be performed with commitment, and the actors must make them real for themselves, while heightening the reality by inhabiting the outrageous given circumstances. When a parade of vegetables (brought to life by a furious magician) enters from the garden to take over the throne room of the dissolute King Fridolin XXIV of Krokodyne in Offenbach and Victorien Sardou's 1872 political satire *Le Roi Carotte* (King Carrot), the cynical courtiers are astounded, and they whisper mockingly to each other, singing in a jaunty, cheerful march tune with contained mirth that wants to burst forth into laughter and merriment:

Ah, quels drôles de costumes!	[Ah, what funny costumes!
Ils ont tous l'air de légumes!	They all look like vegetables!
Est-ce qu'ils viennent tous du bal?	Are they all coming from a ball?
Ou sommes-nous au carnaval?	Or are we at the carnival?]

Their sneering turns to shocked silence as King Carrot enters with a glare and sings his grinding introductory character song, "Je suis le roi Carotte" (I am King Carrot), with its grating accompaniment and its chilling but hilarious menace: "Malheur à qui s'y frotte!" (Woe to whoever rubs me the wrong way!).

The courtiers' snickering and sneering must be done with awe and at the same time with a sense of cynicism. The chorus must enter into the given circumstances and treat the absurdist, fantastical occurrence as if it were absolutely real, and their reactions and responses to what is happening must be within the world of the play. The same principle is true of performing the side-splittingly funny *Giroflé Girofla* by Charles Lecocq; the endearing and hilarious *La mascotte* (The Mascot) by Edmond Audran; the charming *Mam'zelle Nitouche* (Miss Touch-Me-Not) by one of the fathers of operetta, Hervé; and the whole host of brilliant nineteenth-century French comic operas. They all require not only entering into the given circumstances and a sense of the style in which they should be performed, but a knowledge of the period, its history and mores and social attitudes.

Gilbert and Sullivan owe much to Offenbach, both satirically and musically. Their wildly successful, silly spoof of the social class system, *The Pirates of Penzance* (1879), with its Verdian parodies, was inspired in part by *Les brigands* (The Brigands, 1869), which Gilbert had translated into English. After hearing Offenbach's outrageous, if tuneful *Les deux aveugles* (The Two Blind Men, 1855), Sullivan was inspired to write *Cox and Box* (1866), to a libretto by Punch editor and humorist F. C. Burnand. But for all his acerbity, Gilbert was no Molière or revolutionary. His mild satires were not iconoclastic or even particularly mordant. He never suggested that the class system should be overthrown, only that he found it faintly ridiculous and objectionable, and a fit subject for mockery. Underlying the satire is the idea that this was just the way things were, and that the basic system had to be accepted.

In 1882, Richard D'Oyly Carte, the producer responsible for the series of Gilbert and Sullivan comic operas, mounted *Iolanthe, or The Peer and the Peri*. It was the closest the collaborators came to real political satire. It also provided Sullivan with an opportunity to satirize Wagner's music, particularly in the opening scenes, which take place in a meadow in Arcadia—the rather un-Wagnerian setting that is the dwelling place of the Fairies, "tripping hither, tripping thither."

The basic idea for performing these whimsical comic operas remains the same throughout, no matter what the material: What seems ludicrous and ridiculous cannot appear so to the performers; it must be left to the audience to laugh, as in the following excerpt from act 2, where Lord Mountararat and Earl Tololler, old friends and, at the same time, rivals for the hand of the Arcadian Shepherdess Phyllis, discuss their relationship seriously. Phyllis finds "nothing to choose between you." Since neither will give way to the other, they may have to fight a duel:

> LORD TOLL. It's a painful position, for I have a very strong regard for you, George.
>
> LORD MOUNT. [*much affected*] My dear Thomas!
>
> LORD TOLL. You are very dear to me, George. We were boys together—at least I was. If I were to survive you, my existence would be hopelessly embittered.
>
> LORD MOUNT. Then, my dear Thomas, you must not do it. I say it again and again—if it will have this effect upon you, you must not do it. No, no. If one of us is to destroy the other, let it be me!

After some more of the same, Phyllis convinces them that she is not worth fighting over. She is right, says Lord Mountararat, "The sacred ties of Friendship are paramount!" And the two peers burst into song, exclaiming in a sentimental duet that "the things are few" they "would not do in friendship's name."

This brilliantly silly exchange must be played as absolutely unconsciously hypocritical, or it will only have the effect of being extremely calculating. What makes it so funny is, of course, the unconsciousness of the incongruity between the expression of friendship and the willingness to go so far as to kill a dear friend, supposedly in order to spare that dear friend pain! The regal pose of noble self-sacrifice must not be played as a conscious pose, but rather as an unconscious one, with a real, if superficial sense of true nobility and a protestation of love.

As we have seen, comedy depends on timing, on tempo, and on the rhythm set up by the comedians. In Gilbert and Sullivan's first great success, the one-act operetta *Trial by Jury*, the Learned Judge has entered to great acclaim to the strains of Sullivan's brilliant parody of a Handelian chorus, which is followed by this recitative—the reply to the Chorus of spectators, lawyers, and others in the court. It is delivered by the Learned Judge, now seated at the bench:

> For these kind words accept my thanks, I pray.
> A breach of promise we've to try today.
> But firstly, if the time you'll not begrudge,
> I'll tell you how I came to be a Judge.

The Chorus then sings, "He'll tell us how he came to be a Judge!" in a continuation of the Handelian parody. And all of this music may be sung as if it were one of the most solemn numbers from the *Messiah*. It is extremely funny that way.

But it is possible for the Judge to interpret the recitative differently, and to ignore Handel. This is just what British music hall comedian and comic actor Frankie Howerd (1917–1992) did in a television version. He sang the first line straight, as a simple thank you (his attitude/intention), at the same time picking up the sheet of paper with the list of cases. Then, using his trademark "Ooh!" (opening his eyes in blank surprise), he ad libbed that syllable before the second line—dividing one note into two, thus using rubato to keep everything ultimately in tempo—as if he had not seen the docket before, and was surprised and excited by the forthcoming case. He uttered the words "breach of promise" as if they were some of the most salacious and titillating in the language; in other words, he instantaneously changed his attitude/intention. He then immediately changed it again and resumed his decorous judicial demeanor: with a twinkle in his eye, he sang the last two lines, leading perfectly into the tongue-in-cheek song "When I, good friends, was called to the bar." The parameters of acting, theoretically limited by the music, were actually only limited by the amount of time taken, as predetermined by the rhythm of the music, along with its sacrosanct, invariable pitch patterns. There is plenty of room for the actor/singer's interpretation.

Howerd's timing was perfect, as was his technical choice of dividing the recitative into three separate, contiguous sections, making them all seem spontaneous. He observed Gilbert's periods after "pray" and "today" as the briefest of pauses—called for in the music and for purposes of breathing—and also observed the commas after "firstly" and "begrudge." As Stanislavsky points out, the pause after a comma immediately draws the audience's expectant attention: What is he going to say next?

Whether this interpretation happened naturally, born of Howerd's long experience, or was indeed calculated or contrived, it is impossible to say. In any case, it seemed real and spontaneous, and the effect was electric, magical, and absolutely hilarious.

Once again, what all these works and many more besides them have in common is a droll, tongue-in-cheek humor that demands from the performers a knowledge of how funny the material is, and why. This will enable them to assume the mantles of the characters, and, with the help of an able director, to bring them to life for contemporary audiences, allowing the spectators to see how germane the satire is to current life.

Stanislavsky and Acting in Opera

Stanislavsky was in love with the opera. In fact, he had wanted to be an opera singer, as he tells us in *My Life in Art*, but he didn't quite have an operatic voice. At the same time, he was appalled by the stiffness of the singers in performances of works that should have overflowed with the romantic yearnings and unfulfilled strivings of the characters they were supposed to be portraying. So, at the end of a long, distinguished career, he decided to try to reform the operatic stage by directing opera himself and teaching opera singers how to act. His legacy is seen today in the wonderful acting in Russian opera companies.

In opera, passionate vocal acting that conveys the emotions and action through the music—to which all else is subordinate—is paramount. One of the problems in acting in opera, in the many tragic stories, such as Puccini's *Tosca* or Wagner's *Tristan und Isolde*, is to find specific actions. Too often, the acting is very general, which is partly due to the melodramatic nature of the way the characters and libretti are written. And very rarely do the singers take it upon themselves to be specific in dealing with all the issues involved, so caught up are they in the music itself. The fact that they have to deal with their voices and with the music is a very poor excuse for not really acting the parts they often sing so beautifully, and act vocally.

There are plenty of examples of wonderful acting in opera. For instance, at the Pushkin Opera Theatre in Moscow, Stanislavsky's production of

Tchaikovsky's *Yevgenyi Onegin*, which I saw in a museum restaging in Moscow in 1983, was performed with great realism: the acting was as engrossing and beautiful as the singing. Performed on a postage-stamp stage, the great dance numbers went for nothing, although the delightful music and the sprightliness of the three couples the stage could accommodate still lent them great charm. Presentations on a larger scale at the Bolshoi in Moscow, where Tchaikovsky's opera is given an elaborate and riveting production, are equally realistic. So are the operas performed at the Mariinsky, called the Kirov under the Soviets, in St. Petersburg. I saw them there, when the city was still called Leningrad, and in New York when they performed at the Metropolitan Opera House. The Stanislavsky tradition of realistic acting in opera had obviously taken hold, and every individual in the crowd scenes—for instance in the opening scene in the pleasure gardens in Tchaikovsky's *Pikovaya Dama* (The Queen of Spades)—was a specific, distinctive character: a mother with her daughters, a nurse wheeling a baby carriage, soldiers, and old and young men out for a stroll, or looking for a conquest.

In the Moscow Art Theatre's Opera Studio, Stanislavsky worked with singers on acting, and he had two further goals in mind, as Pavel Rumyantsev, his coauthor, informs us in *Stanislavski on Opera* (Routledge, 1975): The first was "to achieve impressive, incisive diction," so that the sung words could be completely understood; the second was "the complete freeing of their bodies from all involuntary tensions and pressures." Stanislavsky was well aware that projection of the voice during singing required the working and consequent tensing of "certain muscles (of the diaphragm, the intercostal muscles, the larynx)." But he felt that these technical, necessary habits should not interfere with acting, and that other kinds of tensions, born perhaps of nervousness, should not result in generalized gestures, which he characterized as "random and trashy," and to which singers were all too prone. In other words, he made the distinction between the necessary muscular tension activated during singing, and the superfluous, largely unconscious tension that had nothing to do with singing or acting, and hindered rather than helped the singers.

Many of the physical exercises at the Opera Studio were specifically timed to music, in order to teach the singers relaxation and the free flow of the rhythm in their bodies. He also had them do exercises in walking and gesturing to music, and he insisted that each exercise be specific: there had to be some reason for a pose or gesture. "Action is all that counts," he said, "a gesture all by itself is nothing but nonsense." In other words, each gesture had to be related to what was happening in a scene, and not to be one of the clichéd repertory of movements, poses, and learned gestures so typical of opera singers who were not acting their roles, but were concentrating only on their vocal technique. He taught acting according to his system, which, as he said, is a guidebook: "The 'system' helps the actor to express what the author wished to say." And, one might add, it helps the opera singer to bring to life what both the author of the libretto and the composer of the music wished to express.

"You have to hear [in the music] the reason for what you are doing," Stanislavsky said. It is the music that reveals the character's thoughts, and the feelings and reasons behind them. And you have to create for yourself the circumstances given in the words, so that you can enter into them truthfully. A character in love is not in love in general, but with someone specific, and no generalized acting or singing will do: Everything the singer/actor does must be personalized and particularized, exactly as in a spoken drama, but with the music added to it.

Stanislavsky also had the actors do individual songs and ballads as exercises, and he followed the same principles elucidated by Lotte Lehmann: namely, that the singer had to be singing about something, not just displaying a beautiful voice and vocal technique. He asked one young lady, who had a gorgeous voice but did not know what she was singing about, if she merely wanted the spectators to notice her stunning looks or her silvery voice. Of course, she wanted more than that. She wanted to convey what the song was all about, and how she felt, but astonishingly, she hadn't bothered to explore the meaning of the words! Stanislavsky put her through a series of questions searching both music and text for meaning, and this was a revelation to her. Difficult as it is, singers must also act, or their performances are pointless.

Some brilliant mid-twentieth century opera singers, among them Tito Gobbi (1913–1984), Nicolai Ghiaurov (1929–2004), Cesare Siepi (1923–2010), and Maria Callas (1923–1977), portrayed their characters with great realism and gave compelling, riveting performances. So do such contemporary singers as Brenda Harris, Richard Bernstein, Ann Murray (b. 1949), Cecilia Bartoli (b. 1966), Neil Shicoff (b. 1949), Tiziana Fabbricini (b. 1961), Felicity Lott (b. 1947), Placido Domingo (b. 1941), Natalie Dessay (b. 1965), and many others. They inhabit the tragic and comic characters they portray as much as any speaking actors, and their performances are engrossing and involving. The audience is invited into their world when they sing. When opera singers act their roles, the experience is one of the greatest the theater has to offer.

CHAPTER SEVEN

Finishing Touches: Outward Appearances, Costume, and Makeup

Outer Form: What the Audience Sees

In a letter (quoted by Maria Ignatieva in *Stanislavsky and Female Actors*), Stanislavsky gave the following advice to Olga Knipper, when they were rehearsing Turgenev's *A Month in the Country* in 1909: "Start thinking about your costume, hairdo and all the rest to envision yourself from head to toes the sooner the better." He also wanted her to "memorize the text" as soon as possible.

Those who think of Stanislavsky as dwelling only on the psychological side of characterization—an impression I have tried to correct in this book—may be surprised at these directions. Even when his methods and the system had evolved, the character's outward appearance and look always remained extremely important to him as both actor and director.

In performance, before the actor has made a move or uttered a word, the audience's first impressions are always of costumes and how they look. And costumes say a great deal about the character. Certain visual statements about characters can be obvious, as in the difference in professions signaled by uniforms, waiter's jackets, and the like: these costumes speak instantly to the audience as eloquently as spoken lines or physical actions. It is quite evident who the Nazi officer is, and who the Hassidic Jew is in Arthur Miller's *Incident at Vichy* (1964), to take two extreme examples. They may behave in any way dictated by the exigencies of the script, but the initial visual statement of who they are will remain with the audience, who will automatically have certain ideas about them, based on prior knowledge, beliefs, and perceptions.

The audience's ideas may be erroneous, of course. They may be set up to believe certain things. Appearances can be deliberately deceiving, as witness the many plays, operas, operettas, and films in which someone is in disguise when we first see him or her. In some plays, an aristocrat is masquerading as someone from a lower social class, just as in Rossini's opera *La Cenerentola* (Cinderella) the Prince masquerades as his own valet in order to evaluate more truly the people he meets: they would bow before a prince, but behave naturally towards a servant.

Aside from those obvious deceptions that are aided by costume, a character's general outer appearance may be deceiving: A serial killer may appear meek and be dressed in ordinary, nondescript clothing. Such people can move through society undetected, their mild appearance masking an inner sickness and turmoil. In the case of political leaders, the benign or authoritative presentation of self that the character shows to the world may mask deep insecurities, compensated for by sartorial splendor. And, as in the case of the fascist leaders in World War II, an impressive uniform can hide the personality of a psychopathic mass murderer beneath the façade of an authoritative military bearing.

Aside from being technically helped by the designer's costume and by makeup, how is the character's outer appearance, which will convey information about character to the audience, arrived at? What does the actor have to do to assume the character's appearance? Whatever is achieved is brought about through the correct mindset: The actor arrives at the physical manifestations of character by entering fully into the given circumstances so that the outward appearances have the forms that correspond to the inner life.

What is within cannot always be shown directly, but must nevertheless be there—the character's inner stream of consciousness, for instance. But, as we have said, the character's appearance should illuminate the audience's understanding. For instance, on Hamlet's first appearance, at the court ceremony, he may be sloppy or very neat in his attire, attesting to the mental state the actor wishes the audience to perceive. He may be neat, because he automatically dresses as a prince for an appearance before the assembled court, or he may be sloppy because he is so unhappy that he doesn't care about his appearance. The "trappings and the suits of woe" may be disheveled or tidily worn. Either way, they say something about Hamlet. And the appearance will be based on what the actor has developed in rehearsals. As the fine actor Kieran Mulcare, who has played Hamlet, points out, the choice of neatness is perhaps the better one: the slovenliness might be best reserved for later in the play, when the prince is wandering around the castle and dealing with Ophelia. Otherwise, the actor has nowhere to go with that aspect of the character's outward appearance, which indicates his inner turmoil as he neglects his clothing more and more. To add to this impression with makeup, he might even show that whereas the prince was clean-shaven in act 1, later on he has a five o'clock shadow. Although he begins calmly enough, in "trappings and the suits of woe," as circumstances change, so does his way of wearing his clothing. And as Mr. Mulcare says, "Each time Hamlet flies off the handle, it is in response to some great violation of trust. Discovering that Ophelia is a tool of the king's and her father's psychological experiment and eavesdropping" is one of the worst of such occasions. When he walks about with "his doublet all unbraced," Ophelia makes plain to her father that she finds it a startling change.

To take another example, the well-dressed, elegant, wealthy Lord Goring in Oscar Wilde's *An Ideal Husband* appears at first to be callous, flippant, and quite amusing, much given to witticisms. As we later learn, this is the pose of a sensitive and loving friend, who is shy and retiring and does not like to have his private good deeds known in public. Part of the first impression of superficiality comes from the excessive neatness of the character's dress, a certain touch of soigné elegance: too much attention has been paid to appearance, to his "buttonhole"—the flower he wears in his lapel—which sends a message to the audience that dressing superbly is what this character really cares about. Of course, he does care about elegance, but the first impression of superficiality, consciously created to deflect attention from the character's real preoccupations, will ultimately be dispelled.

It is also important to note that costume conditions the way actions are played and carried out. A man encumbered by a heavy medieval gown will not be able to fight with swords readily, for instance. And a lady in a long Victorian or eighteenth-century dress is constrained to move in certain ways, also conditioned by the footwear.

I cannot emphasize enough that such externals as particular physical movement and appearance, enhanced by costume and makeup, will ideally grow organically out of the rehearsal process, as Stanislavsky thought. You should find a character's way of moving, that is, the character's physical life, developing by itself. If it does not, you must dedicate time to it at the end of the rehearsal process.

There are any number of ways of exploring the outward appearance of a character: first, there are techniques such as Michael Chekhov's psychological gesture (see chapter 10), which will help to transform the actor physically. There is also the deliberate assumption technically of physical form that can be predetermined and then arrived at by imposition, which is exactly what I advise against. Although not the ideal way to proceed, with time at a premium in a short rehearsal period, such an external technique may prove necessary.

Another technique for assuming the character's appearance: Stanislavsky believed that models could be used consciously, in a calculating way, for the physicality of a character. He famously did so himself for his creation of Dr. Stockman in Ibsen's *Enemy of the People*, as he tells us in *My Life in Art*. He modeled the character physically on several people. But note that he had arrived at his models from his earlier work in rehearsal: They suggested themselves to him as a result of what he had found about the character's actions. He was then able to incorporate these models into his characterization so that they felt natural and real to him, and not imposed from without. The makeup was drawn from portraits of the composer Nicolai Rimsky-Korsakov (1844–1908). His idiosyncratic walk as Stockman—neck and chest thrust forward because of myopia— was in imitation of people he had observed in the street. And his gesture of sawing the air, thumb extended, forefinger and middle finger held together, was drawn from motions the realist playwright Maxim Gorky (1868–1936) used when making a point.

Some actors develop unconscious vocal or physical mannerisms, as opposed to those created for a character. The eminent English actor Sir John Gielgud (1904–2000) has said that soon after he began acting he was aware that he was posing and prancing around gracefully, because, presumably, he was well received for doing so and wanted to be at his most graceful and becoming. However, once he realized what he was doing, he took steps to eliminate mannerisms that ultimately not only interfered with character creation and with acting itself, but made him into a mechanical kind of actor, who resorted to what was comfortable rather than making the effort required to live in the part. Other actors have had similar mannerisms, but have not worked on them, and their performances in films, for instance, are disconcerting: their mannerisms immediately break the illusion of reality they are trying to create.

On the other hand, there are times when the author has written a character with certain mannerisms, and the actor must work to create these. In Chekhov's monologue *On the Harmfulness of Tobacco*, for instance, the lecturer, Nyoukhin, has a nervous tic which causes him to blink his right eye when he is lecturing in front of an audience, out of sheer nervousness. This must be worked on until it becomes a natural, organic reaction. It is not easy to do (I have played the part a number of times), because it must appear to be unconscious, and the actor must keep up the blinking while pursuing the character's objectives, playing the actions, and continuing the monologue. Nyoukhin, however, finally tells us that he is aware of this nervous tic and the reasons for it, and he asks the audience to ignore it.

As an object lesson in how to fuse the inner life of the character with the outer appearance, manner of walking, gesturing, moving, voice, and accent, see Christopher Guest's characters in his own films, discussed in chapter 5.

Costumes and Accessories

Costumes are clothing. That's it, pure and simple. And, as Meyerhold pointed out, the costume is part of the body: it moves with the body as much as the body would move if it wore nothing at all. Costumes are the way the character dresses, in any era in which a play may be set. You should be as familiar with the clothing of a historical period as you are with your own everyday and more formal wear, from foundation garments to the outerwear. And you should always wear something to rehearsal that reminds you of the costume, and that allows you to move in a similar way.

In Alfred Hitchcock's *To Catch a Thief* (1955), there is a grand fancy dress ball in a villa on the French Riviera, and everyone is in Louis XV costume: the women in voluminous gowns, the men in powdered wigs and knee breeches, with lace jabots and colorful embroidered coats. Some of the guests are policemen in pursuit of a jewel thief, who may or may not be at the party. They behave with slight awkwardness (without making an obvious point of it), as if they feel a bit silly and uncomfortable in their unaccustomed garb, as opposed to how they might behave if the film were actually set in the mid-eighteenth century, when all the characters are simply wearing their own natural clothes. The point is this: It is of primary importance to know the exact circumstances in which a costume is worn.

Similarly, in documentary films made during the aftermath of the 1906 San Francisco earthquake, people are just walking around the streets looking at the terrible destruction, and their clothing, which seems pretty heavy and clunky to us today, is just their usual dress; it is not a costume. The women's full-length skirts seem awkward and a little difficult to handle, and the men's clothing seems too heavy for comfort, but it is all naturally worn, right down to the stiff collars that are fastened with studs to the shirts, in the days before collars were sewn on as an integral part of them.

Early in rehearsal, you will usually be shown costume designs, which will help you to decide what to wear in the way of garments that simulate the actual costume. Proper shoes should also be worn, and the actual shoes should be provided as soon as conveniently possible, since they obviously condition how people walk. The equivalent of proper accessories should also be used: fans, pipes, swords, canes, and snuffboxes need to be worked with. See the next chapter for some advice on what to wear as rehearsal costumes, if you will be dressed in period style. Of course, in a modern-dress, updated production, all that is required for rehearsal is simple, comfortable modern clothing that enables you to move freely.

Makeup

As photographs of him in his many roles show, Stanislavsky was an expert makeup artist who seemed to know every trick of the trade. He transformed his physical appearance radically, fulfilling his idea of creating "the life of a body in a role." Every actor should learn the art of makeup, even if he or she rarely actually has to apply it. In the media, in opera houses, and in certain large theaters, makeup and wigs are often done by professional makeup artists and hairdressers; special effects and prosthetics are necessary for many productions. But in small theaters, in summer stock, and in general, actors are expected to be able to apply their own makeup. Or makeup may not be used, and the actor will rely on character rather than applied appearance, as John Barrymore did in his virtuosic performance of the title role in the silent film version of Robert Louis Stevenson's *Dr. Jekyll and Mr. Hyde* (1920).

Every actor should have at least an elementary makeup kit consisting of the makeup materials themselves and the tools or implements necessary for their application. A fishing tackle box, with its tiers and drawers, serves very well as a makeup kit, although there are also specially designed makeup boxes available. The following basic list can be supplemented by other materials, such as nose putty, latex, and extra, personal hairpieces, mustaches, sideburns, and beards, which are usually supplied by the company:

1. Base or foundation (greasepaint, pancake, or crème)
2. Makeup sponges
3. Rouge and shadow
4. Powder and powder puffs

5. Eyebrow pencils, which are also used for lining

6. Eye shadow

7. Eyeliner and mascara

8. Spirit gum for the application of false hair, beards, sideburns, and mustaches; and for wig joins, so as to conceal the gauze from view

9. Q-tips, cotton balls, makeup remover, and a soothing skin lotion, since this stuff can be quite rough on the skin

In Sarah Bernhardt's *The Art of the Theatre*, she gives extensive advice on makeup in an appendix, "Hints for Making-Up." She explains that a face with very strong features must have them "shaded off"; that is, those features must have shadows applied, as a sculptor shapes a face, in order to soften them. On the other hand, a face with small features must be made up in such a way as to bring the features out and make them more prominent under the lights. Among her hints, still applicable, especially in larger houses, we find the following:

> . . . rouge on the cheeks, penciling round the eyes, and the darkening of the eye itself can work a transformation in a featureless face, giving it the accentuation desired.
>
> An insipid face with small eyes is especially to be dreaded. It may be mitigated by an enlargement of the eyes effected by means of a blue or chestnut-colored pencil which stretches the eyelids. . . .
>
> Each face requires special treatment.

Later on, she has this to say:

> Making-up is not the same thing for men as for women. It may be more elaborate in the case of women . . .
>
> But women cannot all make-up according to the same rules. A brunette may not treat her face in the same way as a blonde.

Men should not use too much rouge, for instance, because it "effeminates the features." Darker-skinned women should use a dark foundation, and a lighter powder to set and blend the makeup. And the forehead should be made up with a slightly lighter shade, in order to bring out the features below it. Blondes should use rouge to help bring out and accentuate their features, much more than is used by women with darker skin, and blondes should also use a lighter-colored eyebrow pencil when lining the eyes. Bernhardt recommends a blue or chestnut-colored pencil. Mascara may be used by everyone, to lengthen the eyelashes and bring out the luster of the eyes. Most importantly:

> In a general way make-up should be related to the dimensions of the theatre. The larger the house, the heavier the "make-up." And this is understandable. The actor's features are diminished by distance so that the spectators scarcely perceive them.

Even in small theaters some elementary makeup should be used, because lights tend to wash out even strong features, no matter what the actor's skin color. A lightly applied, small amount of foundation, some shadows, and especially eyeliner are all that is necessary.

Putting on makeup is very much akin to building up the layers in a classical portrait, with the skin as the natural canvas that needs to be primed before the artist can proceed to paint the portrait, applying first shadows and then highlights. When selecting colors, choose a foundation that is very close to your own natural skin tones, and highlights and shadows that are only slightly lighter or darker than the base, unless, of course, you have a specific reason for choosing colors that are far away; for instance, if you are playing someone who is very ill and has to look wan and pale, or someone who is much older and whose skin is therefore mottled or wrinkled, which will require the wrinkles to be painted in, subtly. Makeup experts in stores that sell actor's makeup can be very helpful in matching the correct foundation, or foundations—you will want more than one, depending on characters you are playing.

The following guide applies to putting on straight makeup that is meant simply to bring out the actor's natural features. The techniques apply equally to men and women, and to people of all skin colors and shades. Crème is similar to pancake, so the techniques listed for it apply equally. The main difference is that crème makeup is not as greasy, but it still requires powdering to set it for the stage. More specialized techniques for character makeup are discussed below.

Always have plenty of Kleenex and makeup remover on hand.

Bear in mind that the use of white greasepaint to bring out certain features, such as the eyes, must be very judicious, so that it is blended in well and merely exists as a highlight. White, which must be used sparingly because it is so glaring, or a pale color (depending on the actor's natural skin color) may also be used to block out contours, and makeup that creates the new, desired contours may be applied over it, as with the mouth, where the shape of the lips may be changed as necessary for certain characters requiring thinner or thicker lips than the actor's own.

A Step-by-Step Guide to Applying Straight Stage Makeup

1. If necessary, clean the skin with an astringent to get rid of any sweat, grease, or oil. This helps the foundation to go on better.

2. Put on your foundation, which should be hypoallergenic and selected for your particular skin color, covering the skin lightly. Working with greasepaint is akin to painting in oils: when it is wet, other colors, lights, and shades can be blended into it; it is then dried and set with powder. Faster-drying pancake, on the other hand, is more like watercolors: because blending other colors with wet pancake is usually difficult and chancy, it is more usual to wait until the pancake has dried to apply further colors— at which point, however, seamless blending is harder to achieve than with greasepaint. To apply greasepaint daub a few dots onto the forehead and cheeks, then spread evenly using the fingers. You will find that you don't need very much: it spreads quickly and widely. Be sure to cover the ears, and the neck as far as necessary, including around to the back, where it will show above the collar.

3. Now, using small tins of color, apply the shadows to the cheeks, under the eyebrows, and wherever necessary. Take whatever color has been selected—it should not be too much darker than the foundation—and, using very small amounts, spread the shadow evenly following the natural contours of the bones. Unless you are making up as a grotesque character, the idea is to look as natural as possible.

4. Next, apply the highlights, using a color that is slightly lighter than the foundation. Avoid white, except either when specifically called for; or in order to achieve certain effects, such as blocking out the contours of the lips in order to reshape them. This is a bit more tricky than applying the shadows. Again, use the same techniques, and apply the highlights above the shadows, following the natural contours. They should be narrower than the shadows, which are generally more extensive.

5. It is now time to bring out the main features even further: that most important feature, the eyes, in which the audience should be able to read reactions and responses as in a book, and thus to

understand the inner workings of the character/actor's mind; and any lines or wrinkles you wish to make apparent. Using eyeliner pencil (eyebrow pencil), darken the eyebrows, and draw a line along the upper eyelid. Unless you have dark skin, do not use a black pencil for this, but a chestnut-colored, brown, or gray pencil, depending on the foundation. Black pencils stand out and have the effect of makeup, which is undesirable, since you want to look natural; only in such specific cases as plays or operas set in ancient Egypt do you want to use black, and then only to create the effect of makeup being used. Then draw a line partway along the lower eyelid, but not all the way, unless you have a specific reason for doing so (if you are lining the eye completely to look like an ancient Egyptian, you will want to extend the liner out). Apply shadow just below the eyebrow, but do not cover the entire space between it and the eyelid, above which you should now apply a little highlight. Blend shadows and highlights to soften them and make them look real under the lights. If you wish, and if necessary, you may now apply mascara to the eyelashes.

6. If bringing out certain lines and wrinkles, such as those going from the sides of the nose to the mouth, or crow's feet, begin by using eyebrow or eyeliner pencil in a natural color, such as brown, and follow the natural outlines of the wrinkles. Again, the lining color you select depends on the skin color imparted by the foundation. After blending them lightly, apply highlights above them, or to their outer sides, and blend the highlights. Now apply powder to set them, in the same way as you did earlier. Even if you are trying to make yourself look older, do not draw lines straight across your forehead: you will simply look as if someone has printed a staff of music on it. Break up the lines, be sure to highlight each one, and blend them so they look natural and not painted or drawn on. In any case, the broad touches (that is, bringing out the broad features of the face with shadows and highlights, and emphasizing them if necessary to make the actor appear older), are usually more effective than a mass of wrinkles that do not read from beyond the first of second row.

7. You have now completed the basic face. If you have used grease-paint, apply powder to set the shadows and highlights. Dab it on generously with a powder puff, being sure not to smudge the shadows and highlights, and press it in as necessary. Brush off all

the excess using a fine powder brush or powder puff. Apply powder over pancake as well, since you will have used grease liner to apply shadows and highlights (or you may use other colors of pancake, using wet sponges, but this is more difficult). The application of powder not only sets the makeup, but will help prevent its melting off under the hot lights as the actor perspires. In addition, it further serves as a blending agent.

Some Specialized Character Makeup Techniques

When you are working with professional makeup artists, they will often take care of making you look older and applying prosthetics, putty noses, wigs, facial hair, and so forth. The first rule when you are working with them is to relax in order to allow them to do their work. The second is to follow instructions: when you are told to close your eyes, do so. This is especially important when hairspray, powder, or other potential irritants are being worked with. If anything is unclear to you, always feel free to ask. And be sure to ask questions about how soon you can put on certain costume pieces—in other words, how long it takes the makeup to be set so that it won't rub off.

In opera especially, hairdressers put on wigs and headdresses, which can be quite elaborate. And professional makeup artists are usually employed, particularly in the big houses, and especially where character makeups are concerned.

Should you be doing your own makeup, the following techniques should prove useful:

1. Old age: You may use prosthetics to give yourself a jowly look, or you may paint in jowls using highlights and shadows, as in the technique described above. Remember, if you must have a wrinkled forehead, break up the lines, and make them light. Use a gray or light-brown pencil, and a cream-colored or brown highlight, depending on your skin color. Crow's feet and bags around the eyes, and the pronounced, deep wrinkle that proceeds from the side of the nose down past the mouth should be drawn in using the method of highlighting described above. They should be very light and well blended, or they will simply look painted on. If you are not wearing a wig, and need to apply white to the hair, there are several materials you may use. White cream makeup may be judiciously blended into the hair in strategic places, such as the

temples, using a brush. Pancake, wetted and applied with a brush, then blended with the fingers while it is still wet, can be very effective. You must make sure, however, that it is really well blended, or it will look artificial. Or gray or silver hairspray may be applied and brushed carefully in. Be cautious when using hairspray: it contains particles that may severely irritate the eyes or mucous membranes, and some people are allergic to it, so be careful to apply it away from the other people in your dressing room.

2. Mottled or pockmarked skin: There are a number of ways of achieving such a look. I used the following technique in a regional theater production of *Uncle Vanya* when I played Ilya Ilyich Telyeghin, known as Waffles: First, I applied the ordinary makeup described above. Over that, I stippled dots in red-brown on my cheeks and forehead. Next, I applied an alcohol-based liquid called *collodion*. It is a bit dangerous; do not use this technique if your skin is very sensitive, or if you are allergic. Collodion seizes up and becomes wrinkled, remaining somewhat shiny and yet transparent. It takes a bit of time for it to dry. The stippling shows through, but must be gone over again and reinforced before being powdered down, largely to remove the shine. When you remove the makeup, the collodion peels off easily. Use a soothing lotion afterward to keep the skin moist. Another technique is simply to stipple, highlighting each dot, and then to powder over, so as to set the pockmarks.

3. Scars: Collodion may be used to create scars. It is applied over the makeup, and the scar is then drawn in with red-brown and gray eyebrow liner pencil, and highlighted, before being well blended and powdered down, so as to set it. You may eliminate the collodion and simply paint the scar on, but it may not be as effective. You may also make a reusable scar from latex, which will be applied with spirit gum for each performance.

4. Beauty spots (eighteenth-century plays), moles, and other skin features are usually simply painted on, highlighted, blended, and powdered. But in some cases, they may be made of latex and applied with spirit gum; they must then be well blended, so as to look real, except in the case of artificial beauty spots.

5. Putty applications to change the shape of the nose, cheeks, etc.: Soft, pliable, flexible putty can be purchased in makeup stores, and must be kept at room temperature when used. It can be

molded into any shape you desire, and is applied before makeup, sometimes with the help of spirit gum to ensure that it will stick even if you perspire. The edges must be blended seamlessly with the skin, so no bumpy joins show, and the makeup that is applied over it must also be well blended.

6. Applying facial hair and blending wig joins: In order to ensure that the edges of wigs, mustaches, and beards—which are usually built up by hair being woven through rather flimsy netting—do not show (as they occasionally do on a high-definition DVD), they are applied and flattened down before makeup, which is applied over them and carefully blended into the other makeup. This is comparatively easy with wig joins. To apply a mustache, first smile, so that the skin stretches, then brush on the spirit gum. Then brush a layer of spirit gum onto the netting on the back of the mustache. Let the spirit gum on the mustache and on your skin get sticky before applying the mustache carefully, while you are still smiling. This is to ensure that the mustache will assume a position in consonance with the natural contours of the face, after you cease smiling. Press the mustache into place, holding it firmly until you are sure the spirit gum is hard, then relax from a smiling to a neutral position. Tamp down any edges with your fingers. Similarly, when you put on a beard, stretch the skin and apply the spirit gum all round the edges of the netting and all round the area of skin where you wish to apply the beard. Let it get sticky, then carefully fasten it in place, holding it down and letting go of it only when you are sure the spirit gum is dry.

Period Styles:
The Theater as a
Reflection of History, or
Every Play in Its Time

Stanislavsky's Approach to Period Styles

As Michel Saint-Denis says in *Theatre: The Rediscovery of Style*, "Each period has its own style even though we are not conscious of it as we live." I remember the 1950s quite well, for instance, as Saint-Denis did the 1920s, and I echo his words: "I never thought it would become a 'period'." Such a thought would never even have occurred to me, in fact, nor did it for any of the succeeding decades through which I have lived, which may be history to many of you, but are simple, living reality to me.

History is all our yesterdays—the larger sociopolitical context of our personal pasts—but life is not, as Macbeth would have it, a tale told by an idiot, full of sound and fury, signifying nothing. On the contrary, history is part of the significant mental world of the people who lived it, whether they were idiots or not. To them, of course, it was not history, but the living, breathing reality of their daily existences, as it is of the characters in plays and films set in those times.

Stanislavsky was well aware of the relation between outer behavior and inner, sociocultural attitudes, born of a worldview anchored in historical circumstances. And his attention to the external details of deportment and manners was astonishing. As Jean Benedetti informs us in *Stanislavsky: A Biography* (Routledge, 1990), at a White House reception given for the Moscow Art Theatre by President Calvin Coolidge during their 1924 American tour, Stanislavsky could not resist demonstrating eighteenth-century deportment to his future translator, Mrs. Elizabeth Reynolds Hapgood. He showed her formal greetings, no doubt, and bows of various kinds. He must have kissed her hand in the proper eighteenth-century manner: make a show of doing so, but do not actually touch the lips to the hand. Invited onto the expensive set to see some of the filming of *Monsieur Beaucaire*, Stanislavsky had already observed Rudolph Valentino and the rest of the cast making a hash of eighteenth-century deportment. He had looked on, dumbfounded: the actors were not even adept at wearing the costumes and using the accessories correctly, let alone at behaving with the manners and decorum of the France of Louis XV. They simply hadn't bothered to do their research or to practice moving about in costume. To the great Russian, this was immediately unreal: both the period and acting styles presented to the audience were false, and he, at least, found this totally unacceptable and impossible to overlook.

Nikolai Gorchakov tells us in *Stanislavsky Directs* that part of Stanislavsky's directorial method when doing period pieces was to demonstrate how costumes should be handled. For Stanislavsky, such plays were meant to be historical recreations, reflections of what history itself must have been, and of how life was lived in the period of the play, so clothing was of primary importance.

In 1924, he directed a revival of Alexei Tolstoy's *Tsar Fyodor Ioannovich*, a historical drama set in the seventeenth century. It had been the Moscow Art Theatre's first production in 1898, and one of its great hits. As Gorchakov, who was acting in the revival along with other recent graduates of the MAT school, tells us, "He demonstrated how the boyar's fur coat should be worn, how one should gird himself in the long wide boyar belt, how to 'play' the rich embroidered shawl or the caftan stitched with gold."

Stanislavsky's preparations for the 1898 production had been exhaustive, as he makes clear in *My Life in Art*. He and members of the company ran around the country visiting museums and antiques fairs, immersing themselves in the period, buying cloth and props such as ancient wooden plates and "carved wood for furniture, Oriental couch covers," and so forth. They "sailed down the Volga to Yaroslavl with the current, stopping at cities on the way to buy Tatar materials, coats and footgear." They were even able to buy all the boots for the production. Of course, Stanislavsky was from an extremely wealthy family, and he could afford to do all this. Back in Moscow, he used many of his purchases as models, as he consulted with the costume and props departments:

> On the stage, not all that glitters is gold, and not all that glitters looks like gold. We learned to make the most of stage possibilities and to pass as gold and jewels simple buttons, shells, stones especially cut and prepared... My purchases gave us new ideas.

In Stanislavsky's productions, every detail of period style was filled with intentions, whether a courtier was bowing to a king or a lady using her fan to conceal her emotions. Because of his wealth of knowledge, his productions were infused with a reality often lacking in late twentieth- and early twenty-first-century period presentations, where the actors seem to have merely a nodding acquaintance, if any at all, with the era and the culture with which they are supposed to be intimately familiar.

When he was working on a period play, Stanislavsky read everything he could find about the era. Indeed, among the best research tools for exploring and personalizing a period is its literature, and most especially fiction, autobiographies, and firsthand accounts of events. In them, the era comes alive, so read! Read more! And then read more! You will grow accustomed to the language of the period, to its archaic grammar and vocabulary, so that they will become second nature to you. And attitudes, customs, and everyday behavior and personal relationships are portrayed with a sense of reality that may be absent in purely historical accounts that sometimes lack personality, as many medieval chronicles do, for instance. On the other hand, Greek and Roman historians, such as Tacitus in his *Annals*, provide great insights into personality as well as everyday living. And the long-drawn-out medieval period has also left us wonderful examples of autobiography, many of them now all but forgotten, and such personal accounts as the Byzantine Procopius's (late fifth century– after 558) rewarding and scandalous *Anecdota or Secret History*.

As American actors, we have been educated in the history of the United States, but we also need to know the traditions from which our theater comes, and they are largely European. So I have concentrated in this book on French and English theater and history, as well as on the plays of Chekhov, with forays into Russian theater practice (Meyerhold; Vakhtangov, in part 3); the theater of ancient Greece and Rome; Italy (the commedia); Germany (the Meiningen Company; Brecht); and Norway (Ibsen), since these are some of our roots as theater people. The historical information about France and England is meant to show you the kind of background you need when doing pieces from any country.

In the introduction to his *English Social History: A Survey of Six Centuries / Chaucer to Queen Victoria* (David McKay Company, Inc., 1942)—a book very much worth consulting—the distinguished Cambridge University historian G. M. Trevelyan (1876–1962) writes, "It is the detailed study of history that makes us feel that the past was as real as the present." Any actor doing a period piece might take that sentence as a motto and a suggestion.

In chapters 11, 12, 13, and 14 you will find sections on the years 1693, 1793, 1893, and 1936, as examples of the detailed research you should do as background for your character. They are certainly all very interesting years, but any year could have been chosen. Everyone who lived then would have known the major events and personalities as well as we know those of our own day. The wealth of material available for each year, and indeed each week or day, cannot but enrich the inner mental world of any character you play. You will not remember every detail, but salient important events and personalities will form part of your mental road map and give you access to the mindset, attitudes, and awareness of the characters regarding religion, developments on the world scene, science, important people of the time, and, of course, human relations.

Some Sources for Information About Costumes

The best book for purposes of researching costume in Europe, from Greece and Rome (as well as ancient Egypt) through modern times, is the astonishing, detailed work by François Boucher, *20,000 Years of Fashion: The History of Costume and Personal Adornment* (Harry N. Abrams, Inc., expanded edition, 1983). It is copiously and gorgeously illustrated, and contains a complete glossary of costume terms, as well as explanations about the changes clothing went through in each of the different periods. Boucher provides a wealth of detail about accessories, and even about the routines of daily life. All of this is necessary grist for the actor's mill: not merely incidental knowledge, but part and parcel of the given circumstances of a play, film, or television project set in the ancient or modern world.

For more on the clothing of the ancient European world, consult volume 2 of Mary G. Houston's three-volume *A Technical History of Costume: Ancient Greek, Roman and Byzantine Costume and Decoration* (Adam & Charles Black, 1947). The book is copiously illustrated, and explains exactly how the articles of dress were worn, in all their variations. The richness of Byzantine costume throughout the long history of Byzantium is portrayed as well in all its magnificent array in Boucher's book.

There are several superbly researched works by Alice Morse Earle specifically on the costumes of the British North American colonies; among them, *Costume of Colonial Times* (Charles Scribner's Sons, 1894), which contains an extensively researched glossary, detailing sources from colonial newspapers to wills and other court documents.

The native costumes of the North American Indians have also been extensively documented in many sources.

And there is an abundance of material on the costumes of all parts of Asia, including the extensive *Asian Costumes and Textiles: From the Bosporus to Fujiama* by Mary Hunt Kahlenberg (Skira, 2001). The costumes of the South Pacific nations are beautifully recorded in *Oceania (Cultures and Costumes)* by Charlotte Greig (Mason Crest; 2002). And the costumes of Africa are amply covered in *Africa (Cultures and Costumes)* by the same author (Mason Crest, 2002).

Each chapter in this part ends with advice on what to wear for rehearsal purposes.

CHAPTER EIGHT

Ancient Greece and Rome

The years 462–458 BCE saw the establishment of Athenian democracy, with 457–404 BCE witnessing the long-drawn-out Peloponnesian Wars between the city-states of Athens and Sparta. Many of the tragedies of Aeschylus, Euripides, and Sophocles are period pieces set in the Mycenaean era (1600–1100 BCE). They concern heroic deeds and the suffering of heroes in the aftermath of the Trojan War, which ended in 1184 BCE with the victory of Agamemnon's allied Greek forces. The Athenian audiences must have found them relevant in light of their own experiences with the Peloponnesian Wars. And the plays offer a paradigmatic depiction of moral dilemmas involving the most elemental human passions, and the struggle of mankind against inhuman fate, all taking place against the background of an indifferent, if not actively hostile universe. This must have seemed very real to those who suffered the privations and hardships brought on by conditions they felt powerless to control. The relevance of the tragedies to the spectators' own lives must have been brought home to them even more because the plays were done in modern dress; that is, in costumes contemporary to ancient Athens. The masks all actors wore were easily understood as representing particular characters. This was important because each of the few actors permitted to playwrights by the rules of the festivals (in addition to the Chorus) often played several roles.

The surviving comedies of Aristophanes, satirical and full of allusions and clever wordplay, deal mostly with contemporary Athenian subjects. In *Lysistrata*, for instance, the Athenian women, led by the title character, a faithful wife, refuse to have sexual relations with the men until they stop making war with Sparta. This is the playwright's most popular work. It has even been used as the subject of several musical theater pieces, including a 1902 operetta by the German composer Paul Lincke (1866–1946); the Broadway show *The Happiest Girl in the World* (1961), an Offenbach pastiche with lyrics by E. Y. Harburg and a book by Fred Saidy; and an opera by Mark Adamo, *Lysistrata or The Nude Goddess* (2005), with a libretto by the composer.

Similarly, the Roman comedies of Terence and Plautus deal with their own times. Their plays, often adapted from Greek plays now lost to us, are domestic in nature, even when they deal with mythological subjects: the gods at home, as it were, as in Plautus's *Amphitryon*.

In ancient Athens, several sources tell us, chorus members were assigned to playwrights by the directors of the Dionysia, the annual theater festival in honor of the god Dionysus. Writers directed and choreographed their own plays, and sometimes performed in them. And they trained and rehearsed the chorus rigorously for eleven months, using a series of physical exercises and training them in vocal technique. Their job was supplemented later by professional acting teachers, who, it is presumed, eventually took over actor training entirely. The Chorus was made up of citizens who were amateurs and practiced other professions, so rehearsals must have taken place for only a part of each day. But we don't know what they actually did when they rehearsed, aside from undoubtedly repeating the lines and the moves the playwright had devised.

From a number of different sources, including vase paintings and the accounts of contemporary authors, conjectures can be made about conventional, standardized gestures and movements that the actors used when performing tragedy—the ancestors of the Delsarte system, as it were. These gestures were presumably well established by the fifth century BCE, along with dances, of which you will find a descriptive list in *Using the Stanislavsky System*. Such gestures may still be useful in performing these plays, depending on how they are staged. Among the possible gestures, probably based on those used in religious rites and ceremonies, are:

1. **Grief:** a) The actor covers his (masked) face with his cloak. Or b) The actor looks downward, perhaps making a gesture with the arms at the same time.

2. **Mourning:** The actor rends his garments and tears at his hair and face.

3. **Supplication:** The actor kneels and throws his arms around the person to whom he is pleading, and simultaneously takes hold of that person's beard or chin.

4. **Prayer to an Olympian god:** The actor turns his palms upward and stretches out his arms.

5. **Prayer or plea to Pluto or other figures from Hades:** The actor looks down and stamps his feet.

6. **Swearing oaths:** The actors grasp each other's arms or hands.
7. **Madness, illness:** The actor makes wild gestures with the arms and head.

The vase paintings of performances show not only gestures, but also the masks and, often, huge phalluses that the actors displayed in honor of Dionysus. You can see reproductions in a most informative book by Klaus Neiiendam, *The Art of Acting in Antiquity* (Museum Tusculanum Press, 1992).

Although we don't know much about performance practice in the ancient Greek or Roman theater, we do know that all actors were what we would now call "triple threats": They not only spoke and declaimed the lines, but they could also sing and dance. They had to have powerful voices, to be able to project in the huge open-air amphitheaters where most performances took place. And they had to know how to gesture and move elegantly and eloquently, all the more so because they wore their character masks. From Tacitus and other sources, we know that well-known actors had their fans. There were claques in Rome, and we know from the dedications of Terence's plays, and from other sources, that instrumental as well as vocal music was used in the performances. Here, for instance, is part of the dedication to "The Self-Tormentor by Terence from the Greek of Menander": "Acted the first time with pipes bass and treble, the second with two bass. The adapter's second comedy." His first was *The Lady of Andros*, "The Play wholly from the original Greek of Menander." Not having the originals, we do not know if these were translations, or if they were reworkings by Terence.

We know also that in the era before Christianity was accepted as the official religion of the Empire, there were adherents of the new religion who thought that theater was sinful, decadent, and degenerate. This was a reaction to the fact that it had proliferated over the centuries of paganism and was one of the most popular forms of entertainment in the Roman Empire. Needless to say, its detractors also disapproved of actors and of acting. Here, for instance, is what the fulminating polemicist Tertullian (180–220), an ascetic Berber convert—who characterized theater as "idolatry" and referred to a theater built by Pompey the Great as "that citadel of all uncleanness"—had to say in his treatise *De Spectaculis* (On the Spectacle, written ca. 207–208): "[Acting is] an escalating series of falsehoods. First the actor falsifies his identity, and so commits a deadly sin. If he impersonates someone vicious he compounds it..." Actors were therefore all damned to hell.

While adapting Greek comedies for the Roman stage, Plautus transforms them into distinctly Roman pieces, with his numerous allusions to and portrayals of Roman customs and ways of behaving. His plays are some of the best source material for what the actor must be familiar with: the way life was actually lived.

For ancient Rome, one of the two sources of information we have about houses and living spaces, as well as public areas (the marketplace, the forum, the baths) are excavations—for example, the Roman Forum, Pompeii, Herculaneum, and Ostia Antica, the seaport of ancient Rome. The second major source is *De Architectura*, known as *The Ten Books of Architecture*, by Vitruvius (70/80 BCE?–25 BCE), an architect and engineer about whom little is known; he may have served with Julius Caesar in Gaul as a military engineer. But neither Vitruvius nor other Roman writers thought it important to discuss the ground plans, because the layout of the rooms and their functions were taken so much for granted.

The actors in Rome were mostly slaves whom their masters perceived as talented. Free citizens of the lower economic orders also sometimes became actors. The slaves earned money for acting, and, although much of it went to their masters, they were allowed to keep some of it and could sometimes save enough to purchase their freedom. The profession was considered beneath the dignity and honor of free citizens of means, so the privileged classes did not practice it until much later in Roman history. The slaves were trained by experienced professionals, who were themselves slaves, much as gladiators were trained in gladiator schools.

Roman actors were expected to develop both physical and vocal skills that would permit them to be flexible in playing many roles. Like Greek actors, they wore masks and were trained in mask work. In the second century CE, Julius Pollux, a Greek or possibly Egyptian rhetorician and tutor to the emperor Commodus (161–192; reigned from 180), wrote a dictionary, the *Onomasticon* (a list, book, or other reference work of names or terms; the word derives from the Greek *onomázein*: to name), which described the masks for tragic and comic characters, for young and old men, and for women characters and others.

But we don't know how the Romans rehearsed plays. We do know that in the many *ludi* (games) that included theatrical presentations members of the upper classes participated as amateurs, for a lark. And of course the emperor Nero fancied himself as a great singer-actor. He rehearsed on his own, and studied with teachers, who must have trembled and praised every note that came out of their illustrious pupil's mouth. Nero won every contest he entered. None of the judges would dare have voted for anyone else, because everyone knew he was a murderous psychopath and matricide. We have no idea if he was talented. Tacitus doesn't tell us. For all we know, Nero may have been the Florence Foster Jenkins of his day.

Aeschylus's *Agamemnon*

If you are doing a Greek tragedy, read Rush Rehm's magisterial book *Greek Tragic Theatre* (Routledge, 1992). Professor Rehm has worked on Greek tragedies as both an actor and director, as well as translating and preparing a performance version of the *Oresteia*. His analysis of the trilogy is essential reading.

There were strict formulaic rules laid down for authors of tragedies, and these were used by Aeschylus in *Agamemnon*, the first play in his trilogy about the House of Atreus, called the *Oresteia* because its central story is that of Orestes, son of Agamemnon and Clytemnestra. In the next two plays, *The Libation Bearers* and *The Eumenides* (The Furies), we follow the destiny of Orestes, who, urged on by his sister Electra, kills their mother Clytemnestra in revenge for their father's murder. Both suffer cruelly at the hands of the gods for having done so, which is in accordance with the superobjective of the plays, namely that what the gods decree will come to pass: Everyone lives out his or her predestined fate, and no action you take will help you in avoiding the consequences of evil deeds. In the end, however, the gods may grant pardon, and Orestes is ultimately forgiven by Apollo. Euripides and Sophocles both wrote their own plays about this same myth. The following synopsis shows you the traditional structure in which the story of a tragedy was usually framed; the judges at the play contests took account of this when awarding prizes.

The Chorus is a ubiquitous device in Greek plays that served both to represent the people as a whole or some particular segment of society, and to inform the audience of events and of what their moral attitude to those events should be. In *Agamemnon* they are reputable, highly placed citizens:

1. *Prologos:* The prologue could be for one, two, or three actors; it was most often a monologue, as it is here. Late at night, a sentry keeping watch on the palace roof at Argos complains of his weariness. His ever watchful nights are rewarded with the sight of

a beacon announcing the return of the victorious King Agamemnon from the Trojan War. The sentry descends and rouses Queen Clytemnestra and the other palace residents from their slumbers.

2. *Parodos*: The Chorus enters in dread, and tells briefly the story of the war and its causes, and of the tragic House of Atreus, from which Agamemnon is descended. They wonder why they have been awakened at this late hour. Clytemnestra herself appears and informs them of the reason: The war is over, and the Greeks have won. She orders that they give thanks to Zeus and prepare to celebrate the return of the victors. A Herald enters and confirms the victory to the incredulous Chorus.

3. **The Body of the Play:** The story now unfolds as follows: Agamemnon arrives and is greeted by Clytemnestra, who pretends that she still loves him. In reality, she has been plotting revenge against him ever since he sacrificed their daughter Iphigenia to the gods in order to secure their favor in his prosecution of the war. And Clytemnestra has been unfaithful to Agamemnon and taken the effete Aegisthus as her lover; he is cordially disliked by the populace at large. She leads the exhausted king, whose arduous journey home across the sea was fraught with peril, into the palace and prepares a bath. Their daughter, the prophetess Cassandra, sayer of doom, who has accompanied Agamemnon to Troy and back, is full of dread and foreboding, as she tells the Chorus. Nevertheless, she enters the palace, and Clytemnestra kills them both. The palace doors open to reveal the overwrought queen standing over the bodies of her murdered husband and daughter. She tells the horrified Chorus why she has done the foul deed. Aegisthus now arrives and claims the throne in exultation. The muttering Chorus is in a rebellious mood.

4. *Exodus*: This is the play's conclusion. The Chorus's final warning to the rulers is followed by the Chorus's exit. Clytemnestra tells Aegisthus that the Chorus is howling in impotent rage, and that the real power lies with her. But this is not so, as the rest of the trilogy will reveal.

As we have seen, the murders of Agamemnon and Cassandra take place off stage. In Greek tragedies, violent acts were considered far too unseemly and horrible to be shown to an audience. Instead, the characters and the Chorus tell the audience what has happened.

Once Agamemnon had incurred Clytemnestra's wrath, and the ire of the gods who were on her side, his doom was sealed. But because other gods were on *his* side, he won what those gods considered a just war. He still had to pay the price for murdering his daughter Iphigenia, as the gods who supported him conceded after they had helped him achieve victory. The instruments of the gods' justice are Clytemnestra and her helper and lover Aegisthus, whose turn to suffer justice will soon come. For they, too, having committed murder—however justified in their eyes—must pay the price. The people are muttering against them as the curtain falls, and Agamemnon and Clytemnestra's children, Orestes and Electra, will avenge their father's murder, and suffer in consequence of their matricide.

The play should be performed with a sense of humanity and reality, but there are stylized grand speeches and a sense of ceremony that also enter into the presentation. From a technical point of view, this is no different from performing in a contemporary drama: the same vocal technique, the same approach to character creation, and the same sense of flexibility and agility in movement are necessary. There may be some stylized movement, particularly if the play is staged with choreography based on the ancient Greek dances we surmise were used. All of this, of course, depends on the director's approach to the piece.

In *The Water's Edge* by Theresa Rebeck, a 2006 Off-Broadway drama based on *Agamemnon* and set in modern times, the contemporary relevance of this ancient piece was vividly brought home. Helen and Richard, husband and wife, have been separated since the death of their daughter seventeen years ago, and Richard comes to revisit his childhood home, which he wants to repossess. Helen has managed to reconstruct her life, repressing her contradictory emotions and the despair and depression she has lived through while raising her two young children in their father's absence. The return of Richard reawakens long-dead feelings. She has always felt that he was responsible for their daughter's death, and after much soul searching, she decides to carry out what she considers justice, by killing him. Ancient motives are contemporary and vivid, as real today in their modern variations as they were in the past.

Aristophanes' *Frogs*

Frogs, written in 405 BCE and performed at one of the Dionysia—the festivals in honor of the lubricious god, Dionysus—involves a contest in Hades sponsored by Dionysus (disguised as Hercules) and umpired by

Sophocles. Will Aeschylus or Euripides be selected to return to earth and revive the dying art of tragedy? Dionysus had thought Euripides would win, but in the end he prefers Aeschylus and returns with him to the world of the living. The Chorus of Frogs mostly croaks, and that is their comment on the proceedings.

In Victorian England, where every public school boy learned ancient Greek, even the rather obtuse Major General in Gilbert and Sullivan's *The Pirates of Penzance* says that he knows "the Croaking Chorus from the *Frogs* of Aristophanes." Of course, the Croaking Chorus, which simply imitates frogs, does not require any knowledge of Greek. It speaks volumes about Major General Stanley's education that this is what he retains from his study of ancient Greek: "Brekkekkekkek Co-ax Co-ax!" He can also "tell you every detail of Caractacus's uniform." Caractacus was a legendary ancient Briton who fought the Romans: his uniform probably consisted of a plain tunic, a helmet, and little else; he might even have been stark naked and painted blue—nobody knows. Gilbert is being satiric on the subject of public school education very much as Aristophanes himself might have been, maintaining that it concentrates on the trivial, not to say the useless, and teaches nothing worth knowing.

Stephen Sondheim and Burt Shevelove "freely adapted" *Frogs* in 1974, and turned it into a musical that was performed at the Yale University gymnasium swimming pool. In a revised version, it had a limited Broadway run (92 performances) in 2004 at the Vivian Beaumont Theatre. The rivals were William Shakespeare and the man who didn't think much of him, George Bernard Shaw.

In 1905, Shaw delivered a lecture at the Kensington Town Hall, London, on Shakespeare: "a gentleman of my own profession" and "a narrow-minded, middle-class man." While he paid Shakespeare due tribute as the greatest master of the English language and of its verbal music, his numerous theater reviews are replete with droll, mordant anti-Shakespearean remarks, such as the following critique of *Julius Caesar*, in his introduction, "Better than Shakespear [sic]?," to his own play, *Caesar and Cleopatra*:

> It is impossible for even the most judicially minded critic to look without a revulsion of indignant contempt at this travestying of a great man as a silly braggart, whilst the pitiful gang of mischief-makers who destroyed him are lauded as statesmen and patriots... Regarded as a crafty stage job, the play is a triumph: rhetoric, claptrap, effective gushes of emotion, all the devices of a popular

playwright, are employed with a profusion of power that almost breaks their backs.

Yet Shaw avers that as playwriting, it is "the most splendidly written political melodrama we possess." As the critic Edwin Wilson points out in the introduction to *Shaw on Shakespeare* (Dutton, 1961), "Shaw feels that *what* he says [in his own play] is better than Shakespeare, but not his *way* of saying it."

Despite Shaw's resentment of Shakespeare, and his vaunted sense of his own superiority as a philosopher-playwright (a verdict with which few would agree nowadays), Dionysus brings the poetic, philosophical Shakespeare back to the world, in order to improve it. The prolix Shaw, verbose and tiresome, must remain in Pluto's dark dominion. As in Aristophanes' original, it is the earlier playwright, from a time when the art of playwriting was newer, who has seen the world more clearly and has had more talent to translate his vision into drama. Once again, ancient themes have become contemporary. They constitute a lesson in how to perform the Greek comedies: Take the same approach as an actor as you would to modern material.

Plautus (254–184 BCE)

Among the social customs described in Book II of Tacitus' *Annals* is the manner in which women's sexual appetites were dealt with. He tells the story of one Vistilia, from a patrician background, who registered with the aediles (magistrates) "her availability for illicit sex." This was in fulfillment of an ancient custom which held that confessing and proclaiming one's outrages was a sufficient punishment and disgrace. Her husband, Titidius Labeo, who must have loved her, declined to demand that she be sentenced for the felony of adultery, but she was exiled to the island of Seriphos anyway.

Even in the decadent, ribald atmosphere prevailing in Rome, with its many debauched public ludi and festivals, the Juvenalian games were especially known for their obscene presentations. The area where they took place was filled with temporary, hastily erected taverns and sexual meeting places. Both men and women performed:

> Neither nobility nor age nor the holding of offices served as a hindrance to anyone's practicing the art of a Greek or Latin actor, right

down to gestures or rhythms which were quite unmanly. Indeed,
illustrious ladies too gave grotesque performances...

Many of Plautus's plays contain such characters as those described
by Tacitus. The playwright was considered especially unsavory in the
Victorian era. He is more alive to us today than other Roman playwrights because some of his plays were adapted for the hit Broadway
musical comedy *A Funny Thing Happened on the Way to the Forum*
(1962), with music and lyrics by Stephen Sondheim and a book by
Larry Gelbart and Burt Shevelove. Plautus was fond of constant wordplay, jokes, and puns, which appealed to Roman taste, so his Latin is
considered all but untranslatable. Nevertheless, his sense of humor
comes out in the situations and characters.

The story of Plautus's *Amphitryon*, based on an ancient Greek myth,
since used in other plays, is as follows: Jupiter has fallen in love with the
mortal Alcmena, wife of the general Amphitryon of Thebes. That valiant
warrior is away fighting a war against the Telobians in defense of his
country and king, Creon, successor to Oedipus. Jupiter transforms
himself into Amphitryon and descends to earth, accompanied by his son
Mercury, a sly rapscallion of a god, disguised as the grumbling slave
Sosia, who had accompanied Amphitryon to the war. Jupiter seduces
Alcmena, and Mercury assists him in duping both servant and master on
their return. The furious Amphitryon berates his wife and accuses her of
adultery. He and Jupiter exchange insults, accusing each other of being
the false Amphitryon. The pilot of the ship that brought Amphitryon
and Sosia home from the war, the bluff Blepharo, is appointed arbiter,
but he is unable to decide who is the real Amphitryon. The truth is at
last revealed. Amphitryon forgives his wife, and Alcmena gives birth to
twin sons: one is Jupiter's, the other Amphitryon's.

To the Victorians, such a humorous and sly display of adultery, which
all the characters ultimately take in stride, was shocking and disreputable. For the Romans, adultery, while criminalized, was nevertheless a
source of comedy. The deceived husband was always a figure of mockery,
a theatrical tradition kept alive through the centuries by such playwrights
as Molière. Among other ancient plots he used was that of the risible
older man in love with a younger woman, who is, of course, in love
with a man her own age. It is the inappropriate and the incongruous
that make for laughter, then as now.

In *Amphytrion*, we see domestic life as it was lived in an age before the
conveniences of technology allowed humanity a respite from constantly

working to prepare all necessities from scratch. And we see the nature of social relationships: The display of deference between the classes allows us a glimpse into how to play the characters and the actions. We also see typical Roman farcical humor, as in this scene from act 1, where Sosia arrives home from the wars, only to discover Mercury, disguised as Sosia (1916 translation by Professor Paul Nixon):

MERCURY. Is this the house where you belong?

SOSIA. That's what I say.

MERCURY. Who is your master, then?

SOSIA. Amphitryon, now in command of the Theban army, and his wife is Alcmena.

MERCURY. How say you? Your name?

SOSIA. Sosia the Thebans call me, Sosia, son of Davus.

MERCURY. Ah! 'twas an evil hour for thee, when thou camest here, thou pinnacle of impudence, with thy premeditated lies and patched-up fabrications.

SOSIA. You're wrong, I vow: I've come with my tunic patched up, not my fabrications.

MERCURY. Ha, lying again! Thou dost clearly come with thy feet, not thy tunic.

SOSIA. (*dryly*) Naturally.

MERCURY. And naturally now get thrashed for fibbing. (*advances*)

SOSIA. (*retreats*) Oh dear, I object, naturally.

MERCURY. Oh well, naturally that is immaterial. My "naturally," at least, is a cold hard fact, no matter of opinion. (*beats him*)

SOSIA. (*squirming*) Easy, easy, for Heaven's sake!

MERCURY. Durst say that thou art Sosia when I am he?

SOSIA. Murder! Murder!

MERCURY. (*continuing to beat him*) Murder? A mere nothing compared with what is coming. Whose are you now?

SOSIA. Yours! Your fists have got a title to me by limitation. Help, Thebans, help!

And so forth and so on, with more wordplay and slapstick. The Romans, whose sense of humor could be bloodthirsty, enjoyed the spectacle of gladiators fighting each other to the death, and, later, of Christians thrown to the lions. They loved puns, and adored this sort of knockabout farce in which somebody got a sound drubbing. This kind of brutal, barbaric attitude is seen as well in the history of certain of the emperors, such as Nero and Caligula.

William Shakespeare's *Julius Caesar*

The ethos of savagery underlies not only these plays, but Roman life itself, in its coarser manifestations and raw seeking after power. Cassius in Shakespeare's *Julius Caesar*, under the guise of patriotism, displays his jealousy of Caesar's popularity and masks his own barbaric disposition. This is contrasted with Brutus, whose gentle nature is at odds with many of his compatriots, hence Mark Antony's praise of him at the end of the play (act 5, scene 5):

> All the conspirators save only he
> Did that they did in envy of great Caesar;
> He only, in a general honest thought
> And common good to all, made one of them.
> His life was gentle, and the elements
> So mix'd in him that Nature might stand up
> And say to all the world, "This was a man!"

Note in particular the spelling of "mixed" with an apostrophe: pronouncing the "e," thus making the word two syllables, was falling out of fashion, but it was still necessary to indicate this newly favored pronunciation by using an apostrophe.

Shakespeare's period piece, like his other history plays set in ancient Rome or Greece, actually partakes more of Elizabethan attitudes and customs and ways of behaving than it does of life and manners in ancient Rome. However, it is usually presented in an ancient Roman setting, with the proper historical costumes and majestic scenery as production elements.

In 44 BCE, the assassination of Julius Caesar saw the end of the Roman Republic, followed by the founding of the Roman Empire. The well-known plot of Shakespeare's play shows us Julius Caesar returning in triumph from the wars. He is assassinated by a group of conspirators, with the senators Cassius and his trusted friend Brutus at their head, who fear that he intends to overthrow the republic and make himself king. In the event, civil war breaks out between the army of the conspirators and the army of their opponents, led by Caesar's trusted confidant, Mark Antony, and Caesar's nephew, Octavius, who will become the first Roman emperor, Augustus. When the conspirators lose, the end of the republic is nigh, just as they had feared.

Shakespeare, who was a man of wide-ranging humanitarianism despite his sometimes parochial prejudices, portrays the conspirators sympathetically, but their opponents are shown to be more effective in their actions. By implication, the monarchical system is upheld as the superior and more natural form of governance. In fact, the "rabble" in the play are shown to be not only unthinking, but easily controlled and manipulated.

In 1903–1904, Nemirovich-Danchenko directed a production of *Julius Caesar* for the Moscow Art Theatre. Stanislavsky played Brutus, and the experience was not a happy one for the actor: he disagreed with Nemirovich-Danchenko about the interpretation of the role. But the director was ecstatic about the production. He had gone to incredible lengths to research the period thoroughly, and to have the designer produce as accurate a replica as possible of the Forum. The Senate House (Curia) where Caesar was assassinated is a surprisingly small building made of flat red bricks, rebuilt after the fire of Nero's day, not the vast portico with Doric columns that I had been expecting to see when I went to Rome. Nemirovich-Danchenko reproduced it, and had the Forum in his ultra-realistic production filled with Roman types from all walks of life. He had even made a special trip to Rome with his designer, Simov, to see where it all took place, and to make notes in preparation for the sets. The production, which concentrated so much on technical aspects, and on a portrayal of Rome as almost too clean, did so to the detriment, it seems, of the performances.

Rehearsals were painstaking and endless. There were extensive rehearsals for makeup and for costumes, and everything went on far into the night. But the psychology of the roles was left largely unexplored, and Stanislavsky therefore thought the production artistically stagnant. His portrayal and his acting got a mixed reception from his colleagues and the critics, and he was dissatisfied with himself. Even Nemirovich-Danchenko acknowledged in his memoirs that only the actors playing Caesar and Mark Antony were really happy with their parts in the production. A caveat: When doing period pieces, do not get so caught up in reproducing the externals that you neglect the psychology of the character.

Plutarch (circa 46–120 BCE), on whom Shakespeare relied for several of his plots, including that of *Julius Caesar*, thought that we delight in acting because we know the actors are not really living through the terrible events of the tragedy they are playing, and do not really experience grief and anger, any more than they do consternation or confusion when they perform a comedy. Actors imitate emotions, and that is what the audience enjoys. Others disagreed. In *Noctes Atticae* (Attic Nights), Aulus Gellius (ca. 125–ca. 180 CE) praises the ancient Greek actor Polus for really experiencing the emotions of his character, Electra, thereby moving the audience. And in the *Institutions of Oratory*, Quintilian (ca. 35–ca. 96) says that actors should always feel the emotions they portray. Acting was considered a branch of oratory, and the most famous orator of ancient Rome, Cicero (106–43 BCE), who studied speechmaking with Roscius, also maintained that truly felt emotion was required for effective oratory, both in politics and in the theater. Stanislavsky, of course, believed this, too, but in Nemirovich-Danchenko's production he was almost obliged to imitate, that is, to indicate.

What to Wear for Rehearsal

Ancient Greek clothing was loose: Togas are draped over and around the body, and in rehearsal, the actor should bring along a sheet, a large shawl, or another large piece of cloth to simulate one. Women should wear floor-length rehearsal dresses, as well as using a piece of material to simulate the toga. Both men and women should wear sandals, since they were the most often worn footwear, or something approximating whatever footwear the designer has decided upon. Boots for men playing soldiers may be worn.

The clothing of ancient Rome is similar to ancient Greek costume, and much the same advice for rehearsing applies. Stanislavsky and his fellow actors in Nemirovich-Danchenko's production of *Julius Caesar* practiced wearing togas assiduously: how to drape them, how to move in them, and how to use the toga's corners to throw over their shoulders, and, occasionally, to emphasize a point. They also wore boots that resembled the soldiers' boots, laced at the front, they would be wearing in performance

CHAPTER NINE

The Medieval Period

Medieval Theater in England and France

Just as European medieval life appears to us pervaded with religious strife and fervor, so the medieval dramas that have come down to us are steeped in the fundamentalist version of Christianity prevalent in the European Dark Ages. Its truth was taken for granted by the vast majority. As a result, the rightness of the social hierarchy, where everyone occupied a preordained place, was also accepted as a given. At the head of the social order, the monarch ruled by divinely ordained power, and his word was therefore sacrosanct. The mindset and worldview of characters in plays and films set in the medieval era are conditioned by these elementary facts.

The Passion Plays, dealing with the life of Jesus Christ, and the Mystery Plays concerning the lives of saints are seldom done nowadays. They are highly stylized, and the characters are stereotypical, yet they can be compelling in performance. To some extent this period in the theater overlaps with the Old English (Anglo-Saxon) literary period, lasting from roughly 450 to 1066; one of its major works is the saga of *Beowulf*. The Middle English period, from roughly 1066 to 1500, is the era of the theater's evolution toward more secular forms. Yet its farces and dramas, rustic and moralistic, in verse as often as not, are as rife with religion as liturgical plays.

Among the best-known English plays of the very late medieval/early Renaissance period, by which time secular theater had been well established, are *Gammer Gurton's Needle*, presumably produced in 1533, depicting the life of the lower economic classes, the peasants and serfs; and Nicholas Udall's (1505–1556) popular farce *Ralph Roister Doister*, produced in 1553. The plot concerns a wealthy affianced widow, whom Ralph Roister Doister woos. When his suit is unsuccessful, he and his friends try to abduct her. But their plot is foiled by the arrival of her fiancé, a wealthy merchant. The story has a lot in common with ancient Roman farces, and may have been adapted from a lost play.

The history of French theater really begins with France's first important playwright, the *trouvère* (troubadour), composer, and secular dramatist Adam de la Halle (1237?–1288), whose life was spent at the courts of Count Robert d'Artois and Charles of Anjou, King of Sicily and Naples. He wrote the piece often considered the first opera, *Le Jeu de Robin et Marion* (The Play of Robin and Marion) in 1275, a story of Robin Hood and Maid Marion.

Of the few famous anonymous medieval plays, one of the most celebrated is the witty *La Farce de maître Pierre Pathelin* (The Farce of Master Pierre Pathelin), apparently written around 1465. It is a political satire with five characters, and its performing time is about one hour, which is about what the actors could expect audiences to stand for (literally). The plot concerns the dishonest, manipulative village lawyer, Pierre Pathelin; his wife, Guillemette; and a clothier, Joceaulme, whom Pathelin convinces to give him six yards of cloth on credit. When Joceaulme shows up to collect his money, Pathelin, aided and abetted by Guillemette, pretends to be deliriously feverish in bed, and raves in several French dialects. The clothier gives up. But he now takes Thubault Aignelet, a shepherd, to court, because the man has been stealing his sheep for years. The shepherd's lawyer is none other than Pathelin, who tells him to answer "Baa" to every question the Judge—the only honest character in the play—puts to him. That way, the shepherd will seem insane, and the Judge will rule in his favor. Of course, the clothier recognizes Pathelin and tries to sue him at the same time, confusing and befuddling the Judge, who, in his discombobulated state, rules against the clothier. When Pathelin tries to collect his legal fee from Aignelet, the shepherd only answers, "Baa."

The next great dramatist in French history is the poet Pierre Gringoire (1470–1538), who plays a prominent role as a gallant character in Victor Hugo's (1802–1885) romantic novel *Notre-Dame de Paris* (The Hunchback of Notre Dame), written in 1831. Gringoire was a secular dramatist who wrote light pieces and satires, mostly for the Paris acting company Les Enfants sans souci (The Carefree Children), a guild founded in 1388. They had no fixed theater, but traveled around performing in public squares and at fairs. They were known for being costumed as court jesters, with the famous cap and bells. Authorized to perform by King Charles VI (1368–1422), they did farces and morality plays.

Liturgical dramas sponsored by the Church, and secular fairground comedies were performed throughout much of the medieval period. Audiences were usually not stationary, but wandered by the places where the plays were being performed, and would stay awhile, then move on, particularly at the fairgrounds. The plays were done by groups of strolling players, or by amateurs who got together to do specific projects. One of the first established professional theater companies was the Confrérie de la Passion (The Brotherhood of the Passion), which eventually succeeded Les Enfants sans souci. They were authorized by King Charles VI to perform their plays in Paris in 1402. The Confrérie had been founded in 1398 to present Mystery plays.

Throughout the rest of France, too, at major courts and in large cities, a great many secular tragedies on ancient Greek and Roman subjects, as well as on biblical themes, were written and performed. Among the latter is *Les Juives* (The Jewish Women), written in 1583 by the religious Catholic Robert Garnier (1545–1590), considered the greatest of the pre-classical dramatists. This verse drama, notable for the majesty and lyricism of its poetry, is set in ancient Babylon in the time of Nebuchadnezzar, the villain of the piece. As a play, it is static in the extreme, and seems meant to be read, rather than performed—a perfect example of "closet drama." This tragedy is the product of the author's reactions to the endless and horrifying wars of religion through which he lived. As a distinguished magistrate, loyal to the system, he did not suffer personal hardship, but the suffering he observed left an indelible mark of pain and torment on his psyche, reflected in the play as the chorus of Jewish women and the Jewish matriarchs try to answer the questions of how long God's anger against his people will last, and why God is so angry with mankind, whom He himself has created with a sinful nature. For once, the Jews are not seen as villains; symbolically, they stand for the Catholics persecuted in Protestant lands. The play was probably not performed during its author's lifetime, but we read of a few performances after his death, and of some at the beginning of the seventeenth century.

Medieval rehearsal practice is almost entirely unknown. The style in which medieval dramas were performed was said to have been lively, not mannered or posed, and costumes depicted the characters in a fairly standardized way. Satan was usually the audience's favorite character. He and his legions were meant to be terrifying and thrilling, but they were comical figures as often as not. God in his majesty, the personification of earthly kings, sat on his throne in heaven and decreed the fate of the malignant evildoer as well as of the virtuous. But the audience sometimes scoffed at the miracles in the plays. All this was reason enough for the Paris Parlement (the governing body of the city, subject to royal command) to ban the Mystery plays that had begun to bring religion into disrepute. In 1548, they did so, around the time that the monopolistic Confrérie de la Passion, who had the performance rights for all religious drama, had completed the building of its theater, the Hôtel de Bourgogne, in what is now Paris's 2nd arrondissement. It was eventually torn down, but was still in use in the late eighteenth century. Plays by Jean Racine, Pierre Corneille, and other classical seventeenth-century dramatists were performed there, starring such great actors as Montfleury (1640–1685), mocked off the stage as a ham by Cyrano in act 1 of Edmond Rostand's (1868–1918) verse drama *Cyrano de Bergerac* (1897). The Hôtel de Bourgogne was the home for a time of the Comédie-Italienne and of Molière's Comédie-Française. Its auditorium could accommodate 1600 audience members, most of whom stood in the central well or pit of the theater, while wealthier patrons sat in the galleries, balconies, or private boxes that surrounded the standees on the sides and at the back, or on the stage itself.

In medieval productions, there were songs, and incidental music supplied by tabor, fife, and drum. Lively dances were also part of the entertainment. Among them, in England, was the Morris dance, whose name is a corruption of the adjective Moorish, pertaining to the Moors of Spain and North Africa. By the sixteenth century, this had become the general English term for dance that was part of a theatrical presentation. Originating at country fairs, the dances were supposed to resemble those of North Africa, and the performers blackened their faces. Because they were Muslims, the Moors, along with the Arabs, Persians, and Turks, were viewed as heathens and pagans. And the Turks, who had waged wars of conquest and attempted to impose Islam wherever they went, were feared and hated.

The Islamic World in the Medieval Era and Beyond

From ca. 630 to 1260, the establishment of the Islamic Empire in the Middle East and North Africa changed the world as Europeans knew it. The Emperor Charlemagne, who reigned from 742 to 814, fought the Muslim incursion north of the Pyrenees. The enmity felt by the Christians towards those whom they considered heathen would result two centuries later in the Crusades, brutal wars of conquest by European invaders of the Holy Land that were waged from 1095 to 1272. But the enlightened development of Islam in the Middle East was eventually to have an impact on Europe in every way.

The Koran was written in the Arabic of Islam's founder, the Prophet Muhammad (ca. 570–630), who was born in Mecca on the Arabian peninsula. With the establishment of the Islamic Empire, Arabic became the lingua franca of the non-European lands surrounding the Mediterranean. United by its strong religion, and despite the eventual internecine sectarian strife of Sunni versus Shiite, the empire of Islam was more cultivated, more powerful, and scientifically more advanced than fragmented Europe. It included Spain, largely isolated from the rest of the Islamic world; the Muslims would be definitively driven out by the Christians in 1492. Sicily, which changed hands several times, was conquered by various European powers, which shared the island with Islamic potentates until 1068, when the Normans drove them out after a protracted conflict. They all left their marks not only on the history of Sicily, but on the superb Sicilian cuisine and on the island's unique architecture as well.

Eventually, the Ottoman Turks became the rulers of the Islamic world. In 1453, Mehmet [Mohammed] II (1430–1481), the seventh successive ruler of the house of Othman, for whom the dynasty was named, came out of Anatolia to conquer Constantinople, capital of the Byzantine Empire of the Eastern Orthodox Greeks. The Byzantines had styled themselves the last Roman Emperors after the schism between east and west had led to the existence of two Roman Empires: the Greek-speaking Byzantines and the Latin-speaking Romans. Renamed Istanbul, the city, built on seven hills at the confluence of the Bosporus and the Golden Horn, straddling Europe and Asia, became the capital of Islam. Mehmet, known as Fatih (The Conqueror), who spent most of his life making war, went on to vanquish Serbia, the Crimea, and Greece—except for Rhodes, where he met defeat—and to wage war and make peace with Venice.

A man of contradictions, the highly cultivated Mehmet II was a brutal murderer who had his baby son strangled so as to avoid wars of succession—a tactic that did not succeed, since upon his death the conflict between his two surviving sons broke out anyway. But some of his successors were far worse than he, killing sons, brothers, and nephews in order to avoid future problems with the succession. As contradictory in his nature as Napoleon, Mehmet II was also an educated, philosophical man who presided over a Renaissance court in Istanbul; read Plato, Aristotle, and Homer; and encouraged all the arts, which flourished during his reign. His sense of architecture was supreme, and the beauties of the Turkish architecture of the period are to be seen in Istanbul to this day. With a degree of tolerance unusual for the era, whatever his motives, he allowed the establishment of Jewish and Christian *millets*, or national communities (Venetians, Armenians), in Istanbul, where Jews were also received after they were expelled in 1492 from Spain.

Because of his savage massacre of those in numerous places who had surrendered on the promise of their lives being spared, and because of his many invasions and conquests, even into the boot of Italy itself, Mehmet was the terror of Europe. For more information, and an excellent summary of the period, politically, religiously, and artistically, as well as for some of the details of architecture, art, and daily life, read John Freely's *The Grand Turk: Sultan Mehmet II—Conqueror of Constantinople and Master of an Empire* (The Overlook Press, 2009). Among the fascinating period sources he quotes is Richard Knolles's (1550?–1610) *Generall Historie of the Turkes*, published in 1603, from which Shakespeare obtained information on the Turkish navy that he used in *Othello*, first presented in 1604. If you are doing *Othello*, which is set during one phase of the Turkish-Venetian wars, both Freely and Knolles are prime background reading material and will give you a real sense of the issues involved in the conflict. Othello is a Christian North African general, heading the Venetian fight against the Muslim Turks, ruled by the weak Sultan Selim II (1566–1574) in Cyprus in 1573, nearly a century after the death of Mehmet II.

The Ottoman Empire of the Turks, which extended around the Mediterranean and included Greece, Albania, and the Balkans, was a major power in world affairs until its demise in 1922 after the end of the First World War. The threat to western Europe was definitively ended in 1683, when the Turks were defeated before the very gates of Vienna. In gratitude, the city's bakers invented the croissant, the buttery roll in the shape of a crescent, symbol of Islam. By 1922, the authority and extent of the Ottoman Empire had been gradually whittled away, as various independence movements in Greece, Bulgaria, Albania, and the Balkans took shape. But the influence of the religion of Islam remained strong, of course, even after the demise of the Ottomans.

The world of Islam had created a brilliant literature, including the famous *Thousand and One Nights*, which gives a picture of that world in all its aspects, including its myths, drawn not only from Arab legends but also from Persian and Turkish stories. The *Rubáiyát* of the Persian poet Omar Khayyam, in Edward Fitzgerald's Victorian translation, became famous throughout the English-speaking world. Islamic scholars contributed to the world great knowledge in the different branches of mathematics: It is to them that the world owes the system of Arabic numerals, adapted from the Hindus. And it was they who ensured the spread of the concept of zero. Their discoveries in the fields of chemistry, pharmacology, astronomy, and medicine would eventually be retrieved and understood by Europeans. The origin of these discoveries is evident in a vocabulary whose etymology we have now largely forgotten: alchemy, algebra, algorithm, alkali, amalgam, calibrate, chemistry, zenith, and zero are all from Arabic. As Europeans made progress in all those areas, the Islamic world declined into its own Dark Ages. This was due in part to the destructive wars initiated by Christian Europeans and known in the West as the Crusades. But before that, the Islamic world had preserved the knowledge of ancient Greece and Rome (translating its literature into Arabic), which eventually made its way back to Europe, thanks to them.

The Ottomans invented a lifestyle that was comfortable, at least for the wealthy, and rich in the arts of sumptuous cuisine, architecture, calligraphy, drawing, painting, interior decoration, and weaving. The famous Persian carpets, and the divans set against the wall with embroidered cushions and pillows, were very different from the hard wooden stools and chairs of Europe. And it is awe-inspiring to gaze at the gorgeous blue, turquoise, and gold minarets and mosques of Samarkand in the Central Asian republic of Uzbekistan. Unlike Europe in the Middle Ages, the world of Islam was hygienic, and it is to Arab doctors that we owe the concept that keeping clean and bathing regularly helps to prevent the spread of disease. The Arabs (again, unlike the Europeans of the time) used soap, toothpaste, and deodorizing perfumes as well.

The Sultan of this stratified class society (despite the admonition in the Koran that all are equal), enlightened though he might be, was the supreme ruler. Everyone else was technically his slave, including even the Grand Vizier, who was the Sultan's chief adviser and prime minister.

Clothing in the hot climates where Islam flourished consisted of loose gowns for both men and women. These floor-length garments, versions of which are still seen today, were able to cool the body in the terrible heat. Women wore the veil except in the privacy of their own homes. Their voluminous gowns made them move in a slow, stately manner. Men wore a long or short cloth headdress secured with rope-like ribbons. In the desert, to ride on the ubiquitous horses and camels, men wore breeches or the gowns folded between their legs to resemble trousers. Muslim soldiers wore breeches and jackets. Men's heads were covered either with long cloths secured with braid, as in Saudi Arabia today, or with turbans or the fez in Turkey.

The *dhimmis*—citizens of other religions, particularly Jews and Christians; treated as second class—wore special clothing, hats, or badges that set them off from the rest of the population. There were restrictions on such things as the height of their houses of worship, which could not rise higher than the mosques, and where they could reside, but they were allowed to practice their religions in freedom. And Jews, for instance, were generally tolerated and lived in less fearful conditions than they did in the Christian Europe of the same medieval era. They were honored as people of the book, despite what the Koran sometimes says derogatorily regarding Jews. Moses is one of the prophets revered by Muslims, and both claim descent from Abraham. So there was at that point in history a relationship and an affinity between Jews and Muslims, only tempered by the rejection by Jews of Mohammed as the last prophet of God. This rejection was, of course, the crucial factor in the establishment of the disabilities under which they lived.

The two worlds of Islam and Christianity fully encountered each other first in the realm of war, in the form of the first crusade of 1095, as the fanatical Christian Europeans invaded and attempted to capture the Holy Land from the people they thought of as heathen and condemned to spend eternity in Hell. This attitude was ingrained, and most European characters in plays or films set in this period would take it for granted that it was the incontrovertible truth. In other words, Muslims, like Jews, were dehumanized in the eyes of the Europeans of that period. In the name of their Lord, the Crusaders committed untold crimes and massacred Jews and Muslims in a most savage, barbaric, unchristian fashion. The news of these wars that filtered back to Europe from the Middle East would be known to any character you might be playing.

What to Wear for Rehearsal

Women should wear long rehearsal gowns. Men and women should wear capes or use a sheet draped around the shoulder to simulate cloaks, and men should also wear gowns, if that is required, and tights as well, if possible. A long raincoat is useful, and may simulate a cloak as well, if worn draped around the shoulders. Ordinary walking shoes may be worn, or boots, as necessary. Wear sandals if you know you will be using them, but not sneakers. If you are doing a play with Muslim characters, you may need to simulate the appropriate headdress, such as veils for women, for which you can use kerchiefs. Skullcaps or headdresses for the men may be simulated by wearing an ordinary woolen fitted cap, or a kerchief.

CHAPTER TEN

The Renaissance: Elizabethan England; William Shakespeare

In an age of great dramatists, Christopher Marlowe (1564–1593) is often considered second only to Shakespeare, although he wrote only seven plays. He was killed in a tavern brawl while still a young man. But so brilliant and exciting is his writing style, despite some ponderousness, that there are those who believe he was the real author of Shakespeare's works, that his death was faked, and that he was spirited away, to continue writing in secret. There is no credible evidence for this bizarre theory.

Ben Jonson wrote a number of plays set in his own times, and Shakespeare's *The Merry Wives of Windsor* also has a contemporary setting (see below). Thomas Dekker's (1572–1632) delightful *The Shoemaker's Holiday* (1599) shows us the world of urban craftsmen and depicts middle-class domestic life; the holiday of the title is Shrove Tuesday, honoring London apprentices with banquets. But these plays are the exceptions: Most surviving Elizabethan dramas are period pieces, like Marlowe's plays. Among them are *Edward II*, a biographical play about the medieval English king; and *The Tragicall Historie of Dr. Faustus*, based on a number of German legends. Both are still occasionally performed, as is Thomas Kyd's (1558–1594) *The Spanish Tragedy*, written sometime between 1582 and 1592; its most recent revival was in 2010. Set in medieval Spain, this gory drama, with its overheated dialogue and perfervid situations, was copied and burlesqued by other playwrights. It was one of the most popular of the "revenge tragedies" that appealed to Elizabethan and Jacobean tastes.

These period pieces may be set in times long ago and places far away, but certain Elizabethan assumptions about culture, politics, social hierarchies, manners, and expectations in relationships underlie their stories and form the characters' background. Thus, Elizabethan plays set in ancient Greece or Rome owe more to Elizabethan English attitudes than they do to those of Greeks or Romans, which the Elizabethans assumed were like their own.

As in medieval days, the anointed monarch, Queen Elizabeth I (1533–1603), considered the representative of God on earth, was theoretically the supreme dictator of the state; her reign began in 1558. Although she and her Privy Council of aristocratic advisers promulgated laws, the question of how much these were obeyed the farther one got from the center of power is still one that historians debate. Elizabeth's rule was not and could not be monolithic and absolute: the institution of Parliament ensured that it would not be.

Although the monarch had the power to summon, dissolve, and overrule Parliament, with its Lords and elected Commons, the institution, with its inherently democratic tendencies, was at least established. But the queen had the final say on legislation, which required her signature in order to become law. It is also significant that Parliament sat for only three years in toto during her long reign. It provided advice and passed tax laws. Laws began as bills subject to debate; they were either "public," applying to everyone throughout the kingdom; or "private," applied in specific localities or to individuals.

Along with the political system that forms the background to Elizabethan drama is an accepted pecking order with which everyone was familiar and which they took for granted. At the top, of course, was the queen herself, and just below her was the noble class, the aristocracy. The rank of duke was highest, followed by the ranks of marquis, earl, viscount, baron, and knight. The esquire, or gentleman, was the lowest rank of minor nobility. This hierarchy was paralleled by a Church hierarchy, Anglican by that time, and, as in the Roman Catholic church, the top began with the rank of cardinal and then that of archbishop, followed by the bishops, equal to the earls. Even lower on the social scale, and next after the bishops, were the archdeacons, priests, and deacons. The Mayor of London was of an equal rank with a bishop or an earl, but the rural landholders, the yeomen, were pretty low on the social and economic ladder, along with craftsmen and tradesmen. Just below the urban craftsmen were their apprentices, who might have been born in the city, or have come to it from the countryside. Servants and laborers were their equals. Merchants and such professionals as doctors and lawyers, who had been to university, were the equivalent of the esquire, which made them equal to the minor nobility, both socially and economically.

Of course, how well any of these people lived depended on how much money they earned, or had inherited. A nobleman could be expected to make approximately £2500 a year, mostly from his tenants' rents and the sale of crops from his estates. This was around $1,250,000 in today's currency, whereas a laborer might earn only twenty-six shillings and six pence a year, or $668 today. This was barely enough to live on even then, especially for those with families, and working people suffered severe deprivations. Child mortality was high, and children were set to work or accepted by craftsmen as apprentices at a young age. Only by dint of the greatest ambition could they change their lot in life, becoming master craftsmen, or perhaps university students or clergymen, or even apothecaries, doctors, or lawyers.

As an actor, you must understand the value of money and translate it into contemporary terms. When we think of a penny, we think of a virtually useless small coin, but an Elizabethan penny was a silver coin worth between two and three dollars of today's currency. It could buy you a loaf of bread, considered an expensive commodity back then. For a halfpenny, you could purchase a quart of beer or ale, which were thick, nourishing brews. A shilling, which was worth twelve pence, or between twenty-five and thirty dollars by today's standards, was what a skilled craftsman could expect to earn per day. And he would be doing extremely well at that rate. A bed at an inn cost a penny, and a meal cost two shillings—rather expensive, at between fifty and sixty dollars, which is often what a dinner at a New York restaurant costs per person today. Clothing was extremely expensive, and was usually passed down from parent to child. Discarded noblemen's clothing was given to servants, who supplemented their incomes by selling it, sometimes to theater companies for use as costumes.

Elizabethan rehearsal practices are pretty much of a mystery. Perhaps there were one or two rehearsals of a play, which might have only a few performances, like contemporary summer stock. Maybe there was an extensive rehearsal period, particularly for more complicated pieces. The actors who were "sharers" in the company were its chief joint owners, under the aegis of their manager and of their noble patron. They hired others to be members of the company, either as "hirelings" or as "apprentices." Among the sharers, there could be a playwright, like Shakespeare. The company probably got together and arranged movements and dealt with such necessary details as the logistics of moving the "sick chair"—an armchair in which an ill character, like the King of France in *All's Well That Ends Well*, was carried on and off the stage. Whether a scene took place on the main stage platform or in the "inner below"—a curtained area beneath the covered balcony, called the "above" or the "inner above"—would have been determined at rehearsals. But we are not even sure that the latter were acting areas: the inner above may have been an expensive gallery for some of the well-to-do spectators; the inner below may have been a small backstage space where some of the actors waited to make entrances.

European actors during the medieval and Renaissance eras were expected to have skills in vocal and movement technique, to understand stock characters, and to know the conventions of elementary blocking, such as adjusting the stage picture by moving left or right when another character entered. Apparently, they played types, rather than individuals, as in the Italian commedia: the young lover, the braggart warrior, the king and queen were expected to behave and to speak in certain ways; they could rehearse the standard gestures and comportment on their own. They dealt with the actions and emotions of their own parts, without the help of a director, although they could be instructed in their roles by the playwright, who would explain the character to them. In all of this, hirelings and apprentices were trained by those who were already experienced.

Prompters or company directors would copy out the parts for each actor by hand, since printing was so expensive. The actors were required to understand the whole play, even though they were not given a script. Instead, they were given a plot summary, with scenes listed, along with their cue script, much like the sides given to actors auditioning for film or television today. During performances, a list of scenes in order, and the characters in them, was (presumably) posted backstage. It appears that stage fights were rehearsed, and exits and entrances gone through, from cue to cue, under the instruction of the actor-manager or playwright. But there was no director in the modern sense. There was little scenery and no lighting in the outdoor theaters, where plays were performed during the afternoons, using natural light. Indoor theaters were lit by candles and torchlight, and perhaps by cressets: iron containers in which fuel was burned for light and heat. Cressets were very smoky, and were sometimes used outdoors during cold weather. They may not have been used indoors except to light entranceways or areas on either side of the stage. For an excellent summary of what we know about the Elizabethan theater, and an introduction to all the available source material, consult *Lighting the Shakespearean Stage*, 1567–1642 (Southern Illinois University Press, 1999) by R. B. Graves.

William Shakespeare's *The Merry Wives of Windsor*

Of all Shakespeare's plays, this comedy is the only one actually set in Elizabethan England, in his own place, day, and age. The information about government, rank, and the currency system given earlier in this chapter is an essential study in doing this piece, and is the kind of thing to be discussed by the director with the company during the preliminary table work.

Technically, the characters of Sir John Falstaff and his henchmen belong to an earlier period in history, that of the Wars of the Roses (1455–1485), the dynastic wars between the houses of Lancaster and York, which ended when Elizabeth's grandfather mounted the throne as King Henry VII (1457–1509), and which are the subject of Shakespeare's history plays, from *Richard II* through *Richard III*. Falstaff is the mentor who teaches Prince Hal, the future King Henry V, about life, and helps him sow his wild oats. The prince discards him when he becomes king and the bibulous old knight has become an embarrassment. Falstaff is crushed. The character in this comedy, however, abused as he may be by those whom he would con, is far from annihilated.

The story: Portly and almost always a bit soused, Falstaff is a member of the minor nobility, just above the lowest rank of esquire or gentleman, to which Ford and Page belong, putting them squarely in what we would now call the middle class. His just slightly higher rank enables Falstaff to lord it over them, although his haughtiness is actually pretentious and misplaced. He trades on his station, not paying his bills (he has no money) but living high on the hog and getting away with mayhem. Merry and down at heel in his retirement after a tumultuous life, he connives at various schemes, especially amorous ones, in what almost seems like a French bedroom farce.

Sir John spends most of his time at the Garter Inn in the company of his low-life companions and henchmen, Bardolph, Nym, and Pistol. The knight attempts to seduce Mistress Alice Ford, wife of the irascible, jealous Ford, and Mistress Meg Page, wife of Page, a calm but incisive man. Falstaff, thinking himself very clever, and not knowing how close the women are as friends, has sent them identical love letters. They show the letters to each other and have no intention of giving in to him. He gets his comeuppance when he goes into the forest to keep what he thinks is a rendezvous with his two prospective conquests. The two wives, who make a fool of him, have conspired to play on his superstitions with the connivance of Mistress Quickly, servant to the temperamental French

Dr. Caius, a stereotypical character who shows just how far chauvinistic nationalism was beginning to be the order of the day. Ford's daughter, Nanetta, ends up betrothed to her beloved, Fenton, a gentleman, and therefore of the same rank as Ford. Their love develops behind his back, and despite his attempts to betroth her to Dr. Caius. Among the other characters are the stereotypical Sir Hugh Evans, "a Welsh Parson"; and Justice Shallow, Esquire; and his prideful cousin, Slender. The latter two are of equal rank with Ford and Page. Of the major characters, Mistress Quickly is, of course, lower on the social scale, which does not preclude her having a sense of self-importance and a quick wit.

The observation of domestic customs and habits provides great lessons in the ordinary ways Elizabethan life was lived. We see the way laundry was done, for instance; and the way people behaved in public houses. The ubiquitous tendency to believe in superstition is also realistically portrayed. Shakespeare's language is drawn from the everyday speech of real people, as in the following excerpt from the opening of act 1, scene 3, which takes place in a room at the Garter Inn. Falstaff—whose clever use of language is one of the things that Shakespeare uses to characterize him perfectly—and his three conniving reprobate henchmen are hanging about, hatching schemes as usual:

> FALSTAFF. Which of you know Ford of this town?
>
> PISTOL. I ken the wight: he is of substance good.
>
> FALSTAFF. My honest lads, I will tell you what I am about.
>
> PISTOL. Two yards and more.
>
> FALSTAFF. No quips now, Pistol! Indeed, I am in the waist two yards about; but I am now about no waste; I am about thrift. Briefly, I do mean to make love to Ford's wife: I spy entertainment in her; she discourses, she carves, she gives the leer of invitation: I can construe the action of her familiar style; and the hardest voice of her behavior, to be Englished rightly, is: "I am Sir John Falstaff's."

Of course, Falstaff is deluded when he thinks Mistress Ford is responsive to his overtures. In any case, Falstaff's ultimate goal is to get at her husband's money: "Now, the report goes that she has all the rule of her husband's purse; he hath a legion of angels," says Sir John. The angel was a gold coin with a picture of St. Michael on it, in use since the reign of Edward IV (1461–1470); it went out of circulation after 1643. At the time of Shakespeare's play (1597–1598), it was worth ten shillings (up from its original value of six shillings and eight pence), between $250 and $300 in today's currency. A "legion of angels" is, of course, a punning allusion to religion.

In the next lines, Falstaff tells his followers that he has also written to Mistress Page, whom he thinks is enamored of him: "Here's another letter to her, she bears the purse too: she is a region in Guiana, all gold and bounty. I will be cheaters to them both, and they shall be exchequers to me: they shall be my East and West Indies, and I will trade them both." The New World, discovered by Europeans more than a century before, is by now well known to the Old World, insofar as it has been explored up to that time, and its riches are already being mined and looted; its native populations suppressed, exploited, and massacred; all in the name of the superiority of the religion the conquerors considered the only true one. As with Mistress Ford, Falstaff is deluded into thinking she is madly attracted to him, and mistakes her politeness for flirtation. The plot is launched.

Although some of the English is antiquated and strikes us today as picturesque, most of it, including the puns, is immediately comprehensible. Once again, it is the actor's job to make it as clear as possible to the audience. "I ken the wight" means "I know the fellow." The meaning is clear not only from the context, but also because we have not yet forgotten those obsolete words. The sentence, "I can construe the meaning of her familiar style" is perhaps fairly obscure, and Falstaff, who obviously delights in linguistic preciosity, makes up phrases, and uses "big" words when small ones would do. This is an endearing side of his character that amuses the audience and puts them on his side, so that he remains sympathetic despite his scurrilous antics. To construe, in this context, according to the OED, means "To give the sense or meaning of; to expound, explain, interpret (language)." Her "familiar" style means just what it might mean today: close, intimate, even flirtatious: *She behaved familiarly*. The word does not mean, in this context, merely acquainted with. The line might be delivered with a leer or a wink, to communicate meaning to the audience with a visual cue that accompanies the words, delivered in a lecherous manner, with sexual subtext: "I know what she means, behaving in that familiar way, inviting me with her suggestive looks."

What to Wear for Rehearsal

For plays set in the earlier part of the period, and done in period costume, much the same advice for rehearsal applies as with medieval clothing.

Men should wear short jackets (a blazer will do) and tights for plays set in the middle period, and longer coats and vests for men in the early seventeenth-century period. Once you see the costume designs, you will know better how to proceed. If you were playing Justice Shallow in *The Merry Wives of Windsor*, for instance, your costume might consist of a long gown, and you should wear something to simulate that, since it determines so much about how you can move. Women should wear long gowns, because almost all the costumes will be ankle length. Wear a hat if you know one will be part of your costume. Regular shoes and boots may be worn.

CHAPTER ELEVEN

The Seventeenth Century in France and England: Molière; William Congreve

The Theater Experience for Actor and Spectator

Starting in the 1660s, most acting companies held sporadic rehearsal a few times a week, usually for a few hours in the morning. The actors would also get together just before shows simply to make sure they didn't bump into each other during a performance. In many cases, there was no real need for rehearsal from the point of view of the management, because a standardized system of blocking—with the star in the center, surrounded by the other actors, who adjusted their positions on stage without upstaging the star—was the norm. During performances, as we learn from a study of the many extant Restoration promptbooks, actors were given a warning (entrance cue) for each entrance, much as singers are today in opera productions, where they are told exactly when to enter by someone from stage management standing with them or signaling them from behind a desk or console. Giving actors such warnings was necessary since there was so little rehearsal, and plays were mounted in much more haste than we are used to today.

The theaters were run by associations of actors, and it seems that authors like the founder of the Comédie-Française, Jean-Baptiste Poquelin (better known as Molière, 1622–1673), when they were in positions of power, had a great say in the casting of their plays, but beyond that we know nothing of the process by which plays were brought to life on the stage. No doubt special tricks and commedia lazzi were taught by those practiced experts who trained apprentices.

As Georges Mongrédien informs us in *Daily Life in the French Theatre at the Time of Molière* (George Allen and Unwin Ltd, 1969), we don't know if curtains were used throughout the seventeenth century to mask the stage from the audience, or even when their use began.

Seventeenth-century theaters were badly lit, and there were audience members, mostly aristocrats, seated on the stage, which sometimes led to confusion. Mongrédien quotes the Abbé Michel de Pure (1620–1680), historiographer, adviser to Louis XIV (1638–1715), translator of Quintilian, playwright, novelist, and author of the informative book *Idées des spectacles anciens et nouveaux* (Ideas on Ancient and Contemporary Spectacles, 1668):

> How often, when the actor had to declare: "*Mais le voici!*" [But here he is!] or "*Mais je le vois!*" [But I see him!] the audience confused the actor with a well-dressed, well-built man who suddenly entered the stage looking for his seat even after several scenes had already been acted.

And Molière himself put a character into his play *Les Fâcheux* (The Bores), "who drags his chair into the middle of the stage, in front of the actors, instead of sitting to one side."

Many actors in seventeenth-century European theater were expected to have mastered the art of declamation, as opposed to a vocal technique that would allow the actor to sound natural. Declamation, a false and artificial, not to say bombastic way of intoning dialogue, and especially verse, is to be generally avoided nowadays, except when specifically called for in the context of imitating the old-fashioned delivery of lines.

From the sixteenth through the nineteenth and early twentieth centuries, declamation was not uncommon on the stage, and audiences applauded individual speeches, such as well-known Shakespearean soliloquies, for their fine points of virtuosity, much as audiences applaud a particularly fine display of bel canto singing in an opera by Rossini. On recordings made at the beginning of the twentieth century, you can hear late-nineteenth-century Shakespearean actors intoning and declaiming the verse, and it sounds execrable. But alongside declamation, there was always a more realistic approach to behavior on stage, particularly starting in the late seventeenth century in both France and England.

Some actors, like Michel Baron (1653–1729), creator of leading roles for Corneille and Racine, and a member of Molière's company, had learned to avoid such practices, and experimented with a more natural style of playing and speaking. The actor/dramatist Antoine-François Riccoboni (1707–1772), son of the actor Luigi Riccoboni (1674–1753), director of the much admired Comédie-Italienne in Paris, wrote in *L'Art du Théâtre* (1750): "The celebrated Baron...was the only one who had no declamation. He was nevertheless the most admired...He played with more force than anybody, yet his playing was never forced...They say that in his youth, Baron declaimed like the others, but in the course of thirty years he had lost those early habits." And Antoine-François' mother, the actress Elena Riccoboni, née Balletti (1686–1771), said of Baron: "He always listens to his fellow-actors, a thing to which actors, as a rule, pay little heed, and his attention is accompanied by such movements of face and body as are required by the nature of the speech to which he listens. When speaking, his talk is real conversation."

Those of us in the Anglophone world, used to the active plays of Shakespeare and other Elizabethan and Jacobean dramatists, may find the classical tragedies of Pierre Corneille (1606–1684) and Jean Racine (1639–1699) static and lacking in action, as Michel Saint-Denis pointed out in his brilliant study *Theatre: The Rediscovery of Style*, which every actor should read. The action, as he says, is internal. It is expressed in alexandrine verse, which consists of lines of twelve feet; that is, each line is twelve syllables long, often divided in the middle by a caesura. The alexandrine is the equivalent in French of iambic pentameter in English, in that it reflects the reality of the language's rhythms and seems a natural manner of poetic expression.

Dealing with this style demands the utmost mastery of speaking verse so that it sounds like real thoughts. We are not in the realm of naturalism or even realism, but of heightened fantasy that must be made to seem real to the audience. This can only be accomplished if the actor understands the nature of internal, psychological action and how to translate it technically into verbal action. The plays are, after all, more verbal than physical action, and Stanislavsky's internal "psychotechnique" is of paramount importance. If the actor simply declaims, the audience will not get anything from these plays but a sense of boredom and will leave the theater in a state of exhaustion. So will the actors, who will also not enjoy the experience.

Read the plays of the era, especially all of those by Molière, Racine, and Corneille. The English Restoration comedies of George Farquhar (1678–1707) include *The Beaux' Stratagem* and *The Recruiting Officer*, one of the most popular plays of its day. Thomas Otway's (1652–1685) most notable successes are *Venice Preserv'd* and *The Soldier's Fortune*. And Sir George Etherege (1635–1692), who, incidentally, had a distinguished diplomatic career, wrote such masterpieces as the brilliant satiric comedy *The Man of Mode*. His first play, written in 1660, has the delightful title *The Comical Revenge or Love in a Tub*. Other notable, witty plays include Sir John Vanbrugh's (1664–1726) *The Relapse* and *The Provoked Wife*; and William Wycherly's (1640–1716) often revived *The Country Wife*, as well as *The Plain Dealer*. Read as well the plays of the first noted woman dramatist, Aphra Behn (1640–1689). Among them is *Abdelazer, or The Moor's Revenge*, Behn's only tragedy and a great success when it was produced in 1676. There are echoes in it of *Hamlet*, *Macbeth* and *Othello*, and of Jacobean revenge tragedies. It starred Thomas Betterton, who had been much acclaimed for his Othello, in the title role of the Moor. After Behn's death a revival of *Abdelazer* with music by Henry Purcell (1659?–1695) was highly successful. The plot is extremely complicated, as is so typical of the era, which delighted in abstruseness and convolutions. The influential works of the poet laureate and translator of Virgil's *Aeneid*, John Dryden (1631–1700), include such diverse pieces as *Amphitryon* and *Marriage à la Mode*. He was so famous in his day that the period in which he lived and wrote is often referred to as the Age of Dryden.

William Congreve's *The Way of the World*

In the Restoration England of King Charles II (1630–1685), social satire was the order of the theatrical day. The relief felt at not having to bow down to Puritan religion led to an outpouring of licentiousness. The complicated, passionate relationships this gave rise to were satirized in *The Way of the World* (1700) by William Congreve (1670–1729), and in many other Restoration comedies. The edition edited by Anthony G. Henderson for the Cambridge University Press is particularly helpful.

The story of this wry, somewhat cynical five-act comedy is so complicated that it has been considered a model of Byzantine plot construction. Briefly, Mirabell and Millamant are in love and want to get married. In order for Millamant to receive her dowry in full, Mirabell must obtain the consent and approval of Millamant's aunt, Lady Wishfort. She is an embittered, cynical lady who wants Millamant to marry Sir Wilful Witwoud, her nephew. In addition, she loathes Mirabell, who once "falsely pretended to love her." A subplot involves Mirabell's friend Fainall (Millamant's cousin), who has been having an affair with Mrs. Marwood, while his wife, Mrs. Fainall, has an affair with Sir Wilful Witwoud. After much trickery and deception and many twists and turns in this round robin of relationships, everything works out for Mirabell and Millamant.

Mirabell was played by an actor known for his strong and rebellious personality, John Verbruggen (?–1708), who is supposed to have been "intuitive," without a methodical way of working, relying instead on inspiration. Thomas Betterton created the part of Mr. Fainall. In the following excerpt from the very opening of act 1, scene 1, they are in a "Chocolate-House," finishing a game of cards:

MIRABELL: You are a fortunate man, Mr. Fainall.

FAINALL: Have we done?

MIRABELL: What you please. I'll play on to entertain you.

FAINALL: No, I'll give you your revenge another time, when you are not so indifferent; you are thinking of something else now, and play too negligently: the coldness of a losing gamester lessens the pleasure of the winner. I'd no more play with a man that slighted his ill fortune than I'd make love to a woman who undervalued the loss of her reputation.

MIRABELL: You have a taste extremely delicate, and are for refining on your pleasures.

FAINALL: Prithee, why so reserved? Something has put you out of humour.

MIRABELL: Not at all: I happen to be grave to-day, and you are gay; that's all.

FAINALL: Confess, Millamant and you quarrelled last night, after I left you; my fair cousin has some humours that would tempt the patience of a Stoic. What, some coxcomb came in, and was well received by her, while you were by?

MIRABELL: Witwoud and Petulant ["Followers of Mrs. Millamant"; Witwoud is Sir Wilful's half brother], and what was worse, her aunt, your wife's mother, my evil genius—or to sum up all in her own name, my old Lady Wishfort came in.

FAINALL: Oh, there it is then: she has a lasting passion for you, and with reason.—What, then my wife was there?

MIRABELL: Yes, and Mrs. Marwood and three or four more, whom I never saw before; seeing me, they all put on their grave faces, whispered one another, then complained aloud of the vapours, and after fell into a profound silence.

FAINALL: They had a mind to be rid of you.

MIRABELL: For which reason I resolved not to stir. At last the good old lady broke through her painful taciturnity with an invective against long visits. I would not have understood her, but Milla-mant joining in the argument, I rose and with a constrained smile told her, I thought nothing was so easy as to know when a visit began to be troublesome; she reddened and I withdrew, without expecting her reply.

You will notice immediately how modern the language in this gossipy scene is, and yet how antique it sounds at the same time. This is because of certain grammatical constructions that were natural and normal in their day, but that we no longer use. We would never say today, as Mirabell does, "You have a taste extremely delicate, and are for refining on your pleasures." But we understand immediately, although we might say, rather more crudely, "You have great taste—you really appreciate the finer things in life." Nor would we say, "whispered one another," but rather, "whispered to each other."

All of this background, and the information in the following section, provides grist for the actor's mill and serves to plunge him or her into the heady waters of this roistering, rambunctious period. In such a libertine age, despite the continued existence of the Puritan attitudes towards sexuality, the social veneer of manners and formal language served sometimes to cover the arrogant hypocrisy and narcissism that pervaded the English upper classes, newly restored to prominence along with the monarch. But this phenomenon was hardly confined to the tight little island.

Manners and Hypocrisy

In a letter to the famous diarist Samuel Pepys (1633–1703) of October 4, 1689, his friend, the diarist John Evelyn (1620–1706), tells him that "the late Earle of St. Albans [Henry Jermyn (1604–1684)]...took extraordinary care at Paris, that his Young Nephew should Learne by heart, all the Formes of Encounter, and Court Addresses...and the French, if I mistake not (who are Masters in these Civilities to excess) *l'Entre-gens* [manner of discreet communication between people]." Dr. Martin Lister (1638–1712) remarks in his book *A Journey to Paris in the Year 1698* that "The French Nation value themselves upon Civility." And, says he, "'Tis certain the French are the most Polite Nation in the World, and can Praise and Court with a better Air than the rest of Mankind."

But there were also bad manners and lapses in taste: In a public place, so the writer on etiquette Antoine de Courtin (1662–1685) informs us in his famous *Treatise on Civility*, "a husband who caresses his wife in front of everyone is absolutely ridiculous." No doubt many men did caress their wives in public, hence the reason for this criticism.

Note that the proper sort of behavior prescribed by de Courtin, including the importance attached to rank, applies to plays of this period whether they are set in France or England, or elsewhere in Europe. French fashions, manners, and civility were the fashion all over the continent, especially by the end of the century. As Simon Callow (b. 1949) points out in his book *Acting in Restoration Comedy* (Applause Acting Series, 2000), bowing and curtseying, sometimes quite elaborately and with great flourish, were natural to the characters in plays of this period. The automatic reflex to bow or curtsey was much the same then as shaking hands is in the United States today or kissing someone on both cheeks is in France.

Like civility and deference to those of higher rank, religion, too, was pervasive and paramount in this period, and only by the end of the century had a certain tolerance for religious differences begun to creep into European society. The Latitudinarians, who wanted to allow latitude of opinion within the Anglican church, also ushered in a more tolerant atmosphere, although skeptics were still ridiculed, atheists were anathema, and differences even among orthodox believers were regarded with suspicion. But there were even more startling ideas floating around that contradicted the prevailing repressive approach to religion and to what constituted human as opposed to divine nature: The English philosopher John Locke (1632–1704) maintained that, contrary to seventeenth-century religious ideas about creation, we do not have inborn, innate ideas at birth, but are born with our minds a *tabula rasa*—a blank slate—and that the self exists as a continuity of consciousness. Jansenism, an important French reform movement, smacked of Calvinism to more orthodox Catholics, because it professed a belief in predestination and seemed to downplay the idea of free will. Among its adherents was the playwright Racine. It was as dangerous to be a Jansenist in the France of Louis XIV, who banned the movement, as it was to be a Communist or Communist sympathizer in the United States of Senator Joseph McCarthy. But it was worse to be a Protestant.

A certain hypocrisy with regard to both religion and social interactions among the upper classes is apparent in the characters in Molière's plays. In *The Misanthrope* (1666), Alceste, angry at the cynicism of mankind in general, is furious over the hypocritical displays of affection and flattery between his friend, Philinte, and a marquis he is barely even acquainted with. But Philinte maintains that without such politeness life is impossible: manners are the lubricant that allows life to glide along painlessly. Everyone knows his place and keeps it in comfort. Alceste, and the revolutionaries who came a century after him, disagreed: false politesse cemented hypocrisy and inequality. Sincerity and truth were to be preferred, even at the risk of unpopularity. People should be confronted with the truth. Nobody should say one thing to a person's face and another behind his back. But in a society where even the privilege of handing the king his handkerchief at the morning dressing ceremony was a coveted honor, the behavior despised by Alceste and satirized by Molière was perhaps a natural concomitant of the rigid, controlling system of rank and court etiquette.

Historical Developments: 1693, A Sample Year

The seventeenth century, particularly as it neared its end, appears to us now to be a period in transition between the antiquated naïveté of blind religious faith (not yet gone from the scene, of course, even today), and the developing faith in science as painting a truer picture of what life is and where it comes from; and also as providing the technological means for a better life in this world. The year 1693 seems like one of the watersheds in that transition, and also in the growing awareness of the necessity for such liberties as freedom of the press.

The Salem witch trials in the Massachusetts Bay Colony, which had occupied most of 1692—the year in which Arthur Miller's play *The Crucible* (1953) takes place—finally came to an end. Miller's play uses the witch hunts as a metaphor for the injustices and demonizing fear tactics of the McCarthy era of the early 1950s, when Communists and suspected Communists and sympathizers were dealt with ruthlessly.

Governor Sir William Phipps (1651–1695) countermanded the January 3 order of Judge William Stoughton (1631–1701), the colony's lieutenant governor, to execute the remaining accused, most of whom were consequently released from jail. In May, Phipps finally pardoned all those who were still incarcerated.

The end of the trials, which had riveted the colony and kept it in a state of dread, was heralded by the courage of two highly respected clergyman, towering figures in the colony's history. On October 8, 1692, possibly heeding the request of clergyman Cotton Mather (1663–1728), Phipps had finally forbidden the use of so-called spectral evidence at the trials. This sort of specious, suspect evidence had also been denounced by Increase Mather (1639–1723), father of Cotton Mather and president of Harvard College. Although he had written in defense of the trials, he famously wrote, "It were better that Ten Suspected Witches should escape, than that One Innocent Person should be condemned." Before the trials were over, some twenty people had been brutally done to death—and even after them, four died in prison—based on the ludicrous belief in witchcraft and its power. Perhaps as many as two hundred people had been accused. On April 5, the church of Plymouth had set aside a day of Thanksgiving, in gratitude that "the Government over us is yet in the hands of saints."

The year 1693 saw terrible natural and man-made disasters. Earthquakes in the Mediterranean caused as many as 93,000 deaths in Naples and 60,000 in Sicily. France suffered from a famine that lasted well into 1694, and two million people died.

The second of the disastrous wars waged by Louis XIV, the War of the League of Augsburg, also known as the Nine Years' War (1688–1697), among its other appellations, was raging. The League of Augsburg was an alliance of German states, Sweden, and Spain that fought against France and a European coalition. There were battles as far afield as India, the Caribbean, and North America. On May 22, in yet another horror of that tragic conflict, the French destroyed the city of Heidelberg and laid waste the Rhineland. The Duke of Luxembourg, an ally of Louis XIV, gained a decisive victory over his enemies at Neerwinden on June 29. In August, however, Louis failed to take the fortress city of Liège and retired from the battlefield for good, although, of course, his generals continued to wage war even while, in December, he began the drawn-out process of negotiating peace. In Pennsylvania, William Penn (1644–1718) published *The Present and Future Peace of Europe*. No irony was intended by the title: Penn proposed a European federation as the solution to the continent's problems.

In the world of education, the College of William and Mary was founded on February 6 by Virginia Anglicans. It was the second college founded in the New World ; Harvard was the first. The English philosopher John Locke (1632–1704) published *Some Thoughts Concerning Education*, containing his innovative ideas on teaching upper-class boys to be moral human beings.

And in New York City, the printer William Bradford (1663–1752), having arrived from Philadelphia, began publishing the first books in the colony of New York. As New York's official printer, he also printed paper money. In 1692, he had been involved in a notorious civil case in Philadelphia. Bradford had published a pamphlet by George Keith (1638–1716), which contained remarks that the Quaker leaders found highly objectionable. Keith, a Scottish missionary who eventually became an Anglican priest, thought the Quakers had gone too far in their rejection of orthodox church doctrines. The case resulted in a hung jury, but was an important landmark in instituting freedom of the press. In 1693, still in Philadelphia, Keith published the first antislavery pamphlet, *An Exortation [sic] and Caution to Friends [Quakers] Concerning buying or keeping of Negroes*.

In the world of technology and science, Dutch mathematician, physicist, and horologist Christiaan Huygens (1629–1695) announced the theory of the conservation of mechanical energy. He had invented the pendulum clock in 1657, and began designing his new "perfect marine balance" clock in 1693; it would remain unperfected at his death. In England, Cambridge professor John Woodward (1665–1728) published a paper to prove that fossils were the actual remains of formerly living creatures. Isaac Newton (1643–1727) suffered a nervous breakdown. He had been embroiled in a controversy over whether he or Gottfried Wilhelm Leibniz (1646–1716) had invented calculus, and had ended an intense, possibly romantic relationship with the Swiss mathematician and scientist Nicolas Fatio de Duillier (1664–1753), who had supported him in the quarrel. The pressure of all this was too much, but fortunately, he recovered quickly.

In the theater, William Congreve's *The Old Bachelor* and *The Double Dealer* were produced. The Molièresque satirical comedy *Les Bourgeoises à la mode* (The Fashionable Middle-Class Ladies), by the aristocrat Florent Carton Dancourt (1661–1725), was produced in Paris with great success. Dancourt wrote sixty plays and was also a noted actor, acclaimed for his performance as Alceste in Molière's *The Misanthrope*. Eventually, he gave up life in the theater and retired to his chateau. His plays have a reputation for witty dialogue and realistic characterizations, and are excellent research material for the manners, etiquette, social attitudes, and deportment of the era.

John Dryden published a book of miscellaneous poems, and *A Discourse Concerning the Origin and Progress of the State*. John Evelyn published his book on horticulture, *The Compleat Gardener*. And Cotton Mather published *Wonders of the Invisible World*, defending the belief in witchcraft, despite all the horrors of Salem. On May 25, the great French writer, author of the brilliant psychological historical novel *La princesse de Clèves* (1678), Madame de La Fayette (b. 1634), died at her home in Paris.

On May 1, the first postal service between Boston and New York was established.

On August 4, the monk Dom Perignon invented champagne.

What to Wear for Rehearsal

Men should wear long coats—a raincoat or light winter car coat perhaps—and vests, and women should wear long dresses. If possible, use the footwear provided with your costume, because its high heels require much practice. If this is unavailable, high-heeled boots or shoes should be worn. Graceful, almost balletic movements of the limbs are also natural among the aristocratic classes in this period. Coats should be used for rehearsal, because the costume coats condition how you move and gesture, and you need to get a feeling for the movement as early as possible. When these movements become habit, they create an incomparable atmosphere and flavor the proceedings, but they must not be used too extravagantly, except for extravagant characters: such movement must be natural and not pretentious. Nor should the gestures or other movements draw attention, except where they occur in elaborate ceremonies during which the execution of the movements is meant to be noticed. Hats should usually be worn, for entrances—fedoras, for instance, but not winter hats with earflaps.

CHAPTER TWELVE

The Eighteenth Century: The French Revolution; the Napoleonic Era; the Dawn of the Romantic Age

Some important dates:

1714–1820 Reigns of George I–George IV: the Georgian and Regency eras.

1775–1781 The American Revolution, also called the War of Independence.

1783 Treaty of Paris affirmed the independence of the United States.

1787–1789 Promulgation of the Constitution of the United States.

1789–1795 French Revolution and counterrevolutionary insurrection; overthrow of the Bourbon monarchy; Declaration of the Rights of Man; African slaves freed in French colonies and given full citizenship; Jews emancipated and given full French citizenship.

1795–1804 Five-man Directoire (Directory), followed by Consulate, a triumvirate with Napoleon as First Consul.

1804–1815 French Empire under Napoleon I, and Napoleonic Wars ending in Napoleon's defeat at the battle of Waterloo.

1815 In France, Restoration of the Bourbon Monarchy, overthrown in the Revolution of 1830; Louis-Philippe becomes king of France.

France

In any play or film set in eighteenth- or early nineteenth-century Europe, where France was the most prominent united country on the continent, the inner road map of what the world was like and the mind-set of the characters would have included the following general information.

Most of the population of France was rural. Many people lived in remote, virtually self-governing hamlets with their own customs, laws, and dialects, as they had for centuries. They barely knew of the centralized monarchy that considered them its subjects. And they were largely isolated even from their neighbors in the next valleys. Some were ministered to by French-speaking priests, and there was a local, still feudal aristocracy. Banditry and marauding thieves were rife. The Revolution would begin to do away with all those conditions. People would start to think of themselves as French nationals, but the process would take another century, and the distinction between Paris and the Provinces prevails even today.

The principal French money unit was the livre (pound), in existence since the days of Charlemagne, who named it for the worth of a pound of silver. There was no one-livre coin, but there was the écu (shield), worth six livres. And there were coins worth one-half, one-fourth, and one-eighth of an écu. These were called "sols" (suns), and were worth sixty, thirty, and fifteen sols, respectively. The largest minted coin was the louis d'or (gold louis), worth twenty-four livres. There were also copper coins, valued at one and two sols, and copper deniers, minted in values of six and three deniers. By the time the livre was replaced by the franc, in 1795, during the Revolution, it was worth approximately four dollars in today's currency.

The wildly unequal distribution of wealth was one of the primary causes of the French Revolution. Vast sums were involved in royal expenditures, while working people and craftsmen earned comparatively little. The merchant class did well, but naturally wanted to do better. The semi-feudal system prevailing in the countryside, with peasants paying heavy rents to the lords who owned the estates, was burdensome in the extreme, and was increasingly perceived as unjust. In 1776 alone, Queen Marie Antoinette (1755–1793) spent 500,000 livres ($2,000,000 by today's standards) on just her clothing (over the years it filled three large rooms at Versailles), when her budgetary allowance was only 150,000 ($600,000). Over the course of sixteen years, she paid Léonard (1751–1820), her hairdresser, 300,000 livres ($1,200,000) for his services. When you know what these very large sums amount to in today's currency, and that other members of the royal family were similarly extravagant, while people were starving, you have an even more outraged sense of what was going on. Almost needless to say, none of these people paid taxes. No wonder the queen was nicknamed "Madame Deficit."

Before Marie Antoinette had even arrived from her native Austria to marry the Dauphin, the treasury had already been virtually depleted because of the disastrous wars fought during the reign of King Louis XV (1710–1774). In 1759, his Controller-General had been a man named Etienne de Silhouette (1709–1767). His attempts to balance the budget and ease the national debt through a policy of austerity were highly unpopular with the aristocracy, whose pensions and subventions he reduced. When Silhouette attempted to limit the budget of the royal household, the furious monarch showed him the door. So mocked and ridiculed was he in a decade when outline portraits done by hired artists were the rage at society parties, that it was said he had decorated his house with such drawings to avoid the expense of buying paintings. The word "silhouette" became part of the language. And the king's most famous saying echoes down through the ages: "After me, the deluge!"

Under Louis' shy, inept grandson and successor, Louis XVI (1754–1793), the treasury was again nearly bankrupt: the money had gone to help finance the American War of Independence, and to pay for the extravagant life at Versailles. Louis XVI, who loved eating more than anything else, reigned with his queen in obtuse, unconcerned, egotistical, oblivious splendor until the French Revolution overthrew the monarchy. The deluge had indeed arrived. And the royal family had very little idea why.

On the evening of his wedding to Marie Antoinette, Louis XVI, who loved lamb chops and called lambs "walking cutlets," stuffed himself to the point of sickness, despite his grandfather's warnings to restrain himself. After his trial for treason during the Revolution, when the death verdict was announced, the distraught monarch immediately upon returning to prison devoured an enormous meal of chicken, eggs, and veal cutlets, and drank two glasses of wine and a glass of sherry.

The use of such accessories as snuffboxes and fans is of particular importance in this period, when dressing well and criticizing or even ridiculing the dress of others was almost an affectation among the upper classes. Louis-Antoine, Marquis de Carracioli (1719–1803) writes a brief and revealing analysis in the first chapter of *Le livre de quatre couleurs* (The Book of Four Colors, 1757), "On the Different Ways of Using the Fan," that is replete with irony, ridicule, and a touch of horrid misogyny, all of which are typical of the period:

> [Fans] are charming, useful, interesting; they fulfill the function of zephyrs; they preserve modesty, allowing everything one might wish to show; they are a mask to those who do not wish to make themselves

known; they serve to avoid the sun's rays, which, without regard, burn the skin of a princess as well as that of a peasant; they preserve one's eyes in front of a fire; they hide ugly teeth, malign smiles, humorous grimaces; they prevent others from hearing the little secrets of refined malicious gossip; they express caprices, and sometimes they even speak . . .

After the overthrow of the Bourbons, the gains of the revolution were lost when Napoleon Bonaparte (1769–1821) declared himself emperor. Life at court resumed its frivolous course.

The emperor could be horrid to individuals he took a dislike to, as he did to Madame Regnault de Saint-Jean d'Angely (1775–1857). At a ball one evening, when she was twenty-eight, she was dressed charmingly in (as Laure Junot, Duchesse d'Abrantès [1784–1838] tells us in her memoirs), "a petticoat of white crape trimmed with alternate tufts of pink and white roses; and not a headdress worn that night had so beautiful an effect as the lovely roses which Madame Regnault had embedded in the soft velvet of her glossy black hair." As "a bitter smile played upon his lips," Napoleon, examining her, said in his "clear and sonorous, though solemn, bass voice," "Do you know, Madame Regnault, that you are ageing terribly?" The other court ladies were delighted, in their jealousy, because the emperor whose attentions they craved had insulted her. But she replied, "What your Majesty has done me the honor to observe might have been painful to hear had I been old enough to be frightened by it." In spite of their envy, a "low murmur of approbation" ran round the assemblage.

In a letter to her father on 5–6 May, 1802, the celebrated diarist and novelist Frances Burney, Madame d'Arblay (1752–1840), paints a vivid portrait of the emperor at a review of troops to which she and her husband had tickets; she stood very close to Napoleon as he passed by:

[His face] is of a deeply impressive cast, pale even to sallowness, while not only in the Eye, but in every feature, Care, Thought, Melancholy, and Meditation are strongly marked, with so much of character, nay, Genius, and so penetrating a seriousness—or rather sadness, as powerfully to sink into an observer's mind . . .

What an act Napoleon must have been putting on! If he had not been a player on the world scene, he would no doubt have made a great actor on the stage, like his favorite tragedian, François-Joseph Talma (1763–1826), usually known by his last name.

At the dawn of the romantic movement in the arts, the striking, handsome actor with the beautiful voice was renowned for his passionate playing of the protagonists in classical tragedies as suffering, doomed heroes, struggling alone against inexorable fate. They were compared to Napoleon himself. Talma's friend, Jacques-Louis David (1748–1825), painted an idealized portrait of the dashing general crossing the rugged Alps in 1800. It depicts the future emperor as the epitome of the romantic hero, his red cloak swirling in the wind, reining in his rearing horse, urging the army forward with grim determination. Such an image masks his brutality, and his unspeakable crimes against humanity, but for his deluded, chauvinistic followers, the "Little Corporal" could do no wrong: Was he not exporting the egalitarian ideals of the French Revolution, and overthrowing tyranny everywhere? It is estimated that more than 6,500,000 people died in the wars he waged.

The term "romantic hero" could be more suitably applied to three of the great, innovative artists of the movement, who expressed in their art and in their lives the humanitarian ideals of liberty, equality, and fraternity, and the will to fight against the forces of evil and despair: the composer, Ludwig van Beethoven (1770–1827); and the writers George Gordon, Lord Byron (1788–1824), and Victor Hugo (1802–1885).

The music of the temperamental, passionate, troubled composer, whose adult-onset deafness did not prevent him from continuing to compose masterpieces, is the quintessence of romanticism. The style of his *Third Symphony in E flat*, called the "Eroica" (composed in 1804), considered transitional by many musicologists, is often said to enclose romantic content within classical forms. Beethoven had at first admired Napoleon as the embodiment of Revolutionary ideals, when he was First Consul of the French Republic, and the symphony was meant as a tribute. Horrified and outraged when Napoleon made himself emperor, the composer thrust a knife through the name "Bonaparte" on the title page, ripping it apart.

The bisexual English poet Lord Byron was famous for his handsome looks, his wit, his extravagance, and his tempestuous love affairs. But, forsaking the comforts of a sybaritic life, he fought for his ideals on the battlefield in 1823, in the cause of Greek independence from the Ottomans.

High-minded and prolific, the French novelist, poet, and playwright Victor Hugo practically invented romanticism in the theater: He rejected the rigidity of classical play construction, with its idea of the "unities" of time, place, and action—every play must happen within the course of one day, in one place, and tell one story—replacing it with a looser and freer form of storytelling. In the French legislature, he fought for human rights, and in 1851, when the first Napoleon's nephew declared himself Emperor Napoleon III, Hugo's political and moral idealism led him and his family into self-imposed exile. Hugo's personal life was full of the most terrible suffering, over his daughter Adele's mental illness, and the deaths of his sons, Charles and François-Victor.

In America, as we know, things were in ferment, and generally a bit more relaxed than Europe both in manners and in dress. Courtesy and politesse were by no means absent. As a result of an initial shortage of women settlers in Virginia—one man to every ten women—men often treated those who made the dangerous voyage with special respect, politeness, and consideration. At the same time, women were largely confined to roles assigned to them because of gender, just as they were in New England, where the ratio of women to men was more equal.

Some things have not changed: Of fashion in one great metropolis, the French émigré J. Hector St. John de Crèvecoeur (1735–1813) writes in *Letters from an American Farmer* (1782), "If there is a town on the American continent where English luxury displayed its follies it is in New York...In the dress of the women you will see the most brilliant silks, gauzes, hats and borrowed hair."

Historical Developments: 1793, A Sample Year

The French Revolution was in full swing. In the banner year 1793, after his death was overwhelmingly voted by the National Assembly, Louis XVI was executed on January 21 in the spacious Place de la République, formerly the Place Louis XV, now the Place de la Concorde. The site of the main guillotine of Paris that saw so many executions is just near the foot of the famous Avenue des Champs-Elysées. The king had sworn to be a constitutional monarch, and had betrayed his trust. It was a raw, blustery morning, and the roll of the drums drowned out his last words.

Two days later, Poland was torn apart and partitioned by Prussia and Russia for the second time.

France was in ferment, beset by counterrevolutionary conspiracies from within and the threat of invasions from across its borders. The queen's Austrian family was horrified and appalled by the events in France, and would gladly have invaded the country to restore the gilded Bourbon monarchy to its full reactionary splendor. On February 1, the

Republic declared war on its enemies, Great Britain, Holland (the United Provinces), and Spain, and annexed what is now Belgium and was then the Austrian Netherlands. Britain now formed the first of several coalitions against France, this one with Austria, Prussia, Spain, the Netherlands, and Sardinia. France was in a state of siege and, in a panic, set up the Committee of Public Safety on April 6, with "The Incorruptible" Maximilien de Robespierre (1758–1794), he of weak eyesight and sea-green glasses, and the centrist Georges Danton (1759–1794) at its head. The radical Jean-Paul Marat (1743–1793) was acquitted at his trial on April 24, and immediately agitated for the overthrow of the ruling party, the Girondins, who had brought him to court in the first place. He wanted a complete radicalization of the Revolution in the direction of dictatorial socialism, but he was assassinated in his bath on July 13 by Charlotte Corday (1768–1793), who was tried and executed four days afterward.

That same month of July then saw the overthrow of the centrist bourgeois Girondins by the fear-stricken and dictatorial Committee of Public Safety, and the beginning of the mass guillotining of its opponents. Thus began the Terror, with its public trials and parades of victims through the streets of Paris to the guillotine that would forever be the symbol of the Revolution. Its gains in human rights would be largely forgotten by many, and the cataclysmic year of 1793 would be remembered as the apogee of public sadism and mob rule, with a people drunk on blood and thirsting for vengeance, dragging justice in its wake and trampling it underfoot—a cliché with much in it that is false and some that is true. But the Revolution's most revolutionary act was the Declaration of the Rights of Man, adopted by the French National Assembly on August 26, 1789, and never forgotten. More even than the gains of the American Revolution, it changed people's thinking radically and completely.

By August 28, the allies were massing on the French border, and had already occupied parts of Alsace. Less than two months later, on October 16, the queen, Marie Antoinette, having been found guilty of treasonable correspondence with her Austrian family, was guillotined. After being besieged by the Revolutionary army, France's second largest city, Lyons, in the hands of the counterrevolutionary forces, fell to the Republicans, and mass executions began there. In December, more counterrevolution broke out in the Vendée, the southwest region, and troops had to be sent in by the Paris government. Napoleon would soon defeat the British, who had invaded at Toulon on the Mediterranean, making him a hero of the Republic that he would later undermine. On December 23, the insurrection in the Vendée by the Chouans, as they were called, was quelled, after nearly 500,000 people had been killed in bloody civil reprisals. But mass executions in other areas continued.

In November, despite the political turmoil, the French government had passed progressive laws, abolishing Christianity as the state religion, but replacing it altogether on the other hand with a tyrannical "cult of reason" that citizens were more or less obliged to subscribe to. They made education compulsory for all children beginning at the age of six. And to curb the growing inflation, they passed a law fixing wages and decreeing maximum prices for such goods as bread. Paper money had severely fallen in value, and disaster loomed. But the celebrated "loi du maximum," much touted by Robespierre, would prove in its turn to be a catastrophe, and to have a most deleterious effect on the economy. It would be the ultimate cause of Robespierre's downfall the following year, which also saw the end of the Terror.

Such was Europe in 1793, while half a world away, in the fledgling United States, on February 25, newly reelected first President George Washington (1732–1799) convened the first cabinet meeting ever. There were only four cabinet posts: the Secretary of the Treasury, the Secretary of War, the Postmaster General, and the Attorney General. Later that year, despite the opposition of such figures as Alexander Hamilton (1755/1757?–1804), who supported the British coalition, and Thomas Jefferson (1743–1826), who favored the French, Washington issued a Proclamation of Neutrality, on April 25. It would prove to be problematic.

On February 12, the infamous Fugitive Slave Act had been passed by Congress. It was now illegal to help runaway slaves in any way; they were to be returned to their masters when caught. And they would suffer horribly at the hands of the vindictive, sadistic overseers when they arrived back at the plantations from which they had escaped. Meanwhile, émigrés from France arrived in droves in England and America, escaping to freedom in exile.

The Theater

Our view of rehearsal procedure in the eighteenth century is not much clearer than that of practices in preceding eras, although we know there was usually morning rehearsal. A "call man" was hired by the management of such theaters as the Drury Lane in London to go around to the actors' lodgings and give them their rehearsal and performance calls for that day or the next. Each actor memorized his or her part, along with the standardized gestures that accompanied certain emotions, if such gesticulation was actually used; we don't really know that either.

We do, however, have a glimpse into the methods of actor-manager David Garrick at the Drury Lane, and we are clearly at the dawn of modern rehearsal technique. He would begin the rehearsal period by reading the play to the assembled acting company, a practice that was the norm even in the late nineteenth century, when, for example, W. S. Gilbert would read the libretto of the new Gilbert and Sullivan piece aloud to the actors at the first rehearsal. Garrick would then discuss the play, and talk about each of the characters. When he put the play on its feet, he would play all the characters, demonstrating to the actors exactly what he wished them to do. They were then expected to imitate him more or less exactly. So there was little freedom for an actor to interpret the part on his or her own, except for stars of Garrick's stature, such as Mrs. Sarah Siddons. Garrick and the company would run through the play, perhaps several times, and that was that: it was considered ready for performance.

We learn something about the haste with which plays were mounted in Garrick's two-act farce *A Peep Behind the Curtain; or, The New Rehearsal* (1767), which revolves around a dress rehearsal for the first act of a burletta based on the legend of Orpheus. A burletta, from the Italian, meaning "little joke," is a late eighteenth- and early nineteenth-century English three-act farce with at least five songs, to get around the licensing laws that allowed spoken plays to be performed only at certain patent theaters, which were playhouses licensed by royal fiat to particular managers. The plot of this burletta, act 1 of which is performed in act 2 of the farce, inevitably reminds one of the story of Offenbach's *Orphée aux enfers*, but the French librettists and composer can have had no acquaintance with Garrick's long-forgotten parody of the myth. I cannot resist quoting the words to the first verse of Orpheus's solo:

> Tho' she scolded all day, and all night did the same,
> Tho' she was too rampant, and I was too tame;
> Tho' shriller her notes than the ear-piercing fife,
> *I must and I will go to Hell for my wife.*

This is very Offenbachian indeed!

Full dress rehearsals were apparently quite unusual, and especially of only one act of a piece, as in this farce. Actors were expected to go on without having dealt with the technical details of scenery, special storm effects, or the actual furniture they would have to use. The following dialogue is revealing: The theater's Manager, Patent, who is the equivalent of a modern producer, and is also responsible for certain production elements and some of the staging, and Hopkins, the Prompter—the equivalent of a modern stage manager—are preparing for what we now call an invited dress:

> PATIENT: Make haste with your scenes, Saunders; so clear the stage, Mr. Hopkins, and let us go to business. Is the extraordinary Author of this very extraordinary performance come yet? [Saunders is the Carpenter: he was not only responsible for scene construction, but was also head of the running crew. Patent is telling him to set up the scenery for the rehearsal.]
>
> PROMPTER: Not yet, Sir, but we shall be soon ready for him—'Tis a very extraordinary thing, indeed, to rehearse only one act of a performance, and with dresses [costumes] and decorations [scenery], as if it were really before an Audience.
>
> PATIENT: It is a novelty, indeed, and a little expensive too, but we cou'd not withstand the solicitations that were made to us; we shan't often repeat the same experiment. [Patent means that the self-important, fatuous author of the burletta, Glib, has pressured the management so that his aristocratic patrons can have the novelty of seeing a rehearsal.]
>
> PROMPTER: I hope not, Sir,—'tis a very troublesome one, and the Performers murmur greatly at it.

A bit later on, we learn that another of the prompter's jobs was to handle complaints from actors, just as a modern stage manager does. And we learn that he had a say in casting, and that it was usually the playwright who "instructed" the actors in their roles. Referring to an actor who wants to play the first Lord and not the second, the Prompter says, "Well, well, if the author can make him speak English, I have no objection." And in act 2, we find the following interesting stage direction, which tells us how much authors were involved in what we now conceive of as directing. Of course, this is also supposed to be quite funny, but it still shows us the kind of thing that must have gone on during rehearsals:

> [*During the Burletta*, Glib, *the Author, goes out and comes in several times upon the Stage, and speaks occasionally to the performers, as his fancy prompts him, in order to enliven the action, and give a proper comic spirit to the performance.*]

Plays were usually done in contemporary dress. Even Shakespearean tragedies were performed without any attempt to create period costumes. Garrick, who had played Macbeth in 1747, mounted a new production in 1768. As the American theater historian Charles E. L. Wingate informs us in *Shakespeare's Heroes on the Stage* (Thomas Y. Crowell and Company, 1896), and as period engravings show, Garrick played the part in "the full court-dress of the time of George II—scarlet coat, gold-laced waistcoat, powdered wig and all." Even in 1768, when it was suggested to him that he might want to wear Highland dress for the part, he was adamantly opposed to the idea. Besides, he was terrified: "You forget that the Pretender [Bonnie Prince Charlie (1720–1788), who had led the 1745 Highland uprising] was here only thirty years ago, and egad! I should be pelted off the stage with orange-peel."

His performance as Macbeth received high praise, including that from Thomas Davies. In his second book, published in 1784, *Dramatic Miscellanies: Consisting of Critical Observations of Several Plays of Shakespeare with a Review of His Principal Characters and Those of Various Eminent Writers as Represented by Mr. Garrick* (and the title continues!), Davies describes Garrick and Hannah Pritchard (1711–1768), a leading lady in his company for twenty years (this was her last role, played shortly before her death), in act 2, scene 2, just after the murder of Duncan:

> Garrick's distraction of mind and agonizing horror were finely contrasted by Pritchard's seeming apathy, tranquility, and confidence. The beginning of the scene after the murder was conducted in terrifying whispers. Their looks and actions supplied the place of words. You heard of what they spoke, but you learned more from the agitation of mind displayed in their action and deportment. The poet here gives an outline of the consummate actor: "I have done the deed!" "Didst thou not hear a noise?" "When?" "Did you not speak?" The dark coloring given by the actor to these abrupt speeches makes the scene awful and tremendous to the auditors. The wonderful expression of heartfelt horror which Garrick felt when he showed his bloody hands, can only be conceived and described by those who saw him.

In his *Memoirs of the Life of David Garrick, Esq.*, Davies has this to say of Garrick's acting in general:

> Mr. Garrick's easy and familiar, yet forcible style in speaking and acting, at first threw the critics into some hesitation concerning the

novelty as well as propriety of his manner. They had been long
accustomed to the elevation of the voice, with a sudden mechanical
depression of its tones, calculated to excite admiration and to entrap
applause. To the just modulation of the words, and concurring
expression of the features from the genuine workings of nature, they
had been strangers, at least for some time. . . .

Mr. Garrick shone forth like a theatrical Newton; he threw new
light on elocution and action; he banished ranting, bombast, and
grimace; and restored nature, ease, simplicity, and genuine humor.

She Stoops to Conquer

The Anglo-Irish author Oliver Goldsmith's (1730?–1774) wry five-act
comedy of manners was first produced in 1773, and was an immediate
success. It sends up social and class attitudes, and is at the same time
precursive of the romantic era's sensitivity and sentimentality in matters
of love.

Squire Hardcastle and his wife, Lady Hardcastle, await the arrival of
Mr. Marlowe, a prospective fiancé for their daughter Kate. Although an
aristocrat, Marlowe is uncomfortable and shy around upper-class
women, but forward and at ease around lower-class women. Kate realizes
immediately that in order to win him, she will have to pose as lower
class, so she pretends to be a barmaid, and thus stoops to conquer. There
are droll misunderstandings, and plot complications involving subplots
as well as the main thread, but in the end Kate succeeds in her plan.

In this scene from act 1, we have a real glimpse into mid-eighteenth-
century rural English life, in its drollest aspects. This scene shows,
among other things, that the classes in the countryside were closer
together than is generally thought nowadays; but it also portrays clearly
the unrefined rusticity and ignorance of the peasant classes, however
astute and intelligent they may have been. Their master is no less rustic
than they, and no less provincial, but he knows etiquette, or thinks he
does. Hardcastle has told us at the opening of the play that he likes
everything that is old: old wine, old friends, old books—but does he
read them, or does he simply like to look at their beautiful bindings?

Enter HARDCASTLE *followed by three or four awkward Servants.*

HARDCASTLE. Well, I hope you are perfect in the table exercise I have
been teaching you these three days. You all know your posts and

your places, and can show that you have been used to good company, without ever stirring from home.

OMNES. [Latin for ALL]. Ay, ay.

HARDCASTLE. When company comes you are not to pop out and stare, and then run in again, like frightened rabbits in a warren.

OMNES. No, no.

HARDCASTLE. You, Diggory, whom I have taken from the barn, are to make a show at the side-table; and you, Roger, whom I have advanced from the plough, are to place yourself behind my chair. But you're not to stand so, with your hands in your pockets. Take your hands from your pockets, Roger; and from your head, you blockhead you. See how Diggory carries his hands. They're a little too stiff, indeed, but that's no great matter.

DIGGORY. Ay, mind how I hold them. I learned to hold my hands this way when I was upon drill for the militia. And so being upon drill . . .

HARDCASTLE. You must not be so talkative, Diggory. You must be all attention to the guests. You must hear us talk, and not think of talking; you must see us drink, and not think of drinking; you must see us eat, and not think of eating.

DIGGORY. By the laws, your worship, that's perfectly unpossible. Whenever Diggory sees yeating going forward, ecod, he's always wishing for a mouthful himself.

HARDCASTLE. Blockhead! Is not a belly-full in the kitchen as good as a belly-full in the parlor? Stay your stomach with that reflection.

DIGGORY. Ecod, I thank your worship, I'll make a shift to stay my stomach with a slice of cold beef in the pantry.

HARDCASTLE. Diggory, you are too talkative.—Then, if I happen to say a good thing, or tell a good story at table, you must not all burst out a-laughing, as if you made part of the company.

DIGGORY. Then ecod your worship must not tell the story of Ould Grouse in the gun-room: I can't help laughing at that—he! he! he!—for the soul of me. We have laughed at that these twenty years—ha! ha! ha!

HARDCASTLE. Ha! ha! ha! The story is a good one. Well, honest Diggory, you may laugh at that—but still remember to be attentive. Suppose one of the company should call for a glass of wine, how will you behave? A glass of wine, sir, if you please (*to* DIGGORY).— Eh, why don't you move?

DIGGORY. Ecod, your worship, I never have courage till I see the eatables and drinkables brought upo' the table, and then I'm as bauld as a lion.

HARDCASTLE. What, will nobody move?

FIRST SERVANT. I'm not to leave this place.

SECOND SERVANT. I'm sure it's no place of mine.

THIRD SERVANT. Nor mine, for sartain.

DIGGORY. Wauns, and I'm sure it canna be mine.

HARDCASTLE. You numskulls! And so while, like your betters, you are quarrelling for places, the guests must be starved. O you dunces! I find I must begin all over again...But don't I hear a coach drive into the yard? To your posts, you blockheads. I'll go in the mean time and give my old friend's son a hearty reception at the gate. [*Exit* HARDCASTLE.]

As with *The Way of the World*, you will notice how contemporary the language sounds, and yet how very much in period it is, with expressions and grammatical constructions that we no longer use. It was written nearly three quarters of a century after Congreve's brilliant comedy, so its language is already closer to our own, of course.

The eighteenth century not only saw class prejudice coming to the fore, but the rise of nationalism and nationalistic prejudices as well, precursive of nineteenth- and twentieth-century attitudes, just as Elizabethan attitudes had been forerunners of eighteenth-century prejudices. In fact, nationalistic prejudices against "foreigners" and their ways seem to be the order of the day, on all sides. The author who would be known for that Gothic horror classic *The Castle of Otranto* (1764), Horace Walpole (1717–1797), visited Paris in 1739. He wrote, "The French love show, but there is a meanness through it all. At the house...the room was hung with crimson damask and gold, and the windows were mended in ten or dozen places with paper." From this specific place, the acerbic, bitterly prejudiced Walpole felt entitled to generalize about the French and French taste. And in 1787, Arthur Young (1741–1820), writing of his grand tour in 1792 in *Travels in France*, simply found Paris "vastly inferior to London." In other words, quite simply, he preferred his home, which is understandable, but why generalize about the cities as he did?

What to Wear for Rehearsal

Upper- and middle-class men wore knee britches, lace jabots, and long coats. Aristocratic women wore long gowns and, sometimes, bustles. Working-class men, sailors, and carpenters wore long or knee-length, broad trousers. Carpenters and blacksmiths wore aprons when working, and the actor would do well to bring an ordinary kitchen apron to rehearsal to simulate the real one. For rehearsal, women should have a floor-length skirt, and men should wear a raincoat or other appropriate long coat, a vest, and a scarf tied around the neck. If you have knickerbockers, wear them as well as the knee-length socks that go with them. Men should wear hats, which they usually did when entering from outdoors. The hats were often removed and held under the arm thereafter, when they were not handed to a servant. Women often wore hats outdoors, and married women wore lace caps indoors. Use something to suggest them for rehearsal. Ordinary walking shoes, loafers, or shoes with high heels should be used by both men and women.

The same advice applies to the romantic era as to the immediately preceding eras, except that men should wear long trousers instead of knickerbockers. Ordinary footwear, including boots, should be used.

CHAPTER THIRTEEN

The Later Nineteenth Century: Victorian England and Beyond

Some important dates:

1837 Victoria (1819–1901) becomes Queen of England, marking the start of the Victorian era.

1848 Mass European uprisings against the established order; Louis-Philippe overthrown and the Second Republic established in France; mass emigration to America, especially from Germany, still a collection of individual states, dukedoms, and kingdoms, the largest being Prussia and Bavaria.

1851 As the result of a coup d'état, Napoleon I's nephew, who had been President of the Republic, becomes Emperor Napoleon III (1808–1873).

1861 Unification of Germany under Prussian hegemony.

1860–1865 American Civil War.

1865 End of slavery in the United States; assassination of President Abraham Lincoln (1809–1865).

1866 Italy, freed of Austrian occupation, is unified under the constitutional monarchy of Victor-Emmanuel II (1820–1878).

1870–1871 Franco-Prussian War, ending in France's defeat, the brutal suppression of the Communard Uprising in Paris, and the establishment of the French Third Republic.

Victorian Style

In Victorian England, the convoluted writing style considered elegant was sometimes unwieldy. The overdone, serious prose of the era coexisted with its heaviness in dress and with cluttered, stuffy, overheated interiors, as if the entire period had conspired to make itself one ponderous behemoth lumbering toward modern times. But John Ruskin's (1819–1900) writing is unique: He had true elegance. No other writer of the period in English has his way with words or his lyricism. Yet nobody writing today would ever write in the Aesthetic style he chose. Here is the opening of his beautiful book *The Stones of Venice*, published in 1853 and illustrated with his own drawings and watercolors. The quite obvious imperialistic attitude, and the ethnocentric assumption of superiority it represents, embodies the reality of the world political situation, when the power of the British Empire was at its height. You will notice that Asia and Africa count for nothing, as if they had never had the virtues and vices of great empires and cultures, nor ventured upon the seas. The opposite is the case, of course, as the history of Ethiopia alone shows, with its vast commercial seagoing enterprises. But this attitude underlies the thinking of the era, and is part of the mental construct of characters in its theater, even if the attitude remains unspoken.

Note the apt use of the now all but gone subjunctive in the last sentence: "if it forget their example":

> Since first the dominion of men was asserted over the ocean, three thrones, of mark beyond all others, have been set upon its sands: the thrones of Tyre, Venice, and England. Of the First of these great powers, only the memory remains; of the Second the ruin; the Third, which inherits their greatness, if it forget their example, may be led through prouder eminence to less pitied destruction.

Victorian dress, while it was heavy and meant to conceal the human form, and to provide warmth, was in the process of becoming lighter. Lillie Langtry (1853–1929), the actress of whom Oscar Wilde was enamored, describes his appearance in her memoirs; this excerpt is reprinted in E. H. Mikhail's *Oscar Wilde: Interviews and Recollections* (Harper & Row, 1979):

> His customary apparel consisted of light-colored trousers, a black frock coat, only the lower button fastened, a brightly flowered waistcoat blossoming underneath, and a white silk cravat, held together by an old intaglio amethyst set as a pin.
>
> ...He was ridiculed and he was imitated. When he wore a daisy in his buttonhole, thousands of young men did likewise. When he proclaimed the sunflower "adorable," it was to be found adorning every drawing-room...

Even before he became one of the greatest playwrights of the era, Wilde was a noted speaker, and a noted society wit and raconteur, known for his mellifluous voice. Unfortunately, we have no recordings, but we do have Helen Potter's account of Wilde in her *Impersonations* (Edgar S. Werner, 1891). Potter toured the United States in the 1880s doing impersonations (in drag, when called for) of such famous personalities and actors as Tommaso Salvini, Oscar Wilde, Edwin Booth, and Susan B. Anthony. She impersonated Wilde after seeing him give his lecture on aesthetics during a tour of the US, where he was sent by Richard D'Oyly Carte to publicize Gilbert and Sullivan's *Patience* (1881), a satire of the aesthetic movement. In Appendix B of Richard Ellmann's splendid biography *Oscar Wilde* (Alfred A. Knopf, 1988) you will find a lecture of Wilde's, reprinted from *Impersonations*.

Potter gives the reader an exact indication of how Wilde sounded, and of his delivery, with the pauses he took, and with information on both his pronunciation and his intonation patterns. It is most instructive reading. The symbols that indicate tone and intonation are as follows:

1. A single vertical line [|] represents a brief pause after a word.

2. A double vertical line [‖] represents a long rhetorical pause.

3. A backward slash [\ ] means that the following syllable is spoken on a falling tone, from high to low.

4. A forward slash [/] means that the following syllable is spoken on a rising tone, from low to high.

5. The sign [°] represents a high note on the syllable that follows it.

6. The sign [(o)] represents a low note on the syllable that follows it.

7. A double hyphen [- -] means that the following words are delivered in a monotone.

You will note, even in this brief excerpt, that Wilde speaks in a very measured, deliberate, musical way:

> - - We | in our Renaissance | are seeking to create a sovereignty | that shall still /be \ (o) England's | when her yellow leopards | are weary of /wars [Wilde pronounced it "waːz"], | - - and the rose | on her shield | is crimsoned °no /(o)more [Wilde pronounced it "mow ah"] | | with the blood | of /(o)bat °tle.

Oscar Wilde, born and bred in Dublin, learned to speak with an upper-class English accent while at Oxford. The word "Renaissance" is pronounced "ri NAY səns," or "sa:Ns"; the latter pronunciation was prevalent in the Victorian era, when French phrases were used in conversation as a matter of course. In General American it is pronounced "REN i sa:ns."

The pronunciation of the word "wars" is much the same as it was in General American in the Victorian era, except that the final "r" was pronounced by American speakers ("wa:r"), as one can hear on the recordings made by Woodrow Wilson, Theodore Roosevelt, William Howard Taft and William Jennings Bryan on In *Their Own Voices: The US Presidential Elections of 1908 and 1912* (Marston Records 52028-2 CD, 2000). The pronunciation is still heard in areas of the Middle West. It is interesting to note that although Wilson came from Virginia, Roosevelt from New York City, Taft from Ohio, and Bryan from southern Illinois, they all speak with the same learned upper-class accent, expected by the public of their political leaders. To speak with any other accent, or with poor diction, apparently did not convey a sense of paternalistic reassurance, and failed to instill confidence. Only in more recent times have regional and urban accents been deemed acceptable by the voting public and the audiences of nightly news broadcasts.

A Nineteenth-Century Realistic Drama: *A Doll's House* (1879)

The major theme of Norwegian realist Henrik Ibsen's (1828–1906) iconoclastic drama was considered subversive in its day: He dared to assert that women should assume the responsibility for their own lives: taking their freedom into their own hands, making clear to others their needs and desires, and bearing the consequences. The play's superobjective, its major overall theme, is that women have an inalienable right to absolute equality with men.

The throughline of the plot: Nora tries obliquely to get her husband to treat her as an equal marriage partner, not daring to state her case. The twists and turns of the plot reveal her husband to be the narrow-minded, selfish, egotistical prig she always really knew he was. She finally works up the courage to take action, and leaves him.

There is an important, compelling counter-throughline in the form of the general societal pressure to conform, and to fulfill the role society has decreed for one's gender, no matter what the adverse circumstances of a marriage might be. There are thus inevitable attempts by Nora to adjust to her situation, to be accommodating, and to submit to social pressure.

At the opening of the play, everything appears to be set in an ideal home. Nora merrily comes indoors after a cold afternoon of Christmas shopping. The house is gaily decorated for the season, and it seems cozy and warm. As befits the home of a wealthy banker, it is beautifully furnished and comfortable—Nora has seen to that. Domestic arrangements are her province. But not everything is as wonderful as it appears to be, and we learn gradually that Helmer, Nora's husband, is an insensitive male chauvinist who treats her like a doll in this doll's house that she has decorated. And so the story begins. It will soon become much more complicated, with the blackmailing scheme of Krogstad, who wants to keep his job at the bank and threatens to reveal that Nora forged Helmer's name to borrow money for their trip to Italy. Krogstad eventually gives up his blackmailing scheme, but as the characters' secrets are gradually revealed, so is the quagmire of social corruption.

Ibsen's themes become apparent as the play proceeds. Marriage can be a sham when both partners are not equal. And, despite the appearance of an equal division of labor, with Nora in charge of the home and Helmer in charge of earning money through his work, they are not equal partners. Nora is in a subservient, almost menial position, and she has never been given her intellectual due, because Helmer thinks women are emotional, childlike beings, intellectually inferior to men and indeed incapable of reasoning. In fact, he himself is an emotional, childlike man with a veneer of sophistication, and he seldom reasons very clearly. For the era in which the play was written, this was all novel. This drama exploded social conventions and shocked audiences.

The style of the play is realistic, but the dialogue is verbose, in typical nineteenth-century style. And there are touches of melodrama that seem inevitable. In performing Ibsen, you must use all the internal, psychological techniques of the Stanislavsky system, and you must deal with the stilted Victorian style in which most translations are written. The passionate nature of the themes about women's rights and equality will help to enliven your desires, actions, and objectives. The contrast between increasingly progressive Scandinavian sociocultural attitudes and those of regressive Victorian England is striking, despite the continued pressures of bourgeois conformism and sexual repression in Scandinavia.

Just seven years before the play was produced, Susan B. Anthony (1820–1906), the great champion of women's rights, and especially of the right to vote, was put on trial and convicted of the offence of voting in the 1872 election for Ulysses S. Grant. She was fined $100, which she refused to pay, but she was not imprisoned. It is unclear to me whether Helen Potter, who deeply admired Susan B. Anthony and writes as if she knew her personally, actually attended the trial in Canandaigua, New York, but she had certainly seen Anthony speak and knew her voice and manner, which she was able to recreate as one of her impersonations. Here is part of an impassioned speech given by Anthony in her own defense; Potter took it from the court transcripts:

[The judge says, "Has the prisoner anything to say why judgment should not be pronounced?"]

Miss A. [*rising.*] Yes, your honor, | I have (\ ) many things to say; | for in your ordered verdict of guilty, you have trampled underfoot | every | vital | principle | of our (\ ) government. < My (\ ) ∘ natural rights | my (\ ) ∘ civil rights, my ∘ political rights, | my (\ ) ∘ judicial rights | are all alike | ignored. Robbed of the fundamental privilege of citizenship, | I am degraded | from the status of a citizen to that of a subject; | and not only myself indivi (/) dually, but all of my (\ ) sex, | are, by your honor's verdict, doomed to political sub ∘ (\ ) jection | under this so-called Re ∘ publican form of (\ ) government. < Your denial of my citizen's right to (/) vote, | is the denial of my right to consent | as one of the (\ ) governed | the denial of my right of representation | as one of the (\ ) taxed; | the denial of my right | to a trial by a jury of my ∘ (\ ) peers | [the word "as" is spoken on a low note] as an offender against (\ ) law | therefore, | the denial of my sacred rights | to life, | liberty,—property.|

[Judge's Voice: The court orders the prisoner to sit down.]

Miss A. [*still standing.*] But your honor will not deny me this one and only poor privilege against this high-handed outrage | upon my citizen's rights. May it please the court to remember | that since the day of my arrest last Novem (\ ) ber | this is the first time | that either myself or ∘ any [the word "person" is spoken on a low note] (\ ) person | of my disenfranchised (/) class | has been allowed a word of defense before judge or jury—

After the judge's interruption there are no indications of intonation patterns or pauses until after the word "outrage," which shows us that the sentence is meant to be spoken fairly rapidly and on one breath, as a hurried protest. The speech clearly arises from deep emotion and anger and is a passionate expression of Anthony's political and personal feelings. We are shown its surface, like the tip of an iceberg. But if we ourselves wish to deliver it with power and meaning, we must personalize it and make it real from below the surface, from the inside. Why, for instance, does Anthony take the pauses shown by Potter? Why does her voice rise or fall at particular places? If you work on the emotions internally, you should be able to find the answers.

Helen Potter's final advice to anyone performing this speech on stage: "If recalled, enter quickly, bow abruptly and retire." It was the nineteenth-century custom to applaud major speeches in plays, just as operagoers applaud arias. Actors usually took a curtain call after each scene, as we learn from theatrical memoirs of the period. Potter's stage direction to "bow abruptly," and other directions throughout *Impersonations*, smack of melodrama, with its one-dimensional character writing and simplistic subtexts, which allowed the actor a limited range of emotions, generally black or white, with few shades of gray.

A melodrama was, originally and literally, a play with incidental music (*melos* is Greek for "music"), meant to create or enhance emotional effects, like background music in movies. It began as eighteenth-century French salon entertainment, with dramatic monologues, duologues, or poetry recited to musical accompaniment. The idea was then adapted for the theater, and the form evolved in the nineteenth century into full-length "well-made" plays (pieces in which all loose plot threads are neatly tied up), moralistic in tone and often violent in content. The villain frequently appeared in lurid "green lime," i.e., in the greenish glare of the limelight, a follow spot with an extremely hot light, shining on whoever was speaking at the moment. And the music consisted of overtures, entr'actes, and short incidental pieces such as the ubiquitous "hurry music," fast-paced instrumental compositions played during action or chase scenes.

Melodrama has the reputation of presenting a reductio ad absurdum of life, as opposed to the crystallization of reality that one expects of a drama where characters are portrayed with psychological depth. The genre is indeed replete with stock, one-dimensional types, e.g., dashing heroes, faithful in love; delicate, virtuous, long-suffering damsels in distress; scowling, maniacal villains. But even a superficial, cardboard character has a life. A waiter in a restaurant or a messenger has his own circumstances that have been lived through in order to arrive with that plate of corned beef and cabbage or that message. There is no reason to play even a flat character without a sense of reality.

Gilbert and Sullivan, in a now instructive parody of a lost genre, satirized not only the popular Victorian "transpontine" melodrama (so called because many of them were performed in theaters "across the bridge" in Southwark, on the south bank of the Thames), but also Regency frivolity and lechery, in *Ruddigore* (1887). Its "bad baronets" and its Chorus of Bucks and Blades arrive in the Cornish fishing village of Rederring (red herring) to seduce the local maidens, to whom they give flattering Romantic, poetic names: "Come, Amaryllis, come Chloe, come Phyllis." Gilbert's very funny writing will give you all the clichés you need to know.

Edmund Lester Pearson (1880–1937) describes in *Queer Books* (Kennicat Press, 1970; first published in 1928) a performance he attended of Timothy Shay Arthur's (1809–1885) popular temperance melodrama *Ten Nights in a Bar-Room* at the Newburyport, Massachusetts City Hall, "probably in the early '90s," that was full of "dramatic realism":

> When the drunk-crazed father hurled the rum bottle into the *left* wing,
> the little daughter obediently trotted on from the *right*, exclaiming:
>   "Oh, Papa, you have killed me!"
> Then she fell dead in the centre of the stage...

Now there's style for you! And the acceptance by the general public of the conventions of melodrama made all of it fine for the audience, who, if they could not entirely suspend their disbelief when such incidents occurred, at least left the theater vastly entertained. The influence of melodrama is still ubiquitous, when it comes to both characters and plots. Much of nighttime television and many films are melodramas. And it remains as exciting and entertaining as ever, no matter how it is disguised in modern dress.

Oscar Wilde's *Lady Windermere's Fan: A Play about a Good Woman* (1892)

This charmingly dated late Victorian comedy of manners, a melodrama in four acts, could only have been written in the days when ladies regularly used fans as an accessory, as they had since at least the sixteenth century in Europe, as well as in ancient Greece and Rome. The style of fan had changed over the centuries, and the one most in use in the Victorian era was the folding fan made of slats fastened together at one end, with a band or ribbon at that end so that the fan might be dangled from a lady's wrist.

Social attitudes toward illicit love affairs and adultery were not much different from what they are today: disapproval and scandal that ended in the divorce court were very much a part of the scene. We have many unfortunate examples of celebrity divorces to remind us of society's titillated and prurient disapproval of extramarital affairs, and the hurt they inflict on the people involved. But divorce was considered far more scandalous than it is today, when it is unfortunate and emotionally wrenching and may even be a tragedy, but there is nothing particularly disgraceful or ignominious to us now about the separation of two people who, for whatever reasons, are incompatible.

The title has a double meaning: The puritanical, judgmental Lady Windermere, whose husband has presented her with a beautiful, elaborate fan as a twenty-first birthday present, has a great fan and admirer in the slightly disreputable if witty Lord Darlington, in whom she confides. It is he who utters the famous line "I can resist anything except temptation." Lord Windermere has apparently been having an affair with a certain Mrs. Erlynne, of dubious reputation. She may be a courtesan, a profession as much in evidence in this period as it is rare in ours, despite the continued existence of various forms of prostitution. At any rate, Lord Windermere has been giving her large sums of money. When Lady Windermere confronts him, he is forced to admit that he has been doing this, but he maintains that he has been a faithful husband. When his wife leaves, he says, in a typical melodramatic line, "What shall I do? I dare not tell her who this woman is. The shame would kill her." Angry and upset when Lord Windermere invites Mrs. Erlynne to her birthday ball over her protests, Lady Windermere leaves him and goes off to be with Lord Darlington, who has professed his love for her. Mrs. Erlynne goes to her and tries to persuade her to return to her husband, all too aware that "A moment may ruin a life. Who knows that better than I?" Mrs. Erlynne is actually Lady Windermere's mother, forced to give up her daughter years before to be raised by an aunt. Mrs. Erlynne decides to sacrifice her reputation, and therefore her life as she has heretofore lived it, in order to save the Windermeres' marriage, but in the end her noble self-sacrifice is satisfactorily explained, and she makes a good marriage to Lord Augustus Lorton. Lady Windermere returns to her husband. And everyone manages to keep the various secrets that would otherwise ruin each of them.

Brilliantly written, with great humor and a sense of witty repartee, the play's language is nevertheless somewhat stilted, in typical Victorian, melodramatic fashion. We would never say nowadays, as Lady Windermere does in the following scene, "Our child is but six months old," but rather, "Our child is only six months old." The fact that the play is in four acts is another sign of the times; nowadays, we expect a play to be in two acts, or even in one long act with no intermission. And who is the "good woman" of the subtitle: Lady Windermere or Mrs. Erlynne? Perhaps it is both. Mrs. Erlynne is certainly a good woman, who has learned from her mistakes in life and is therefore more tolerant and forgiving and less judgmental than her daughter, who is more conventional in her attitudes and will possibly remain so. But Lady Windermere is also a good woman in her own rather self-righteous way, and Wilde himself—with his own secrets, soon to be exposed before a shocked and viciously homophobic public—approves of her. In the following exposition scene from act 1, we see her reactions to the information revealed by the gossipy, malicious Duchess of Berwick, who is paying a call on Lady Windermere:

LADY WINDERMERE. Oh, I can't believe it!

DUCHESS OF BERWICK. But it's quite true, my dear. The whole of London knows it. That is why I felt it was better to come and talk to you, and advise you to take Windermere away at once to Homburg or to Aix, where he'll have something to amuse him, and where you can watch him all day long. I assure you, my dear, that on several occasions after I was first married, I had to pretend to be very ill, and was obliged to drink the most unpleasant mineral waters, merely to get Berwick out of town. He was so extremely susceptible. Though I am bound to say he never gave away any large sums of money to anybody. He is far too high-principled for that!

LADY WINDERMERE. [Interrupting.] Duchess, Duchess, it's impossible! [Rising and crossing stage to C.] We are only married two years. Our child is but six months old. [Sits in chair R. of L. table.]

DUCHESS OF BERWICK. Ah, the dear pretty baby! How is the little darling? Is it a boy or a girl? I hope a girl—Ah, no, I remember it's a boy! I'm so sorry. Boys are so wicked. My boy is excessively immoral. You wouldn't believe at what hours he comes home. And he's only left Oxford a few months—I really don't know what they teach them there.

LADY WINDERMERE. Are all men bad?

DUCHESS OF BERWICK. Oh, all of them, my dear, all of them, without any exception. And they never grow any better. Men become old, but they never become good.

LADY WINDERMERE. Windermere and I married for love.

DUCHESS OF BERWICK. Yes, we begin like that. It was only Berwick's brutal and incessant threats of suicide that made me accept him at all, and before the year was out, he was running after all kinds of petticoats, every color, every shape, every material. In fact, before the honeymoon was over, I caught him winking at my maid, a most pretty, respectable girl. I dismissed her at once without a character. [a referral letter about character, recommending the bearer to a prospective employer]—No, I remember I passed her on to my sister; poor dear Sir George is so short-sighted, I thought it wouldn't matter. But it did, though—it was most unfortunate. [*Rises.*] And now, my dear child, I must go, as we are dining out. And mind you don't take this little aberration of Windermere's too much to heart. Just take him abroad, and he'll come back to you all right.

LADY WINDERMERE. Come back to me? [C.]

DUCHESS OF BERWICK. [*L.C.*] Yes, dear, these wicked women get our husbands away from us, but they always come back, slightly damaged, of course. And don't make scenes, men hate them.

We see the cynical Duchess confronting the naïve Lady Windermere with what everyone takes to be her husband's infidelity. She is shocked and conflicted immediately. This shows that she is innocent in worldly matters. These attitudes, which still are not gone from the scene when it comes to relationships and what people expect from each other, prevailed in a distinctly Victorian upper-class milieu, and against the background of the hush-hush privacy of that even more socially inflexible age. Again, the language, too, while perfectly real for the era, strikes us today as somewhat antiquated. You have to be careful not to make it feel or sound stilted. You can avoid this in part by assimilating and personalizing the language, and then by playing the actions and the objectives in a real way.

Historical Developments: 1893, A Sample Year

After his great success of 1892, Oscar Wilde had another triumph in 1893 with his brilliant comedy of manners *A Woman of No Importance*, which opened on April 19.

Gilbert and Sullivan, who had quarreled and had not collaborated on a comic opera for several years, presented to an eager public the much anticipated *Utopia Limited; or, The Flowers of Progress*. It opened on October 7, but closed after 245 performances. This politically satiric work is rather heavy-handed, not to say hamfisted, and also unclear as to the targets of its satire, although Gilbert has supplied some clever, acerbic lyrics. The pleasant but not terribly inspired score contains several sparkling numbers and particularly ingenious orchestrations. George Bernard Shaw, reviewing the opening night performance for the newspaper *The World*, thought it wonderful, especially Sullivan's contribution. The plot revolves around the attempt by King Paramount of the South Sea island nation of Utopia to reform his country along British lines, with the help of his English-educated daughter, Princess Zara, and the team of Flowers of Progress she has imported from England. Each one represents an aspect of the English sociocultural and economic system.

Other notable works were produced that year, including Maurice Maeterlinck's symbolist play *Pelléas et Mélisande*, opening on May 17; it is more famous as Claude Debussy's opera, which premiered in 1902. Henrik Ibsen's *The Master Builder* was published in 1892, but it was considered too outrageous in his native Norway, and was first performed in Berlin on January 19, 1893. Arthur Wing Pinero's well-made play *The Second Mrs. Tanqueray*—it seems terribly dated today in a way that Wilde, for instance is not—opened on May 27 at the St. James's Theatre in London. Giacomo Puccini's *Manon Lescaut* premiered at the opera house in Turin on February 1. And on February 9, La Scala in Milan saw the triumph of Giuseppe Verdi's last opera, and one of his greatest, *Falstaff*, based on Shakespeare's *The Merry Wives of Windsor*. The musical world also listened with pleasure on October 28 in St. Petersburg to the premier of Pyotr Ilyich Tchaikovsky's new *Symphony No. 6 in B minor (Pathétique)*. On December 16, Antonín Leopold Dvořák's *Symphony No. 9 in E minor (From the New World)* premiered at Carnegie Hall in New York, the composer having been resident in America since the previous year; he would return to Europe in 1895.

The literary world saw new, now obscure books by Stephen Crane, Arthur Conan Doyle, George Gissing, Jules Verne, and H. Rider Haggard. Robert Louis Stevenson published *Catriona*, the sequel to *Kidnapped*. Anatole France published his wry, philosophical *La rôtisserie de la reine Pédauque* (At the Sign of the Queen Pédauque). The mystery writer Dorothy L. Sayers was born on June 13; and the wit, short story writer, and poet Dorothy Parker on August 22. Guy de Maupassant died on July 6.

In the political and economic world, 1893 was a disaster, a precursor of the Great Depression of the 1930s. On May 5, the stock market on Wall Street crashed, ruining investors and throwing millions out of work. More than six hundred banks were forced to close, and railroad companies and many businesses went bankrupt, while other firms just managed to stay afloat. The depression lasted four more years. The United States, which had been off the gold standard since 1890 and the passage of the Sherman Silver Purchase Act, repealed it and returned to the gold standard on October 31. The price of silver immediately collapsed, worsening the catastrophe.

Later that year, the labor leader Charles Kelly led an army of the unemployed on a march of protest to Washington, D.C., all the way from California. And Eugene V. Debs founded the American Railway Union. The movement for workers' rights was under way, and whatever was done to secure them would be over the sometimes physically brutal opposition of the capitalist bosses.

In the imperialistic world, of which *Utopia Limited* was a mild satire, it was just another year in the European and American scramble for colonies. The wholesale plunder of sub-Saharan Africa by European powers was well advanced. On March 10, France declared that the Ivory Coast was its colony, and earlier in the year, Laos had been forced to become a French protectorate. Their possession of an empire in Indochina was progressing, and French hegemony in Southeast Asia would end only in the 1950s. The French also declared Dahomey (present-day Benin) in west Africa to be their protectorate, on November 17; there was no opposition to this wholesale theft.

The situation in South Africa was volatile, and developments were rapid: On May 10, Natal, under British rule, became self-governing. And on October 23, the British South Africa Company brutally suppressed the revolt of the Matabele people in what is now Zimbabwe, using machine guns to massacre the populace. On November 11, their king, Lobengula, went into exile, dying the following year. And on November 13, the Boer Republic of the Transvaal annexed Swaziland, an African state. All of this bloody competition between the British and the Afrikaans-speaking Boer farmers would lead by 1899 to the Second Boer War, which ended with the defeat of the Boers in 1902. The British instituted concentration camps in which they imprisoned Boer farmers; these notorious hellholes would later prove an example and a model to the Nazis.

This was also the year that the United States declared the islands of Hawaii an American protectorate, on February 1, after the abdication of Queen Liliuokalani on January 17. The Hawaiians promulgated a republic, with the help and connivance of the US resident minister and the Marines, who had landed in order to secure American interests, but in reality with the intention of taking over the country.

In a happier development, New Zealand became the first country in the world to allow women suffrage. And the first open-heart surgery was performed by the American Dr. Daniel Hale Williams in Chicago. For conditions in health, hygiene, sanitation, and developments in medicine that apply to the general era of the 1880s through the 1890s, read the fascinating *The Great Stink of Paris and the Nineteenth-Century Struggle against Filth and Germs* (The Johns Hopkins University Press, 2006) by David S. Barnes.

And read the novels of Emile Zola (1840–1902), the naturalist writer and staunch defender of human rights. He showed sides of life that other writers generally avoided, and dealt with such subjects as the seedy working-class life of Paris, in *L'Assommoir* (1877)—an untranslatable title; the word means a place whrere one is beaten down, from the verb *assommer*: to beat someone, to kill someone, to be prey to utter exhaustion. Zola wrote about prostitution in *Nana* (1880); and about working-class conditions in *Germinal* (1885), often considered his masterpiece. Germinal is the name of the seventh month in the French Revolutionary calendar, corresponding to the early spring season: the title refers to the planting of the seeds of hope for a better future among the miners. These books are all part of a monumental saga that portrays the history of the Second Empire of Napoleon III, ending with the Franco-Prussian War and the Commune, through the story of a family and its varying fortunes, *Les Rougon-Macquart* (The Rougon-Macquart Family). Zola published the first in the series of twenty novels, *La Fortune des Rougon*, in 1871, and completed it in 1893 with *Le docteur Pascal*.

Shakespeare in the Nineteenth Century

We know more about nineteenth-century Shakespeare productions than we do about those in earlier periods because there are promptbooks, accounts of productions, descriptive theater reviews, books of criticism about actors, and many photographs and engravings. Scenery and costumes could be elaborate. And the promptbooks tell us many details of the staging, no doubt arranged by actor-managers.

Nowadays we generally confine Shakespeare to summer festival productions, but throughout the Victorian era, a London or New York season would have been unthinkable without the presentation by one of the great actor-managers of a repertoire of classic plays, mostly by Shakespeare. New plays and musical theater pieces were done, of course, but to many people theater meant Shakespeare performed by the actor-managers' companies. There were touring Shakespeare companies as well, and great stars toured when not in the metropolitan centers for the usual season. Stars crossed the Atlantic in both directions, bringing their productions to New York from London, and vice versa. Sometimes they even performed with each other, as Booth and Irving did at the Lyceum, Irving's London theater.

The "facsimile prompt-book" for the English actor-manager William Charles Macready's production of *King John*, edited by Charles H. Shattuck, was published by the University of Illinois Press in 1962. Macready mounted the play in London in 1842, and the promptbook was later given to the English actor-manager Charles Kean (1811–1868), who used it for a New York production in 1846; he was the son of the famous actor Edmund Kean (1789–1833). The production was much acclaimed for its "glorious pageantry," less so for some of its acting, which critics found too violent.

In the promptbook, which is full of cut lines and speeches, we find the positions for people in the difficult crowd scenes, which had to be carefully managed, marked clearly in the margins; music cues ("Loud Flourish of Trumpets"); and such directions for staging as the following, for act 2, scene 2, during a speech by the First Citizen, on the lines concerning the marriage proposed between "That daughter there of Spain, the lady Blanch" and "Lewis the Dauphin" of France:

> The Nobles, l-c, have broke into various groups, by the end of this speech, and appear to be remarking on the proposal, and its effect on the Kings, —Elinor is u-l gently speaking to K. John, —Lewis to Philip, in debate, on R; are joined by Austria.

The details must have been carefully rehearsed for blocking, but the actors were expected to follow such directions as "appear to be remarking on the proposal" without further help or interpretation from Macready, because they were supposed to know their business. At any rate, we can see by now a more modern approach to staging plays.

The Story of My Life by Dame Ellen Terry (1847–1928), who was Henry Irving's leading lady and came from a theatrical family, is perhaps the most valuable book of its kind for what it imparts about Victorian theater and Shakespearean production; it was published in 1908. The revised edition of 1933 is more serviceable than the original, because of the notes to each chapter written by Edith Craig, Terry's daughter, and Christopher St. John.

Ellen Terry's first engagment, in 1856, when she was a child, was with the "Charles Keans," as she calls them. She played Mamillus in *The Winter's Tale*. There were no formal acting schools, and actors were trained as part of a company. Her parents had taught her elocution, and she was trained and instructed in roles by Ellen Tree, who was Mrs. Kean (1805–1880). She had movement training as well, conducted by Oscar Byrn (1795–1867), "the dancing master and director of crowds at the Princess's":

> There was the minuet, to which he used to attach great importance, and there was "walking the plank." Up and down one of the long planks, extending the length of the stage, we had to walk, first slowly, and then quicker and quicker until we were able at a considerable pace to walk the whole length of it without deviating an inch from the straight line. This exercise, Mr. Byrn used to say, and quite truly, I think, taught us uprightness of carriage and certainty of step.
>
> "Eyes right! Chest out! Chin tucked in!" I can hear the dear old man shouting at us as if it were yesterday.

For Kean's production of *The Winter's Tale*, "Rehearsals lasted all day, Sundays included, and when there was no play running at night, until four or five the next morning." In 1858, she played Prince Arthur in Shakespeare's King John, in which she was eager to do well:

> I used to get up in the middle of the night and watch my gestures in the glass. I used to try my voice and bring it down and up in the right places. And all vanity fell away from me. At the first rehearsals of "King John" I could not do anything right. Mrs. Kean stormed at me, slapped me. I broke down and cried, and then, with all the mortification and grief in my voice, managed to express what Mrs. Kean wanted and what she could not teach me by doing it herself.

"That's right, that's right!" she cried excitedly. "You've got it! Now remember what you did with your voice, reproduce it, remember everything, and do it!"

Much Shakespearean acting in this period was in a declamatory style, some of it quite unacceptable by today's standards, as recordings made at the beginning of the twentieth century show. Many luminaries of the Victorian theater, such as Lewis Waller (1860–1915) and Arthur Bourchier (1863–1927), deliver Shakespearean speeches with a bombast and a fearful noise, full of tacked-on meaning, so it seems, rather than heartfelt emotion. They almost sing, rather than speak the lines. They declaim and intone, and it is very difficult to know sometimes what they are talking about, even though one knows the speeches so well. Frequently, they seem as intent upon creating vocal effects as on making clear the intentions of the lines, despite the clearest articulation, the best diction, and what must obviously have been complete audibility in the theater, to judge by their stentorian delivery into the acoustic horn.

Sir Henry Irving, while eccentric and individual in his declamation—and, according to many accounts, in his movement on stage, as we saw in chapter 3—is perhaps an exception to the rule. For descriptions of Irving as Shylock, see pp. 68; 71. He, like Booth and Salvini, was perceived by many of his contemporaries as an uneven, inconsistent actor. Even William Winter says of Booth that "he was an uneven actor and of many moods, not a machine; but no words can describe the glow of his spirit and the music of his tones when once his spirit had been fully aroused..." Yet all three had astounding charisma, and were much admired and appreciated as well. And the recordings of Booth, with his deep, sonorous voice; Irving, with his reedy voice and heartfelt, sometimes calculating delivery; and Ellen Terry, with her tremolo, show them to have been more real in their delivery than those I have just described. And all three are absolutely fascinating. They must have been superb on stage.

Here are two examples of old-fashioned delivery—both are described in various accounts, but were never recorded—done by two very great actors. The excerpts from Booth's and Salvini's performances are drawn from Helen Potter's *Impersonations*. You can use these brief excerpts as exercises. First, imitate the pattern, once you have figured out what the symbols mean (see p. 257); and, second, try to assimilate it and make it organic. Analyze and understand why it was spoken as it was, then speak it again.

Edwin Booth as Hamlet

Edwin Booth had a beautiful, resonant baritone. He made two recording for Thomas Edison on wax cylinder in 1890: the speech to the Senate from *Othello*, available on a Pearl CD, *Great Shakespearean Actors*; and the famous soliloquy "To be or not to be," which seems to be unavailable in any format, except in library archives inaccessible to the general public. As Othello he is grave and serious in his delivery of the speech, and, except for his period stage diction, he sounds surprisingly modern, especially when compared with his colleagues. For Ellen Terry, "Booth was a melancholy, dignified Othello, but not great as Salvini was great." On the other hand, "Salvini's Hamlet made me scream with mirth."

In the role of Hamlet, Booth was the most melancholy of Danes, and the most real anyone had seen up to that time. Accounts of his Hamlet include those by his friend and biographer, William Winter, *Life and Art of Edwin Booth* (T. Fisher Unwin, 1893); and that by Mrs. Goodale, whom we met in chapter 4. The following excerpt, with Helen Potter's markings, is from the graveyard scene, act 5, scene 1:

> (o)Alas! [soft] °poor (o)Yorick! [Turns] I knew him, Horatio; a
> (o)fellow of °infin \ite /(o)jest, (o)of most °excell \ent (o)fan °/cy.
> (o)He hath °borne me (o)on his °/back (o)a °thousand (o)times.

It is interesting to note that we have a possible indication of how the originator of the role of Hamlet in 1602, Richard Burbage, may have played this scene. The poet John Raynolds (?–1650?), also spelled Raynold or Reynolds, published *Dolarnys* [anagram for Raynolds] *Primerose, or The First Part of the Passionate Hermit* in 1606. And in it, he describes an actor handling Yorick's skull, that actor most probably being Burbage, the only player Raynolds would have seen in the role:

> He held it still, in his sinister [left] hand,
> He turn'd it soft, and stroakt it with the other,
> He smil'd on it . . .

There is a great deal of source material on exactly how Edwin Booth performed his most famous role, as Charles H. Shattuck informs us in *The Hamlet of Edwin Booth* (University of Illinois Press, 1969), among them Booth's own notebooks, promptbooks, and an extensive description by Charles H. Clarke (1848–1940), a great admirer. He saw Booth eight times. In the graveyard scene, after "I knew him, Horatio":

He drops the skull to his waist and looks at Horatio. "A fellow of infinite jest, of excellent fancy (slight upward accent). He hath borne me on his back a thousand (slight upward accent) times (slight upward accent). And now how abhorred in my imagination it is!" He draws back his head and gives a gesture of disgust.

One can conjecture that this way of playing and delivering the speech was fairly set, but always alive and organic. Indeed, although Clarke may have seen Booth do it this way, it is by no means certain that he did it that way every time. In any case, fascinating as the description is, it can only ultimately give a vague idea of what Booth's performance was really like. Theater, like great cooking, is an ephemeral art. You have to have been there!

Tommaso Salvini as Othello

Potter writes of Tommaso Salvini's voice that it is "a basso profundo, of great power. He can strike terror to the heart of an adversary, or melt into tenderness; and ring all the changes of grief, remorse or despair." And she feels his performance as Othello has never been equaled. He acted in Italian, while the rest of the cast performed in English. For the edification of Anglophone audiences, an authorized bilingual edition was published in New York by A. Seer's Printing and Engraving Establishment, some time between 1875 and 1886. Many people at the time felt he owned the role, just as Edwin Booth owned Hamlet. Here is an excerpt from the last act:

And °say, (o)be /sides, that in Aleppo /once,
- - Where a malignant | and turban'd Turk
Beat a Venetian, | and traduced the /state,
I took by the throat | the circumcised /dog
/(o)And smote him— || °thus!

[*He drives the scimitar into his throat, reels heavily to the floor, and dies.*]

Salvini performed in his own truncated, slightly redone version of the play, which begins with him and Iago having a conversation in which Othello responds to Iago's questions about what is going on by telling him he is married.

In 1890, New York City literary critic and author Edward Tuckerman Mason (1847–1912), who had been going to Salvini's performances of the play since 1881 and making notes about it (as he had about Booth's

Hamlet), published a fascinating little tome, *The Othello of Tommaso Salvini* (Putnam, 1890; reprint, General Books LLC, 2009), which is a detailed description of his performance. It obviously would have been subject to change from evening to evening. For instance, Mason informs us that during Brabantio's speech to the Senate in act 1, scene 2, "She is abused," Salvini "sighs, and turns slightly to the left, wearied and disgusted. The action is very slight, not emphasized." But it is improbable that he did this every time without variations; after all, nobody else was involved in this individual reaction to Brabantio's vituperative slanders; that is, nobody else's physical action or blocking depended on Salvini's playing at this point, so he probably varied his reactions in an organic way, as he felt them.

Still, the descriptions are intriguing, affording us the only glimpse we are ever likely to have of this great actor's performance, as in this excerpt from act 3, scene 3:

IAGO. Is't possible, my lord?

OTELLO. Villain, be sure thou prove my love a whore;
Be sure of it; give me the ocular proof…

On hearing anew the voice of Iago, Othello gradually recovers himself. Sitting upright, and convulsively grasping the arms of the chair, he turns upon Iago, who stands, left of center, near the front. Seated thus, and shaking his head like an angry lion, he utters "Villain!" (*"Sciagurato!"*) in a low voice, expressing the extreme of deadly menace—the first muttering of the storm which is about to break. Still seated, and somewhat louder, with increasing intensity, he says, "be sure thou prove," etc.; then, starting from the chair, as he continues, "Be sure of it," etc., he rushes upon Iago, clutches him by the throat, and forces him down upon his knees. The rest of this speech, and the following two speeches, he delivers holding Iago by the throat, at time menacing him with his clenched right hand while he holds him with his left hand, at times seeming almost to twist Iago's head from his body.

This sort of thing would perhaps account for Ellen Terry's reaction to Salvini's performance:

…his Othello was the grandest, biggest, most glorious thing. We often prate of "reserved force." Salvini had it, for the simple reason that his was the gigantic force which may be restrained because of its immensity. Men have no need to dam up a little purling brook. If they do it in acting, it is tame, absurd and pretentious. But Salvini held himself in, and still his groan was like a tempest, his passion huge.

In his colorful *Leaves from the Autobiography of Tommaso Salvini* (The Century Company, 1890), the great actor says of his performances as Othello, "It is very seldom that I have attained satisfaction with myself in that role; I may say that in the thousands of times that I have played it I can count on the fingers of one hand those when I have said to myself, 'I can do no better.' " This is a great lesson for actors: Who indeed is ever really satisfied with his or her own work? We all know we can do better, and we know the faults and flaws in our performances, even when they are not always perceived by others. So what do we do? We work on ourselves and on our roles, exactly as Stanislavsky advised us to do so long ago!

What to Wear for Rehearsal

The same advice applies as with the immediately preceding two eras: long gowns or dresses for the women; long coats, vests, and long trousers for the men. A raincoat may simulate a man's frock coat quite adequately. If you have a stiff collar, wear it, along with a tie, or an ascot if you do not have a shirt with a collar. Men's shirts usually required a collar to be fastened on with studs, and could be quite uncomfortable. Clothing was heavy, so you might choose heavier garments for rehearsal, unless the rehearsal rooms are too hot. You want to simulate the feeling of the clothing, but not at the risk of dire discomfort. But a coat for men is certainly advisable, because movement is limited by it. As that brilliant master technician Vsevolod Meyerhold points out, "In a tail coat one must keep to half movements. Elbows have to be held closer to the body. Gestural thrusts must be short, movements light." Ordinary footwear should be used, particularly good, solid, heavy walking shoes. They will give you a sense of weight that is part of the feel of the heavy costume of the period.

CHAPTER FOURTEEN

The Turn of the Twentieth Century; World War One; the Roaring Twenties and the Great Depression; World War Two

Some important dates:

1914–1918 World War One, also known as the Great War; the Allies—Great Britain, the United States, France, and Italy—defeat the German and Austrian coalition and promulgate the Treaty of Versailles, which ended the conflict but was perceived by the losers as one-sided and unjust. The Austro-Hungarian and Ottoman Empires disappear as political entities; the maps of Europe and the Middle East are redrawn by the imperialist winners of the war.

1917 Russian Revolution; overthrow of czarism and establishment of Communism; soon after the October revolution, the Russians withdraw from the war, in which they had been aligned with the Allies.

1922 Fascists take over government of Italy.

1919–1933 Weimar Republic in Germany; flowering of the arts and the German avant-garde.

1929 Start of Great Depression, with the October crash on Wall Street; its repercussions are disastrous and worldwide.

1933–1945 Nazi dictatorship in Germany; the Holocaust begins with the persecution and eventual segregation of German Jews as soon as the Nazis take power: anti-Semitism was the cornerstone of their program.

1933 Franklin D. Roosevelt is elected President of the United States; start of the New Deal.

1936 The Germans defy the Treaty of Versailles and march into the Rhineland.

1936 The Italians attack, defeat, and take over helpless Abyssinia (Ethiopia).

1936–1939 Spanish Civil War, ending the Republic and establishing Phalangist dictatorship.

1938 The Germans annex Austria and, despite the Munich Agreement, occupy all of Czechoslovakia; immediately, persecution of Austrian and Czech Jews begins. On November 9–10, the Nazis stage a huge anti-Jewish pogrom, known as *Kristallnacht* (Crystal Night), or the Night of Broken Glass, because of all the smashed shop windows, in reprisal for the assassination in Paris of a German embassy official by a Jewish youth.

1939–1945 World War Two, ending in victory for the Allies against the Nazis and Fascists and Imperial Japan; the United States enters the war after the Japanese bomb Pearl Harbor on December 7, 1941. The war was fought in Europe and the Pacific theaters and had repercussions in South America and Africa, making it indeed a world war. More than 56,000,000 people lost their lives.

Marcel Proust (1871–1922)

Technological devices, such as the icebox, the old-style New York subway and Paris Métro cars, and the telephone operator's plug board, in use in the first decades of the twentieth century, would disappear, replaced by the end of the century with more efficient machines and methods that accomplish the same things. Fashions such as ladies' floor-length dresses and men's detachable shirt collars (around since 1827 and largely gone by 1930), and customs like presenting visiting cards when paying a call, would all be outmoded around the World War I era. These things, once so common, now appear to us quaint and picturesque.

Considered in some circles a fair way of settling differences and bitter quarrels, the duel is gone, too, replaced by lawsuits, the divorce courts—or the commission of punishable crimes. As long ago as 1679, Louis XIV had issued an edict forbidding dueling, but it did not have much of an effect. Though the practice was often condemned, only at the end of the nineteenth century did we finally hear its swan song.

Alexander Hamilton (1757–1804), Mikhail Lermontov (1814–1841), and Alexander Pushkin (1799–1837) were famously killed in duels, and many dueling scenes in literature are famous: those in *Hamlet* (in the form of a fencing match that turns into a deadly duel); Pushkin's *Yevgenyi Onegin*, in which the hero kills his best friend in an incident that seems in retrospect like a premonition of the author's own death; and Alexandre Dumas' (1802–1870) *Three Musketeers* and *The Count of Monte Cristo*.

Against his despairing mother's wishes, Marcel Proust (1871–1922) fought a pistol duel in 1897 with the scandalmonger Jean Lorrain (1855–1906), a journalist who had practically accused him in a scathing review of Proust's first book, *Les Plaisirs et les Jours* (Pleasures and Days), of having a relationship that went beyond friendship with Lucien Daudet (1883–1946), the son of the famous author Alphonse Daudet (1840–1897). They exchanged shots, but both aimed high, and nobody was hurt. In fact, later on, Proust feared that he might be put on trial for obscenity. He maintained that people would never speak to him again once they had read certain sexually explicit episodes in his book, particularly those relating to the extravagant homosexual Baron de Charlus in *Sodom and Gomorrah* (1922). This is the fourth tome in the Modern Library edition of Proust's novel, *A la recherche du temps perdu* (In Search of Lost Time), published from 1913 to 1927. (Several volumes of the novel were published posthumously.)

If you are doing a play set at the turn of the twentieth century, you owe it to yourself to read Proust's insightful, broad-ranging masterpiece, which is a first-person narrative that draws heavily on incidents in the author's life without actually being an autobiography.

Proust's profound understanding of behavior and psychology is brilliantly embodied in a gallery of memorable characters. Some of his observations parallel those of his famous contemporary Sigmund Freud. For instance, the self-analyzing narrator experiences as a child the conflicting emotions of what Freud called the Oedipus complex. And like Freud, Proust understood the nature of the unconscious and its drives, and gave his characters (including the narrator) motivations of which they themselves are unaware, as you will see in the selection below.

The portrayal of character and motivation has always been the province of literature, but by the end of the nineteenth century, psychology was also emerging as an important area of scientific study. Its new insights influenced Stanislavsky profoundly, and would have a major impact on playwriting. Chekhov, as we saw in chapter 2, was a master psychologist, and very modern in his conceptions. His characters, like those of Proust, have reality and depth, as do the characters of both Henrik Ibsen and the iconoclastic, misogynistic Swedish dramatist August Strindberg (1849–1912).

To show you the kind of sociocultural and psychological information that would be useful to you as an actor, here is a brief character study from *Swann's Way*, the first volume of Proust's novel (my translation):

> [Legrandin, unconsciously a snob, enamored of duchesses, to whom he attributes superior virtues and graces, is a friend of the narrator's family. The aristocratic Guermantes are a family of ancient lineage, and their chateau is near the village where he and the narrator's family spend their summer vacations. Asked if he knows them:]

> Legrandin the talker replied, "No, I have never *wanted* to know them." Unfortunately, he only replied as a second person, because another Legrandin, whom he had carefully hidden deep inside himself, which he did not reveal (because that Legrandin knew compromising stories about our Legrandin and his snobbery)— another Legrandin had already replied by a wounded look, by an involuntary twist of the mouth, by the excessive seriousness of the tone of his reply, by the thousand arrows with which *our* Legrandin had been pierced and laid low, like a Saint Sebastian of snobbery, "Alas! How you hurt me, no, I don't know the Guermantes; do not awaken the great sorrow of my life." And this mischievous child Legrandin, this master blackmailer Legrandin—even if he did not have the facility with language that the other had—was infinitely more prompt with his own language, composed of what one calls "reflexes"; when Legrandin the talker wanted to impose silence on him, the other one had already spoken, and our friend regretted in vain the bad impression that the revelations of his alter ego must have produced, but he could only undertake to soften it.

> And this certainly did not mean that Legrandin was not sincere when he railed against snobs. He could not know, at least by himself, that he was one, because we only know the passions of others; and what we come to know of our own, we can only have learned from others... Legrandin's snobbery... charged his imagination, so that a duchess appeared to him adorned with all the graces. Legrandin approached a duchess, convinced that he was yielding to that

attraction of spirit and virtue unknown to the most insignificant snobs. Only other people knew he was one, because, thanks to their inability to understand the intermediary work of his imagination, they were confronted directly with Legrandin's worldly activities and their primary cause.

How does an actor play a snob? The days of duchesses and aristocrats who were regarded as the true elite are long gone, and you might have to substitute a great movie star to understand Legrandin's feelings. But read the selection above, and you have a perfect lesson in playing a subtext that is opposite to the direct statement in the text.

Proust describes the ways in which Legrandin's mind works: 1) Legrandin is conscious of being hurt, and consciously pretends to be indifferent; 2) Legrandin is unconscious that he has revealed his inner self by his automatic, nonverbal body language; and 3) Legrandin is unconscious that the hurt he has unwittingly revealed brands him as a snob. He would not characterize himself as a snob, and does not realize he is one. Legrandin is lying, even to himself. On a conscious level, he knows he is hurt by not knowing the Guermantes, and he lies about that to his interlocutors. On another, unconscious level, he is lying to himself about the reasons for his hurt, and shielding himself from the knowledge that he is a snob.

Why is he a snob? What needs in him are served by his snobbery? He needs to feel superior, and does so by associating with a class of people he considers superior, because in an even deeper layer of the subconscious reside feelings of inferiority. Searching within, the actor can find those feelings of inferiority and superiority and insecurity and the tension created by the conflict between them, all of which will enable him or her to play such a part perfectly.

What would be the physical actions here, if this were a scene in a stage play? Simply follow Proust's description: While maintaining a correct distance from your interlocutor, suitable to the period, say the line (the verbal action) "No, I have never wanted to know them." This will perhaps come out in a very serious tone, and smile. The use of a substitution for "them" in this instance should help to awaken that wounded feeling in you. You might incline your head slightly, and even doff your hat in deference to the Guermantes name. And you might also consider the possibility of using a falling intonation pattern in Legrandin's utterance. These technical, physical aspects of playing are meant to convey the character's inner life.

Historical Developments: 1936, A Sample Year

In the decades after the Great War, the Fascists ruled in Italy, led by Benito Mussolini (1883–1945), who took power in 1921–1922. And the Nazis under Adolf Hitler (1889–1945) governed Germany, starting in 1933. On February 4, 1936, Wilhelm Gustloff, the Swiss Nazi Party leader, was assassinated by a Swiss-Jewish youth, David Frankfurter.

The year 1929 had seen the start of the Great Depression, beginning in the United States. In 1936, as the Depression continued, important events were premonitory of things to come: On March 7 the Germans marched into the Rhineland, against the provisions of the Treaty of Versailles that had ended the Great War. The League of Nations, precursor to the United Nations, did nothing to stop them. This was a first step toward World War II, and the Nazis were allowed to get away with it. The Italians occupied and annexed Ethiopia, then called Abyssinia, which surrendered on May 5. Again the League of Nations, even after an urgent appeal and the denunciation of the use by the Fascists of chemical warfare by the deposed Emperor Haile Selassie I (1892–1975), whose dynasty had been in power since the thirteenth century, did nothing to oppose the Italian takeover. On June 17, the sinister Heinrich Himmler was appointed head of the German police. And on June 19, the German boxer Max Schmeling (1905–2005) defeated the African-American champion Joe Louis (1914–1981), much to the glee of the Nazis, who used the match for propaganda purposes, touting the superiority of the so-called "Aryans." The Olympic Games opened on August 1 in Berlin, bringing a temporary, relaxation for propagandistic purposes of the persecution of the German Jews. The respite for Jews ended as soon as the Games closed on August 16.

Britain's occupation of Egypt, in force since 1882, officially came to an end, but under the provisions of the Anglo-Egyptian treaty of 1936, some British soldiers remained in Egypt. The country was used as a base for Allied North African operations during World War II, and the last British troops would not leave until 1952. The British maintained their mandate over Palestine, where Arab anti-Jewish riots broke out on April 15, 1936.

In the United States, Franklin D. Roosevelt had been President since 1933, and his progressive programs to help end the Depression, with its dust bowls, soup kitchens, massive unemployment, and terrible poverty, were in force. In February 1936, the first Social Security checks were mailed. There were still unrest and terrible labor strikes. Roosevelt was nevertheless reelected by a landslide in November.

In France, the Popular Front government of Socialist Léon Blum (1872–1950) took power on June 4 for the first time. His first ministry would last until June of the following year; his second was in 1938. He was immediately denounced by the right wing because of his Jewish ancestry.

The Cunard ocean liner *Queen Mary* had left Southampton on May 27 on its maiden voyage, arriving in New York on June 1.

In the world of literature, Rudyard Kipling, author of *The Jungle Book*, died on January 18. Penguin Books was founded. And Stanislavsky published *An Actor Prepares*, translated by Elizabeth Reynolds Hapgood. George Orwell (1903–1950) published his novel *Keep the Aspidistra Flying*, and James Cain (1892–1977) wrote *Double Indemnity*. Both books were later made into films, as was, of course, Margaret Mitchell's (1900–1949) runaway best seller of the year, *Gone with the Wind*.

In the theater, Terence Rattigan's first play, *French Without Tears*, was produced in London to great acclaim and established him as a leading dramatist; it was made into a film in 1940. Richard Rodgers (1902–1979) and Lorenz Hart (1895–1943) produced *On Your Toes* on Broadway; George Abbott (1887–1995) cowrote the book and directed. Noël Coward (1899–1973) premiered *Tonight at 8:30*; while Eugene O'Neill (1888–1953) presented *A Touch of the Poet*. O'Neill won the 1936 Nobel Prize for Literature.

King George V of England (b. 1865) died on January 20 and was briefly succeeded by his son Edward VIII (1894–1972). Edward was never crowned, and, under tremendous pressure from all sides, he abdicated, after a storm of controversy, to marry "the woman I love," a twice-divorced American socialite, Wallis Warfield Simpson (1896–1986). The royal family found Mrs. Simpson unsuitable and unbearable, and always refused to receive her. The political establishment, led by Prime Minister Stanley Baldwin (1867–1947), made it clear to Edward that they were sure the people would never accept her as queen, and that a constitutional crisis would be precipitated if he remained on the throne. Once crowned, Edward would have been head of the Church of England, so marrying a divorcee, and one with two living ex-husbands at that, was shockingly problematic at best. In addition, Edward's pro-Nazi stance was completely unacceptable; during the war he was shunted off to the Bahamas as governor. His brother, who immediately upon Edward's abdication became King George VI (1895–1952), created him Duke of Windsor.

The Spanish Civil War between Francisco Franco's (1892–1975) fascist Phalangists and the Republican Loyalists broke out on July 18; the war would last until 1939. Germany, who had sent the Condor Legion on November 18 to help Franco, and Italy, which also intervened on the Phalangist side, recognized the Franco government. On August 19, the Phalangists murdered the gay Spanish playwright Federico Garcia Lorca (1898–1936). On December 27, Great Britain and France agreed not to intervene in Spain. Individuals from those countries and the United States did, however, join the anti-Franco forces.

On July 29, in the United States, the first television program was broadcast by RCA.

On October 10, the Arab Higher Committee in Jerusalem decided to end the murderous riots against Jews. On October 25, Hitler and Mussolini signed the treaty that formed the Berlin-Rome axis, a further prelude to war.

On November 23, the first issue of *Life* magazine was published. The first men's trousers with a zip-up fly, introduced by Hart, Schaffner & Marx, went on sale.

To show you how recent this is in psychological terms, however distant it may be in time: My mother, Ruth Blumenfeld, born in 1915, was twenty-one. Her uncle, Herman Wohl (b. 1877), a noted composer and conductor in the New York Yiddish theater, died in October of gangrene, then incurable. She remembers how her grief-stricken mother screamed with the pain of her loss. And she remembers her uncle's funeral on Second Avenue. She was there with her older sister and younger brother. It was attended by thousands of mourners.

For the performing styles of this era, look at the films that were made; and for styles in the theater, see some of the great movie musicals, made directly for the screen. You might start with *Broadway Melody of 1936* and *The Big Broadcast of 1936*. The Nazi documentary *Olympia*, Leni Riefenstahl's film about the Olympic Games, is also available on DVD, and it may send chills up and down your spine, as it did mine.

In addition to animated cartoon features and shorts; cliffhanger serials; comedy series starring Harold Lloyd, the Marx Brothers, Charlie Chaplin, Buster Keaton, and many others, more than fifty Hollywood feature films were released in 1936. Among them are *Show Boat*, directed by James Whale (1889–1957), starring Paul Robeson (1898–1976), and based on the Broadway hit by Jerome Kern (1885–1945) and Oscar Hammerstein II (1895–1960). Other big hits that year were *Anthony Adverse*, an eighteenth-century historical drama based on the novel by Hervey Allen;

After the Thin Man, one of the films in the detective series starring William Powell and Myrna Loy as the sophisticated, urbane society couple Nick and Nora Charles (Nick loves his martini; the prohibition of alcohol has been repealed in 1933); *The Bohemian Girl*, starring Laurel and Hardy in a version of Balfe's opera; George Cukor's *Camille*, based on the play by Alexandre Dumas fils that was also used as the basis of Verdi's opera *La traviata*, and starring Greta Garbo and Robert Taylor; George Stevens' *Swing Time*, starring Ginger Rogers and Fred Astaire; *Dodsworth*, based on the Sinclair Lewis novel about the medical profession; *Follow the Fleet*, starring Fred Astaire and Ginger Rogers; *The Great Ziegfeld*, starring William Powell as the Follies producer Florenz Ziegfeld (1867–1932) and featuring magnificent production numbers—it won the Academy Award for Best Picture, and Luise Rainer won for Best Actress; *My Man Godfrey*, a screwball comedy, starring William Powell and Carole Lombard; *The Petrified Forest*, starring Leslie Howard and Bette Davis (who says "What a dump!"—famously recalled in Edward Albee's *Who's Afraid of Virginia Woolf?*); Rudolf Friml's musical *Rose Marie*, starring Jeannette MacDonald and Nelson Eddy; *Romeo and Juliet*, starring Norma Shearer and Leslie Howard; *The Story of Louis Pasteur*, starring Paul Muni, who won the Academy Award for Best Actor; Frank Capra's *Mr. Deeds Goes to Town*, with Gary Cooper; the anti-marijuana propaganda film *Reefer Madness*; *San Francisco*, with its famous title song and its stars Clark Gable and Jeannette MacDonald; Alfred Hitchcock's *Secret Agent*; *Things to Come*, a futuristic H. G. Wells story; and Charlie Chaplin's *Modern Times*, one of the last silent films. This is an amazing number of brilliant films for one year. It was the era of the studio system, when they used to churn them out like mad, and many of those years are full of cinematic masterpieces. You will notice that three of the films listed starred William Powell, and that Fred Astaire and Ginger Rogers appeared in two films, as did several other stars. The studio actors were always working. They customarily made more than one film a year, and that even in the midst of the Depression.

Among modern films about this period, Christophe Barratier's moving, charming *Paris 36* (its original French title is *Faubourg 36*), released in 2008 but set in 1936, is an excellent recreation of what Paris was like, with its political ferment and struggles to survive. The film provides a wonderful recreation of the Paris music hall, with the amusing musical numbers done in perfect period style. It deals peripherally with Léon Blum's socialist government, and shows union movements as well as conditions in the theater.

Elmer Rice's Street Scene

One of the first things you will notice in reading Elmer Rice's (1892–1967) Pulitzer Prize–winning play, *Street Scene* (1929), written as the Great Depression was about to descend, is that the technology of the period conditions the behavior of the characters in a very important way. Wood-burning iron stoves were the norm, and my mother, who was born in New York, has often told me how my grandmother used to get up at the crack of dawn to load the stove with wood and light it for the day, even in summer. There were iceboxes, but no electric-powered refrigerators. Most importantly, there was no air conditioning, although there were ceiling and table fans, as well as the handheld fans the characters use as they sit on the stoop in front of the New York City apartment building in which they live. As a result of these conditions, much of the city's life took place during the steamy summers on the teeming streets, with their vendors and carts and horse-drawn wagons— still common at this time—as well as automobiles and trucks. People spent less time in their baking apartments, which they used largely to sleep in at night. If they were too hot, they slept on the fire escapes of the crowded tenement buildings. Many people had radios and listened to music, weekly radio dramas, soap operas, and comedy series. There were movies to go to, but, of course, no such thing as television. And theaters and movie houses were not air-conditioned.

The role of the super, or maintenance man, in a New York apartment building was very important, as indeed it still is. But there is no longer a regular delivery of milk, which was always put into in glass bottles and left outside the apartment doors, like the newspapers. And there are no longer milk bill collectors, like Rice's character Mr. Sankey, whose job it was to make the rounds for the company. You could order cream, and the milk also came with cream on top: it could be skimmed off and used separately, leaving skim milk for drinking, or the bottle could be shaken to homogenize the milk.

In his autobiography, *In the Moment: My Life as an Actor*, the distinguished actor Ben Gazzara (b. 1930) describes what his childhood in a tenement apartment on Thirty-ninth Street on the East Side of New York City in the 1930s was like, before the family was able to move to a building his father had bought. The family lived in a typical three-room "railroad flat": the first room as you entered was the kitchen, which you passed through in a straight line into the living room, from which you entered the bedroom. The bathroom in the hall outside the apartment was shared by two families. There was only cold water, and the bathtub was a small one that could be attached to the kitchen sink to bathe the babies. The parents would take sponge baths at the sink, and for a full wash they would go to the then ubiquitous public baths. But Gazzara's family had some hot water, because his father "had rigged up a small boiler in the kitchen." When the Great Depression struck, they had a hard time of it; like so many families, because of the dreadful economic stagnation, they could never break even.

The activities or stage business that actors have to do has changed considerably, because of the advances in technology. I smiled during a recent rerun of an episode of *Murder, She Wrote*, from the 1980s, when a young lady's beeper goes off as she is sitting in a restaurant and she says to the waiter, "Bring me a phone." The technology, which seemed advanced at the time, is so out of date in the age of cell phones; yet it was only twenty-five years ago. Indeed, even by the end of the series, with very large cell phones and the first laptop computers, the technology is very dated: floppy discs are still in use, for instance; and the computers are large and clunky. Once upon a time, as in the era of *Street Scene*, you wound a crank on a wall telephone, then talked to an operator: "Hello, Central? Get me Cypress 1-345, please"; or, perhaps in a small rural town, "Hi, Gladys [the operator was always a woman], can you get me Doc over at the grocery store?"

One of Rice's characters, Rose Kaplan, works in an office. There, too, the technology was almost totally different from today's computer and internet world, with its instantaneous exchange of e-mails and its Google searches. Secretaries, who were mostly women, took dictation of letters and other documents from their bosses in shorthand with a pad and pencil. Typewriters were manual, and ribbons had to be changed fairly frequently, where today we change printer cartridges. And the keys were very hard to the touch, and difficult to press: we had such typewriters up through the sixties, all the time I went to high school and college and graduate school, until the invention of the electric typewriter, which was followed by the word processor, ancestor of writing programs like Word for today's computers. And carbon copies of documents were made, using inked carbon paper between sheets of typewriter paper; only a limited number of copies could be made this way. There were also mimeograph machines, which one cranked by hand, since replaced by today's Xerox copy machines. And such was the world. And it seemed very modern and up to date!

The plot of *Street Scene*: On a terribly hot day, a group of New Yorkers are out on the street in front of their building, which is cooler than in their baking apartments. They are the city's inhabitants in microcosm, a cross-section of many of the groups in the 1930s population, including the native-born, and fairly recent immigrants from Germany, Sweden, Russia, and Italy. The bookish Sam Kaplan is in love with Rose, a secretary. His schoolteacher sister, Miss Kaplan, is unhappy about her brother's involvement with Rose. Their socialist immigrant father, Mr. Kaplan, gets into political arguments with his more conservative neighbors. Rose is the daughter of the jealous, angry stagehand, Mr. Maurrant, who keeps a strict eye on her and is abusive to his wife, Anna. She is having an affair with Mr. Sankey, the milk bill collector and a married man with children. All the neighbors gossip about it, except Sam, who can't stand such behavior. Mr. Maurrant suspects Anna, but does not know whether she really has a lover. One day, when he is supposed to leave for an unexpectedly postponed out-of-town tryout in New Haven, he comes home to find the two lovers in his apartment. He goes berserk and shoots them.

The themes of this melodramatic play, which is discussed succinctly by Paul A. Firestone in his magisterial *The Pulitzer Prize Plays: The First Fifty Years, 1917–1967* (Limelight, 2008), are immorality and bigotry. The prejudices of the period are more prominently portrayed in the play, less so in the film, and even less so in the 1947 "Broadway opera" by Kurt Weill (1900–1950), with a book by Rice and lyrics by Harlem Renaissance poet Langston Hughes (1902–1967), so that the major theme of racist and xenophobic prejudice is diffused by the time we get to the musicalization. But Weill's version is very effective, as two productions beautifully directed by Jay Lesenger in 2008, first at the Manhattan School of Music, then at the Chautauqua Opera, demonstrated.

This is the era of Jim Crow laws and de jure segregation of African Americans in the South, and of their de facto segregation in northern urban ghettos such as New York's famed Harlem. Interracial marriage was illegal in at least twenty states. Armed forces units were segregated, and there were segregated black colleges. Films with African-American casts were produced, but in mainstream Hollywood, African Americans usually played stereotypical maids or Pullman porters and others in subservient positions; the roles were usually walk-ons. Because of anti-Semitism, Jewish actors regularly changed their names to conceal their ethnicity and to open up greater possibilities for employment. The movement for civil rights would not really get under full steam until the

1960s, when prejudice and segregation were still heavily entrenched. Even in 1965, when I played the patter-song roles for Dorothy Raedler's American Savoyards, she insisted that I change my name to Robert Fields: Blumenfeld was "too ethnic," she said. Perhaps overly eager to play those parts, I complied. The season over, I immediately changed my stage name back. ("Too ethnic"—in New York?!)

Street Scene includes representatives of almost all the immigrant groups of the period: the Jews of Eastern Europe; the southern Italians of Naples and Sicily; the Germans; the Scandinavians (the Olsens, who are the janitors in the play; in the musical, Olsen is the super and the janitors are African American). The Maurrants and Officer Murphy, the Brooklyn cop, are native New Yorkers of Irish background. One of the nursemaids who come to gawk at the murder scene is an Irish immigrant. And there is the Jones family, representing the WASP (White Anglo-Saxon Protestant) majority, in this case, lower class, ignorant, and bigoted, with ingrained prejudices against immigrants and Jews. The ruling classes are not represented: the characters in this slice-of-life, realistic melodrama are all lower-middle- and middle-class types. There are no Asian characters, and no Hispanic or Caribbean characters, though all these groups were already in New York. But in the 1930s, the Chinese population, for instance, lived largely segregated in Chinatown in lower Manhattan, and not in Hell's Kitchen, where the play takes place. All of this is just prior to the Great Depression and several years before World War Two.

The play also takes place against the background of surviving Victorian attitudes, including that of Maurrant toward his daughter, Rose, and of the neighbors towards Mrs. Maurrant, whose affair with Mr. Sankey they know about and disapprove of. Of course, such attitudes are still with us: parents want to make sure their children are not indulging in sex, and few people would approve of adulterous affairs or marital infidelity. But Rose is already grown up, even though she lives at home, as many women in those days did until they were married, even when they had jobs. The condition of women was largely subservient to men, and an independent woman executive, lawyer, or doctor was a rarity. Even when women had jobs, they could not always afford their own New York City apartments. As the Depression continued, whole families would live in a few rooms. It was also not uncommon for young children of the same gender to sleep three or four in the only bed the family could afford, but this was the case even before the stock market crash. The Depression is heralded as well by the eviction of the Hildebrand family. Mrs. Hildebrand has been deserted by her husband, and she can no longer afford to pay the rent.

There are also character types of the period: the cad, represented by Harry Easter, the office manager who makes advances to Rose and is a descendant of the seventeenth- and eighteenth-century libertine, and the stereotypical Don Juan/Casanova figure. The type is still with us, of course. And some of the characters are stereotypical: the jovial, ice-cream loving Italian musician and music teacher, Mr. Fiorentino (better, certainly, than the later Mafia stereotype); the politicizing, outspoken Russian-Jewish leftist immigrant; his son, the unassuming Sam Kaplan, who doesn't want to fight; Miss Kaplan, the spinsterish intellectual schoolteacher daughter; Murphy, the wisecracking Irish-American Brooklyn cop; and the Irish-American Mr. Maurrant, who has a drinking problem.

The language of the play is almost more antique to us today than that of *Lady Windermere's Fan*, particularly because Rice employs such slang expressions as "I'll knock da stuffin's out o' him, dat's what I'll do!" And the old New York and Brooklyn accents of the period have long disappeared from the scene. Seldom does one hear such words as "work," "first" and "third" pronounced with the "oy" in "boy" anymore.

Mrs. Jones, the quintessential bigot and busybody neighbor, speaks poorly, and uses an expression that was clearly understood to be incorrect but that, oddly enough, is heard ubiquitously today, wrong as it is: "Between you and I..." The correct locution is, of course, "between you and me," since a preposition is followed by an object pronoun (me), not a subject pronoun (I). The use of such poor English shows the ignorance and low status of Mrs. Jones, who thinks so highly of herself. Her grammar is a great clue as to how to play the character. At one point, referring to Mr. Sankey, she says, "Ain't men the limit? What do you suppose he come walkin' by here for?" The dropping of the "g" and the use of "ain't" again show her lack of education, although nowadays "g" is regularly dropped, but "ain't" is still considered incorrect—it is seldom heard anymore in any case, except sometimes as a joke. The expression, "to come walking by" (rare today) should be past tense: came.

Mrs. Maurrant, too, uses substandard grammar sometimes: "My husband don't like it if he [their young son, Willie] stays out late." The use of "don't," instead of "doesn't," although incorrect nowadays, and even then, had been common in the Victorian era, where it sometimes seemed rather affected, as opposed to merely wrong.

At one point, Mr. Maurrant asks, "What's become of me wife?" This pronunciation of "my," common for the period, had been in use since the Victorian era and earlier, and was a regular feature of stage diction: You can hear Edwin Booth use it in his 1890 recording of Othello's act 1 speech to the Senate, whom he calls "Me very noble and approv'd good masters." Nowadays, it is purely dialectical, associated with Irish accents in particular. The fact that Maurrant is Irish-American would seem, however, to have nothing to do with this pronunciation, common to people of all backgrounds at the time.

Some Recommendations for Further Study of the Period

For the period of the Roaring 1920s, the Prohibition era, and the Great Depression, read Frederick Lewis Allen's *Only Yesterday: An Informal History of the 1920s* (Harper Perennial Classics, reissued, 2000), first published in 1931; and *Since Yesterday: The 1930s in America* (Harper and Row, reissued 1986), first published in 1939, on the eve of the war. These are popularizing histories, full of details about daily life, popular music, theater, movies, current events, and technology. These two books will give you wonderful background and a real feeling for the period. They deal almost exclusively with the United States. The second book covers some of the politics of isolationism, as well as the repercussions of Franklin D. Roosevelt's New Deal, but for a history of events in Europe you have to look elsewhere.

Although it is not a movie made in the era, one of the best films to see about what was going on in Italy in the mid-1930s is *Cristo si è fermato a Eboli* (Christ Stopped at Eboli, 1979), brilliantly researched and brilliantly acted. Directed by Francesco Rosi (b. 1922), this beautiful movie, which breathes authenticity, is based on the semi-autobiographical 1945 novel of the same name by Carlo Levi (1902–1975), an Italian-Jewish painter, writer, medical doctor, and antifascist political activist. His uncle, Claudio Treves (1869–1933), was an important socialist political leader. In 1935, Carlo Levi was exiled by the fascist government to a tiny mountain village near the larger town of Eboli, where the train stopped. His exile among the friendly villagers was not unhappy, and it turned out to be his good fortune, since he survived the war. His story is so very different from that of Anne Frank, discussed below.

The Italian population by and large was not anti-Semitic, and helped their Jewish fellow citizens at the risk of their own lives. After the war, Levi did a series of striking paintings of the people he had known and befriended there. Other Jews were not so lucky, and his namesake (no relation), the chemist Primo Levi (1919–1987), who later wrote about his experiences in several books, survived the horrors of the concentration camp.

In this film, available on a subtitled DVD from Facets Video, you can hear the colorful local dialect, very instructive to listen to. (There are sixteen groups of Italian dialects.) And you have a loving glimpse into the kind of life these people led, and into their attitudes. Many of them were very religious Catholics, for instance; and they were not terribly interested in fascism, which they simply accepted as the government's way of doing things. They were the salt of the earth, warm-hearted, and mired in poverty, but generous with what little they had. Their isolation and provincialism, the lack of modern technology, and the picturesque if rundown village houses and streets give you a perfect feeling for the life of the period.

World War Two

The war began on September 1, 1939 with Hitler's invasion of Poland, and ended in Europe on May 7–8, 1945 with the German surrender to the Allied forces led by the United States and Great Britain, after a bitter, hard-fought campaign spearheaded by the July 6, 1944 Normandy invasion. France had been occupied by the Germans since 1940 but had resisted the occupation heavily, despite the numerous collaborators and the pro-Nazi Vichy government centered in the unoccupied southern zone, which the Germans later occupied. The US had entered the war after December 7, 1941, when the Imperial Japanese navy had bombed the American fleet at Pearl Harbor, Hawaii, but the Japanese empire went down to defeat in August 1945, again after a brutal, drawn-out war in the Pacific theater, capped by the Americans dropping the atomic bomb on the Japanese cities of Hiroshima and Nagasaki.

As early as 1722, more than fifty years before the American Revolution, Benjamin Franklin penned an essay, "On Titles of Honour," in which he derided the necessity for distinguishing, hierarchical titles, particularly when it came to aristocratic designations; such titles would later be banned by the new US Constitution. In Marcel Ophuls' documentary *Le chagrin et la pitié* (The Sorrow and the Pity, 1970), there is a perfect example of the survival of the attitude that only the titled are worthy of consideration and respect. This point of view was known as "Old France." It was the right-wing, pre–World War I feudal attitude: everything that is *peuple* (people), and therefore not noble, is unworthy. The semi-feudal deference paid by some of the peasants to their lords and masters is exemplified in interviews with the peasant who works for the son-in-law of the sinister Vichy collaborator Pierre Laval (1883–1945), Count René de Chambrun (1906–2002), who was a descendent of the Marquis de Lafayette (1757–1834), of American and French Revolutionary fame. Physically, the peasant displays abject deference, and we can see him repressing any anger and resentment, smiling and glancing down. We get the impression that he would have been a counterrevolutionary during the French Revolution. Such feudal attitudes seem to lead in a direct line to fascistic and Nazi attitudes about superior and inferior people. The documentary deals in depth with the brutal Nazi occupation of the southern French city of Clermont-Ferrand, formerly in the so-called free zone, and by extension with conditions in general. If you do any project concerned with the war, make it your business to see this film.

The most central, horrifying events of the war for most of us are the use of the atomic bombs against Japan, and the Holocaust in Europe. The slaughter of people for the crime of being who they were and simply existing on this earth is so well documented that we know in detail what happened to six million Jews (close to half of them Poles), three million Christian Poles, including the intellectual class of university professors and scientists, five hundred thousand Gypsies; innumerable homosexuals; and as many as five thousand Jehovah's Witnesses, who all lost their lives. And those are only some of the groups marked for extermination in the name of one of the most vicious, pseudoscientific ideas ever invented: the fraud of racial purity, based on the scientifically false idea that there is such a thing as race. In any case, the arrogance, inhumanity, and hypocrisy of those who became mass murderers—the incredible egotism, sense of entitlement, and presumption of the criminals who considered themselves superior members of a master race—are as well documented as they are appalling.

But even in the face of the Nazi onslaught, at least some of the victims retained a sardonic sense of humor. In 1938, before the Nazis would let the aged and ill Sigmund Freud leave Vienna, they forced him to sign a declaration stating that they had treated him well. He dared to add a note: "I can highly recommend the Gestapo to everyone." The officials in charge either did not perceive or chose to ignore his sarcasm.

In doing what they did to the Jews, the Nazis' gangster regime gave the lie to the fiction of Jewish power and world domination: In Germany, the Nazis segregated the Jews, excluding them from public life as much as possible. Jewish children were not allowed to attend schools with "Aryan" children. The Nazis deprived Jews of their livelihoods by dismissing them from various jobs and professions, beginning with the civil service and education, and then deprived them of citizenship as well. Eventually, this created an impoverished class of people who had to be cared for on state welfare programs. Naturally, when they realized what they had done, the Nazis insisted that the Jewish community provide its own welfare programs. The Jewish community was unable to do so, however, in any meaningful or efficient way. Also, in legally prohibiting Jewish doctors from having non-Jewish patients, the Nazis ensured that all of a sudden many non-Jewish Germans would be without the medical care of their trusted physicians. However, the Germans implemented the dismissal of all Jewish doctors from their hospital posts and practices as slowly as possible, because they realized the implications. There were endless problems involving Jewish veterans of the Great War, Jewish converts to Christianity (still considered Jewish by the Nazis), and the Jewish spouses of Christian Germans, among other classes of people. In short, the blundering Nazi attempt to get rid of the Jews of Germany was a bureaucratic and humanitarian mess, aside from being incredibly stupid. Instead of realizing that Jews were simply one part of a whole integrated society and helped it function just as all its other elements did, the Nazis based their belief in the Jewish conspiracy on the delusion that the Jews were a race of interloping subhumans who had taken over most of the important positions in Germany, did not belong there, and were not German at all.

Another example of Nazi illogicality and stupidity: the Hungarian-born Emmerich Kálmán (1882–1953) was one of the greatest Viennese operetta composers. He wrote some two dozen tuneful, vibrant scores. Among his enthralling successes are the richly Hungarian-flavored *Csárdásfürstin* (The Csárdás Princess, 1915) and *Gräfin Mariza* (Countess Mariza, 1924); and the American jazz-influenced *Die Herzogin von Chicago* (The Duchess of Chicago, 1928). He was also a Jew. Despite that, he was one of Hitler's favorite composers! In 1938, after the Anschluss (the annexation of Austria), Hitler offered therefore to make him an "honorary Aryan," so his operettas could continue to be performed! What becomes then of the vaunted Nazi desire to eliminate so-called "Jewish" influence in the arts? One second before the granting of this "distinction," the music was evil, underhanded, nefarious, seductive of "Aryans," and a distraction from the Jewish conspiracy to take over the world; one second afterward, it was suddenly no longer even composed by a Jew—although it cannot be denied that it had been! Kálmán, of course, refused the "honor." His music was banned, except for presentations at the German *Jüdischer Kulturbund* (Jewish Cultural Organization), where performances by Jews only, for Jews only, took place. They put on *Gräfin Mariza*, with a censored libretto that eliminated references to Goethe, Schiller, and other "Aryans"—Jews no longer had any right even to mention the great "Aryans," or to include them in their culture: it was a contamination of his illustrious name and an insult to Goethe for a Jew to pronounce it! The composer was forced to emigrate, eventually going to the US, but returned to Vienna in 1949. He spent his last years in Paris, where he settled in 1951.

Once the war got under way, the Jews of Poland were among the first to be incarcerated in ghettos before the extermination camps were set up, in order to make it easier to ship the survivors off when the time came. Not even working for the Nazis in the virtual slave factories that made army uniforms could save them.

Half a million Jews were imprisoned behind the walls of the Warsaw Ghetto, when it was at its height, in horrendous conditions meant to kill off as many as possible gradually. They died of starvation and disease, or were shot in one of the almost daily raids, before the ghetto was destroyed by the Germans during the famous, heroic uprising of April 1943, mounted by those who remained after most of the population had been deported to death camps and murdered.

Here is an authentic Warsaw Ghetto joke: A man is standing on a corner in the ghetto, reading the Nazi newspaper, when a friend comes up to him and reproaches him. "How can you read that filthy rag? It's disgusting! I can't believe you!" "Well," says his friend, "I'll tell you. If I read the Jewish newspaper, what does it say? Twenty thousand Jews have been deported to the east from such and such a city, who knows where? More Jews are being rounded up from the countryside and brought to Warsaw. New discriminatory laws are being enacted. All Jewish males to be inducted into forced labor battalions, and so forth. But if I read the Nazi newspaper, what does it say? Jews control the world's finances. Jews run the media. Jews pull the strings. It makes me feel better!"

A Romantic Movie: *Casablanca* (1942)

Made in the midst of the war, which the US had entered at the end of the previous year, this classic film is also an authentic period piece. Its heroic theme, bound intimately to wartime conditions, is that there are times in your life when doing something for the greater good of mankind is more important than indulging your personal desires, where they are in conflict with that greater good. It takes great strength of character and great determination to do something as noble as sacrificing what you want more than anything in the world. If you don't know the full plot of this great classic film, I won't ruin it for you. By all means, see it! If you don't shed a tear at least once, well, then you are not fit for treasons, stratagems, and spoils.

Casablanca, which won the Oscar for best picture of the year in 1942, was made on a shoestring budget. Written by Howard Koch and the Epstein brothers, Julius and Philip, the Academy Award–winning script, with its memorable lines of dialogue and superb atmosphere, is often cited as one of the greatest screenplays. And the film was directed by the masterful Michael Curtiz, who also won an Oscar for best director.

The story takes place in occupied Casablanca, Morocco, during World War II. The city, run by the Vichy French government—a puppet regime under the thumb of the Nazis, symbolized by the police captain Renault (played by the urbane, charming Claude Rains)—is a way station for people wanting to escape to freedom. But many of them do not have the means to do so.

The hard-boiled American Rick (Humphrey Bogart) runs a café that is a meeting place for all kinds of people, and caters to well-heeled German officers such as Major Strasser (Conrad Veidt [1893–1943]; a staunch anti-Nazi, he left Germany for England in 1933), as well as to penniless European refugees. Rick is neutral and takes no sides, refusing to be involved in politics. One day, Ilse Lund (Ingrid Bergman) shows up with her husband, Victor Laszlo (Paul Henreid), a very important, underground leader of the Resistance to the Nazis. Ilse and Rick have a history; they were lovers in Paris while Victor was in a concentration camp from which he eventually escaped, precipitating Ilse's sudden disappearance. Left without any explanation, Rick was baffled and deeply hurt. Now, when she turns up unexpectedly at his café with Victor, the wounded Rick has adopted a cynical veneer that makes him seem impervious and lacking in empathy. The Laszlos need Rick's help to elude the Nazis and the Vichy police. Will he help them, or turn Victor over to the authorities and certain doom? There are, of course, many plot complications involving other characters, and the cast is practically a who's who of Hollywood character actors of the period, including S. K. "Cuddles" Sakall, Sydney Greenstreet, and Peter Lorre, all of whom turn in marvelous performances. The film is perfect for background and the general atmosphere of the period.

The Diary of Anne Frank

The successful 1955 Broadway play *The Diary of Anne Frank*, by Frances Goodrich and Albert Hackett, revived on Broadway in 1997, is often done in regional theaters. The play was first made into a film in 1959, with a script by the playwrights, and with Joseph Schildkraut as Otto Frank, reprising the role he had created on Broadway. There have since been other media versions, including a 1980 television film, which is quite good; two television miniseries in 1987 and 2009; and a 1967 television film. All versions are based on the world-famous book, *Anne Frank: The Diary of a Young Girl*, published in 1947 (first English translation, 1952), in an expurgated version that eliminated passages thought to be too personal by her father, Otto Frank (1889–1980). He had been given the diary and other papers when he revisited the rear annex above the shop, where the family had hidden before being betrayed to the Nazis and arrested. The diary had been retrieved from the ransacked hideout by one of the people who cared for the Franks and brought them food while they were in hiding, the heroic and self-effacing Miep Gies (1909–2010). The full version was finally published by Doubleday in 2003, in a revised and updated edition. If you are doing this play, naturally the first thing you will do is to read the book, which fills in many details that are of help in bringing the characters to life.

Anne Frank, a teenaged Jewish girl living in Amsterdam, wants to be a great writer, to be treated like an adult, and to be taken seriously. Helped by empathetic friends, soon after the Nazis occupy Holland, she and the rest of her German immigrant family—her father, Otto; her mother; and her older sister, Margot—go into hiding in a rear annex attic above the shop that houses Otto's spice importing business. They share the space with a Dutch Jewish family, the van Daans. Anne falls in love with Peter van Daan. The families are later joined by the fussy dentist Dr. Dussell, who is used to living alone. They are betrayed to the Nazis by someone unknown to this day, and shipped off to a concentration camp. Otto is the only survivor.

Except for the Frank family, the characters in the play were fictionalized, based on the real people discussed in the diary; and they are portrayed from Anne's own particular point of view. During the play, Anne is actually beginning to achieve all three of her objectives, as she starts to mature and to grow up emotionally, and to understand the nature of love and desire.

Of course, as an actor you have to deal with the fictionalized character you are playing. You can't worry about how or where it departs from the actual historical personage. For dramatic reasons, the characters have been given certain traits that allow for conflict with the other characters, whether or not the conflicts were historical.

What to Wear for Rehearsal

Modern dress is all that is required for rehearsal, with the proviso that the actor should dress formally or informally, depending on the role and the given circumstances. Do try to wear any special costume pieces, such as a soldier's helmet, or at least a hat to simulate it. The wearing of hats was certainly widespread, and the actor in any outdoor scene, or when making an entrance from outdoors, will probably want to wear one for rehearsal. Women wore hats and gloves and carried purses outdoors, so, again, women will want to do this when rehearsing, unless they know they will not be doing this in performance. Generally speaking, actors should not wear sneakers to rehearsal, unless they are specifically required for the play. Wear sensible, good walking shoes: most of the time, this is the kind of footwear that will be worn during performances. A performance note: Since men and women's hairstyles changed over the decades, these should be studied, and carefully done for all the characters, so as to keep in period. The wrong hairstyle is very distracting to anyone in the audience familiar with the era.

Some Post-Stanislavskian Approaches to Theater, Character Creation, and the Art of Acting

INTRODUCTION

Dissent and Variations

All of the early- to mid-twentieth-century theorists and practitioners discussed in this part, including the Russians, the Americans, and those Russian-born Americans who became actors and teachers in New York and Hollywood, taught their own interpretations of Stanislavsky, each one emphasizing different aspects of the system. In some cases, notably those of Yevgenyi Vakhtangov, Vsevolod Meyerhold, and Michael Chekhov, they eventually departed radically from Stanislavsky. All three added valuable imaginative tools to the actor's kit.

Berthold Brecht's theories about theater as a politicizing instrument for positive social change, as well as his plays, had an enormous influence, reflected in Poland in the productions of Jerzy Grotowski, in Norway's Odinteatret with the presentations of the Italian director Eugenio Barba, and in the United States in such companies as Joseph Chaikin's Open Theater. The Brazilian director Augusto Boal, with his ideas about the anthropology of the theater, followed suit. The English director and theoretician Peter Brook, headquartered in Paris, exerted enormous influence on the theatrical avant-garde with *The Empty Space: A Book About the Theatre: Deadly, Holy, Rough, Immediate* (Touchstone, 1968). In the same way, the iconoclastic, half-mad playwright, actor, and director Antonin Artaud (1896–1948), Brook's rather strange and off-putting avant-garde precursor in France, was considered far-reaching in his productions. They could be stark and difficult, and many were considered failures, but they were meant to change the audience and to awaken them to their political and social situation. In that, Artaud resembled playwrights Samuel Beckett and Eugène Ionesco, with their theater of the absurd. Both dramatists wrote plays considered startling and almost indecipherable when they were produced, but we now find them amusing, entertaining, and quite comprehensible in their symbolism. Despite their iconoclastic ideas about theater, Stanislavsky was their actual precursor when it came to the art of interpreting characters, no matter how much they may have professed to disagree with his principal idea that an actor embodies a character.

If a system or a method of acting doesn't give you the freedom to soar, to take off, doesn't inspire you, doesn't allow for spontaneity, then it is useless. If it imprisons you and stifles your creativity, and if you feel you have to follow it obsessively and slavishly, then you are already heading in the wrong direction. At the Moscow Art Theatre, Meyerhold, Vakhtangov, and Michael Chekhov felt that Stanislavsky's system, as he taught it, had made actors do just that, even though many of his principles were sound and his ideas praiseworthy as well as practical. These dissenters proceeded to modify the system so as to leave even greater room for the imagination than they felt Stanislavsky had done. Vakhtangov and Michael Chekhov wanted the actor to feel free and creative, to enter the life of the character with gusto and passion and even with abandon. For acting to have the feeling of "as if for the first (and only) time," it had to have the unique feeling of being improvised every time, however carefully a play had been rehearsed, and however minutely the details had been worked out. Some students and teachers at the MAT Studio thought that Stanislavsky had not actually solved this paradox. And Meyerhold veered in another direction entirely, considering the actor almost like a machine whose movements were what communicated story and character to the audience; his stylized "biomechanical" productions reflected his ideas.

In any case, it is important to bear in mind that the Stanislavsky system is the basis of the acting technique required for film and television, as well as for most plays in today's theater. The audience still expects to see actors behaving like real people. And there is no other system that allows actors to do so. I include in this idea such variations on the system as the Meisner technique, Uta Hagen's teachings, and even Strasberg's more eclectic Method, all discussed below.

You will find many useful ideas and techniques in the following pages, and they may all be added to your actor's toolkit. They will be additions, not subtractions, to all the basic elements you must consider when bringing a character to life.

CHAPTER FIFTEEN

The Russians:
Vsevelod Meyerhold;
Yevgenyi Vakhtangov

Vsevolod Emilievich Meyerhold (1874–1940)

A leading figure in Soviet Russian theater, Vsevolod Meyerhold was a fiercely energetic, dynamic stage director who split away from the Moscow Art Theatre and Stanislavsky artistically while remaining attached to him personally. In fact, Stanislavsky admired him. Meyerhold was a committed Communist but remained a staunch advocate of individualistic artistic rights. Unfortunately, he ran afoul of the Soviet authorities with his innovative, abstract productions. In the tense atmosphere of the 1930s, he had not paid enough attention to the principles of Socialist Realism. He paid for his dissidence and innovations with his life: Stalin had him murdered.

Meyerhold, nurtured first on the vast corpus of classic Russian literature (Lermontov, Pushkin, Turgenev, Gogol, Dostoevsky, Tolstoy), was fascinated by symbolism, the late nineteenth-century European movement in the arts that was a revolt against realism and naturalism. One of its main ideas is that everything can be viewed as a sign, or a symbolic representation of something else. The movement was a precursor of the contemporary critical school of semiotics and deconstruction.

Well before the literary movement formalized the symbolic approach to composition, objects stood for or symbolized abstract qualities or emotions. For example, in the old-fashioned language of plants and flowers, the acacia flower symbolizes secret love; the bay leaf, strength (as in the Roman laurel wreath awarded to the conquering hero); and the red rose, "I love you." Symbolism, in the form of metaphor, has always been part of poetry. The movement was typified in late nineteenth-century France by such poets as Paul Verlaine, Arthur Rimbaud, and Stéphane Mallarmé, and by the Belgian dramatist Maurice Maeterlinck, whose play *The Blue Bird* Stanislavsky, intrigued by symbolism and fantasy, began to rehearse in 1907.

Symbolism and symbolist drama deal in vague moods and dreamlike atmospheres, as in Debussy's impressionistic opera of Maeterlinck's *Pelléas et Mélisande*. The staging of symbolist plays demands a different directorial approach from the plays of Chekhov, for example, and a different way for actors to approach character. There is a greater emphasis on the plastic side of the character (movement, posture, gesture, physicality) and less on the character's emotional, inner life. Chekhov himself was influenced by symbolism, as witness, for example, his use of timepieces in *Three Sisters*. It was just this sort of drama and these ideas that attracted Meyerhold and caused him to want to go off on his own to experiment.

He was an extremely inventive technician and director who understood the actor's process and wanted to reinvent it for his own "biomechanical" productions. "Biomechanical acting" is Meyerhold's term for precise, perfectly timed movements, gestures, and expressions that become automatic once they have been rehearsed. For him, movement constituted the essence of the actor's art, as opposed to the psychological approach of Stanislavsky. The term "biomechanics" includes the process and the plastic techniques involved in such acting.

Meyerhold wanted actors' movements to be concise and expressive, in the service of his abstract and sometimes circus-like productions. This meant the movements, like those in dance, had to be repeatable exactly, without variations. It also meant that no movement could be extraneous or meaningless: every move was in the service of the character and the situation. And in the case of certain timed movements and tricks in farce or comedy, the ability to repeat such movements and to time them exactly has to be part of the actor's technical equipment no matter what the approach to character creation.

As a director, Meyerhold chose not to work out detailed staging until later in the rehearsal process, preferring to absorb and know the play thoroughly, and to let it work on his unconscious imagination. This is also useful for an actor, whose interpretation and physical embodiment of a role should not be set until a more complete understanding of the material has been attained organically through the rehearsal process.

In his grotesque, futuristic productions, Meyerhold used everything he could think of: masks; stylized adaptations of the already stylized Japanese kabuki and martial arts techniques of movement; acrobatics and circus tricks; machine-like assembly line movement; and realistic interpretations of characters, as well as outright caricature. These could be all mixed together in productions that sometimes used abstract sets suggestive of Picasso paintings, full of angles and angular lines, abstract shapes and forms, influenced as well by the look of factories and smoke-stacks. Meyerhold has indeed been called the Picasso of the theater. He believed passionately in the dynamic theatrical and dramatic nature of the experience he wanted both actors and audience to have, an experience that would take them beyond the reality of their lives into the heightened realm of fantasy.

He was an extravagant visionary who never wrote down in any systematic way what he believed and how he worked, but his student and close associate Aleksandr Gladkov kept extensive, detailed notes on everything Meyerhold said and did, and his book *Meyerhold Speaks Meyerhold Rehearses* (Routledge, 1997) is an invaluable compendium of ideas and principles. Meyerhold wanted his actors to take pleasure in their work, to find the pleasure in every move they made. He was a master stylist and technician of acting whose pithy style was itself an expression of his ideas on actors' precision. He worked with actors on the music, rhythm, and overall composition of a piece, as much as on the nature of their individual performances.

Meyerhold's concept of biomechanics called for the actor of the future to be trained thoroughly in order to become "biomechanical." He discussed the nature of how action takes place in time and space. By action, he meant actual physical movement, which he thought of in terms of the following categories, for which he devised études (exercises):

1. **Backing off:** Proceeding in the opposite direction from the direction one started in.

2. **Braking:** Stopping a movement and remaining in the attitude assumed when the stop occurred.

3. **Gesture close-ups:** Concentration on a particular movement while all else around it remains still.

4. **Contrast:** The difference between moving and remaining still at the desired moment, as in braking.

5. **Dispatching:** Concentrating on the main movement.

6. **Repetition and Variation:** Doing the same movement several times with a slight difference each time.

The results of his biomechanics may strike us nowadays as technical and old-fashioned, though they were considered highly innovative at the time. Meyerhold's ideas about acting are closely related to clowning and acrobatics, and even to the mechanical work of assembly lines in factories. But it is true that no matter what school of acting one subscribes to, precision is clearly a necessary component of the art. In realistic dramas, for instance, in such situations as fistfights or swordplay, every movement must be precisely reproduced every time, or else there is danger of injury and worse.

Among other ideas related to precision was Meyerhold's division of every action into three parts, in accordance with the idea that each action has a rhythm: preparation, actually doing the action, and ending the action, leaving room for the possibility of a new action. Part of his training of actors consisted of having them break down actions into their components. They would then put the components together smoothly and accurately.

When analyzing emotions, Meyerhold thought in terms of what he called "montage": the origin of an emotion could be understood by juxtaposing the elements from which it was synthesized. As Jonathan Pitches tells us in *Vsevolod Meyerhold* (Routledge, 2003), two disparate things are put together, and "our *psychological* response to those things is to create a third 'representation.' " For instance, put an eye and water together, one after another, and you come up with crying. The approach seems rather simplistic when it comes to acting, but is very useful for directors or designers, who can juxtapose disparate visual elements that will have an immediate effect on the audience. The idea had a great influence on the filmmaking techniques of Serge Eisenstein. You can see this quite clearly in the two parts of *Ivan the Terrible* (1942; 1946) and *Alexander Nevsky* (1938), all of which are extremely melodramatic and highly stylized.

Meyerhold techniques that we still use today in the theater include working with masks in both the classroom and rehearsal. This is meant to free the actor of certain inhibitions, but it simultaneously limits the possibilities for expression. Masks encourage the actor to be spontaneous and physical in the approach to creating a character. Also derived from Meyerhold is the speed-through rehearsal, where the actors rush through the play in record time. Meyerhold would have his actors do a selective, three-minute version of a play, then list the events they had chosen to include, as a way of zeroing in on what was most important.

Michael Redgrave opined in *The Actor's Ways and Means* that a certain amount of biomechanics was useful as an accompaniment to the Stanislavsky system, which Redgrave himself had espoused. This was as true in performing Shakespeare as in Chekhov and contemporary plays. In other words, a certain amount of calculation in the use of gestures and movements might not be out of place and could be helpful. But, he warned, "It becomes dangerous the moment the audience can spot what is happening and senses the artificial." For Redgrave, nothing must look calculated: everything must appear to happen naturally and organically.

Yevgenyi Bagrationovich Vakhtangov (1883–1922)

The actor and director Yevgenyi Vakhtangov studied with Stanislavsky and was an important member of the Moscow Art Theatre Studio, where he taught. While agreeing with most of Stanislavsky's ideas on acting, he disagreed with him in certain ways. His death at the age of only thirty-five deprived the theater world of one of its most creative minds. He had tried to synthesize Meyerhold and Stanislavsky's ideas into an approach to the actor's art that he called "fantastic realism."

Accepting Stanislavsky's idea of emotional recall, Vakhtangov extended the idea of substitution and dwelt on the overriding importance to the actor of repeated, recollected emotion. He took from Stanislavsky the idea that everything the actor does must be justified and, once again, extended it: the actor should feel free to use anything internal that worked, including the most extravagant fantasy and imagination as needed. And, following Stanislavsky's idea, he told a student at the Moscow Art Theatre Studio after an étude (acting class exercise), "*Action*, not emotion." By this he meant exactly what Stanislavsky meant: Perform the correct psychophysical action, and the correct accompanying emotion will be awakened; don't try to force the emotion into existence. You feel something, or you don't. He talked as well of the necessity of a "circle of attention," which was much the same as the Stanislavskian concept of the creative circle; but he dealt with it in terms of its being an outward radiation that could gradually encompass and include a wider area, even, on occasion, as in the case of a Shakespearean soliloquy, the audience itself.

Also in line with Stanislavskian concepts are Vakhtangov's ideas about the necessity of believing in the truth of what one is doing as an actor, as in this quotation, in Nicolai Gorchakov's *The Vakhtangov School of Stage Art* (Foreign Languages Publishing House, n.d.):

> What does believing mean? You can't believe that a notebook is a box of chocolates because at the rehearsal you see clearly that it is a notebook. And if the actor sees that it is a notebook, he can't believe it is a box of chocolates. But he can make himself look upon it as a box of chocolates. And that's precisely what one needs to make stage truth one's own. The actor knows that the man before him is his friend and not King Lear. Therefore he can't believe it is Lear, but he can learn to treat his friend as the king.

This expresses succinctly the heart and essence of the system, and of Vakhtangov's teaching of it: Do not deny the truth of what you know. Instead, use the "magic if" to project yourself into the circumstances, so that you can treat a notebook "as if" it were a box of chocolates. There is no acting without truth and "as if." In other words, you don't have to pretend that something is what it isn't, only to behave as if it is what it is supposed to be. That, coupled with immersing yourself in the given circumstances, and finding the correct objectives, obstacles, and actions, is the foundation of the system.

Arising from this idea is one of Vakhtangov's important, heretical deviations from the Stanislavsky system, namely his concept of the "object of attention," which has to do with the nature and use of substitution. For purposes of concentrating, the actor has to have selected an internal object on which to concentrate his attention, and, as far as Stanislavsky was concerned, that object must be connected to the play, to the objective or relationship, or to the time and place of the given circumstances. But for Vakhtangov, the virtual originator of the "actor's secret," the object of attention is not necessarily required to have anything whatsoever to do with the material being performed. And neither the director, nor fellow actors, nor the audience need ever know or guess what it is: it remains the actor's secret. The actor can think about anything—what he or she has to buy at the grocery store on the way home, the pleasure or misery of a relationship, the weather outside—anything at all. This helps the actor to relax and to concentrate. But to Stanislavsky, this was not only heresy, it was also ridiculous and anti-art. It has nevertheless persisted in contemporary acting practice, and is a particularly useful technique on camera when the actor is simply being filmed without dialogue and is in the act of thinking.

Vakhtangov's idea of the actor's job as an artist was quite simple: the actor had to understand the character's intellect and objective; feel the character's desires in a visceral, physical way; and adjust all that intellect and emotion to the demands of interpreting a text according to the requirements of a director. The actor then had to perform; that is, to communicate everything clearly to the audience.

In performing the material and using substitution and endowment, the actor is free to make up an entire scenario for what is happening. It may be a completely private scenario, unfathomable to anyone else, but as long as it makes sense to the actor, who is in essence performing his own play in his head, then that actor is free to do as he or she wishes. Provided the actor appears to everyone else involved (including the audience) to be serving the material and to be in consonance with it, and, importantly, as long as the actor continues to relate to the other actors in character and to communicate with them, he or she can make any substitutions at all.

If the character needs to be on tenterhooks, upset and waiting for some result, such as a verdict in a trial or news from a doctor, and if you have never experienced such an event, then the substitution might consist of remembering and recalling a day when you had to wait for the restoration of your internet service. You couldn't do anything but wait. What did you do while waiting? Probably you did some light cooking or made a sandwich for lunch. You made some calls on your cell phone. You read, watched television, tried to doze. You experienced frustration, tension and anger. The memory of all these things, or of a visit to the doctor or dentist when you were kept waiting, or the memory of waiting for someone who stood you up, might serve you very well and give reality to the scene, even in the simple opening scene of Hamlet, where people are impatiently waiting for each other. The guard says, "'Tis bitter cold and I am sick at heart..." and a substitution lends reality to that line. And such a substitution will help you avoid the cliché of pacing back and forth, which is usually merely an indication of frustration rather than the real thing, and was exactly the sort of stereotypical, illustrated, unreal behavior that so annoyed Stanislavsky.

We can all imagine everything. Furthermore, we all have the capacity to act in the most appalling ways in our imagination. Of course, thinking of homicide is not the same as committing it. Nevertheless, even thinking such thoughts can arouse feelings of rage and guilt. And the memory of such thoughts and such feelings may be exactly what is required in order to play a certain character convincingly, really, and specifically.

CHAPTER SIXTEEN

The Russian Émigrés: Maria Ouspenskaya and Richard Boleslavsky; Michael Chekhov

Maria Ouspenskaya and Richard Boleslavsky Bring the System to America

The actor and director Richard Boleslavsky (1889–1937) left the Soviet Union in 1920 and emigrated eventually to the United States. A former member of the Moscow Art Theatre, he was invited to work with the company again when it was in New York in 1923–1924, particularly because he was adept at staging crowd scenes. In the same years, he founded the American Laboratory Theatre, where he taught the Stanislavsky system. But the American Lab was always in financial difficulty, even though it maintained itself until 1930.

After the Moscow Art Theatre tours of the early 1920s, a number of Russian actors defected, deciding to stay in the United States and involve themselves in teaching the system. Among them was Maria Ouspenskaya (1876–1949). She taught the orthodox Stanislavsky system at the American Lab, and in 1928 also gave classes at the new Neighborhood Playhouse, later taken over by Sandy Meisner (see next chapter). She taught what she had learned directly from Stanislavsky in the Moscow Art Theatre Studio classes and productions. Her emphasis was on observing people and life so as to be able to reproduce real behavior; on concentration as an all-important condition for acting; and on affective memory, particularly emotional memory. At the Lab, physical and spiritual exercises and improvisations were part of the training. Ouspenskaya's teaching formed a generation of actors and teachers, right down to her autocratic methods of pedagogy, so that the acting studio teacher became generally as much a star as her pupils. Ouspenskaya could be bitterly sarcastic in her remarks and very difficult to deal with, but she was revered for her knowledge and her ability to transmit it.

Among her students were Stella Adler and Lee Strasberg, both discussed in the next chapter. Whereas Adler met and talked with Stanislavsky about his latest ideas, Strasberg stuck to what he had learned from Ouspenskaya about emotional recall, about which Stanislavsky had changed his thinking. This was one of the causes of the conflict over theory and practice between Adler and Strasberg, as we shall see. It is a shame that Ouspenskaya always refused to write a book setting down her teaching, of which we know a great deal at second hand from her students.

The diminutive actress with the heavy Russian accent played on Broadway for more than ten years, and in 1929 she founded her own Maria Ouspenskaya School of Dramatic Art in New York, in order to promote Stanislavsky's ideas; it lasted until 1949. To help finance her teaching ventures, she went to Hollywood in 1936 to make *Dodsworth*, based on a Sinclair Lewis novel, and remained there to teach and to act, appearing in more than twenty films. Watching her is a true lesson in the authentic Stanislavsky system. After the war, she started teaching again in Hollywood, and renamed the school The American Repertory Theatre and Studio.

Boleslavsky went on to Hollywood, where he became a film director, with more than twenty motion pictures to his credit, including one of his greatest successes, *The Garden of Allah* (1936), and the 1935 adaptation of Victor Hugo's *Les Misérables*, starring Frederic March as Jean Valjean and Charles Laughton as Inspector Javert.

His brilliant, now classic book, *Acting: The First Six Lessons* (Theatre Arts Books, 1933), is still available, having gone through numerous printings. This brief, succinct volume (it is only 122 pages) covers the elements of acting and is eminently readable (however off-putting the author's male chauvinism), as well as very useful for actors.

The six lessons, each one a chapter, are in the form of charming, instructive dialogues between "I" (Boleslavsky) and a "Creature" of eighteen years old who wants to study dramatic art. But art, which is the same thing as talent, says Boleslavsky, cannot be taught. Talent can be developed through education. It is not easy to pursue the ephemeral art of acting, with its temporary rewards, no matter how great the desire to act, unless you are willing to sacrifice much for your art.

The lessons are on the following subjects, each one given its own chapter:

1. **Concentration:** Like all people involved in their work, in solving problems or in other tasks, actors performing a part pay attention

only to what they are bent on accomplishing. That is concentration, and its object is an "invented or imagined" inner life that the actor has created: this is what the actor concentrates on.

2. **Memory of Emotion:** In order to create the imaginary inner life, and its outward manifestation in action, the actor must search within for remembered feelings that will arouse the emotions the actor wishes for the character: "You will have to organize and synchronize the self that is within you, with your part." Also, feelings, which have a special memory of their own, are aroused and work unconsciously, as the result of action.

3. **Dramatic Action:** The writer uses words to express actions, "which the actor performs." An action is expressed in terms of verbs. A series of complementary actions are combined to fulfill the main action.

4. **Characterization:** This aspect of a performance entails far more than simply putting on costume and makeup and looking like the character physically. It is the unique, specific way of expressing the particular character's emotions and inner life that constitutes characterization. Nothing is expressed in a generalized way that could serve for any other character.

5. **Observation:** Watching what people do, how they behave, and how they carry out everyday actions is necessary if the actor is to reproduce real behavior and not present some mechanical, hack cliché.

6. **Rhythm:** Rhythm consists of the fluctuations and changes that take place in time as actions are being performed. Finding the rhythm is the most difficult and demanding actor's task. It does not consist merely of finding a tempo, of speeding up or slowing down, but of variations that are imposed from within and without, and which, once found, sweep you along.

Boleslavsky also deals with acting for the camera in the relatively new medium of talking films and says it is the same in some ways as acting on stage, because you still have to understand the character's throughline and the themes of the script, and to play actions from wherever the scene begins. The main difference between acting for the camera and acting for the stage is that the performance for the camera has to be smaller and more natural, without the voice being projected. Otherwise, script analysis and playing actions in furtherance of objectives is the same, with the proviso that scenes are broken up, and you may do a minute here and a minute there, without playing a scene through from beginning to end. You must "turn on" the character at any time, and at any moment in the script, which means that you must have worked out the arc of the part and the throughline on your own. There is usually only a scant amount of time allowed for rehearsal. As Alice Spivak points out, the actor playing for the camera "accumulates" the character, rather than playing the character through from beginning to end, as in a stage production. And the experience of acting for the camera is therefore different, and cumulative—an exercise in technique that involves the ability to remember and repeat as exactly as possible the same physical positioning from take to take, so that the film can be edited. For more on acting for the camera, see the book Alice Spivak and I wrote, *How to Rehearse When There Is No Rehearsal: Acting and the Media.*

Michael Chekhov (1891–1955)

Perhaps the most truly innovative and lasting departure from Stanislavsky's way of working, or, rather, one of the most innovative extensions of it, is the imaginative and simultaneously practical approach of playwright Anton Chekhov's nephew, Michael Chekhov. He eventually taught in Hollywood, as did his associate George Shdanoff (1905–1998), another Russian immigrant. Shdanoff and his wife, Elsa Schreiber (?–1982), were considered two of the greatest acting teachers and coaches in America, and their influence was enormous. Nevertheless, Chekhov had his dissenters. Strasberg, for instance, was not convinced that Chekhov's way, by itself, was the best method of actor training and practice. He said, "There is value in the psychological gesture, but in the rest I don't agree with him." Strasberg's way of working would have been anathema to Chekhov.

Michael Chekhov was Stanislavsky's star pupil at the First Moscow Art Theatre Studio. He was also a brilliant actor—some have said he was the greatest actor of the twentieth century. His Hamlet was legendary, and Stanislavsky said of him, quite simply, "He is a genius."

It was America's gain and Russia's loss that the political situation in the USSR in 1928 forced him to leave his native country for good. He went first to Great Britain and then to Hollywood, where he appeared in films. You can see him playing an earnest psychiatrist in Alfred Hitchcock's *Spellbound* (1945) and a rather fey ballet impresario in Ben

Hecht's strange film *Spectre of the Rose* (1949), in which Shdanoff also appears. Chekhov taught his way of working to a generation of movie actors who lit up the screen. In fact, the actors who trained and coached with him, and with Shdanoff and Elsa Schreiber, are an astounding who's who of mid-twentieth-century Hollywood. You cannot teach charisma and "radiation," to use Chekhov's word, but the stars who studied with him certainly had it, and the imaginative methods he taught them were no doubt responsible for their developing it further. He himself was terribly afraid of being what he called an "accent clown," and his acting career in the English-speaking world was perforce curtailed by his rather heavy Russian accent. He could play Hamlet in Russian to great acclaim, but he could not even attempt the role in English.

Although based in the Stanislavsky system, without which his ideas are almost inconceivable, he takes the actor into the realm of the imagination in a very original way in accordance with Stanislavsky's dictum: "Not a step should be taken on stage without the cooperation of your imagination." And he by no means neglects such necessary ideas as objectives and actions, concentration and relaxation, and naïve belief and faith in the reality of what the actor is doing. As you are beginning to find the objectives and actions, you can use his techniques to help propel yourself into the character. Chekhov's book *To the Actor on the Technique of Acting* (revised and expanded ed., Routledge, 2002) details his unorthodox methods of work, which some would find tinged with mysticism. It should be on every actor's bookshelf.

The way Chekhov has actors use their imaginations is amazing, very freeing, and does not rely on personal experiences in the Stanislavsky mold, but makes use of visualizations and improvisations that take the actor out of him- or herself and into the character. His idea was that the character's ego should be paramount, and the actor's subordinate to it. And there was no reason why purely imaginative substitutions could not be used.

Michael Chekhov's techniques are designed to propel the actor into action, to make the actor dynamic, and to awaken the character's dynamism as well. It takes time to find the psychological gesture, the center, and the images. They are not simply instant ways of approaching a character, but must be carefully considered, experimented on, and worked with. You can learn more about the following techniques from Lisa Dalton's *From Russia to Hollywood: The 100-Year Odyssey of Chekhov and Shdanoff* (Singa Home Entertainment DVD, 2004), a wonderful, informative documentary in which many of the actors who studied with Chekhov and Shdanoff are interviewed, as well as Shdanoff himself:

1. **The psychological gesture:** The actor, after having begun exploring the character, has feelings about who the character is and what the character's overall nature is. He or she then finds a physical gesture that will awaken and free the desired feelings, emotions, impulses to action, and wants, both in specific scenes and moments, and will also arouse the general psychology of the character, so that the actor can begin to inhabit the character's inner world. You can think of the psychological gesture in terms of a verb: to grasp, to hug oneself, to jump, to fling one's arms in the air, to reach out, to hold. In *Lessons for the Professional Actor* (Performing Arts Journal Publications, 1985), based on classes he gave in 1941, Chekhov suggests this way of working with the psychological gesture:

   > Take a certain gesture, such as "to grasp." Do it physically. Now do it only inwardly, remaining physically unmoved. As soon as we have developed this gesture, it becomes a certain "psychology," and that is what we want. Now on the basis of this gesture, which you will do inwardly, say the sentence, "Please, darling, tell me the truth." While speaking, produce the gesture inwardly... Now do them both together—the gesture and the sentence. Then drop the physical gesture and speak, having the gesture inside only.

   When he played Hamlet, Michael Chekhov used what he called a "gothic" gesture, looking heavenward with his hands above his head in a kind of arch, hands touching, much like the arch over the portal of a Gothic cathedral.

2. **The character's center:** This involves the use of images for a character's psychological "center" and for arousing emotions and actions. The character's center—where the character "lives"—can be located anywhere on the body. The character leads from that center. A snob's center might be the tip of the nose, and the nose would be the center of the actor's concentration. The center of a character like Julius Caesar or Othello might be his right arm, in which he grasps the sword. Perhaps such a character's instincts are to be aggressive and to react with anger, which must then be controlled. Juliet's center might be her heart, and her instinct would be to love and to want to enfold someone in her embrace.

3. **The use of images for specific situations:** The actor uses imaginative visualizations in the playing of specific situations or moments; or uses the images to launch him- or herself into the situation. If a character is petrified, for instance, perhaps the imagined feeling of being chained to a wall and unable to move except in the most limited way may serve to arouse the necessary feelings and consequent actions. In *From Russia to Hollywood*, Leslie Caron talks about the idea that a quick and witty character, who may be very pleased with himself, and in a humorous, cheerful mood, might see the lines dancing before his eyes like a butterfly. This makes the character funny without the actor's even trying to be funny, as her droll demonstration shows us. As an exercise, try this with some of Oscar Wilde's sparkling dialogue or with a patter song from one of the Gilbert and Sullivan operettas. Aside from relaxing you as an actor, and giving you what Michael Chekhov called that all-important "feeling of ease," such a technique allows you to communicate to the audience with immediacy and liveliness, so that they can enjoy the performance as much as you do.

Similar exercises were already in use by Stanislavsky himself: In Toporkov's *Stanislavski in Rehearsal*, the actor describes an exercise Stanislavsky gave him when he was having difficulties finding a certain way of bowing peculiar to Chichikov during rehearsals of the adaptation of Gogol's *Dead Souls*. He had Toporkov imagine a drop of mercury rolling carefully off the top of his head, and down his back, without falling off his heel to the floor. This exercise succeeded, and the strange upward movement of the head that begins the bow led to the arching of the back as the actor bent forward, raising his heel slightly.

CHAPTER SEVENTEEN

The Americans: Stella Adler; Lee Strasberg; Sanford Meisner; Morris Carnovsky; Uta Hagen

Stella Adler's Classic Approach; Lee Strasberg's Method

Derived from Stanislavsky, but departing from his ideas in some ways, Stella Adler's (1901–1992) teachings are succinctly expressed in her book *The Technique of Acting* (Bantam Books, 1988). It contains her neat, compact, and clear approach to the art, filled with Adler's unique insights, gleaned partly in the days when she was a member of the Group Theater. An influential New York theater company and collective, the Group Theater was founded in 1931 by director Harold Clurman (1901–1980), producer Cheryl Crawford (1902–1986), and Lee Strasberg (1901–1982), who was an actor at the time, and who conducted acting classes for the company members. The Group, as it was colloquially called, lasted until 1941, and was known for its productions of plays by Irwin Shaw (1913–1984) and Clifford Odets (1906–1963), and for its realistic, Stanislavskian approach to acting. It was also known for presenting plays with social messages, and for the leftist political leanings of many of its members, who came under fire from the House Un-American Activities Committee and from the destructive Senator Joseph McCarthy in the 1950s. Among its famous members were actors Morris Carnovsky (1897–1992); his wife, Phoebe Brand (1907–2004); Sanford "Sandy" Meisner (1905–1997)—all of whom were also acting teachers—and director Elia Kazan (1909–2003), whose brilliant films, among them *Gentleman's Agreement* (1947), *A Streetcar Named Desire* (1951), *On the Waterfront* (1954), and *East of Eden* (1955) are legendary.

A member of the Communist Party, Kazan later betrayed his friends, whose names he gave to the House Un-American Activities Committee, and he was still justifying his actions years later. He cofounded the Actors Studio and opposed the hiring of Strasberg when the Studio was looking for an acting teacher. Kazan lost that fight, and, as we know, Strasberg eventually took over the Studio. I acted in a project there sometime in the late 1980s, an act from Mikhail Bulgakov's *A Cabal of Hypocrites* (also known as *Molière in Spite of Himself*). The play is an allegory, in which Louis XIV stands for Stalin, and Molière for Bulgakov, who was having his problems with the Soviet dictator. Kazan was the moderator for the session, and, instead of critiquing the project, he proceeded essentially to harangue us about how horrible Stalin was, and how dangerous American Communists had been—an attempt to excuse and justify what many of us perceived as the evil thing he had done.

Of all the members of the Group Theater who also taught acting, Adler's ideas seem closest to those of Stanislavsky. In company with Harold Clurman, she met Stanislavsky in Paris in 1934, when his earlier ideas about the extensive use of emotional recall had already been replaced by his "method of physical actions," and talked with him about his system. What she learned led her to disagree with Strasberg.

Stella Adler emphasizes the need for the actor to be knowledgeable in the arts and to have a general culture in order to gain the necessary background for interpreting plays. When it came to doing period plays, this was in complete accord with Stanislavsky's ideas.

The chapters in her book cover all the topics, beginning with elementary techniques of relaxation, communication with the audience, and muscular memory. The book continues with the use of the imagination, the necessity for specificity, dealing with the given circumstances, playing actions, creative justification, and developing characters. Chapter 9, "The Vocabulary of Action," includes details and exercises on such subjects as reminiscing, talking, chatting, conversing, discussing, arguing, explaining, dreaming, and philosophizing. These are extremely important elementary actions that characters, like people in real life, carry out all the time.

For Adler, as for Stanislavsky, the most important place to begin work on a play is the text itself, and script interpretation is a cornerstone of her way of working. You will find in the text all you need to know about the character's actions and objectives. The play comes first, and what the author says is paramount. You must project yourself into the given circumstances and make them real and personal by using your imagination and sense memory. But there is no necessity as far as Adler is concerned to use emotional memory in any extensive way, or to confuse the actor's needs and desires with the character's, even though you find analogies to those desires within yourself. In this way of approaching substitution, she differed from Lee Strasberg, who insisted on the actor's use of the self, and on emotional recall as the paramount actor's technique. For Strasberg, this was of prime importance for bringing a character and a scene to life. From Strasberg's point of view, early script interpretation could have the deleterious effect of limiting creativity and setting a performance before it had really been worked on and found in rehearsal. The controversy over these differing approaches was a bitter one for Strasberg and Adler, and for their followers. One of the reproaches directed against Strasberg's famous Method was the unassailable one that it differed considerably from Stanislavsky's system, which Strasberg was the first to admit: he felt that his approach was in fact superior to that of the great master, that he had gone beyond him.

It is worth noting that both Adler's and Strasberg's roots were in the old Yiddish theater, now largely gone. It flourished on New York's Lower East Side, among other venues, at the turn of the twentieth century, and was the product of Eastern European Jews, who brought it with them when they came to these shores. Influenced by what they knew of theater in Russia, they were probably the first people in the United States to adhere to the basic idealistic, lofty ethical principles of the Stanislavsky system, and they were passionate about it. In fact, passion was the basis of Yiddish theater: the passion of love and delight in performing everything to the hilt, taking emotion and exuberance as far as they could go. The influence of Yiddish theater on the surrounding English-speaking American theater and its acting styles was enormous. Actors who learned English, or their children who grew up with English, left the more parochial, limited Yiddish stage for the larger, majority theater, and people like Adler and Strasberg transmitted Stanislavskian methods, which have had a lasting impact.

Stella Adler was from one of the great Yiddish theater families. Her father, Jacob Adler, was one of its most renowned and beloved stars. A theater aficionado from the old days, who had seen many productions of *King Lear*, his favorite play, is reported to have said, "Everybody does it in English! But Jacob Adler, ah, he is the real King Lear: he does it in Yiddish!"

Artificiality, posing, and overacting apparently had their place alongside realism in the Yiddish theater, especially in domestic melodramas, fraught with intergenerational conflict and dysfunctional family problems. The actors jocularly called these sentimental, tearjerking dramas *onion plays*, a literal translation of the Yiddish word *tziblshtick*. They were done alongside the classics, which were performed with great feeling and realism, and also sometimes with a naturalism that must have been astonishing. There was also a very popular Yiddish musical theater: Operas were performed in translation, there were songs composed for Yiddish vaudeville, and original operettas were written. In short, Yiddish theater was rich in all genres and in all styles.

Lee Strasberg's books *A Dream of Passion* (Penguin Plume Books, 1987) and *Strasberg at the Actors Studio: Tape-Recorded Sessions*, edited by Robert H. Hethmon (Theatre Communications Group; fifth printing, 2000) show exactly what he was up to, so that there is no mystery. His own succinct summary of the Method (the capitalization is his), in the indispensable volume *The Lee Strasberg Notes*, edited by Lola Cohen (Routledge, 2010), is this: "The Method is an amalgam of the work of Stanislavski, Vakhtangov, Meyerhold and the Group Theater."

A well-read man, Strasberg was influenced by such authors as Marcel Proust and by the ideas of Sigmund Freud. This was different from Stanislavsky, who had been influenced by Ivan Pavlov (1849–1936), with his famous experiments on reflex reactions—which had a great influence on Meyerhold's ideas of biomechanics—and Théodule Ribot (1839–1916), Freud's French precursor. Ribot's emphasis (in keeping with his nineteenth-century scientific orientation) was on the physiological and neurological bases of psychology. Stanislavsky used these concepts to form his own ideas on psychophysical motivation and resultant actions. Richard Boleslavsky, impressed by both Freud and Ribot, combined their approaches in the study of the character's psychological motivations.

Strasberg's core idea about character interpretation is the belief, based on the idea of truthfulness on stage, that the actor is him- or herself always, and that the character can therefore really be none other than the actor who infuses him or herself into the role. However, he adds the following important idea as a kind of caveat against confusing the actor with the character: "To search for the reality, ask yourself what the character would do in each situation—not what you would do." In other words, nothing in his Method is to be preconceived, or imposed or superimposed from without. The actor's aim is to be truthful and organic, and that implies *using* the self as the character: It is I who live through the play, and behave as the character, but not according to some predetermined conception of what the character should be or do. And for this, I need to find substitutions from my own life for the events and people in the play, so that I can relate to them viscerally, and therefore be truthful as the character. In going so far with the idea of emotional recall, Strasberg ignored Stanislavsky's later ideas because he felt the earlier ideas were better.

One of his most famous class exercises, the *private moment*, was considered very controversial, largely because it was caricatured and ridiculed. It was also willfully misunderstood as being psychologically dangerous for actors. The actor does something that usually demands complete privacy, and that the actor would perhaps be embarrassed to be seen doing, such as talking aloud to oneself (many people do this without even being aware of it), singing or dancing in the living room, weeping uncontrollably, or even something as mundane as shaving the hair off one's legs. By overcoming the inhibitions of the actor with regard to what was significantly private for him or her, this exercise was meant to inculcate a sense of public solitude, to help the actor create the circle of concentration so necessary in performance, and to overcome the actor's concern with results, and with producing results. The results would be whatever they would be. Actors would use their senses and imagination to create the place, such as their own living room, where they felt private when alone. This meant they could be relaxed because there was no pressure from the presence of other people. Actors would also bring in an object to help remind them of the place, and to awaken their imagination—a cushion that was on the couch, for instance. The actor would then do something that he or she would ordinarily not do in public. Talking aloud to oneself was an activity often used for this exercise. Then the actor would add other exercises to the private moment, such as a song, a monologue, or an animal exercise, and the private moment would have helped the actor to achieve that desired sense of pubic solitude.

As Uta Hagen would later point out in her book *Respect for Acting*, people talk to themselves for a reason, which is usually in order to solve some problem. This is of prime importance when delivering a monologue in the theater, because it has to do with the soliloquizer's objective(s) and action(s). As Strasberg said, when he had seen actors talk to themselves in the private moment exercise, people can do whole soliloquies when they are alone, and think nobody is listening: "Before this I thought of soliloquies as a dramaturgic device, as convention. I thought that people didn't soliloquize when alone, but I found that they did."

Another very important teaching tool is the *song and dance exercise*, which is a two-part classroom acting exercise. In the first part, an actor must choose a simple, easily remembered song, such as "For he's a jolly good fellow." The actor must stand facing the class/audience, and maintain eye contact as he or she sings each syllable separately, filling the lungs with air each time and singing as loudly as possible. This part of the exercise helps lead to self-awareness of the tension and inhibition the actor may not be aware of. In the second part of the exercise, the actor takes the same song and sings it again syllable by syllable, doing a dance movement on each syllable. Often, actors will stop and try to think of a movement each time, instead of being spontaneous. The purpose of the dance part of the exercise is to make the actor aware of how much he or she is intellectualizing, instead of living through the moment.

One of the cardinal sins in acting, according to Strasberg, is, in fact, intellectualizing: living too much in the mind, and overseeing every action from the lofty vantage point of judgment, rather than being visceral, feeling the moment, and living in it, as Strasberg opines we all actually do. This principle and way of working has often been perceived as leading to self-indulgence, and the spontaneity of the moment may indeed not be in conformity with the play as rehearsed. The technical side of acting is ignored. In particular, vocal technique is said by the Method's detractors to be neglected. Method actors have the reputation of mumbling privately to themselves rather than communicating with the audience. But this stereotype is not strictly true, and Strasberg was well aware of the importance of vocal technique. He felt, however, that if the actor was really in the moment, the voice would come out correctly, and that all the techniques the actor really needed were the psychological ones he advocated and taught.

Still, the self-indulgence of some actors who had studied at the Actors Studio and would do whatever occurred to them at the moment, whether or not it was suitable to the play, is not entirely without basis. A well-known theater anecdote has it that when Uta Hagen was playing Blanche in the Broadway production of Tennessee Williams's *A Streetcar Named Desire*, Anthony Quinn, as Stanley, used to grab her arms so forcefully in the rape scene that he actually hurt her. She remonstrated with him, but all he said was, "I felt it that way." Finally, unable to bear it any longer, during one performance she lashed out and slapped him resoundingly. Later, in the wings, he told her she had really hurt him, and reproached her for not doing the scene as rehearsed. "I felt it that way," she said. He never gripped her so tightly again. One of the prime rules of performance, as you will recall, is "safety first." You never have a right to injure another actor, and stage fights or other violent incidents must be carefully and thoroughly rehearsed, and constantly gone over before each performance, precisely in order to avoid injury. Although the combat is clearly the result of psychological, characterological motivation, stage fighting is ultimately a purely external exercise in technique. There is a line to be drawn between technical requirements and allowing the emotion aroused by playing psychophysical actions to take over. See Ronald Colman in *A Double Life* (1947): He plays an actor performing Othello, and the role takes over so much that he loses all self-control. And self-control is one of the keys to doing eight performances a week: you must be in control of your performances, just as you must know how to pace yourself, which includes not expending your energy uselessly, but using it in the right places, at the right times.

Sanford Meisner

On Acting (Random House Vintage Books, 1987) by Sanford Meisner, whom everyone called "Sandy," written with Dennis Longwell, presents the influential work of the head of the Neighborhood Playhouse, which Meisner took over in 1935. Like Adler and Carnovsky, he had been a member of the Group Theater and an early adherent of the Stanislavsky system. The Meisner Technique is one of the most important taught to contemporary actors, not only at the legendary Neighborhood Playhouse, but also by James Price, a protégé of Sanford Meisner and a Playhouse graduate, at the studio Mr. Price founded and runs, The Acting Studio, Inc., one of the most excellent schools in New York City.

Meisner's book is full of sound advice and teachings. He talks about the Group and Stanislavsky, Stella Adler and Harold Clurman. Scenes from such plays as Tennessee Williams's *Summer and Smoke* are analyzed, with stage directions crossed out and implicitly ignored so that they do not lead actors to try to predetermine how a moment is to be played. Moments must evolve organically out of exploration. Deciding them technically is a mistake because it precludes acting, rather than helping it along. There is also a DVD, *Sanford Meisner Master Class*, which further clarifies the principles of this dynamic man, who was an excellent actor himself. Important as well, and already a classic, is the volume by the distinguished acting teacher William Esper, in collaboration with his colleague Damon DiMarco, *The Actor's Art and Craft: William Esper Teaches the Meisner Technique* (Random House, 2008). Esper studied and taught with Meisner, and was associate director of the Neighborhood Playhouse's acting department for fifteen years. Aside from running his own William Esper Studio, he was also the founder and longtime chairman of the Professional Actor Training Program at Rutgers University's Mason Gross School of the Arts.

Meisner begins his book, which is in the form of dialogues between Meisner and his students in acting class, with his first principle: "The foundation of acting is the reality of doing": i.e., truly doing and not pretending. Acting is action, in the Stanislavskian sense: internal and external. And acting consists of doing something: "If you do something, you really do it! Did you walk up the steps to the classroom this morning? You didn't jump up? You didn't skip up, right? You didn't do a ballet pirouette? You really walked up those steps." In other words, whatever you do, you have to do not just in a real way, but for real. Actions have a reason. They occur in a specific situation, and in a certain way that is conditioned by circumstances. And the beginning and the foundation for the actor are in performing the action itself.

Meisner's most famous exercise for training in the reality of doing is the repetition exercise, details of which are in the book: its goal is to teach the student actor to listen so as to really hear not just the words, but the intentions behind them. You listen. That's it. You listen, simply listen, and you are able to respond simply to what you hear, which will arouse some feeling, some emotion in you. Some desire will be awakened, if only the desire to respond. Listening and responding accordingly is one of the great principles of acting, and this exercise teaches it superbly. You cannot pretend to listen. You have to listen for real, just as you climb those steps to the classroom. Eventually, you will learn that you listen for a reason and for a purpose. In the obvious case of a police detective interrogating a suspect, two people are listening and responding to each other, one for the purpose of obtaining, the other perhaps for the purpose of concealing information. This is dramatic conflict. The two may be observed also from outside the interrogation room, by other officers equally intent on gaining information, as in many scenes in the superb hit CBS television series *NCIS*. The wonderful cast provides an object lesson in how to do it for real, without indication or anticipation, or any of the other cardinal acting sins.

Morris Carnovsky

The Actor's Eye (Performing Arts Journal Publications, 1984) by the great actor and teacher Morris Carnovsky, written with his colleague Peter Sander, provides an insightful, very practical approach to the actor's art. His system involves three very simple concepts that subsume a world of complications: the action, the object, and the self. The self is the character: Who are you as a person? What are your qualities and defects? What is your background? The object is that at which the character's desires are directed. The term may mean a general objective and is also applied to specific objects, such as Prospero's magic wand or the map that Lear uses to divide up his kingdom. The action is what the character does to fulfill the objective; the concept is the same as Stanislavsky's idea. There is also a brilliant, incisive chapter on performing Shakespeare, which every Shakespearean actor should read.

By breaking down the system into these three major concepts, Carnovsky has immensely clarified the actor's work. He had a long career as a teacher, and taught in 1936 at the Chicago Repertory Group (an offshoot of the Group Theatre) as well as at the Actors Laboratory in Hollywood. The influential Actors Lab was founded in 1941 to teach the Stanislavsky system, and lasted until 1950, when it was forced to close because of the McCarthy witch hunt. As Carnovsky said in an interview in *Theatre Arts* magazine for June/July 1948, "The Lab basically inherited the best ideas and ideals of the Group Theatre." Later, Carnovsky taught his way of working at Brandeis University.

When I met him, he had already been in the theater for more than four decades, from before his days with the Group in the 1930s through his incomparable Shakespeare performances as King Lear, Shylock, and Prospero at the American Shakespeare Festival in Stratford, Connecticut in the 1970s. There I had the pleasure of getting to know him and of talking with him about acting when he did *The Tempest* during the 1970 season. Since I understudied two roles and only was on stage during the Masque scene, working the arms of a huge puppet from inside it, I had the opportunity to watch him the rest of the time. From the back of the house, I saw every single performance of his—an incredible lesson in acting. He had an uncanny reality every time, and mesmerized the audience with his deep, ringing voice. In act 1, scene 2, when he was relating to his daughter Miranda the story of how they came to be on the island, he had personalized all of the other characters he talked about, so that when he said, for instance, "My brother and thy uncle, call'd Antonio,—I pray thee, mark me,—that a brother should / Be so perfidious!—he whom next thyself / Of all the world I lov'd..." his feelings were visceral, palpable, and his terrible disappointment at his brother's betrayal was heartrending. He often paused very slightly after "My brother," as he remembered the pain of what had happened. And he also paused very briefly after "uncle" and after "Antonio" for sense, to impress upon Miranda who this person was to her, and, secondarily, communicating the fact with clarity to the audience. He was very sharp, and almost harsh on "I pray thee, mark me." And, of course, he did not take a pause after the word "should," just because it is the end of a line in the printed script, but treated the line as what it is—a run-on line—thus giving the speech its reality. And he had the uncanny art of being able to repeat his performance exactly every time, and to appear to be living through and experiencing the character's emotions, which I have no doubt he actually did.

In 1969, I was a camp counselor at Buck's Rock, a camp for young people interested in the arts, and we took the kids to see Brian Bedford in the uncut *Hamlet*, with Carnovsky as a very distinguished Polonius—the best I have ever seen. In his self-importance as the character, during the court scene, when he entered, he looked about to see who was observing him. This was immediately riveting. Later, in act 2, scene 1, when he was giving directions to his servant Reynaldo, whom he is sending to Paris to see about Laertes, he had the lines "And then, sir, does he this,—he does,—what was I about to say? By the mass I was about to say something: where did I leave?" The kid sitting next to me whispered, "He forgot his lines!" That is how real Carnovsky's acting was.

Uta Hagen (1919–2004)

Uta Hagen's first book, *Respect for Acting*, remains one of the best books on the subject ever written. Her second book, *A Challenge for the Actor* (Charles Scribner's Sons, 1991) is perhaps less penetrating, but still worth reading. A distinguished and brilliant actor, she taught for many decades at the famed HB Studio, founded by her husband, the Austrian-born American actor and acting teacher Herbert Berghof (1909–1990), on Bank Street in New York City. A student of Max Reinhardt in Europe, Berghof acted in more than thirty films and television plays. He taught with the influential German theater director Erwin Piscator (1893–1966) at the New School for Social Research before starting his own school in 1945.

Imbued with the teachings of Stanislavsky, Uta Hagen was incisive and insightful, although she could also be intimidating. Still, I learned a great deal from her. I remember that she assigned a scene from *Billy Liar*, a play by Keith Waterhouse and Willis Hall, based on Waterhouse's novel. I was to play Billy, who is nineteen, while I was already in my mid-twenties. I said to her, rather stupidly, that it might be difficult for me to play someone so much younger than myself. She let me have it. "I'm fifty-six, and I feel much younger!" she began, angrily stubbing out one of her eternal cigarettes. And she gave us a very instructive lecture on the nature of age and how people view it and feel about it. Age is a given circumstance, but everyone ages differently; some people are still young at the age of sixty, in both their mental outlook and their ability to enjoy life, while others are already beginning to lose it, and to slide toward the grave. And, as Stanislavsky said, even as circumstances such as age change, we remain the same inside; that is, we are the same person, with the same basic needs. Among other things, I learned from Uta Hagen that it was actions and objectives that count, not chronological age. My father, when he was eighty, once said to me, "I feel twenty until I look in the mirror."

An indispensable classic that should be in every actor's library, *Respect for Acting* provides eminently practical advice on exactly what to do not only in generally building a character from the inside out, but also in specific behavior, such as acting drunk or talking to oneself—delivering a monologue or soliloquy—so that all awkwardness disappears, and the actor is comfortable in an inherently unnatural situation. Hagen lays out very clearly the concepts of objective, obstacle, and action, as well as the other Stanislavskian ideas, putting her own spin on them. Also very useful is her album of two DVDs, *Uta Hagen's Acting Class* (Applause, 2002), where you can see her in riveting action.

Hagen's main emphasis, as we saw in chapter 4, is on specificity and detail, and on the use of objects, both inner—images, people, places, etc., and the actor's concentration on them—and outer—stage properties, or props. Equally important is the use of substitutions. Hagen calls substitutions "transferences" in her second book; the words mean the same thing. For her, these analogies to other characters, places, things, or events should be drawn from the actor's personal experience only after the actual feelings have been assimilated and not when they are fresh and raw and traumatic. When you are in a position to have distanced yourself, and can view the experience more objectively, it is of use, but not before.

CHAPTER EIGHTEEN

The Influence of Berthold Brecht: Joseph Chaikin; Jerzy Grotowski

Berthold Brecht: The Theater as a Political Institution

The German writer, librettist, and theoretician of the theater Berthold Brecht (1898–1956) was well known for his iconoclastic plays, and for his collaborations with composer Kurt Weill (1900–1950), including the mordantly satirical *Die Dreigroschenoper* (The Threepenny Opera), *Happy End*, and *Aufstieg und Fall der Stadt Mahagonny* (The Rise and Fall of the City of Mahagonny). Brecht's groundbreaking ideas on theater were linked to his political ideas as a Communist: He thought theater that demanded the audience's rapt attention and elicited manipulated responses was a manifestation of bourgeois capitalism and called unconsciously for the basic acceptance of the system.

Equally influential in world theater, the noted German director and theorist Erwin Piscator (1893–1966) was Brecht's friend and shared his political ideas and his desire for a sociopolitical theater. He had been very prominent during the Weimar Republic, with his own theater in Berlin. When it went bankrupt in 1931, Piscator went to the USSR, where he had been invited to make a film. Brecht left Nazi Germany, and he and Piscator eventually lived and worked in the United States, where their influence was enormous. Under pressure from HUAC and McCarthy's anti-Communist witch hunts, both returned to their homeland. Brecht went to Communist East Germany in 1949, but Piscator, disillusioned by his experiences in the USSR, did not want to work ever again under a Communist regime, and remained in West Germany from 1951 on.

To counteract what he saw as the pacifying effect of conventional theater on the audience, Brecht wanted to create what he called a *Verfremdungseffekt*, usually translated as "alienation effect," or sometimes "estrangement effect," whereby the audience would have to view what they were seeing in a more thought-provoking way. By the term *Verfremdungseffekt*, Brecht meant a didactic, politicizing distantiation between audience and performance. The translation "distancing effect" is perhaps more accurate than the usual renderings. Brecht did not want to alienate or estrange the audience, but to create an awareness during performances that the spectators were indeed watching an artificial event, full of conventions that they had accepted in their willing suspension of disbelief. You cannot believe that what you are watching is real and actual, but you can allow yourself to be caught up in a story and to enjoy it, as you suspend your knowledge of the reality of life outside it. But Brecht wanted to teach by having the audience constantly observe the performance with full awareness of its didactic nature.

To achieve this, Brecht used exposed lighting, ropes, sandbags, and other usually hidden production elements. And he insisted that actors be directed to show, or indicate the character, rather than embodying it. The actor selects "a definite attitude to adopt towards the character," which then enables the actor to show his or her comments on the character to the audience. This attitude must be in consonance with the director's vision of the story as a whole. Thus the actor's outward appearance, movements, and gestures become important at the expense of the character's inner life. The external aspects seen by the audience are no longer the embodiment of the character's psychology, as with Stanislavsky. They are imposed in order to make points. The spectators' job was to learn from this didactic attitude and to be critical observers of the show, always aware that they were looking at a stage, and that a message was being conveyed.

Joseph Chaikin and the American Avant-Garde

Director, actor, and playwright Joseph Chaikin (1935–2003), with his avant-garde approach to theater and acting, represented an American departure from Stanislavsky, although he could by no means escape the pervasive influence of the great Russian master when it came to the system of character creation. Chaikin was heavily influenced by Berthold Brecht's ideas, and like Brecht, Chaikin believed that theater could and should be a tool for expediting societal change through the education of the audience. So did Julian Beck (1925–1985) and Erwin Piscator's student Judith Malina (b. 1926), cofounders and directors of the Living Theatre in 1947. The company is still part of the New York City scene, and tours internationally as well.

Chaikin's famous Off-Off-Broadway company, the Open Theater, founded as a theater cooperative in 1963, was political and iconoclastic in nature. The company lasted until 1973, creating collaborative plays under his direction. In rehearsal, Chaikin concentrated first on improvisation centered around the text. The actual text was only worked on later—a Stanislavskian approach to rehearsal, as we saw in chapter 4.

In 1977, I was one of the actors in Chaikin's production of S. Anski's (1863–1920) classic, *The Dybbuk* (written in either Yiddish or Russian, and translated into Hebrew; nobody seems to know its original language), performed in English at the New York Shakespeare Festival's Public Theatre. In 1979, he also directed the play in Hebrew for Israel's Habimah. Vakhtangov had directed their first production of the play, which had premiered in Warsaw in 1920, and in Moscow in 1921.

We rehearsed mostly in a studio in a building on Lafayette Street across from the theater. The rehearsal day began early, with physical warm-ups and theater games to get everyone limbered up and in the mood to improvise around the text. Some of the final staging of the play was directly drawn from these improvs, when Chaikin would decide that he liked the way the blocking was naturally shaping the telling of the story. He would also stage scenes of text, working improvisationally on the blocking. When we got into the theater, the space would further determine the blocking, for which sightlines in the auditorium had to be considered. The production, even in performance, maintained its improvisational feel and seemed very alive in front of the responsive audiences, who were moved by this tale of the demonic possession of a young bride by the dead student who had been in love with her.

I had toured the US in 1973 with the National Theater of the Deaf's production of *The Dybbuk*, and the rehearsal process was completely orthodox, but with occasional improvisations. Our rehearsal day at the O'Neill Theatre Center in Waterford, Connecticut, always began with physical exercises, which we each did on our own. And we just put the play together scene by scene. The contrast in the two experiences of working on the same play was striking. The deaf actors did the play brilliantly in a heightened version of American Sign Language, which I learned on the job. There were four of us hearing actors who did the characters' voices. The performance was somewhat like dubbing a film: we stood on stage unobtrusively, dressed in costume, and spoke simultaneously with the actors who were playing the roles physically.

Chaikin's book, *The Presence of the Actor* (Theatre Communications Group, 1972; revised 1991), outlines his theories on theater and acting.

The actor's presence, for Chaikin, is paramount: if the actor is mentally not really present, not living the moment, then there is no valid theatrical experience. Performer and audience have a share in each other's presence, and the experience is in the sharing, which can be transformative. In fact, Chaikin was very much in tune with Brecht's ideas on theater as an institution that played its part in suppressing freedom because of its very nature as a reflection of the sociopolitical establishment. For Chaikin, it is the alive experience that is desirable, as opposed to the experience of looking at or doing performances in the media. Direct, visceral communication is paramount. The actor must be more awake than the audience, and not only aware of what is going on inside him- or herself, but also thoroughly aware of the whole world of the play in which he or she participates. As with Stanislavsky, the actor must live through the experience and be aware of the relationship to the other characters as well as to the audience. The actor plays actions that emanate from within, again as with Stanislavsky, and uses emotional memory to seek parallel experiences with those of the characters. And, although aware of the audience, the actor does not pander or play to them. Finally, Chaikin believed that actors should learn to look at themselves as part of the general community, and realize that they are people who sometimes play theatrical roles. Theater, for him, should be part of everyone's lives, in the sense that it should have an effect on the audience, and not be mere ephemeral entertainment.

In the Latter Half of the Twentieth Century: Jerzy Grotowski and Environmental Theater

Jerzy Grotowski's (1933–1999) groundbreaking book on his experiments and methods, *Towards a Poor Theatre* (Odin Teatrets Forlag, 1968), gives many detailed physical exercises that are of use to actors no matter what system or method of character creation they subscribe to, and lays out his ideas on actor training clearly and succinctly. It also gives a great deal of information on his unusual productions. Grotowski was an innovative, highly influential, avant-garde Polish theater director, theorist, writer, and teacher who went beyond Stanislavsky's ideas of psychophysical actions and Meyerhold's biomechanics to develop his own system of actor training and environmental theater: dramatic presentations that surround the audience with a particular ambience. In one production in Norway at the Odinteatret, Eugenio Barba (b. 1936), whose ideas were influenced by and in turn influenced Grotowski, began the evening with the audience seated at dining tables set with china and silverware, and the actors poured wine for the audience.

The so-called "rich" theater was one in which the politics of acceptance of normative social values prevailed, while Grotowski wished in his "poor" theater, with its direct relation of actor and audience, to propagate the values of basic human relations and revolutionary social reforms, in accord with Brecht's ideas, as he makes plain in *Towards a Poor Theatre*. His theater was his experimental laboratory; hence the term *laboratory theater*.

Grotowski's semi-ritualistic plays were acted in various realistic, semi-realistic, and abstract settings in which a symbol or piece of furniture could stand for a place. The audience did not sit in a mass, but in various places on the set. They were often part of the action, as they were, for example, in *Kordian*, which takes place in a mental hospital. Some spectators sat in the bottom half of bunk beds while the doctors dealt with patients placed directly above their heads or right in front of them.

Grotowski also coined the term *theater of sources* to mean the deep, unconscious origin of personal healing and well-being that the actor must use in the creative process in order to create authentic theater that will move the spectators. These ideas, which also influenced Chaikin, came from many other sources, including Brecht, Buddhism, and yoga.

Grotowski saw the actor as a public person, exposing the self in public, not merely privately creating characters. For him, actions that are banal and trivial do not reveal anything to the audience. The actor should therefore search for and perform meaningful actions that will have an effect on the public. The actor must "give away" the performance. And the actor must work "in public with his body, offering it publicity. If this body restricts itself to demonstrating what it is—something that any average person can do—then it is not an obedient instrument capable of performing a spiritual act." Hence Grotowski's emphasis on movement and physical exercises. He thought acting as he knew it was "wretched," and that the actor should use all means to sacrifice him- or herself and to reveal the innermost part of the self, "to construct a psycho-analytic language of sounds and gestures in the same way that a great poet creates his language of words."

We are far removed here from Stanislavsky and the idea of creating real and realistic characters. In fact, we have almost entered the realm of expressive modern dance as the center of the theatrical experience. Grotowski writes further that the actor should "use the role as a trampoline, an instrument with which to study what is hidden behind our everyday mask—the innermost core of our personality—in order to sacrifice it, to expose it." The spectator is implicitly invited to do the same thing, and to transform the self, and thereby to be open to improving life and society.

Physical training becomes paramount in Grotowski's system of educating actors. And the artificiality of the theatrical experience as we generally know it is to be replaced with his idea of environmental theater in which the audience is also part of the show, as we have seen. Intriguing as these ideas are, their practical implications in performance were of limited appeal to audiences, and were never adopted in general as the only way of presenting theater, but rather as a very special, different experience. What most audiences wanted and still want is to see behavior on stage, not sociopolitical harangues, and they want to be entertained in rather traditional ways. And most actors enjoy creating characters, a process in which they feel they expose their own inner lives, behaving in ways that they often keep hidden, but that lurk somewhere in their unconscious. Still, there are always those who prefer the experiment, and who feel that without it, they are not doing their didactic, transformative job of uplifting and educating the audience.

CHAPTER NINETEEN

Some Notes on Contemporary Developments: Augusto Boal; Anne Bogart's Viewpoints and Tadashi Suzuki's Approach

The influential Brazilian stage director and theorist Augusto Boal (b. 1931) is directly political in his approach to theater. He wrote *Theatre of the Oppressed*, published by Pluto Press in English in 1979, in order to present his ideas on a dramatic voice for the masses and on the oppressive nature of theater. Boal perceives theater as a political weapon, serving to reinforce the existing social system. Acting is therefore an instrument of oppression. In this situation, the artist must learn anew to create, and must give us a new view of what it means to make moral choices. The spectator is to become one with the actors, and to undergo a kind of education. This theorizing is very much in line with the ideas of Berthold Brecht. Boal claims that theater was at its inception a participatory experience open to all, and that in essence he is getting back to that ancient idea.

What this means in practice is that the process of character creation and the way plays are performed is often presentational rather than representational: The actor is sometimes called upon to engage the spectator in a Brechtian way, by presenting the character, rather than trying to be the character. In fact, the actor is often him- or herself, rather than a character, although the actor plays a role (parent, child, etc.). In improvisational or scripted performances, there are confrontation scenes between actors, and these, says Boal, must be done in a Stanislavskian way, with actions and objectives considered the foundation of acting. But there is also an extensive use of theater games and improvisations, especially in actor training and rehearsal. In short, this contemporary development is eclectic in its approach to performance. It takes from everywhere, and combines Brecht and Stanislavsky.

Among the most interesting contemporary developments in theater, in actor training, and in the approach to the art of acting is Anne Bogart's system of work, called "viewpoints": Basically, all characters have a point of view; and each viewpoint has its parameters, which must be explored and recreated. Just as Stanislavsky's system consists of deconstructing a text, then reconstructing it based on the understanding gained from the deconstruction, so viewpoints focuses on particular deconstructive areas, used by a performing or creative artist to concentrate on aspects of a project for analytical purposes.

Originally developed by choreographer Mary Overlie in the 1970s, the idea of viewpoints was an attempt to narrow down the focus of concentration for interpretive dance purposes. The viewpoints were space, story, time, emotion, movement, and shape. The viewpoints were further refined by Anne Bogart (b. 1951), who wanted to make them useful for actors, both in class and in rehearsal. Bogart is an award-winning American theater director who teaches at Columbia University. In 1992, she cofounded the Saratoga International Theatre Institute, devoted to actor training, with the influential Japanese theorist and theater director Tadashi Suzuki. With Tina Landau, she wrote *The Viewpoints Book: A Practical Guide to Viewpoints and Composition* (Theater Communications Group, 2005), expounding her theories.

Bogart eliminated emotion and story, since she saw these as too broad and too pervasive in theatrical presentations. She felt they would be a natural part of the process, forming the background to the other viewpoints. In considering space, the actor concentrates on the architectural surroundings of artificially constructed spaces or of natural outdoor spaces, as well as the patterns of movement the character makes in the space. Shape includes the pattern of movement and gesture. Time includes tempo, duration, and the repetition of movement in time. In other words, the given circumstances of place and time are given primary consideration, before objectives, obstacles, intentions, and the actions to be played. All of the latter depend on movement in a particular space and in particular durations of time. These considerations are paramount, partly because they are what the audience sees immediately: actors performing actions in a particular time and space. However, in the course of dealing with the story being told, actions and intentions will emerge, and so will emotion, in accordance with Stanislavsky's dictum that the correct psychophysical action will arouse the required feelings. Hence, too, Bogart's elimination of emotion and story from the viewpoints under consideration.

Tadashi Suzuki bases his ideas on ancient Greek theater, as well as on Shakespearean and traditional Japanese noh and kabuki, with their stress on physical control and stylization. He has also been called the "Japanese Grotowski" because of his emphasis on the actor as making a public sacrifice of the self in what he conceives of as the shared social ritual of theater, with the audience as a participant. In *The Theatre Practice of Tadashi Suzuki: A Critical Study with DVD Examples* (Methuen Drama, 2009), Paul Allain informs us that "Suzuki is also recognized for the emphasis he has placed on the need for companies to create a home for their theatre activities."

Suzuki works not only in Toga, Toyama, Japan, but also in Saratoga Springs, New York. He has written twelve books, including *The Way of Acting* (Theatre Communications Group, 1986), probably his most popular book in English. For Suzuki, the physical life of the character is its most important manifestation. That is why his methods emphasize finding the correct action to play, correctly carried out. The whole body must speak, and must be involved in the character, even if nothing is being said.

In the DVD that accompanies Allain's *The Theatre Practice of Tadashi Suzuki*, the trainer explains that Suzuki's aim is to create a strong performer on stage, both vocally and physically. He wants to create actors with stage presence so powerful that the audience will be riveted to the performers even if they stand there immobile and silent. To that end, initial exercises include the stomp followed by the "sliding step," a kind of glide-and-stop exercise. The student wears loose, comfortable clothing and socks, but no shoes, for this exercise.

For the stomp, the student stamps very strongly on the floor, keeping the upper body still and developing a sense of bodily control, strength, and power. The kabuki-like exercise is done in distinctly counted, almost military four steps: 1. Stamp with one foot. This brings the weight onto that leg. Later, the student will stomp with the other leg. 2. Bring the feet together. 3. Keeping the upper body upright, arms unmoving but relaxed at the sides, move downward abruptly, bending the knees. Later, the student will move down slowly, counting as directed. 4. Stand upright in one simple move, again keeping the upper body still. In later repetitions of the exercise, the student comes up slowly from the crouching position, to a count of ten. Also included, to develop a sense of balance, is shifting the weight to one side or the other to a slow count. In addition, the exercise serves to help develop a feeling of being centered in the middle of the body, which Suzuki divides into the upper and lower half. The center feels as if it is in the abdomen, just below and around the diaphragm that supports the breath.

One of Suzuki's key concepts, as Allain informs us, is the idea of "animal energy": the physical apparatus animated by instinct. But the aim of the Suzuki method, which also concentrates on the nature of spaces, is to integrate the mind and the body, in a way similar to the Stanislavskian concept of psychophysical action. The Suzuki method of actor training concentrates on each important individual part of the body: feet, tongue, eyes, and so forth, so that each is alive and involved. Acting requires a great deal of natural animal energy, and the contemporary theater is replete with such non-animal energy as electricity, used in lighting and special effects. This non-animal, mechanical energy vitiates the power of the actor to communicate. Suzuki tells us that in his training he emphasizes first and foremost the use of the feet, as in the stomp exercise, "because I believe the consciousness of the body's communication with the ground leads to a great awareness of all the physical junctions of the body." And this helps to begin uniting the actor's mind and body so that the performance is fully integrated and finely tuned. The important thing for an actor in performance is to be living organically in the moment. This is exactly the point as well of the Stanislavsky way of working.

Ultimately, then, no matter what the approach to creating theater, we are led back to the logic and methods of the Stanislavsky system. Internal, psychological techniques and external techniques are inseparable in character creation. As we have seen, the external serves to reveal the internal life of the character. Movement and vocal technique are habits that serve the art of communicating feeling through behavior. "You cannot see feeling," said Stanislavsky. But you can see behavior. And that is what interests audiences: real behavior that shows us who people are, as the story of the play in which they are engrossed unfolds before them live, and in real time.

There is no secret to living in the moment when you are performing. Everything you have memorized—words, objectives, actions, physical movements, and so on—enables you to live each moment out. It is important to remember that you cannot repeat an emotional moment. But everything comes flooding back to you spontaneously when you act, and you hardly need to do more than fulfill all you have worked out. I say "hardly," but indeed acting is hard bloody work every time, to paraphrase Sir, the old Shakespearean actor-manager on tour in Ronald Harwood's *The Dresser*.

You have to fulfill the correct psychophysical action every time. Every time, an emotion will be there. Go with it. Live it truthfully. Don't worry that tonight it is not what it was last night. Enjoy the new performance as it happens. You will then feel fresh and alive. You will be performing organically. And that is one of the supreme joys of acting.

An Annotated Glossary
of Acting Terms

A word in **boldface** within an entry is a cross-reference to another entry.

act   **1.** To perform; to do something with a purpose; to carry out an intentional action. **2.** To interpret and play a character in a written or improvised piece; in a film, radio, television program, or internet project; or in a play done in the theater or other performance space. **3.** A large section of a play, musical theater piece, film, or television program that is marked off from the next long section of it by some kind of pause or transition, usually reaches some kind of climax in the story being told, and, in the theater or on television, is often followed by an intermission. An act is normally divided into shorter sections called *scenes*, usually signaled by the entrance or exit of one or more characters. **4.** A sketch, vaudeville routine, or other short performance piece, done without an intermission.

action   Something a character does in furtherance of an **objective**; i.e., to solve some task or find the solution to some problem. Actions must be logical, and a series of actions must follow a logical sequence and be in consonance with the character and the circumstances. Stanislavsky said, "The art of the dramatic actor is the art of internal and external action." Actions may be verbal, in the form of a statement meant to elicit a response. Actions may be external, physical actions, such as embracing the person one loves. Actions may be internal: something that is going on in the character's mind in the form of an "interior monologue," which is a running series of thoughts in a "stream of consciousness"; these may or may not lead to external action. The concept of action is central not only to Stanislavsky's system, but to acting in any form or school of thought. If acting is "doing something with a purpose," then action *is* acting. Hence also the term "movement action," meaning a move or a series of moves made with a purpose and directed toward reaching an objective. For Stanislavsky, every action had to be "genuine": "internally justified, expedient, and productive." Actions can be broken down into specific details, involving how exactly they are carried out; for example, when dueling with pistols or swords, or when exploring a crime scene.

activity   Stage business; a secondary task or job the character does, or could and would do, if something did not prevent it from being done—this is an important addition to the idea of activity by Alice Spivak; the character's physical life, proceeding while the primary action is played out in pursuit of an objective, for instance folding laundry, serving tea, or reading a book. An activity may be interrupted, but could be taken up again at any point, if possible. An activity is not to be confused with an action. Activities are always secondary. If a physical action becomes the primary objective in a scene, it is no longer considered an activity.

actor's apparatus of embodiment   For Stanislavsky, the physical person of the actor, with all the tools necessary to incarnate a character, including skills and abilities in vocal and movement techniques; that is, those external techniques that enable the actor to make clear through physical expression the inner, psychological life of a character.

actor's secret   A substitution or substitutions that only the actor knows. One of Vakhtangov's modifications of Stanislavsky.

adaptation   A mental and perhaps physical adjustment to a change of the character's circumstances, necessitating a new action, perhaps one different from what the character had planned; Stanislavsky's term.

adjustment   1. A conscious, deliberate change of impulse, instinct, and/or action on the part of the actor, particularly when rehearsing a character, sometimes because of a director's instructions to the actor. 2. A change of the actor's position on stage; e.g., a slight counter-cross to adjust the stage picture when another actor has crossed; sometimes, a change made on the director's instructions.

affective memory   The memory of emotions and feelings in any situation, whether emotionally charged or not (*emotional memory*); and the memory of physical sensations—hot, cold, drunk, sick, tired, attracted to something or someone, etc.—(*sense memory*). Emotional and sense memories overlap. The term was coined by the pre-Freudian French psychologist Théodule Ribot (1839–1916) in *Psychologie des Sentiments* (Psychology of Feelings), published in Russia in 1906. It was later adopted by Stanislavsky, who was even more impressed, however, with Ivan Pavlov's (1849–1936) famous experiments in reflexology. For more information, consult *Science and the Stanislavsky Tradition of Acting* (Routledge, 2006) by Jonathan Pitches.

anticipation   1. Along with indication, one of the cardinal sins in acting. To anticipate is to expect the next event, which the character is not in a position to do, instead of allowing it to happen "as if" for the first time. Anticipation can take simple or complicated forms: reaching for a glass of water before it is offered; sitting down before another character has said "Sit down"; or cringing in anticipation of a blow that the other character has not even started to deliver. **2.** A necessary, desirable aspect of timing an entrance or action so as to enter on time, or to perform the action as expected and at the right moment, for instance in stage combat.

arc   **1.** A curving, semicircular, linear shape; hence the "shape" of a dramatic character's journey from beginning to end. **2.** To move in a curving, semicircular pattern on stage, as an actor or dancer is sometimes asked to do.

aside   A theatrical convention in which the actor steps out of the scene to address the audience directly, telling them what he or she really thinks.

"as if" Endowment; Stanislavsky's "magic *if*."   The actor behaves as if he or she were in certain circumstances, and living through a character's life from moment to moment, as if for the first time. The term "as if" also refers to endowment, which is the projection of an imaginary quality or property onto a person, place, or thing, so that the actor treats that person, place, or thing as if the object had that property or quality.

beat; unit   A piece or bit of a scene:
   a) The beginning of a specific moment during which an action is played;
   b) A longer amount of time during which a conflict in a scene is played out;
   c) If and when an objective has been attained, or if and when it has not, there is a change of beat. When one beat comes to an end, another begins. Characters can have individual beats that differ from the longer beats in a scene.

blocking   The director's planning of the actors' moves; the schema of the actors' movements in a scene. Blocking is sometimes set very early in rehearsals, depending partly on the time allowed for rehearsal, and partly on the director's way of working. Ideally, blocking should arise organically and spontaneously from the natural impulses of the actor, which may need to be corrected by a director— that is, the actor may be told to make an adjustment to his or her impulses, in order to accommodate what the director wants, and sees as correct blocking. Sometimes, the actor will have to "translate" directions into language that he or she can understand in acting terms, in order to justify the direction. The direction to be "faster," for instance, may be justified by adding urgency to the action.

business   A synonym for **activity**. Also called *stage business.*

cardboard character   A one-dimensional, flat personage; frequently found in melodrama and romantic operas, where the heroine is a virtuous, long-suffering maiden, the hero a dashing and faithful lover, and the villain a scowling maniac; only the setting in which they function is different. There is not much psychological depth in the writing, but, in opera, the music frequently adds layers of emotion, so that the singer has something to explore, rather than simply playing a stereotype. When you play such a character—who could be a walk-on messenger or a vendor—you must still flesh the character out, using yourself.

character   A fictional person created by a writer, or improvised by an actor in various kinds of presentations. In the theater and the media, the imaginary written character is embodied and performed by an actor, according to his or her understanding and interpretation of the character's psychology and physicality, which are fused with the actor's own personality and attributes, so that the audience sees the character as a real, distinctive person.

choices   Selection among various possibilities for interpreting the character as a whole, as well as for playing each moment or beat in a scene. Although the general arc and shape of a part remain the same once the play is in performance, and the actors are used to the other actors' patterns and to the blocking that has been worked out, individual moments may and should vary and be alive in every performance as choices spontaneously arise.

circumstances; given circumstances   The factors that condition a character's life. Given circumstances are those supplied by the author. Emotional circumstances are internal, and include how the character feels in his or her relationships with the other characters, as well as the character's state of emotional health, and what the character needs emotionally. Physical circumstances include time, place, the weather, the temperature, and the character's state of physical health. Stanislavsky included production elements (staging, scenery, lighting, costumes, etc.) as circumstances the actor had to deal with.

completeness   In Stanislavskian terms, the finishing of a definite gesture; the feeling that something has been fully carried out.

concentration   Focus on the task at hand. Concentration is necessary throughout a performance, whether on stage for an entire play or in front of a camera for a particular take. It allows the actor to relax and to feel private and therefore involved. Stanislavsky talked of a "circle of concentration" and privacy that the actor builds around himself while rehearsing and performing.

counter-throughline   That which opposes the **throughline** of the action leading to the fulfillment of the **superobjective**.

creative apparatus of the soul   Stanislavsky's term for the combination of the imagination and the mind's ideas about the character, using "as if" to project the mind into the character's psychology and emotional life. Emotional and sense memories (affective memories) are two further elements of the creative apparatus of the soul.

creative mood; creative state   The actor's feeling and condition of being ready to rehearse or perform, brought about by a combination of concentration, relaxation, and inspiration.

cue   The technical signal that the actor is supposed to start performing, or to enter. Also, the signal to deliver the next line ("That line is your cue to speak") or to move to a certain place ("Your cue to move is when the lights go on"). The cue to enter may be a hand signal from a stage manager, or a light that flashes on and off, or a word or phrase the actor waiting to make an entrance hears from a character on stage. Cues that are signals to speak or move are part of the action, and have been completely absorbed during the rehearsal process. There is a well-known story about the Barrymores, all of whom were appearing in a play together. At one point, the dialogue simply stopped, for far too long a time, and the stage manager's voice whispered the next line loudly from the wings. Ethel turned towards him and said, "We know the line, darling. We just don't know who says it."

device   Another word for any specific internal or external acting technique.

element   1. For Stanislavsky, a basic aspect of the actor's training and equipment, and of the system of acting used in the creation of a role. Each element can be studied separately: for example, vocal or movement technique. 2. The basic building blocks of character creation, which can be worked on separately, but which must ultimately be fused in order to create the character; no element exists by itself. The elements include the imagination; the understanding of the given circumstances; each action, obstacle, objective, task, and activity; emotional memories; the logic of the character's psychology; movement; and finishing touches of costume and makeup.

embodiment   Stanislavsky's term for the complete incarnation of the actor as the character, but referring especially to the physicality of the character.

emotional memory   See **affective memory**.

endowment   Projection of physical or emotional qualities onto an object "as if" it had the qualities or properties being projected, in order for the actor endowing the object to relate to it in a personal, real way. All of acting is endowment.

étude [French: study]   A term Stanislavsky borrowed from music; the acting exercises and improvisations based around particular themes, scene study, or the performance of a short play, all used as part of actor training at the Moscow Art Theatre studios.

experience   To live through the events of a character's life by actually living the emotions aroused when performing the psychophysical actions; Stanislavsky's term, synonymous with the term **live through**.

explore   Part of the rehearsal process; it consists of trying different ways of playing moments and scenes, perhaps by means of improvisations and other exercises, until certain results may be found that can be more or less set physically, as with **blocking**. Emotional results will always vary slightly from performance to performance.

find   To make a discovery in rehearsal of a moment or an action that the actor has been searching for; for instance, a particular way of playing a scene or a moment, or of delivering a line, dealing with a relationship, etc.

fourth wall   An imaginary wall between the actors and the audience, creating a sense of privacy for the actor, who can then concentrate and behave as if he or she were alone. The "fourth wall" may even be in an outdoor setting, so that the actor can look into the distance as if he or she were in a meadow or at the rail of a ship. The term comes from the proscenium stage, which had three walls of a "box set," with the front of the stage constituting the missing "fourth wall." The concept can also be used in a three-quarters arena stage or in the round, where fourth walls are on all sides of the playing area.

freedom   The actor's liberty to make choices and to play moments spontaneously, while remaining true to what has been worked out about how to interpret and perform a character.

given circumstances   See **circumstances**.

grain   Nemirovich-Danchenko's term for the nub of a story, its essence; the seed that gave birth to it; its main idea; similar to its **superobjective**: its ruling, principal theme. A play's story described in just a few sentences. Also called a *seed*.

immediacy   1. The present urgency of the moment, and of the objective, whether it is the small beat objective or a larger need. 2. The feeling of being present in the moment, and thus prepared to take action right away.

impulse   The spontaneous, organic desire to do something, such as making a move, arising from the situation the character is in at the moment. Such impulses can and often do change as rehearsal proceeds; or when a director tells the actor what to do.

indicate   The cardinal sin in acting, indicating is showing an emotion or an action, rather than feeling or really doing them. Playing drunk or ill, for instance, requires a commitment to real actions, as opposed to staggering about in an exaggerated manner or sneezing in a clichéd way. The actions at any moment of any role have to come from a source, and the actor must know where such actions originate and why before he or she can do them truthfully using sense memory to recall the real way of behaving in such situations.

inspiration   In acting terms, a sudden inner sense that one must do something, serendipitously arising in the moment, leading the actor to play an action or scene in a new manner. But actors, as Diderot, Delsarte, Stanislavsky, and others pointed out, cannot rely simply on inspiration when performing. Everything has to have been worked out thoroughly beforehand in rehearsal. Only then can inspiration be aroused, leading to actions that are in accord with what has been worked out, while at the same time giving actors the freedom to make spontaneous choices.

instinct   1. In acting terms, the general overall feeling or feelings the actor has about what the character is like psychologically, emotionally, and morally, arising from having read and studied the script. 2. Part of the actor's talent and equipment as an artist. Instinct includes the ability to know when something is required, and to do it without prompting, as, for instance, adjusting the stage picture by making a slight counter-cross when another actor crosses in front; facing the audience in such a way as to allow them to see facial expressions clearly; or automatically adjusting to what another actor is doing in performance. Instinct also involves **impulse**; that is, the ability to feel instinctively when something should happen, such as finding the light, if the actor is suddenly aware of being in a dark spot. Such instincts may be inculcated and developed through actor training, and further cultivated by experience.

intention   The underlying, or subtextual, meaning of a line, delivered with the idea of expressing something a character feels, or wishes to convey. Ideally, intentions should happen organically.

interior monologue   The running stream of thoughts in a character's head that goes on while the actions are taking place. The interior monologue takes place also when the character is not speaking, whether the character is listening to what another character is saying or is alone in a scene. Also called *imaginary* or *inner monologue*.

journey   The forward development and arc of a character's life in the course of his or her story, step by step; where the character goes, and how he or she gets there.

justification   Logical, plausible, appropriate reasons for particular actions, and for interpretations both of the character as a whole and of individual moments. Sometimes, an actor will be directed to read a line or do a movement that is not in accord with the actor's ideas, but that the director feels is necessary. It is part of the actor's job to do what the director asks and to justify the new reading or action. There will always be a reason why the director wants something, and the actor has to find it, if the director has not explained it.

life of the body in the role   Stanislavsky's term for the outer, physical manifestations of character, following the character's natural, logical behavior, which itself is in accord with the logic of the way things such as simple actions happen; i.e., when making a drink, writing a letter, crossing from one side of a room to the other; includes the behavior of the character in specific physical circumstances; e.g., when sick, drunk, tired, hot, cold, etc.

life of the human spirit in the role   Stanislavsky's term for the inner psychological workings of character, logically determined by the mind's cognitions, the emotions, the character's unconscious, and the general psychology of the character, all of which must have an outer, physical manifestation in order to communicate or transmit them in an artistic, physical form to the audience.

line reading   An actor's particular interpretation and expression of a bit of dialogue—the way of uttering it, with its inflection, stressed words, and tone. Gone are the days when directors insisted on instructing the actor to do particular line readings, which they would demonstrate to the actors, who then had to imitate them exactly—although even today sometimes, directors will do just that, particularly when they feel an actor is stuck.

live through   Stanislavskian term, synonymous with **experience**: to be involved in the character, to live the character's life when going through the role in performance.

magic "if"   See **"as if."**

mannerism   A particular bit of physical behavior, such as tossing the head back or brushing a shock of hair off the forehead; a nervous tic. Characters may have mannerisms that the actors have worked out in rehearsal, and that are choices for a character's physicality. Or the actor may have an unconscious physical mannerism, perhaps born of nervousness, that should be pointed out to him or her, so that the actor can work to get rid of it, especially when it is inappropriate to the character.

method of physical actions   This is the essential Stanislavsky system: Based on the given circumstances, determine the character's objectives, then the actions, every one of which must have a logical, inner **justification.**

moment of absorption   The split second when the actor takes in what has been said or done and assimilates it; this is just before the moment of reversal, when a **beat** changes and the character moves to the next beat/action.

moment of orientation   The beat that begins a scene; the few seconds or less that a character needs in order to understand what is going on, usually at the beginning of a scene; or to adjust to the entrance of a new character; or to the surroundings, whether they are familiar or unfamiliar. Leaving out the moment of orientation is immediately unreal.

moment of reversal   The end of a beat, when a character has or has not attained the objective for that beat. There is always another beat, whether the character has won or lost, and a consequent adjustment that the character has to make.

moment to moment   Playing a scene without anticipating the next event in it.

move   A particular action taking the character from one place to another on the stage. See also **blocking.**

movement   In terms of acting, physical actions resulting from muscular motion that serves the portrayal of character, and helps the character in the pursuit of an objective and in the performance of a task. A character's movement is psychologically motivated.

object   A person, place, or thing on which the actor concentrates. Objects can be external, such as a cup of coffee or a chair; or internal, such as person one loves, or someone from the character's past or present, who may or may not appear in the play.

objective   What the character wants; the character's goal; the character's aim; the problem the character has to solve; the character's motivation, meaning that which motivates the character psychologically and emotionally, compelling him or her to take action; also called a *problem* or a *task* by Stanislavsky. There is an objective for a beat (beat objective); for a scene (scene objective); and for the play as a whole (play objective). Alice Spivak has innovatively and helpfully broken down the different kinds of objectives into the following categories: for a situation (situational objective); for a relationship (relationship objective); for the character as a whole (the character objective). In Freudian terms, people want pleasure and the relief of tension through the gratification and fulfillment of needs, both physical and psychological; and they flee from unpleasure (the raising of tension): he called this the *pleasure principle*. In seeking pleasure and satisfaction from external sources, people are confronted with the reality of other people's needs and desires, with the world as it exists, and with conditions of life, to which they need to adjust both externally and internally in some way: this is called the *reality principle*. The wish to fulfill the need has *sources*, the body and the self that is indissoluble from it; an *aim*, gratification; and an *object*, an external source that supplies gratification—a useful schema for actors to keep in mind when studying objectives and obstacles .

You can get a good lesson in objectives and actions from watching some of the competition shows on the Food Network, such as *Iron Chef America* or *Chopped*. The chefs' super-objectives are to win the competitions. Their objectives are to prepare dishes that the judges will like, so that they will give the chefs the necessary number of points. And we watch them preparing the dishes, performing the necessary actions: chopping, slicing, dicing, sautéing, braising, roasting, and so forth. These shows are also lessons in concentration and psychophysical motivation.

object of attention   Anything or anyone that an actor fastens his or her concentration on, whether something internal or external. A person on whom one is focused is an important object of attention, whether the person is present or not.

obstacle   Something that is in the character's way, preventing the character from accomplishing an objective. The obstacle may be physical, interpersonal, emotional, internal, etc.

organic   Spontaneous, unanticipated, real behavior resulting from living in the moment and proceeding as the character would from one moment to the next, as if everything were happening for the unique, first, and only time. Such organic behavior must be carefully prepared for during the rehearsal process, which must then be "forgotten."

particularization   Making an **object**, and event, time- and place-specific and individual. A cup, a lamp, a room, and all the circumstances connected with them have to be just as real and specific as they are in real life.

pause   A brief, psychologically or situationally motivated stop in the middle of dialogue; "eloquent silence," as Stanislavsky characterized it. A pause may be the occasion for a look, a movement, or a sound of some kind, such as a sigh or a groan. A pause may also occur before an action, or before the actor begins speaking, thus grabbling the audience's attention; or after the completion of an action, when the character assesses what has happened, while the audience remains all attention to see what will happen next. A pause may be very brief, short, or long, but it must always be filled with action, usually action in the form of the internal thought processes of the character.

personalization   Relating something specific in a script, as well as the script and relationships as a whole, to personal relationships and other aspects in the actor's life, so that everything in the script is personal and real.

perspective   The necessary view by the actor of what is going on, even during performance; part of the double nature of performing, where the actor is the character and at the same time remains aware that he or she is acting, so that anything that happens can be dealt with, including spontaneous reactions by the other actors that call for instant adjustments.

physical action   An external action, arising from an internal motive, carried out and performed by an actor in a specific manner in pursuance of a large or small objective.

place   Where one is located in space; the location where each scene in a play unfolds. Place is an important given circumstance and conditions behavior: we behave differently in a public place than if we are at home, for instance.

playing opposites; playing against   The terms refer both to the playing of characters as a whole and to the playing of specific moments. Recognizing a character's ambivalences, and acting them when appropriate; also, acting in a way contrary to what would be expected when expressing a character's feelings, which adds reality and depth to the portrayal. For instance, a person who is full of rage may smile and speak softly, but the menace underneath, having been felt and experienced by the actor, will be readily apparent to the audience.

preparation   **1.** Getting ready for something to take place. For actors, the initial preparation for the profession consists of training and the study of such subjects as human psychology and behavior. **2.** In rehearsal, preparation consists first of the (pre-rehearsal) reading of the script and making preliminary decisions regarding objectives, actions, relationships, and other elements, prior to reading the play aloud with the assembled company, then putting the play on its feet. While rehearsal is in progress, preparation involves homework, based usually on what has happened in rehearsal sessions, so as to be ready for the next day's session. Physical exercises may also be part of the process, before a session begins. **3.** In performance, preparation consists of arriving at the theater ready to get into the mental and physical creative state necessary for the performance, including putting on costume and makeup. During the show, preparation involves getting ready for each entrance the actor has to make. The questions asked when rehearsing an entrance include: Where have I just been? Where am I now going? What do I want when I get there? What do I expect to find or see when I arrive? These questions will have been assimilated into the acting score, as part of the character's offstage life, and part of the preparation for an entrance consists of the actor reminding him- or herself of the answers.

presentational   The old-fashioned, external, technical, non-organic approach to acting, in which the character is "presented" to the audience by the actor, who does not feel any of the character's emotions, but rather imitates or counterfeits them.

privacy   The feeling of being alone and unobserved during a performance.

psychophysical action   Something the actor/character does as the result of a psychological motivation. All actions are psychologically motivated.

public solitude   The feeling of being alone and private on stage. This feeling can be induced by concentration and by being in the so-called circle of concentration, a useful fiction.

relationship   The nature of the character's connection to other characters, as well to inner and external objects, to place, and to time. Relationship involves how and why the character relates. Relationships are part of the important internal and external circumstances in a character's life; they condition behavior. Here are some of the sorts of questions the actor has to ask when considering relationships; they could be questions asked by the character, or by the actor looking for substitutions: How do I behave when I am in love with someone? How do I behave if I hate someone? How do I behave in the presence of my parents, spouse, lover, partner, children, friends, acquaintances, neighbors, teammates, colleagues, bosses, teachers, doctors, or lawyers? How do I feel about them? How do I relate to them? How do I relate to or react to a change in the temperature, i.e., am I more comfortable in hot weather or in cold, for example? How do I relate to a body of water, if I can or can't swim? Do I have allergies, so that I relate in a specifically fearful way to even the sight of a certain flower or of someone smoking a cigarette? Do I have vertigo, claustrophobia, agoraphobia, or acrophobia? Am I afraid of something or someone? How do I relate to my possessions, to my environment?

relaxation   The absence of extraneous, superfluous tension on the part of the actor, and an inner sense of being at rest, accompanied by a readiness to perform, so that he or she can concentrate on fulfilling the life of the character. Relaxation allows the actor to be loose and flexible and to react spontaneously and organically. There is a desirable actor's tension born of concentration, but the tension the actor might feel because of having to perform must be eliminated as much as possible.

representational   Contemporary acting practice, in which the actor "represents" the character by living through the character's life moment to moment as if for the first time, and embodies the character by feeling the character's emotions and putting him or herself in the character's place, living the character's life.

result(s)   The end product of the search for how to play a moment, together with the emotions that arise when an action is performed. Stanislavsky's famous, all-important dictum: "Never begin with results." Lee Strasberg's corollary: "Never force or push for a result." You find the results in the course of rehearsing, of experimenting and exploring, and, while you may carry out the same physical results in each performance, the emotional results will never be exactly the same. Results cannot be anticipated, or the actor is not living in the moment.

rhythm   The arrangement of slow and fast beats in the playing of a character.

score   The order of the beats in the scene, of the scenes in a script, and of the events and episodes of the story, all integrated together, and showing where the highs and lows of the story occur, with its overall development. Each scene has its own score of actions. The score is personal to each actor, who "scores the beats" on an individual basis—that is, he or she lists them in order.

sense memory   See **affective memory**.

set   **1.** Scenery, in the theater and the media; a particular décor: *the set for the first scene*; *the set(s) for the play*. **2.** In acting terms, to memorize and thus preserve a particular bit of business, a line reading, an acting moment, or the way a scene is played, so that it can be acted in the same way every time, insofar as possible. **3.** To solidify, fix, and gel a whole performance, including its technical aspects, e.g., lighting and scenery cues. The actors will repeat the staging and blocking each time. The basic shape and architectonics of their parts, of each scene, and of the play as a whole will be the same as well. The ability to repeat a performance as rehearsed is one of the most important obligations of the professional actor. But the repetition must never be mechanical: The actor must perform "as if" he or she were experiencing everything for the first (and only) time. Therein lie the paradox and the difficulty of acting.

specificity   Particularity, uniqueness; one of the guiding principles of the Stanislavsky system: Every action taken happens for a specific reason, and in a specific way, which the actor must find. No swordfight is the same as any other swordfight, no meal like any other meal. Each is unique. Every character has a specific relationship with all the other characters: no romantic relationship is the same as another romantic relationship; no parent-child relationship is the same. Every prop the actor uses has a specific meaning to the character, aside from its actual use, and is used in a personal, particular, and specific manner.

spine   The core, or throughline, or main thrust of a scene, or of the play as a whole; also the main life drive or objective of a character.

stakes   The importance to the character of obtaining an objective, whether large or small. How much importance is attached to a goal involves the amount of emotional desire the character has invested in it, and determines the amount of energy put into pursuing it: the higher the stakes, the greater the energy, and the more riveting the pursuit for an audience.

stream of consciousness   American psychologist and philosopher William James's term for the constant river of thoughts that arise from the unconscious and fall back into it; some of the thoughts are dwelt on, and some simply pass by unnoticed.

substitution   The use by the actor of emotions, events, people, relationships, places, or objects from his or her own life that are analogous to or associated with similar things experienced by the character; a conscious replacement of the fictitious objects in the play with objects from the actor's private life. It is important to remember that you must relate directly to the other actor, so that substitutions are more of a rehearsal than a performance tool, and should be forgotten by the time you get to the performance.

subtext   The underlying meaning of the text; the intention and/or desire of the character when speaking. Stanislavsky: "The subtext is what makes us say the words."

superobjective   **1.** The main thrust or aim of the play as a whole—that is, where the arc of the story leads; the main theme and subject of a play or film. **2.** The main, overall objective or life drive of the character.

tempo   The pace at which a scene is played. Tempo includes rhythm and works in tandem with it, hence the frequently used Stanislavskian term *tempo-rhythm*: the rhythm of the scene as a whole, and of each character in it. Even if one character's rhythm is slow and the other's fast, the rhythm of the scene as a whole may be either. It is up to the director to determine tempo. Stanislavsky stated that tempo also depends on the particular tempo of the actor at the moment of playing, so that if an actor were tired, the tempo would be different than if he or she were feeling fresh and rested. Of such variables are performances made. It is also possible, he thought, to concentrate so deeply that the tempo becomes sluggish, without the actor being aware that this is the case. Tempi should have a sense of lightness and energy even in scenes of heavy import, so that the spectator is carried along in the desired way, rather than suddenly experiencing a sense of boredom.

throughline   The ultimate thrust of the story in the play, into which all the individual characters of the play fit. Each scene has its own throughline, or spine. So does each character, with her or his story's arc, or shape, and main objective. The throughline of the actions leads to the fulfilling of the superobjective.

time   The day, hour, and moment when a scene takes place. Time—past, present, and future—is an important given circumstance; the amount of time a character has to perform a certain task is a conditioning factor.

transition   The change from one beat or one moment to the next, involving a change of the character's immediate small, or beat, objective.

unit   See **beat.**

verbal action; vocal action   Speech in furtherance of an objective; usually directed at another character, or to oneself in the case of a monologue or soliloquy. Speaking is an action, and always has some purpose. It is one of the principal stage actions, since the spoken word is one of theater's most important elements.

vocal energy   The strength of the voice when projected, communicating intentions; enabled by proper **vocal technique**, which must become habitual through study and hard work.

vocal technique   The method and way of using the voice to project it in the theater, in the service of portraying a character. In contemporary practice, this is meant to sound as natural as possible, given the fact that the actor is speaking so loudly. In old-fashioned technique, placement helped declamation, and the voice usually sounded artificial.

vocalize   1. To warm up the singing or speaking voice preparatory to performing, in order to make sure that the voice is in good shape and the vocal apparatus is limber. Actors often do vocal exercises, both singing and speaking, but not everyone feels the need for such warm-ups. 2. To practice vocal technique for singing, using exercises such as scales, arpeggios, etc.

vulnerability   Openness to what is happening to the character. Vulnerability leaves the character, and the actor, room for spontaneous, organic reactions in both rehearsal and performance.

warm up   To prepare for a performance by doing vocal and physical exercises, to make sure the body is limber and flexible. A psychological warm-up is the mental preparation for the role. Some actors like to go over their lines in their heads or, occasionally, speak them aloud softly, so only they can hear them. This is perhaps a matter of insecurity: the actor is not sure he or she will remember all the lines. For many actors, though, going through lines just before entering is counterproductive, and is in any case not the proper preparation for an entrance. It may even interfere with being there in the moment, and with living through the role from moment to moment, without anticipation.

Selected Bibliography

Abrams, M. H. *A Glossary of Literary Terms*. 7th ed. New York: Heinle & Heinle, 1999.

Adler, Stella. *On the Technique of Acting*. Foreword by Marlon Brando. New York: Bantam Books, 1988.

Ahart, John. *The Director's Eye: A Comprehensive Textbook for Directors and Actors*. Colorado Springs, CO: Meriwether Publishing Ltd., 2001.

Allain, Paul. *The Theatre Practice of Tadashi Suzuki: A Critical Study with DVD Examples*. London: Methuen Drama, 2009.

Allen, Frederick Lewis. *Only Yesterday: An Informal History of the 1920s*. New York: Harper and Row, 1931; Harper Perennial Classics, 2000.

———. *Since Yesterday: The 1930s in America*. New York: Harper and Row, 1940; Harper Perennial Classics, 1986.

Avilov, Lydia. *Chekhov in My Life: A Love Story*. New York: Harcourt, Brace, 1950.

Babbage, Frances. *Augusto Boal*. New York: Routledge, 2004.

Balatova, Natasha, and Anatoly Svodbodin, compilers. *The Stanislavsky System: A New Authoritative Dictionary of Terms*. From the 1989 Symposium *"Stanislavsky and a Changing World."* Translated by James Thomas. Moscow: Russian edition published by the Moscow Observer and Publishing House, 1994; translation copyright 2009 by James Thomas.

Barnes, David S. *The Great Stink of Paris and the Nineteenth-Century Struggle Against Filth and Germs*. Baltimore, MD: The Johns Hopkins University Press, 2006.

Batson, Susan. *Truth: Personas, Needs and Flaws in the Art of Building and Creating Characters*. Introduction by Nicole Kidman. New York: Rugged Land, 2006.

Benedetti, Jean. *The Art of the Actor*. New York: Routledge, 2007.

———. *Stanislavski: A Biography*. New York: Routledge, 1990.

———. *Stanislavski and the Actor*. London: Methuen Drama, 1998.

———. *Stanislavski: An Introduction*. New York: Routledge, 1982.

———. *The Moscow Art Theatre Letters*. Selected, edited, and translated by Jean Benedetti. New York: Routledge, 1991.

Berry, Cicely. *The Actor and the Text*. New York: Applause, 1992.

Bloom, Harold. *Shakespeare: The Invention of the Human.* New York: Riverhead Books, 1998.

Blumenfeld, Robert. *Accents: A Manual for Actors.* New York: Limelight Editions, 2002.

——. *Acting with the Voice: The Art of Recording Books.* New York: Limelight Editions, 2004.

——. *Tools and Techniques for Character Interpretation: A Handbook of Psychology for Actors, Writers, and Directors.* New York: Limelight Editions, 2006.

——. *Using the Stanislavsky System: A Practical Guide to Character Creation and Period Styles.* New York: Limelight Editions, 2008.

Boal, Augusto. *Theatre of the Oppressed.* Translated by C. and M.-O. Leal McBride. London: Pluto Press, 1979.

Boleslavsky, Richard. *Acting: The First Six Lessons.* Twenty-ninth printing. New York: Routledge, 1987.

Boucher, François. *20,000 Years of Fashion: The History of Costume and Personal Adornment.* Expanded edition. New York: Harry N. Abrams, Inc., 1983.

Bradley, Karen K. *Rudolf Laban.* New York: Routledge, 2009.

Peter Brook. *The Empty Space: A Book about the Theatre: Deadly, Holy, Rough, Immediate.* New York: Touchstone, 1968.

Carnovsky, Morris, with Peter Sander. *The Actor's Eye.* Foreword by John Houseman. New York: Performing Arts Journal Publications, 1984.

Chaikin, Joseph. *The Presence of the Actor.* New York: Theatre Communications Group, 1993.

Chekhov, Michael. *Lessons for the Professional Actor.* From a collection of notes transcribed and arranged by Deirdre Hurst du Pray. Introduction by Mel Gordon. New York: Performing Arts Journal Publications, 1985.

——. *The Path of the Actor.* Edited by Andrei Kirillov and Bella Merlin. New York: Routledge, 2005.

——. *To the Actor on the Technique of Acting.* Revised and expanded edition. Foreword by Simon Callow. Preface by Yul Brynner. New York: Routledge, 2002.

Claire, Thomas. *BodyWork: What Type of Massage to Get—and How to Make the Most of It.* New York: William Morrow and Company, Inc., 1995.

Cole, Toby, and Helen Krich Chinoy, eds. *Actors on Acting: The Theories, Techniques, and Practices of the World's Great Actors Told in Their Own Words.* New York: Three Rivers Press, 1970.

Collins, Beverley, and Inger M. Mees. *Practical Phonetics and Phonology: A Resource Book for Students.* New York: Routledge, 2003.

Craig, Gordon. *Henry Irving.* New York: Longmans, Green, and Company, 1930.

Crystal, David, and Ben Crystal. *Shakespeare's Words: A Glossary and Language Companion*. Preface by Stanley Wells. New York: Penguin Books, 2002.

Darwin, Charles. *The Expression of the Emotions in Man and Animals*. Reprint of 1896 ed. Internet: Kessenger Publishing, n.d.

Downes, John. *Roscius Anglicanus or an Historical Review of the Stage* (1708). Publication Number 134. Los Angeles, CA: The Augustan Reprint Society, 1969.

Dressen, Alan C., and Leslie Thomson. *A Dictionary of Stage Directions in English Drama, 1580–1642*. New York: Cambridge University Press, 1999.

Ellmann, Richard. *Oscar Wilde*. New York: Alfred A. Knopf, 1988.

Esper, William, and Damon DiMarco. *The Actor's Art and Craft: William Esper Teaches the Meisner Technique*. Foreword by David Mamet. New York: Anchor Books, 2008.

Firestone, Paul A. *The Pulitzer Prize Plays: The First Fifty Years, 1917–1967*. New York: Limelight Editions, 2008.

Frank, Anne. *The Diary of Anne Frank: The Revised Critical Edition*. Revised and updated ed. New York: Doubleday, 2003.

Freely, John. *The Grand Turk: Sultan Mehmet II—Conqueror of Constantinople and Master of an Empire*. New York: The Overlook Press, 2009.

Freud, Sigmund. *The Basic Writings of Sigmund Freud*, Translated and edited by Dr. A. A. Brill. *Psychopathology of Everyday Life*; *The Interpretation of Dreams*; *Three Contributions to the Theory of Sex*; *Wit and Its Relations to the Unconscious*; *Totem and Taboo*; *The History of the Psychoanalytic Movement*. New York: The Modern Library, 1995.

——. *Civilization and Its Discontents*. Newly translated from the German and edited by James Strachey. New York: W. W. Norton & Company, 1961.

García, Manuel. *Hints on Singing*. London: Ascherberg, Hopwood, and Crew, Limited, 1894.

Garfield, David. *The Actors Studio: A Player's Place*. Preface by Ellen Burstyn. New York: Macmillan Collier Books, 1984.

Gazzara, Ben. *In the Moment: My Life as an Actor*. New York: Carroll & Graf, 2004.

Gillette, William. *The Illusion of the First Time in Acting*. Foreword by George Arliss. New York: BiblioLife reprint, 2009.

Goodale, Mrs. Katherine (Kitty Molony). *Behind the Scenes with Edwin Booth*. Boston: Houghton, Mifflin Company, 1931.

Gorchakov, Nicolai. *Stanislavsky Directs*. Translated by Miriam Goldina. Foreword by Norris Houghton. New York: Limelight Editions, 1991.

——. *The Vakhtangov School of Stage Art*. Translated from the Russian by G. Ivanov-Mumjiev. Edited by Phyl Griffith. Moscow: Foreign Languages Publishing House, n.d.

Gordon, Mel. *Stanislavsky in America: An Actor's Workbook*. New York: Routledge, 2010.

Gossett, Philip. *Divas and Scholars: Performing Italian Opera*. Chicago: The University of Chicago Press, 2006.

Graves, R. B. *Lighting the Shakespearean Stage, 1567–1642*. Carbondale and Edwardsville, IL: Southern Illinois University Press, 1999.

Greig, Charlotte. *Africa (Cultures and Costumes)*. New York: Mason Crest Publishers, 2002.

——. *Oceania (Cultures and Costumes)*. New York: Mason Crest Publishers, 2002.

Groddeck, Georg Walther. *The Book of the It*. Authorized translation by V. M. E. Collins. New York: Vintage Books, 1961.

Grotowski, Jerzy. *Towards a Poor Theatre*. Preface by Peter Brook. 1st ed., Holstebro, Denmark: Odin Teatrets Forlag, 1968; New York: Routledge, 2002.

Hagen, Uta. *A Challenge for the Actor*. New York: Charles Scribner's Sons, 1991.

Hagen, Uta, with Haskell Frankel. *Respect for Acting*. New York: Macmillan, 1973.

Hall, Peter. *Shakespeare's Advice to the Players*. New York: Theatre Communications Group, 2003.

Hauser, Frank, and Russell Reich. *Notes on Directing*. New York: RCR Creative Press, 2003.

Houghton, Norris. *Moscow Rehearsals*. New York: Harcourt, Brace, 1936.

Houston, Mary G. *A Technical History of Costume* 3 vols. Vol. 2: *Ancient Greek, Roman and Byzantine Costume and Decoration*. London: Adam & Charles Black, 1947.

Hull, S. Loraine. *Strasberg's Method as Taught by Lorrie Hull: A Practical Guide for Actors, Teachers, and Directors*. Foreword by Susan Strasberg. Woodbridge, CT: Oxbow Publishing, Inc., 1985.

Ignatieva, Maria. *Stanislavsky and Female Actors: Women in Stanislavsky's Life and Art*. New York: University Press of America, Inc., 2008.

Jones, Ernest. *Hamlet and Oedipus*. London: V. Gollancz, 1949.

Kahlenberg, Mary Hunt. *Asian Costumes and Textiles: From the Bosporus to Fujiama*. New York: Skira, 2001.

LaBouff, Kathryn. *Singing and Communicating in English: A Singer's Guide to English Diction*. New York: Oxford University Press, 2008.

Laing, R. D. *The Divided Self: An Existential Study in Sanity and Madness*. Baltimore, MD: Penguin Books, 1965.

Lecoq, Jacques, in collaboration with Jean-Gabriel Carasso and Jean-Claude Lallias. *The Moving Body: Teaching Creative Theatre*. Translated from *Le corps poétique* by David Bradby. With a foreword by Samuel McBurney. New York: Routledge, 2000.

Lehmann, Lotte. *More Than Singing: The Interpretation of Songs*. Introduction by Bruno Walter. London: Boosey and Hawkes, 1945.

Lessac, Arthur. *The Use and Training of the Human Voice: A Practical Approach to Speech and Voice Dynamics*. New York: DBS Publications, 1967.

Lewis, Robert. *Advice to the Players*. Introduction by Harold Clurman. New York: Theatre Communications Books, 1980.

Linklater, Kristin. *Freeing the Natural Voice: Imagery and Art in the Practice of Voice and Language*. New York: Drama Publishers, 1976, revised 2006.

———. *Shakespeare's Voice: The Actor's Guide to Talking the Text*. New York: Theatre Communications Group, 1992.

London, John. *Theatre Under the Nazis*. New York: Manchester University Press, 2000.

Lumet, Sidney. *Making Movies*. New York: Alfred A. Knopf, 1995.

Macready, William Charles. *William Charles Macready's "King John."* A facsimile promptbook, edited by Charles H. Shattuck. Urbana, IL: University of Illinois Press, 1962.

Marey, Jules-Etienne. *La machine animale* (The Animal Machine: A Treatise on Terrestrial and Aerial Locomotion). Reprint ed. Internet: BiblioLife, 2009.

Mason, Edwin Tuckerman. *The Othello of Tommaso Salvini*. New York: Putnam's Subjects, 1890; General Books LLC, 2009.

Meisner, Sanford, and Dennis Longwell. *On Acting*. New York: Random House Vintage Books, 1987.

Merlin, Bella. *The Complete Stanislavsky Toolkit*. Hollywood, CA: Drama Publishers, 2007.

———. *Konstantin Stanislavsky*. New York: Routledge, 2003.

Mikhail, E. H., ed. *Oscar Wilde: Interviews and Recollections*. 2 vols. New York: Harper & Row, 1979.

Mitchell, Theresa. *Movement from Person to Actor to Character*. Lanham, MD: The Scarecrow Press, Inc., 2009.

Mongrédien, Georges. *Daily Life in the French Theatre at the Time of Molière*. Translated by Claire Eliane Engel. London: George Allen and Unwin Ltd, 1969.

Moore, Sonia. *The Stanislavsky Method: The Professional Training of an Actor*. Preface by Sir John Gielgud. Foreword by Joshua Logan. New York: The Viking Press, 1960.

———. *Stanislavsky Revealed: The Actor's Guide to Spontaneity on Stage*. New York: Applause Theatre Books, 1968.

———. *Training an Actor: The Stanislavsky System in Class*. New York: Penguin Books, 1979.

Morosova, Galina Victorovna. *An Actor's Plastic Culture: A Short Encyclopedia of Stage Movement Terms*. Moscow: GITIS, 1999.

Muybridge, Eadwaerd. *The Human Figure in Motion*. New York: Dover, 1955.

Nagler, A. M. *A Source Book in Theatrical History (Sources of Theatrical History)*. New York: Dover Publications, Inc., 1952.

Neiiendam, Klaus. *The Art of Acting in Antiquity*. Copenhagen: Museum-Tusculanum Press / University of Copenhagen, 1992.

Nemirovich-Danchenko, Vladimir. *My Life in the Russian Theatre*. Translated by John Cournos. With an Introduction by John Logan, A Foreword by Oliver M. Saylor and a Chronology by Elizabeth Reynolds Hapgood. New York: Theatre Arts Books, 1936.

Pearson, Edmund Lester. *Queer Books*. Orig. ed. 1928. Port Washington, NY: Kennicat Press, 1970.

Pitches, Jonathan. *Science and the Stanislavsky Tradition of Acting*. New York: Routledge, 2006.

——. *Vsevolod Meyerhold*. New York: Routledge, 2003.

Polti, Georges. *The Thirty-Six Dramatic Situations*. Translated by Lucille Ray. Original ed., Boston: The Writer, Inc., 1923. Kessinger Publishing Rare Reprints, n.d.

Potter, Helen. *Impersonations*. New York: Edgar S. Werner, 1891.

Redgrave, Michael. *The Actor's Ways and Means*. Revised edition. New York: Routledge, 1979.

——. *Mask or Face: Reflections in an Actor's Mirror*. London: William Heinemann, 1958.

Rehm, Rush. *Greek Tragic Theatre*. New York: Routledge, 1992.

Rudlin, John. *Commedia dell'Arte: An Actor's Handbook*. New York: Routledge, 1994.

Saint-Denis, Michel. *Theatre: The Rediscovery of Style*. Introduction by Sir Laurence Olivier. New York: Theatre Arts Books, 1960.

Salvini, Tommaso. *Leaves from the Autobiography of Tommaso Salvini*. New York: The Century Company, 1890, 1893.

Shakespeare, William. *Hamlet Prince of Denmark*. Edited by Robert Hapgood. Shakespeare in Production. New York: Cambridge University Press, 1999.

——. *The Merchant of Venice*. Edited by Charles Edelman. Shakespeare in Production. New York: Cambridge University Press, 2002.

Shattuck, Charles H. *The Hamlet of Edwin Booth*. Urbana, IL: University of Illinois Press, 1969.

Shaw, George Bernard. *Shaw on Shakespeare: An Anthology of Bernard Shaw's Writings on the Plays and Production of Shakespeare*. Edited and with an introduction by Edwin Wilson. New York: E. P. Dutton & Co., Inc., 1961.

Simon, Mark. *Facial Expressions: A Visual Reference for Artists.* New York: Watson-Guptill, 2005.

Skinner, Edith. *Speak with Distinction.* Revised with new material added by Timothy Monich and Lilene Mansell. Edited by Lilene Mansell. New York: Applause Theatre Book Publishers, 1990.

Spivak, Alice, written in collaboration with Robert Blumenfeld. *How to Rehearse When There Is No Rehearsal: Acting and the Media.* New York: Limelight, 2007.

Stanislavsky, Constantin. *An Actor Prepares.* Translated by Elizabeth Reynolds Hapgood. Twenty-third printing. New York: Theatre Arts Books, 1969.

——. *An Actor's Work: A Student's Diary.* Translated and edited by Jean Benedetti. (A contemporary translation of *An Actor Prepares* and *Building a Character.*) New York: Routledge, 2008.

——. *Building a Character.* Translated by Elizabeth Reynolds Hapgood. Fourteenth printing. New York: Theatre Arts Books, 1949.

——. *Creating a Role.* Translated by Elizabeth Reynolds Hapgood. Sixth printing. New York: Theatre Arts Books, 1969.

——. *My Life in Art.* Translated by G. Ivanov-Mumjiev. Moscow: Foreign Languages Publishing House, n.d.

——. *My Life in Art.* Translated by J. J. Robbins. Little, Brown and Company, 1924; New York: The World Publishing Co. Meridian Books, 1966.

——. *On the Art of the Stage.* Introduced and translated by David Magarshack. New York: Hill and Wang, 1961.

Stanislavsky, Constantin, and Pavel Rumyantsev. *Stanislavski on Opera.* Translated and edited by Elizabeth Reynolds Hapgood. New York: Routledge, 1975.

Stoker, Bram. *Personal Reminiscences of Henry Irving.* London: William Heinemann, 1906.

Strasberg, Lee. *A Dream of Passion.* New York: Penguin Plume Books, 1987.

——. *The Lee Strasberg Notes.* Edited by Lola Cohen. New York: Routledge, 2010.

——. *Strasberg at the Actors Studio: Tape-Recorded Sessions.* Edited by Robert H. Hethmon. Fifth printing. New York: Theatre Communications Group, 2000.

Suzuki, Tadashi. *The Way of Acting: The Theatre Writings of Tadashi Suzuki.* Translated by J. Thomas Rimer. New York: Theatre Communications Group, 1986.

Terry, Ellen. *Ellen Terry's Memoirs.* With preface, notes, and additional biographical chapters by Edith Craig and Christopher St. John. London: Victor Gollancz Ltd., 1933.

Toporkov, Vasili. *Stanislavski in Rehearsal.* Translated and edited with an introduction by Jean Benedetti. New York: Routledge, 2004.

Trevelyan, G. M. *English Social History: A Survey of Six Centuries / Chaucer to Queen Victoria*. New York: David McKay Company, Inc., 1942.

Turner, J. Clifford. *Voice and Speech in the Theatre*. New edition. London: Methuen, 2009.

Whyman, Rose. *The Stanislavsky System of Acting: Legacy and Influence in Modern Performance*. New York: Cambridge University Press, 2008.

Wingate, Charles E. L. *Shakespeare's Heroes on the Stage*. 2 vols. New York: Thomas Y. Crowell and Company, 1896.

Winter, William. *Life and Art of Edwin Booth*. London: T. Fisher Unwin, 1893.

——. Shakespeare on the Stage. New York: Moffatt, Yard, and Company, 1911; 1915.

Index of People

About the Author

ROBERT BLUMENFELD is the author of *Accents: A Manual for Actors* (1998; revised and expanded edition, 2002); *Acting with the Voice: The Art of Recording Books* (2004); *Tools and Techniques for Character Interpretation: A Handbook of Psychology for Actors, Writers, and Directors* (2006); *Using the Stanislavsky System: A Practical Guide to Character Creation and Period Styles* (2008); *Blumenfeld's Dictionary of Acting and Show Business* (2009); *Blumenfeld's Dictionary of Musical Theater: Opera, Operetta, Musical Comedy* (2010); and the collaborator with noted teacher, acting coach, and actress Alice Spivak on the writing of her book *How to Rehearse When There Is No Rehearsal: Acting and the Media* (2007)—all published by Limelight. He lives and works as an actor, dialect coach, and writer in New York City, and is a longtime member of Equity, AFTRA, and SAG. He has worked in numerous regional and New York theaters, as well as in television and independent films. For ACT Seattle he played the title role in Ronald Harwood's *The Dresser*, and he has performed many roles in plays by Shakespeare and Chekhov, as well as doing an Off-Broadway season of six Gilbert and Sullivan comic operas for Dorothy Raedler's American Savoyards (under the name Robert Fields), for which he played the Lord Chancellor in *Iolanthe* and other patter-song roles. In 1994, he performed in Michael John LaChiusa's musical *The Petrified Prince*, directed by Harold Prince at the New York Shakespeare Festival's Public Theater. He created the roles of the Marquis of Queensberry and two prosecuting attorneys in Moisés Kaufman's Off-Broadway hit play *Gross Indecency: The Three Trials of Oscar Wilde*, and was also the production's dialect coach, a job which he did as well for the Broadway musicals *Saturday Night Fever* and *The Scarlet Pimpernel* (third version and national tour), and for the New York workshop of David Henry Hwang's rewritten version of Rodgers and Hammerstein's *Flower Drum Song*. At the Manhattan School of Music, he was dialect coach for Dona D. Vaughn's production of Strauss's *Die Fledermaus* (2009) and for Jay Lesenger's production of Weill's *Street Scene* (2008), which he also coached for Mr.

Lesenger at the Chautauqua Opera. Mr. Blumenfeld, who currently records books for Audible, has recorded more than 320 Talking Books for the American Foundation for the Blind, including the complete Sherlock Holmes canon (four novels and fifty-six short stories), Victor Hugo's *The Hunchback of Notre-Dame*, Alexandre Dumas' *The Count of Monte Cristo*, a bilingual edition of Rainer Maria Rilke's previously unpublished poetry, and a bilingual edition of Samuel Beckett's *Waiting for Godot*, which he recorded in Beckett's original French and the playwright's own English translation. He received the 1997 Canadian National Institute for the Blind's Torgi Award for the Talking Book of the Year in the Fiction category for his recording of Pat Conroy's *Beach Music*, and the 1999 Alexander Scourby Talking Book Narrator of the Year Award in the Fiction category. He holds a B.A. in French from Rutgers University and an M.A. from Columbia University in French Language and Literature. Mr. Blumenfeld speaks French, German, and Italian fluently, and has smatterings of Russian, Spanish, and Yiddish.